THE CANCELLED PRIME MINISTER

ALSO BY WALTER REID

A Volunteer's Odyssey: Arras 1917
(Tuckwell Press, 2003)

Architect of Victory, Douglas Haig
(Birlinn, 2009)

Churchill 1940–1945: Under Friendly Fire
(Birlinn, 2013)

Empire of Sand: How Britain Made the Middle East
(Birlinn, 2013)

Keeping the Jewel in the Crown: The British Betrayal of India
(Birlinn and Penguin India, 2016)

Supreme Sacrifice: A Small Village and the Great War
(with Gordon Masterton and PaulBirch)
(Birlinn, 2016)

Five Days from Defeat: How Britain nearly lost the First World War
(Birlinn, 2017)

Neville Chamberlain: The Passionate Radical
(Birlinn, 2021)

Fighting Retreat: Winston Churchill and India
(Penguin India and Hurst Publishing, 2024)

WALTER REID

The Cancelled Prime Minister

The Extraordinary Rise and Tragic Fall of Ramsay MacDonald

HURST & COMPANY, LONDON

First published in the United Kingdom in 2026 by
C. Hurst & Co. (Publishers) Ltd.,
New Wing, Somerset House, Strand, London WC2R 1LA
Copyright © Walter Reid, 2026
All rights reserved.

The right of Walter Reid to be identified as the author of this publication is asserted by him in accordance with the Copyright, Designs and Patents Act, 1988.

Distributed in the United States, Canada and Latin America by Oxford University Press, 546 Fifth Avenue, New York, NY 10036, United States of America.

A Cataloguing-in-Publication data record for this book is available from the British Library.

ISBN: 9781805265306

EU GPSR Authorised Representative
Easy Access System Europe Oü, 16879218
Address: Mustamäe tee 50, 10621, Tallinn, Estonia
Contact Details: gpsr.requests@easproject.com, +358 40 500 3575

www.hurstpublishers.com

Printed and bound in Great Britain by Bell & Bain Ltd, Glasgow.

REMEMBERING
JOHN WALSH
1927–2022

CONTENTS

List of Illustrations ix
Acknowledgements xi
Prologue: Peas from Different Pods—Two Foreign Secretaries xiii

1. Background and Beginnings 1
2. A Step to the Side 19
3. Bristol 25
4. Beefsteak Puddings and Hot Water 31
5. The Tessellated Pavement of Radical Politics 41
6. The Steps of the British Museum 49
7. Refining His Philosophy 57
8. South Africa and Beyond 63
9. Westminster 71
10. Family Life in Lossiemouth 81
11. Tragedy 85
12. Leader of the Labour Party 91
13. MacDonald's Ladies 101
14. 1914: Crisis 111
15. Humiliations 123
16. Political Change 127
17. Abroad and in the Wilderness 135
18. The Approach to Power 143
19. George V 159
20. Reflections from the Pinnacle 171
21. Labour in Power 177
22. A Matinée Idol on the World Stage 195
23. Problems Crowd In 203

CONTENTS

24. Out of Office	215
25. Stocktake	225
26. The Second Government	231
27. Crash	245
28. Economic Crisis	255
29. Reaction	269
30. The National Government	277
31. Health and Diplomacy	285
32. National Government without Samuel	293
33. Decline	301
34. Judgement	307
Notes	313
Bibliography	325
Index	329

LIST OF ILLUSTRATIONS

1. The railway comes to Lossiemouth in 1852. Antiqua Print Gallery / Alamy.
2. MacDonald's childhood home in Lossiemouth. Author photo.
3. Ramsay MacDonald, his two elder children, Ishbel and Joan, and his wife Margaret. Colin Waters / Alamy.
4. MacDonald on the platform. World History Archive / Alamy.
5. MacDonald family home, The Hillocks. Author photo.
6. Ramsay MacDonald's bedroom in The Hillocks. Author photo.
7. Ramsay MacDonald's sitting room in The Hillocks. Author photo.
8. The first Labour Government. World History Archive / Alamy.
9. Punch 18 June 1924. Author's collection.
10. Ishbel MacDonald. Circle Archive / Alamy.
11. Lady Londonderry. Alpha Stock / Alamy.
12. John Maynard Keynes at rest by David Low. Historic Collection / Alamy.
13. Jimmy Thomas with his grandchildren. Smith Archive / Alamy.
14. The core of the National Government, MacDonald front row, centre. The Print Collector / Alamy.
15. The historic Labour government of 1945. Associated Press / Alamy.
16. Family gravestone. Author photo.

ACKNOWLEDGEMENTS

As I release my hold on this book I reflect again on the generous spirit which an author encounters in the course of his work. It is a very real pleasure to acknowledge the support and assistance I have received from so many people, some in passing contacts and others who parted with substantial amounts of valuable time to help me.

John Hussey, OBE, and Dr Robert Lyman, MBE, both historians to whom I already owe much, kindly read my manuscript and commented helpfully. Iona Kielhorn is Ramsay MacDonald's granddaughter. I am grateful to her for taking time to answer many questions about MacDonald. She has retired to The Hillocks, the MacDonald family home in Lossiemouth, where she was most hospitable to Janet and me, talking at length about her grandfather's time in the house which he built for his young family and which is very substantially as it was in his time. His books, his papers, his pictures remain as they were, and one half expects to bump into him in his study. That study is to be seen twice in Lossiemouth, because it has been replicated in Lossiemouth Fisheries and Community Museum. I have to thank the Museum Board and their enthusiastic staff for showing me something of their resources. A valuable store of material shreds light on MacDonald's Lossie life.

MacDonald was born and brought up in Lossiemouth. He never remotely lost touch with the town. It was where his roots were planted and where he felt most at home, the place to which he kept returning throughout his life. He never represented the town in parliament, but my old friend Sheriff Alexander Pollock did represent the constituency of which Lossiemouth is part in two parliaments and found himself entrusted with roles relating to the MacDonald family. I am grateful to him for sharing his memories, which reveal the Labour Party's determination to paint MacDonald

ACKNOWLEDGEMENTS

out of their collective memory. Dr John Rhys is an almost equally old friend and a distinguished economist, and I am grateful to him for talking me through financial policies and economics in MacDonald's time. Dr Liz Evans kindly obtained copies of vast amounts of MacDonald materials from the National Archives, for which I am very grateful.

Illegible scribbles, muttered dictation and a confusion of paperwork were turned into an elegant script by my assistant, Gwen McKerrell. And that script was relentlessly probed, challenged and improved by Russell Martin, my copy editor. At Hurst Publishers Michael Dwyer was from the outset marvellously supportive and encouraging.

As always family support means so much. My daughter Dr Julia Reid identified some revealing contemporary cartoons highlighting interesting aspects of how MacDonald was seen before the prism was changed by the National Government. Janet accompanied me on the metaphorical MacDonald journey, and also on the physical one which took us from his birthplace to the churchyard at Spynie, where he and Margaret are buried. The metaphorical journey, the physical journey and so much else wouldn't have been the same without her.

Mas Lou Troumpill, Laroque-des-Albères.

PROLOGUE

PEAS FROM DIFFERENT PODS

TWO FOREIGN SECRETARIES

In the agreeable surroundings of Lausanne in July 1923, in one of the series of conferences at which the statesmen of Europe tried to improve on the crude terms of the treaties which had ended the First World War, the fate of Turkey was at stake. The Conservative Foreign Secretary, George Nathaniel Curzon, First Marquess Curzon of Kedleston, represented his country. A year later when the allies tried to sort out the matter of financial reparations to be paid by Germany, the United Kingdom was represented by the Labour Foreign Secretary, Ramsay MacDonald.

*

The two men had one superficial similarity. They were tall and held themselves well. In Curzon's case the dignity of his bearing was the result of a childhood spinal injury which contained him in a steel corset. But his features were podgy and his cast of countenance inexpressive—a little like that of the leader of his party, Stanley Baldwin. MacDonald had a much more refined expression, an expression which for many people spoke of a nobility of character, eyes fixed on distant horizons and sublime concepts. Altogether he was more impressive than the marquess. He was often described as the best-looking man in the Labour Party.

*

The early Labour leaders were in general a funny-looking lot. Their whiskers and beards and moustaches evoke characters from *The Wind in the Willows*. MacDonald certainly had a fine moustache,

PROLOGUE

ebullient and glossy. In his youth it looked suspiciously extraneous, like a glossy squirrel resting on his upper lip. Later it adapted to its surroundings and looked more a part of him. But his face was substantially free of topiary. With a bow tie and a cigar he had the air of a Café Royal dandy or a Mississippi riverboat gambler. One can see why when George Bernard Shaw first met MacDonald, he thought he was a military man.

But MacDonald was not what he seemed. He and Curzon could not have been more different. He was not only Labour's first Foreign Secretary; he was also leader of his party and Labour's first Prime Minister. Curzon was never Prime Minister. Just three months after Lausanne, Baldwin became Prime Minister, appointed because Curzon, in the Lords, was thought to be ineligible. 'The cup of honourable ambition has been dashed from my lips ... I could never aspire to fill the highest office in the service of the Crown.'[1] He broke down in tears.* He had forgotten Baldwin. 'Not even a public figure,' he sobbed. 'A man of no experience. And of the utmost insignificance.'[2]

The backgrounds of the two foreign secretaries were very different. Curzon, a former Viceroy of India and a member of Lloyd George's War Cabinet, took his title from Kedleston Hall, where he had been born and where his family had lived since the twelfth century. He had been educated at Eton and Oxford. Ramsay MacDonald had been educated at a village school, which he left at the age of fourteen; and he was the illegitimate son of a farm maidservant and a ploughman who had briefly worked on the same farm.

*

Ramsay MacDonald, I repeat, was not what he seemed. Indeed he was not even who he seemed: he was known by a name which was not his. What and who was he? In some ways it is easy to say what

---

* But that was something that happened quite often. Indeed, even at Lausanne, having had to listen to a harangue from the French President Poincaré, he had burst out sobbing. The Italian representative, Sforza, had pulled a silver hipflask from the depth of his frock coat and administered 'an invigorating mouthful of brandy' to his British counterpart.

PROLOGUE

he was not rather than what he was. Before we seek to penetrate the mystery, a few brief facts can be agreed.

He was born in 1866 in Lossiemouth, a small fishing town in the north-east of Scotland. He was brought up by his single mother in circumstances just about as straitened as they could be in Victorian rural Britain. When he left school at the age of fourteen, it was to work on a nearby farm. He could have continued there until his death, like his father, of whom nothing much is remembered.

Instead, he found his way to London and in circumstances of great privation tried to scratch a living from minor clerical jobs, an existence that could have been described by Charles Dickens or George Gissing. But MacDonald's abilities and ambitions were not constrained by his circumstances and his intellectual existence was on a different plane from his physical surroundings. By hard work and conscious self-improvement he emerged into the stimulating world of progressive ideas and politics, the world of HG Wells and Shaw and the new Fabian Society.

The young MacDonald became active in a whole range of bodies which collectively were to fuse into the Labour Party. By force of his industry and abilities he played as important a role as anyone in the creation of that party, although emotionally he was never at its heart. He didn't see it, as subsequent Labour prime ministers like Clement Attlee and Harold Wilson did, as a family or a crusade.

The first unique feature about Ramsay MacDonald, then, is the remarkable journey from farm bothy to the pinnacle of power. The second is the debate which has continued from 1930 to the present day: rather than the creator of the Labour Party, was he a class traitor who set out to destroy it? In January 1924, as leader of the party, he became the first Labour Prime Minister of Britain. The government over which he presided was a minority government. It fell after just a matter of months, but in that time and within the constraints that it operated, this first Labour government achieved a number of successes, particularly in foreign policy, in which MacDonald himself acted as Foreign Secretary as well as Prime Minister.

If MacDonald had died at the end of his first term in office, he would be remembered as a brilliant creative politician, and as the most romantic of phenomena, a man who had achieved the British equivalent of moving from a log cabin to the White House. But he

PROLOGUE

did not die then. He became Prime Minister again in May 1929. This time Labour was the largest party in the Commons. But the great financial crisis, still simply known as 'The Crash', was about to strike Britain, as it struck the rest of the world. As the British economy, indeed the capitalist model, seemed about to collapse, MacDonald chose to abandon party politics. He elected instead to preside over the National Government, a coalition consisting chiefly of the Conservative Party, some Liberals and just a handful of his Labour colleagues.

The great question is why MacDonald did this. His critics—and there were and are many critics—argue that he deliberately abandoned Labour. Some say he had always meant to, that he had been an undercover agent of the right all along, that he had deliberately strangled his own child. Even his kinder critics thought that he had been seduced by his contacts with the aristocracy. He was subjected to abuse and reviled by those who had been his closest supporters. He continued in political life only by the tolerance of his capitalist enemies. His later years were humiliating ones, as his physical and intellectual energies, which he had given in such great measure to the labour movement, ebbed away. He was no more than a shadow that would disappear into the mist.

So this political figure, hugely influential in his time, is now little remembered. The party which he created has done its best to write him out of its history, remembering him, if at all, as the traitor, the lost leader who abandoned his party for the ribbon on his coat.

It's easy to arrive at such a conclusion. MacDonald was an elusive personality, difficult to categorise. His contemporaries all acknowledged this. The influences on and the nature of his personality were complex. He was a romantic, refreshing himself from bogus wells of mythology and the mists of Celtic imagination.

There are a number of MacDonalds. One is the treacherous defector from the Labour cause, and another is his own view of a romantic visionary surrounded by unappreciative pygmies. But if we go to the kernel of his being we can find a complicated consistency, neither entirely commendable nor entirely deserving of criticism, and that is the MacDonald this book seeks to explore and reveal. Its approach will be thematic, influenced by chronology, but not in thrall to it.

1

BACKGROUND AND BEGINNINGS

Using the word in its strictly technical sense, no British Prime Minister since Ramsay MacDonald has been a bastard. Happily, when the next illegitimate Prime Minister comes along, no great interest will be taken in the matter. It's important to understand just how different things were when MacDonald formed his first government in January 1924. Those who were illegitimate suffered legal disadvantage, in relation to succession for instance. Far more significantly, they faced enormous social prejudice. The upper classes connived in elaborate pretence to hide the stain of bastardy, and the lower classes ignored it, but in the middle classes in MacDonald's lifetime and long afterwards the stigma was immense, and MacDonald emerged from the lower into these middle classes to face exposure and humiliation. Some hint of the manners of the times is given by the fact that George V, whose hands he notionally kissed on his appointment as Prime Minister in January 1924 and whose friend he was to become, had ordained that at his court even the 'innocent' party to a divorce would not be received. If the innocent divorcé was unwelcome, what was the fate of the innocent issue of an unmarried union?

*

MacDonald was born on 12 October 1866. In most accounts of his life he is said to have been born in the Highlands. That is really another half-truth. Lossiemouth is on the northern side of the Highland Line, but not deep within the land of the mountain and the flood. The Highland Line doesn't divide Scotland on an east–west axis. It runs roughly from the south-west, as far south as Arran and Helensburgh, to the north-east around Stonehaven. The true north-west highlands, the heart of Gaeldom, lie to the north-west of Inverness; and the coastal area between Stonehaven and Inverness, with Lossiemouth somewhere near its centre, is characterised by relatively productive fishing ports and farmland hugely more fertile than the heathery acid moors to the west.

One of MacDonald's earliest biographers conceded that although the setting was superb, Lossiemouth itself was less than prepossessing, 'A grim little village of fisherfolk and farm workers. A street or two of small unlovely houses on the slope of a hill above the sea, an abrupt rockfall, and below it, more small grey houses within reach of the flying foam.' He goes on to say:

> In spring and summer miles of the surrounding moors are golden with lemon-scented gorse. Pink sea thrift covers the cliffs, white gulls and white cloudlets sail playfully together in the vast blue sky. But autumn and winter last longer and seem more kindred to the place—when the wind screams, and under massed black clouds the ruthless seas are one heaving mass from Moray to the Pole. The village withdraws within itself. Outwardly, save for its courage, its patience under the lash of wind and wave, the place itself is prosaic. But in its surroundings there is all that is needed to stir the imagination.[1]

The writer, who came from gentler climes, may have been a bit hard on the realities of rural Scotland, but he was right in sensing the inspirational romance which Lossiemouth inspired in MacDonald and which he drew on to create his particular persona.

The area's relative fertility doesn't imply a bounteous prosperity. Rural life in the county of Moray had been hard before the arrival of agricultural improvements, and though they brought benefits in the course of the nineteenth century, even in MacDonald's time the benefits, such as they were, were largely enjoyed by landlords and substantial farmers, not by the ordinary farm worker. 'My childhood', MacDonald told the *Sunday Express* in 1929, 'was spent at a time when the larger farmers were turning the people off the land,

BACKGROUND AND BEGINNINGS

and when the good, honest hatred that Scotsman has for landlords was being encouraged and was taking deep root.'²

*

MacDonald's family came from the ranks of these ordinary farm workers. Although for most of his life he was known as James Ramsay MacDonald, his birth certificate named him as 'James MacDonald Ramsay'. Even his name was a fiction. His mother was Annie Ramsay, a farm servant. Although he isn't mentioned on Ramsay's birth certificate, the father was John MacDonald, a ploughman who had worked for a time at the farm where Annie, who left school at thirteen or fourteen, was in service. Lord Elton, who knew the family and was the Cambridge tutor of Malcolm MacDonald, Ramsay's son, describes Annie as being beautiful with 'her mother's darkly flashing eyes and a dignity of bearing which seemed to be hereditary among the Ramsays'.³*

What little we know about John MacDonald comes mostly from the minute book of the Kirk Session of Alves Free Kirk. Annie and John, by now a foreman at Sweethillock Farm, appeared before the Kirk Session on 14 December 1866. Annie named MacDonald as the father of the child and MacDonald acknowledged the fact. They were addressed by the Moderator on the sin they had committed and were exhorted to seek repentance and forgiveness. They received the advice 'in a becoming manner and professed their sorrow and their desire to be forgiven'. The Kirk Session was satisfied,

---

* Godfrey Elton was an unusual man. Rugby School followed by Balliol College, Oxford, where his education was interrupted by the First World War. He was wounded and taken into captivity in the course of the siege of Kut al-Amara, but survived the notorious conditions in which the Turks kept their prisoners. After the war he spent the rest of his life at Queen's College, Oxford, a fellow and praelector in modern history, eventually a supernumerary fellow. He was a genial member of the college and a generous host. Latterly he became a reactionary and could appear to be a disciplinarian. But he was a supporter of the Labour Party, and particularly of MacDonald. When he was elevated to the House of Lords in 1934, MacDonald's son Malcolm, whose tutor he had been, was Under-Secretary of State for Dominion Affairs and the historian LB Namier enjoyed himself: 'In the eighteenth century peers made their tutors under-secretaries; in the twentieth under-secretaries make their tutors peers.'

agreeing that the two young people be absolved from censure 'and be restored to church privileges'.[4]

Lord Elton was a distinguished historian but could well have been a romantic novelist. He tells us that John MacDonald was handsome and quick-witted 'with a certain jovial recklessness in his bearing' and that the farm workers had noticed the development of the relationship between him and Annie. He did some of her jobs around the farm for her, and she put extra cream on his porridge.[5] That is all we know of John MacDonald.

Annie Ramsay was a woman of character. She and John MacDonald are thought to have been engaged but to have quarrelled, with the result that Annie decided she would be better off without a husband. Her own mother, Isabella ('Bella'), was also a powerful personality. She had separated from her husband, William Ramsay. She brought up four children on her own. Isabella thought she was a cut above her neighbours in Lossiemouth, where she earned her living as a seamstress. Indeed her brother was a minister. Her husband, William Ramsay, had been a baker, which had a whiff of a profession about it, and her family had been small farmers in the parish of Spynie, where MacDonald would be buried. Altogether, she regarded her background as superior to that of the farm labourers and fishermen of the town.

Whatever Bella's dreams of ancestral prosperity, Annie started out at the bottom of the social scale. John MacDonald's pay as a ploughman would have been about £20 a year in cash and perhaps another £20 in kind. Annie herself would live on £7 or £8 a year plus keep. We know a little about Annie, who didn't die until 1910. MacDonald remained close to her to the end. Her death was one of a series of blows that had an incremental effect on him.

When David Marquand wrote his biography of MacDonald in 1957, Annie Ramsay was only just disappearing from Lossiemouth memory. Marquand was able to describe her good features and natural dignity, her reserve and also her stubbornness. She, like Bella, was a skilled dressmaker and made hats for half the women in Lossiemouth. She was capable of dignity despite her social status and despite the fact that she continued to work in the fields and even followed the herring fleet around the coast as a fisherwoman, gutting the fish as they were landed. She had strong political views and expressed them. The family milk jug was decorated with a picture of Gladstone. She supported the Boers during the South African War, and when Ladysmith was relieved she lowered her blinds and hung crape on her front door. That wasn't calculated to make her popular: she was burned in effigy on the bonfire that marked the end of the siege. By this time MacDonald was in London, active in national politics. His response to the South African War was very much the same as his mother's, and the reaction to his response was fairly similar too.

So Ramsay spent his early years with these two independent women. Their influence was reflected in the confidence he was to display in his own abilities and the role in which these abilities could be deployed. Bella Ramsay was religious, a committed member of the Free Church of Scotland. The Free Church was born of what is called the Disruption of 1843, when 474 ministers of the Church of Scotland, about a third of the total, walked away from their brethren largely on the issue of whether a patron had the right to install a minister in his parish. This was perhaps the greatest schism of very many in the history of the Church of Scotland, but it was not the last, and Bella had strong opinions on them all. She enjoyed controversy.

She also had a fund of the stories and legends of Morayshire, which she imparted to her grandson, creating or feeding an abiding passion for what he saw as the romance and myth of his heritage. For the whole of his life MacDonald found solace in coming back to the histories and literature of the land which he had left in his search for fulfilment. His need for romance was insatiable and at the centre of his character. This otherworldliness, his feyness, was present not just in his outward personality, when it informed his inspirational speaking, but also in his inner character and definition.

*

If Lossiemouth, perched on the edge of the North Sea, was not truly in the Highlands of Ossian or Sir Walter Scott, it was, all the same, individual and special. In MacDonald's time Lossiemouth—'Lossie' as it was and still is known—was a small town sheltered beneath a spur of rock. It looks over the grey seductive sea. Northwards the mountains of the true Highlands can be seen. Not much more than one hundred years before MacDonald was born and just forty-three miles away as the crow flies from the place of his birth, the last great hopes of Jacobitism were extinguished at Culloden and the true independence of Gaeldom came to an end. Spynie, where his Ramsay ancestors lie, was two miles inland. There is a ruined castle, once a bishop's palace, essential romantic elements for an impressionable boy.

Closed off till then from contact with wider civilisation, the way of life was not greatly touched by the spirit of modernity. Pagan ways continued. Deaths were understood to be preceded by the sight of a ghostly light which would migrate from the cottage in which the death took place to the churchyard. Evil spirits were warded off by a ceremony involving setting a tarred barrel alight and parading it around the town. The church worked to try to suppress the continuing practice of sorcery and witchcraft.[6] Many writers observed the influences of Nordic rather than Celtic culture.

But change was underway and very gradually becoming apparent. The recent agricultural improvements had extended the arable acreage in the area by a factor of three between 1857 and 1881. The traditional agricultural economy knew nothing of green crops. There were no potatoes, and the usual diet was of oats, barley and weeds. A new harbour was built in the 1840s and a railway linked Lossiemouth with Elgin in 1852, but at the time of MacDonald's birth, the population of Lossiemouth was only about 1,300, and the town was just beginning to lose the character of a remote community, essentially on the edge.

The laird, the local landowner, had laid out the town to support its function as a fishing port. The houses he built are of stone and have an air of solidity. The streets are unusually wide and are separated by areas of grass studded with daisies and sea pinks.

Lossiemouth is indeed at the mouth of the Lossie, a substantial stream though hardly one of Scotland's great salmon rivers, which turns as it reaches the coast and flows parallel to it for some distance, its right bank a long sandy spit which separates it from the North Sea and shelters the town. When the spit eventually gives out, a series of wooden bulwarks continue to the pier to protect the

BACKGROUND AND BEGINNINGS

harbour. There are rotting timbers still, to which fishing boats are tied up, that were there in MacDonald's time.

The town faces north. Behind it lies flat, fertile farmland. That flatness, and the open sea on the other side, make for big skies and much light. The whole effect is much more of East Anglia than of the Scottish Highlands, and Ramsay's Gaelic conceit is a fancy from the start. Benjamin Britten would have been at home here.

It is appropriate, then, that there should be a golf course. Golf has always been a more democratic sport in Scotland than in England, but, even so, the golf course and particularly its clubhouse in Lossie are very much what the Scots call douce: respectable and prosperous. It was established in 1889 and the course was initially laid out by the very famous 'old' Tom Morris of St Andrews. More of Moray Golf Club later.

MacDonald's birthplace can still be seen, as can the more substantial house which he built later for his family. More, too, of that larger house in due course.

*

For a farm labourer life was nasty and brutish, lived generally in a 'bothy', a very basic part of the farm buildings, often separate from the farmhouse. The Royal Commission on the Employment of Children, Young Persons and Women in Agriculture of 1867 recorded an unappealing picture of bothy life:

> As a general rule, the bothy consists of a portion of the farm buildings or steading formed into a single room of moderate size. It is supplied with no separate sleeping arrangements and nobody is employed to clean it or make the beds (and the bothy men if left to themselves will never attempt to keep it clean and tidy); a heap of coals will be seen in one corner and of firewood in another; it is furnished with no tables and no seats, so that on returning from work the only place the servants have to sit upon is their chests; and the flags with which it is paved are generally broken into small pieces by having the firewood chopped upon them. In a few cases I have met with bothies attached to the stables where the ventilation (if indeed it can be so called) was of the worst description. I recollect two which consisted of portions of the stables in which cart-

horses were kept and were only separated from the stables themselves by thin wooden partitions, which were broken and defective in many places. These bothies had no means of obtaining air except what came through the stables; and the stables themselves were badly ventilated and contained several horses each ... There can be no question that a life in such bothies as I have last been describing must have the effect of making them rude and boorish.[7]

It is hardly surprising that the divergence between agricultural employer and employee was widening.

MacDonald's experience of the agricultural economy was to inform his political views. The agricultural worker moved in the course of his career from farm to farm and bothy to bothy. It was an unsettled and unsettling life with no intellectual or intelligent component. The distractions consisted of drink, singing 'bothy ballads', some of which have happily lived on to the present time, and periodic escapes from this masculine world to the delights of fornication, usually with maidservants also employed on the farm.

Marriage, for financial reasons and from the circumstances of a nomadic existence, was rarely an option—indeed a ploughman would be dismissed and lose secure employment if he did marry—and among the lower levels of the farming community in Morayshire illegitimacy was not as rare as it would have been in the more rarefied world to which MacDonald migrated. In the county of Moray the rate of illegitimacy was about fifteen per cent—the highest rate in Scotland and probably in Britain. The royal commission was told that the Church had 'all but abandoned ecclesiastical discipline in cases of sexual immorality, and even if such discipline were attempted to be revived it would be now so little regarded as to be quite ineffectual'.[8]

There was no secret of MacDonald's illegitimacy in Lossie. His mother never pretended to be a married woman. MacDonald was a reserved and secretive man, sensitive to the blows and buffets of fate and of the world. In his extensive written reflections it is clear that he felt he struggled against great odds. There are those who thought his illegitimacy mattered to him. His daughter Ishbel, the closest of his children, went so far as to say that his illegitimacy was the central influence on his life.[9] That seems to me an exaggeration.

It's true, though, that he didn't publicise his illegitimacy. It took the publication of a facsimile birth certificate by Horatio Bottomley in the populist magazine *John Bull*, dealt with later, to bring the fact to widespread attention.

In 1896 MacDonald said that 'all my early memories are wretched to me ... As far as I can remember, I had a grudge against the world rankling in me.'[10] But he attributed his local problems to the hostility of respectable relatives and neighbours, rather than to the fact of his illegitimacy.[11] The presence or absence of his father and the fact that he was not married to his mother do not seem to have bulked large with him. His father, who seems to have gravitated to being more of a farmer than a ploughman, he only saw once, 'leading some horses out of a cattle show in Elgin'. That some of his prickliness was the result of the burden of bastardy is an easy assumption. The absence of a father no doubt did have a bearing on his character, but in the world of his youth he would not have been aware of any great stigma. Other factors had a much greater effect on his cast of mind.

*

MacDonald's apartness is crucially important. Although he thought of himself always as part of the working class, *his* working classes were not those of the great towns and cities. The community he felt himself part of was in truth an imagined and romanticised community. He injected into the people he felt he belonged to more sturdy independence than perhaps they felt. He said that the folk of Lossiemouth

> earn their scanty living amidst danger and hardship on the waters, and they are willing that it should be so. They are not tended, fed, pruned and sheltered like the flowers of [a] garden. They are comely people of an easy dignity of carriage like all men and women unburdened by the spirit of servitude and living a life of natural independence.[12]

This is pretty strange stuff. The qualities he described are obviously partly fantasised. Similarly the Scotland he describes. 'Located at the periphery,' as Kevin Morgan puts it, 'beyond the experience of most of his readers, the images had an almost fabulous quality.'[13] This was magical conjuring.

But while MacDonald exaggerated, there was an element of truth in his assertion that the people of Lossiemouth were 'the stout stems of a natural aristocracy'. He said that their bearing was without servility or sycophancy. Given this belief, it was entirely reasonable that this good-looking, six-foot-tall man conducted himself like an aristocrat. Thomas Jones, the civil servant superstar of the inter-war years, 'one of the six most important men in the world and keeper of a thousand secrets', said of MacDonald, 'It is so plain from his distinguished head, his address, his rings, that he is not a TU [trade union] leader, but an aristocrat.'[14] His aristocratic cronies, of whom much more later, accepted him as one of their own. Lord De La Warr said: 'JRM is *not* a snob, but he genuinely prefers the aristocrat to the proletarian as everyday associates.'[15] The Duchess of Sutherland told her sister that 'MacDonald is no Labour man. He is one of us.'[16]

*

MacDonald's predecessor as Foreign Secretary, that George Nathaniel Curzon whom we met briefly in the Prologue, was educated, as has been said, at Eton and at Balliol College, Oxford. It was while he was at Oxford that he appeared in a piece of college doggerel, 'The Masque of Balliol':

> My name is George Nathaniel Curzon,
> I am a most superior person.
> My cheek is pink, my hair is sleek,
> I dine at Blenheim once a week.

James Ramsay MacDonald was, notoriously, to dine, if not at Blenheim, then at Londonderry House, *twice* a week when he was Prime Minister, but he didn't attend Eton or any university. He went first to the Free Kirk School in Lossiemouth. There he was said to have been savagely beaten. We don't know why; it may just have been one of the teacher's little ways. The same man had formerly taught James Barrie in Kirriemuir. After the teacher's death by drowning, MacDonald went to the parish school at Drainie, a few

BACKGROUND AND BEGINNINGS

miles from his home. There was no more beating, and Ramsay had a warm relationship with the school's one teacher, James Macdonald, who presided over the school's two classrooms. MacDonald's formal education ended in July 1881, when he was still fourteen. Curzon's education ended in 1883, when he was twenty-four. He had already been awarded important university prizes and now received the supreme accolade, a prize fellowship at All Souls College.

*

Was MacDonald, then, uneducated and semi-literate? Emphatically not. James Macdonald was a remarkable master. With his pupil-teacher and sewing mistress he presided over about seventy boys and girls. The school inspectors were impressed by their results. The inspectors complained about a certain informality—'humming at work'—and a lack of cleanliness. But the dominie knew what mattered. His drive and the achievements of his pupils in challenging circumstances seem incredible today but were probably not untypical of the commitment to education in village schools throughout Scotland at that time. Ramsay MacDonald wrote later that James Macdonald was part of a

> goodly company of schoolmasters, who teach without putting any goal except knowledge before their pupils, and who present knowledge to them as something which is pursued through a man's life. The work done in the school was of an old order now. It was a steady hard grind to get at the heart of things. We turned everything outside and in, pulled everything to pieces in order to put it together again, analysed, parsed, got firm hold of the roots, shivered English into fragments and fitted it together like a Chinese Puzzle, all by the help of Bain's Sixteenpenny Grammar (which the dominie's pupils must remember as they do the Shorter Catechism), and wrestled with 'deductions'. Then every bolt in our intellect was tightened up. One of the dominie's generalizations was: 'You must master: that is education: when you have mastered one thing you are well on the way to master all things' ... Mental capacity and character are what he strove to produce in his boys. He was Calvinistic enough to see that he did not provide the armour for life's fight. That came

from the Fates who give presents to life at birth. His work was to temper what was given.[17]

Ramsay was no model pupil. He played truant when he felt like it and got involved in fights and generally did what healthy young boys do if they get the chance. But he was in no sense a rebel. At the age of thirteen, he started a diary. He can be seen to be expanding his horizons. He took an interest in national political events—Gladstone's victory in Midlothian, for example. He started a cricket club—not a very Scottish, let alone Highland, thing to do.

MacDonald describes the machinery of education as being 'as old as Knox; the education was the best ever given to the sons and daughters of men'. His teacher fed Ramsay's precocious appetite with Carlyle and Ruskin and Henry David Thoreau. The motto of another Scottish school at this time was blunt and unforgiving: *disce puer, aut abi* (learn, child, or be gone). MacDonald wanted to learn, and he stayed, and he was provided with rigorous reading and instruction which, for an able and ambitious young man, would supply a more solid introduction to social philosophy than an idle young aristocrat would receive at Oxford or Cambridge.

The little school was a concentrated and particularly Scottish and democratic institution. Side by side, young children were taught that c-a-t spelled 'cat', and 'older ones were drilled in Latin, Greek and the mysteries of Euclid. They entered the building as infants and left to go to the university or the bothy, depending on their abilities and ambitions.'

*

It was very nearly to the bothy that MacDonald went when he left school in the summer of 1881 and began work on a neighbouring farm. He enjoyed the work. Like young men of his time, often from much more exalted classes, he found a virtue and an appeal in hard physical exertion. While they took pleasure as he later would in long, testing marches, at this stage he exulted in exhausting work in the fields. He admired the ploughmen with whom he worked, who knew their Burns and their Bible by heart and seemed to him, at least in retrospect, to be constantly singing. It was only by accident—one of the critical accidents of his life, but an accident all the

BACKGROUND AND BEGINNINGS

same, not inevitable—that he was diverted from falling into the mould in which his father had lived: back-breaking manual work, poverty, siring another generation of illegitimate children.

The critical incident was that while Ramsay was working the fields, the pupil-teacher went off for a week to Edinburgh to sit exams. Ramsay was asked to take his place. At the end of the year, the pupil-teacher left permanently and MacDonald replaced him in that role, a role he was to occupy for four years.

MacDonald talked about pupils from his school going straight into university. Financially this was impossible for him, but in his years as a pupil-teacher his intellect was stimulated as it perhaps would not have been at a Scottish university in those days. His diaries reveal a formidable brain, and his interests were not those of the cowshed and the bothy. He would probably not have broken with his hereditary destiny without the activities and mental expansion of these four years; but as a result of them, MacDonald has been described as by far the best educated Labour politician of these years. That depends a bit on how wide the net is cast, but he certainly was extraordinarily well-read, and he continued to read widely for the rest of his life. He read the standards of English literature at school and a daunting library of church histories and sermons belonging to Bella Ramsay. A consumptive watchmaker who ended his days in Lossiemouth lent him volumes of mainstream authors from Shakespeare through to Dickens and Burns. Increasingly he found himself absorbed in the natural sciences, particularly geology and biology.

The conscious self-improvement which had marked voluntary activities at school continued. He founded the Lossiemouth Field Club and went with its members on scientific excursions, where they read papers to one another. The forty-four-page study of the geological structure of the Coulard Hill, which runs above Lossiemouth on its landward side, still exists, together with an attack on 'cruelty to animals', which starts, 'Nero began his long list of cruelties by torturing flies and ended by murdering his mother.' He also joined the local Mutual Improvement Society, one of innumerable such bodies that existed in the country in those days and in which earnest young men and women consciously sought to better themselves. He took part in weekly debates and very soon became secretary of the society. What remains of his early speeches is evidence of a slightly brash self-assurance, typical indeed of undergraduates of his age, tilted towards the controversial and engaging in philosophy and particularly science. Politics also featured. The 1884 Reform Act gave the vote to some agricultural workers and tripled the local electorate. Resentment of the landlord and the propertied classes was increasing, and MacDonald's politics were expressive of these long-suppressed sentiments. Subscribing to the *Christian Socialist*, which advocated reform of the land laws, and reading Henry George's *Progress and Poverty*, he sought what he described in one of his youthful fragments as 'the nationalisation of land'.

The writings of Henry George had a particular influence on Ramsay. George was a hugely popular American economist who flourished in the last third of the nineteenth century. He wrote widely, and his most successful book, *Progress and Poverty* (1879), was a best-seller worldwide. He supported the usual progressive causes, such as free trade, but his main contribution to the political debate was 'Georgism', which held that while individuals should be allowed to flourish as a result of their own efforts, land should be the basis of taxation. In effect, land and other key elements of the economy should be in public ownership. His pragmatic views were based on his own observations, and not on a priori theory, and thus stand apart from Marxism and doctrinaire socialism. This will be seen to reflect MacDonald's own position; he too was little affected by dogma. George obviously informed MacDonald's thinking when he was a young man, but Ramsay's undogmatic approach was part of the settled ballast of his mind throughout his life.

*

The title of the magazine, the *Christian Socialist*, raises two questions: Was MacDonald a Christian? Was he a socialist? He had been brought up by his mother in the strict Calvinist tradition, but although he remained religious and spiritual to a high degree throughout his life, he was not a Christian—certainly not to the extent of subscribing to all the tenets of Christianity. He always attended church during his

BACKGROUND AND BEGINNINGS

visits to Lossie, but otherwise took an interest in religion that was essentially broad and didn't adhere to any particular sect. He believed in Christian ethics, but his commitment to the spiritual life went further than that. He saw an overarching authority and design in the universe. His conviction that there was in and above life something greater than physical existence was fed by his love of nature. He has been described as having been too much of a rationalist to accept all aspects of the faith in which he was brought up, but what was truly significant about him was not the narrow outlook of a rationalist but a searching openness which left a space in his mind for even a belief in myth and magic, indeed second sight.

Whether he was a socialist and, if so, what kind of socialist he was are matters which will be debated throughout this book. At the moment, as he prepares to leave the Lossiemouth nest, he was certainly not a socialist in any technical sense. Socialism, left in the doldrums after the flourishing of the Christian Socialism promoted by Ruskin and Arnold and their contemporaries, had entered a fallow period (from which, however, it would shortly revive). So although MacDonald favoured social and property reform, it was to liberalism that he looked as the machinery of change. Indeed he acted as Liberal sub-agent at a by-election in Elginshire and Nairnshire. His candidate won.

To understand MacDonald's political position, it is important to try to understand what 'socialism' meant for men of his generation. That isn't easy. Socialism meant different things to different people. What it pretty well never meant for MacDonald and for many others was a rigid, doctrinaire or theoretical set of rules. MacDonald was never remotely a Marxist. A 'socialist' outlook meant little more than a benevolent, progressive attitude of mind. Harold Macmillan's father, roughly a contemporary of MacDonald, was a Liberal, but he and his own father were influenced, as Macmillan himself would be, by Frederick Denison Maurice, author of *The Kingdom of Christ*, and Charles Kingsley, who was, like MacDonald, an adherent of the Christian Socialist movement.

Macmillan described the movement:

> It began about the time of the Chartist agitation and the World Revolutionary Movement of 1848. It was, in a sense, a precursor of

THE CANCELLED PRIME MINISTER

the Fabians, although it was fundamentally religious rather than political. In reality it had developed no economic doctrine. It was a social movement based upon an intense feeling for the poor and the suffering. It was applied Christianity ... The fundamental radicalism—the desire for reform—continued to inspire many men and women.[18]

When Macmillan thought back to MacDonald, as he knew him in the 1930s, he recognised it was difficult to know what he really was.

> Was he a Socialist? He was certainly not a Marxist. In some ways I felt that he was much nearer to the old Christian Socialist ideals of my grandfather. That is to say his political attitude was not based on clear economic concepts, but much more upon the general demands of humanity, with a special regard to the needs of the poor and those who had fallen by the wayside.[19]

It is crucial to understand that this generous benevolence was what MacDonald was all about. He was never a socialist in the sense that even the wholly pragmatic Clement Attlee was. It is tempting, if flip, to say that if he was never committed to socialism, he cannot be accused of betraying it.

In his review of the political personages that he had known in the course of his career, Macmillan struggled to understand the enigma of MacDonald. As a fellow Scot and a romantic himself, he came closer to doing so than some Anglo-Saxon historians. 'Some', said Macmillan,

> regard [MacDonald] as a double-dyed traitor who destroyed his own child in 1931; others as a man of high patriotic motives who consciously took the decision which he knew would blacken his reputation but believed to be in the national interest. Where does the truth lie? The answer perhaps lies in the fact that in temperament he was a romantic. He was also vain and, like Sir Willoughby Patterne, he had a good leg.* Born of humble origin in the East

---

* Sir Willoughby Patterne is the solipsistic hero of a novel, *The Egoist*, not by Macmillan's favourite author, Anthony Trollope, but by George Meredith. MacDonald showed his good leg to advantage in the plus fours which he frequently affected. If indeed he was proud of his legs, that may have explained his enthusiasm for court dress and tight breeches.

BACKGROUND AND BEGINNINGS

Highlands he had all the pride and ambition of his race. He was not an economist, although he wrote a rather sentimental book on Socialism which I remember reading with some enthusiasm when I was at school. I am sure he had not studied Marxism.[20]

Macmillan was right: MacDonald was no economist, certainly no Marxist. He was romantic and vain, and it was the combination of these qualities which led him to believe that he had a personal and self-sacrificial role to play in 1931.

*

The records of Drainie School reveal in April 1885 that Ramsay was performing well as a student teacher, but just a month later, with the permission of the school board, he left, on what seems the inevitable next step for an able and ambitious young man who sought to be more than a student teacher in a small Scottish town.

2

A STEP TO THE SIDE

Let us pause for a moment to look briefly at this young MacDonald and why it's worth following him on his journey from Lossiemouth in his search for something—something he hadn't yet identified.

In the first place he was on a unique journey, worth following because of its uniqueness. He was to be the first Labour Prime Minister, and he performed that role in a way that moved Britain from a predominantly aristocratic system of government to a modern, inclusive social democracy and, importantly, did so without the shocks and turbulence which accompanied similar moves in other countries.

Secondly, he effected a change in his personal circumstances of a sort to which no other British politician has achieved, starting from a level far below that of, say, Lloyd George, probably his nearest rival in terms of social mobility, and ending by moving among the aristocracy, the politician closest to George V, and his monarch's friend.

Thirdly, it's fascinating to seek to pierce the shadows of his complicated character. Most politicians are very straightforward. Not all: what made Arthur Balfour tick was obscured by his dreamy languor, and Disraeli was a concoction of faery mystery. But MacDonald went far beyond that. He created an entirely artificial world woven through with the mythological attributes of a Celtic dreamworld which he never inhabited, and he mesmerised himself and his audiences by seeming to live only half in the real world. It is well worth trying to separate reality from the imagination and to do so without oversimplifying the nature of this complicated being.

*

In the course of the narrative of MacDonald's earliest years, some elements of what I propose to argue will have become fairly clear. All the same, as he prepares to move from domestic security towards the national stage, it's as well that I set out my argument in more detail. I shall also outline in this chapter the differing historiographical treatments of MacDonald.

MacDonald's interior world of noble Highlanders, of flights of fancy, of another world of faery dreams and the second sight, is something very unusual. There have been too many attempts to understand MacDonald that simply identify his oddness but leave it unanalysed. That is too facile an approach, and it creates paradoxes in and around MacDonald which have invited attack.

The most obvious line of attack is that he was simply insincere. He emerged from poverty, claiming to want to improve the lot of the poor and downtrodden, but ended by inhabiting and clearly enjoying the company of the rich and famous. He did indeed love his duchesses.

Was he, then, a hypocrite? No: when the economy juddered to a halt in the great financial crisis of 1930–1, he was prepared to separate himself from the bulk of the Labour Party, which he had worked so hard to create, and he presided, in the National Government, over an administration which was overwhelmingly Conservative. He came close to destroying the party that he had claimed to love, and was reviled by former colleagues as the lost leader.

This wasn't the conduct of a hypocrite. He could have chosen to be remembered as a prodigy, a Byronic figure who had risen to dazzling heights from the most obscure of origins: a phenomenon without parallel in British political history. But that's not how he has been seen by history; and how he is seen by history is the result of his choosing what he saw as the path of duty.

He was expelled from the Labour Party and took with him only a handful of his own supporters. With this tiny band, he was now the prisoner of the Conservatives. He behaved with dignity, but the situation was horrible. The cabinet decided to leave the gold standard. At the general election at the end of October 1931 the Labour Party was reduced to just fifty-two seats, fewer than in 1918.

Thereafter it was downhill for the saviour of the nation. His health caused him increasing problems. He suffered from insomnia, depression and glaucoma. He was aware that his intellectual powers were failing. His memory deteriorated and he found it difficult to concentrate. Although he still had presence and charm, he was far older than his years, his morale eroded by the viciousness of attacks from his old Labour friends, only a handful of whom remained on speaking terms with him. The behaviour of his former friends was described as being like hounds straining at the leash to kill.

In June 1935 Stanley Baldwin took over as Prime Minister and MacDonald took *his* job as Lord President of the Council. Three months later, at a general election, he lost his seat by a massive 20,500 votes to his old Labour friend, the engaging old bruiser who started in boxing booths and ended as Minister for Defence, Emanuel Shinwell:* the days when Shinwell had described MacDonald as 'a prince among men' were long past. MacDonald crept back into parliament through a by-election and staggered on almost unnoticed for another two years. Lord Simon, a colleague in the National Government, said, 'The denunciations heaped upon MacDonald's head by many who had previously idolised him were the most violent I have ever known in British politics.'[1] He died a sad and pathetic figure, and his memory disappeared fast into the shadows.

His image continued to fade. Those on the right, possibly ashamed of their support for him, blocked his memory out. Those on the left who remembered him did so as a man who had not merely failed his party but deliberately plotted to destroy it.

In 1976, when the Labour government was considering austerity, Tony Benn circulated minutes of meetings from MacDonald's cabinet. When Neil Kinnock didn't support the miners in the strike of 1984–5, he was disparaged as 'Ramsay McKinnock'.[2]

*

---

* During the First World War Shinwell chaired a meeting in the Charing Cross Hall in Glasgow when MacDonald was speaking about the protection of civil liberties after the promulgation of the Defence of the Realm Act. The leader of the Scottish Patriotic Federation, Neil Jamieson, arrived, intent on breaking up the meeting. Shinwell, who had been an amateur boxer and had considered a professional career, 'ran down and punched [Jamieson] between the eyes. The door was closed and I returned to the platform, where I made a short introductory speech in favour of peace by negotiation' (Shinwell, *Conflict without Malice*, p. 116).

THE CANCELLED PRIME MINISTER

We must look at how MacDonald has been seen from their different perspectives by those who studied him. Philip Snowden's *Autobiography* was published in 1934. Snowden and his views will be looked at later. The first stand-alone biography of MacDonald was by Lauchlan MacNeill Weir, *The Tragedy of Ramsay MacDonald*, published in 1938. Weir was MacDonald's parliamentary private secretary. His book is immoderate and hostile. His motives for writing the book are not entirely clear. He did not receive office from MacDonald beyond that of an unpaid parliamentary private secretary. He wrote the book before most of the materials we now have were available. He had been a journalist, and he writes the book with style as well as bile. There are some good stories, a lot of redundant verse and some pretty pointless criticism about such matters as the number of support staff MacDonald had. If it were not inspired solely by the charge of personal ambition and betrayal, it could have been a mildly interesting book.

Almost equally biased in a different direction was Lord Elton's very sympathetic study mentioned above, *The Life of James Ramsay MacDonald*, published in 1939. Elton had stood for parliament as a Labour candidate and was in the House of Lords as a National Labour peer. He had been the tutor of Ramsay MacDonald's son Malcolm at Cambridge and remained a close friend. His book was meant to be favourable, but only the first volume, covering the period up to 1919, was published and it did nothing to improve MacDonald's reputation. It is written with affection and sensitivity, very much by a member of the family. While it is hugely biased, Elton does have some insights as a result of family knowledge and of the fact that he was writing when memories of MacDonald's childhood in Lossiemouth were still fresh, and the book still deserves to be read. In 1932 Harold Laski, a professor at the London School of Economics from 1926 to 1951 and chairman of the Labour Party from 1945 to 1946, wrote a book which doesn't still deserve to be read but exemplifies the attack from the left.[3*]

---

[*] Laski's complex philosophical journey started off from the widely held belief in eugenics, to pluralism, to an urgent desire for political action not greatly constrained by the courts. Finally he wanted not a liberal, constitutional democracy but a state

A STEP TO THE SIDE

In the 1970s some historians began to look at MacDonald's role in creating the Labour Party and tended to exonerate him from the conspiracy charge. The first substantial study of MacDonald since Elton's was written by David Marquand in 1977. It was a very serious study and, importantly, was written for the first time with access to MacDonald's papers. This magisterial study, just shy of 900 pages, is in every sense substantial.

The detail is enormous. I acknowledge my debt to Professor Marquand. I have made much use of his book, which is well researched and a sound basis for a study of MacDonald and in particular of his contribution to the evolving Labour Party. Why I believe a new study of MacDonald is required is not because of errors or omissions in Marquand's book, but because, after more than half a century, there is room for fresh interpretation of a man who is, by any standard, difficult to interpret. I do not share all of Marquand's conclusions. He depicted MacDonald as decent and honourable, but I would go further than that, finding less to criticise and more to praise. In particular I suggest that Marquand is critical of MacDonald because of the degree of his own commitment to economic theories that are no longer regarded as unchallengeable.

This book will not serve, as Marquand's book does, as a history of the labour movement or of the detailed political events which filled MacDonald's life. After perhaps two generations from the first appearance of Marquand's book (it was reissued in 1997), our view of politics, and of economics, has changed enormously. There have been coalitions and minority governments, which in the 1970s appeared to have been replaced by clear swings from one party to another. The dynamics of political life have become and continue to be much closer to MacDonald's time than in the years following the Second World War.

Marquand wrote at a time when Keynesianism, the doctrine that governments could always successfully stimulate the economy by public spending, reigned unchallenged. Economic thinking has moved on, and MacDonald's views cannot easily be written off, as

---

that was organised and all-powerful, endowed with 'vast powers' and untrammelled by the 'classic formulae of opposition'.

Marquand did, as being backward-looking and unimaginative. Keynes is not the infallible guru that he was thought to be in the 1960s. MacDonald listened to Keynes but preferred the advice of the Bank of England. Many others did so too. Even Churchill, well disposed to Keynes, rejected his advice when he returned to the gold standard. The economic certainties and the apparently self-evident and simple merits of Keynesianism and deficit financing have been displaced by the general acceptance that the austerity for which the National Government was so criticised cannot always be discarded as simplistic and archaic.

*

While MacDonald enjoyed creating a romantic myth about his background and the people who filled it, he believed in that myth and lived it consistently throughout his adult life. He believed in social democracy, but social democracy applied to his notion of society. He had a true grandeur of vision. He was never petty or mean. His concept was wide. He saw men and women as spirits with enormous potential and as players in a great, imperishable theatre. Theory was subordinated to a vision, and that is the key to unlocking a paradox in MacDonald's life. That's why it is worth following Ramsay on his train journey south from Lossie.

3

BRISTOL

For a young Scot on the make, the usual destination was London or one of the major Scottish cities. MacDonald, being his own man, was not, however, looking for streets paved in gold. He had been scouring the advertisements in *The Scotsman* for something that captured his interests more than money ever did. When the train took him out of Lossiemouth for the first time in the summer of 1885, he was responding to an advertisement from a clergyman in Bristol with an interest in Christian Socialism, wonderfully named Mordaunt Crofton, who wanted an assistant to help him set up a Boys' and Young Men's Guild at St Stephen's Church. His worldly goods—a small second-hand suitcase and a bundle of books tied together with string—were on the rack above his head. He was wearing a new suit presented to him by the local draper, and in the pocket of that suit there was a purse containing a one-way railway ticket, a pound note and seven shillings in silver.[1]

Ramsay didn't get on well with the Reverend Mordaunt Crofton, and his employment was very brief. Before the end of the year he returned to Lossiemouth. It was an ignominious return for a promising young man who had headed south so recently. But in the long term the Bristol months weren't wasted. For a start, he was initiated in the world of politics and politics of the left. This may indeed have had something to do with the end of his employment with the Boys' and Young Men's Guild.

Outside London, Bristol was the one place in the United Kingdom where the socialist flame still burned bright. The Christian Socialist activities of the 1860s had been displaced by the growth of collectivism as a response to the increasing power of state and, indeed, municipal authorities. We saw that Ramsay had already been aware of Henry George and his attack on private property. In 1881 HM Hyndman founded the Democratic Federation, three years later rechristened the Social Democratic Federation (SDF)—it's tempting to suggest that this is known as the initial period of the labour movement because of its love of acronyms—and, later still, the British Socialist Party. It was a business-like part of the labour movement. Hyndman was clear about that: 'I do not want the movement to be a depository of old cranks, humanitarians, vegetarians, anti-vivisectionists and anti-vaccinationists, arty-craftys and all the rest of them.'[2] Keir Hardie complained that they drank too much beer.*

Henry Hyndman discovered *Das Kapital* when he was almost forty. He made a point of meeting with Marx, and a product of his conversations was *England for All*. He translated Marx's teachings into fiery rhetoric which he channelled into his SDF speeches. Manny Shinwell recalled hearing him in the City Hall in Glasgow in 1908. 'His pamphlets and his oratory left most of his prospective adherents more mystified about their role in the coming social revolution than before.'[3] His speeches were more suited for a mass audience of serfs in Russia than for working-class industrial audiences, and were all the more outlandish for being delivered by this formal bearded man always dressed in top hat and frock coat. 'Hyndman enthralled minor writers, retired army officers, clergymen and lesser officials whose advanced thinking had set them at odds with the Establishment.'[4]

The Social Democratic Federation, as its name suggests, was socialist. It should be remembered throughout a study of MacDonald, and I shall re-emphasise the point at the risk of irritation, that 'socialism' could mean all sorts of things, very often

---

* The Independent Labour Party (ILP), of which more later, drank tea (Taylor, *The Troublemakers*, p. 106). Bruce Glasier described a difficult day in 1884 which ended in the ILP club at Golcar, in the Colne Valley, and 'an hour's attempted jollity on "hop non-intoxicating" ale' (Bruce Glasier diary, quoted in Pelling, *The Origins of the Labour Party*, p. 166).

denoting no more than a mildly progressive attitude of mind, anything from mild redistribution and protection to out-and-out Marxism. MacDonald was very far away from the extreme end of the spectrum. Hyndman, unlike many people then or since, had read the whole of Marx. He was a stockbroker and had been a Tory. He changed parties but not his dress, wearing to the end a frock coat and top hat. In the long run, left-of-centre politics would end up being informed much less by Hyndman's rigid theories than by the pragmatic incrementalism of the Fabians, who were set up in the same year as the SDF changed its name for the first time; but in these early days Hyndman was more influential than the Webbs.

By the time Ramsay arrived in Bristol, that city's branch of the SDF was already a year old. Bristol and London were the only two branches in the south of England. Ramsay made the acquaintance of the Bristol branch in a British Workman's coffee tavern at 58 West Street. He was immediately entranced and joined at once.

> There was something exotic about it. The odour of sawdust and steaming coffee, the long wooden staircase, the dimly-lit small upper room with the hard penitential forms, impressed the novice with a sense of awe and expectation. That coffee-shop was a cathedral, and its odours were the smells of sacrifice which were being offered up to Demos. A paper on 'Ruskin', to a small audience, was read—and thus I became a full-blown Social Democrat.

Soon he moved to lodgings opposite the home of one of his fellow members. This man and his wife took the young Scot under their wing. Did Ramsay seem awkward and provincial? He considered himself to be shy, though there is little evidence to support that. His accent was unremarkable. To the end of his life, though he spoke with a distinctive Scottish accent, that accent was neither uncouth nor incomprehensible: on the contrary, attractive and alluring.

His neighbours kept an eye on him and he often visited them for a game of cards. Another couple, the leaders of the Bristol branch, also made sure that he was reasonably well fed. 'Reasonably' only, because throughout his life he tended to neglect to feed himself. He wrote home regularly and received food parcels to supplement the intellectual nourishment from reading Plutarch's *Lives*, which absorbed him at this time. Books always mattered to MacDonald. A benefactor gave the branch a gift of £5. The money was invested in books. It was MacDonald who selected them, arranged them, and became their custodian, the branch's librarian.

Outside politics, his interests remained scientific and serious. Geology was still important. He wrote a study of the geology of Bristol. His knowledge was augmented in the course of the long rural walks which were to sustain him throughout his life. It was the Lossiemouth Field Club again.

To that extent, the Bristol months were marked by continuity with his past, but there were important new features. One was simply that he was, for the first time, away from home, making his way in the world, meeting new people and surviving in the urban jungle. More importantly, he was becoming seized by the political life and by new political currents. He and his fellow Bristolians, though under Hyndman's umbrella, rejected the authoritative doctrines that their founder expounded in the SDF newspaper, *Justice*. They were more influenced by the gentler views of Edward Carpenter, the idealistic socialist who had donated the £5 that founded their library. MacDonald argued for this conciliatory tone in the columns of *Justice*.

Visitors from the London branch urged that instead of weekly meetings in the coffee house, the branch should take to the open air and deploy their propaganda on the street corners. One of the Londoners, J Hunter Watts, despairing of the branch's reticence, dragged his diffident Bristol colleagues onto the street and harangued them as the hopeful nucleus of a mass meeting. Mass meetings never did materialise. The tradition is that on MacDonald's first venture into outdoor speaking, he had an audience of three, but he realised how important direct access to the public was. He had started out on his long journey to persuade the world of what politics should be like.

*

The winter of 1885 was an important time for the SDF, and it's interesting that MacDonald, though so recent a recruit to its numbers, should have been as involved as he was. In the general election of November 1885, there were three SDF candidates. John Burns in Nottingham polled a few hundred votes; the other two managed only fifty-nine between them.* This disaster was followed by a letter from the SDF treasurer to the *Pall Mall Gazette* in which he claimed that the Conservatives had funded the SDF candidates. Hyndman haughtily dismissed the allegation, saying that it couldn't be proved and, even if it were, it wouldn't matter: the source of the money was irrelevant. But many members left the SDF and the Bristol branch disaffiliated itself entirely. The precocious twenty-year-old MacDonald drafted two strong letters. In the first, he dealt with the flaw in Hyndman's argument. The source of the money was not irrelevant if the purpose of its donation was to split a Liberal (or Conservative, for that matter) vote. The second draft letter, written in January 1886, was stronger and contained a hint of the kind of socialism that would appeal to him throughout his life, one which had nothing to do with the harsh theories of Marx and Hyndman. He appealed to the 'many who loved the grand principles of Socialism more than the distorted doctrines of the Federation and who have the courage and manliness to act accordingly'.[5]

---

* Burns stood as a Liberal in 1892 and was elected as the member for Battersea. He was a keen attender at cricket matches and in 1894 he was badly injured when he was hit in the face by a cricket ball. He became the President of the Board of Trade in 1914— but, as we shall see, not for long.

4

BEEFSTEAK PUDDINGS AND HOT WATER

Ramsay's tail-between-his-legs return to Lossiemouth didn't last long. He recharged his batteries speedily and early in 1886 he was heading south again. This time his destination was the conventional one: London.

He went in pursuit of a job that had sounded interesting, but when he got there the position had been filled and the prospects of finding another weren't good. There was a serious depression and unemployment was at a high point. His life was grim, and the echoes of the novels of George Gissing are reflected in the fact that MacDonald's own and only novel, never completed, has been said to be distinctly derived from Gissing's *Workers in the Dawn*.[1]

He had only a few pounds to keep him going while he found work. He did what other semi-destitute young men did, walking the streets and looking for any chance of employment, however uncongenial. Like other young Scots in this situation, he received occasional parcels of oatmeal from home (for which he paid his mother). Otherwise he sometimes bought a beefsteak pudding for a few pennies—'it helped to fill up the corners'. Instead of tea or coffee he drank hot water. He lived in 'model' lodgings off the Gray's Inn Road. He had no romantic illusions about his surroundings. They were characterised by 'ugliness, squalor, dullness and noise'. He described his way of life:

> How did I manage to do it? In the first place I used to buy myself whatever food I wanted around the slums of King's Cross ... In the middle of the day I had a meal at Pearse and Plenty's in Aldersgate Street. I don't think I ever spent more than two pence or three

pence on it, although it was the meal of the day ... My food bill worked out at about seven pence or eight pence a day for everything, so that saving was easy.

Just in time, he found a temporary job with the National Cyclists' Union, addressing envelopes for ten shillings (50p) a week. That didn't last long. Another period of hungry tramping followed until he found a job as an invoice clerk at twelve shillings and sixpence a week, with the promise of a rise to fifteen shillings. When we think of his later career, mixing with the highest in the land, from the King downwards, having as it appeared gone native with the aristocracy, it is salutary to remember what he had experienced of a very different level of existence. He had felt the pain and indignity of poverty in his period of unemployment.

His job as an invoice clerk was with a large warehouse in the city, Cooper, Box and Company. Later he said that he lived well—'like a fighting cock'—on his fifteen shillings (75p) a week. Although he talked about squalor and so forth, the 'fighting cock' tone is more typical of MacDonald's reflections on this period of his life. He tended to romanticise and make light of his difficulties. He could not bring himself to share his desolation with his friends in Scotland,[2] and it's as well to look at accounts like those of Gissing to be reminded of just how precarious life was on the margins of society and how near disaster always lay.

It was indeed a grim existence, whatever gloss he put on it afterwards, working from half past eight in the morning until nine in the evening, with just an hour's break at lunchtime. Ramsay was always conscious that he could fall back on another life in Moray, and he was genuinely uninterested in his food and material comforts, to the extent that his health repeatedly suffered. But he did romanticise. He believed that the rigours of a poor young man's start in life nourished 'the aristocratic virtues'. His biographer Lord Elton bought into this strange notion: 'The poor have far more in common with the genuine aristocrat than with the commercial middle-class. Like him, they are free from the pressure of the narrower social conventions, and can be more human because they are more natural.'[3] Poverty was enabling! Elton may have believed this nonsense. He went on to say that MacDonald would, 'in due course, ... figure as naturally in the duke's saloon as in the fisherman's but-and-ben'. But that did not mean, as some of his enemies said it meant, that he had betrayed the fishermen to the dukes.[4]

Whether or not Elton did indeed believe in this romantic tosh, MacDonald certainly did. He believed that the virtues of the allegedly simple people of Lossiemouth constituted a wholesome well on which he could draw to sustain his honest vision and steadfast simplicity. That simplicity, romantic but robust, enabled him to say—and to believe—that the poorest of the Lossiemouth fisherfolk 'receive you with a dignity of gentlemen, look you in the face and bid you welcome in their harbours as though they were receiving you in a drawing room. Their natures are not twisted and contorted by the superficial arts of an artificial society.' If we are to understand this complicated man we have to accept that he sincerely believed in this notion of the nobility of the common folk—or at least the common country folk. The sincerity of the notion, far-fetched though it may seem, is at his heart and is the reason that he felt able to perform contortions later in his career which would otherwise be rightly condemned as hypocrisy.

The lunch break and his brief period of freedom in the evening were obsessively devoted to self-improvement. At midday he read at the Guildhall Library, annotating George Howell's *Conflicts between Capital and Labour* and articles on geology. In the evenings he attended science classes at the Birkbeck Institute. He took courses on botany, agriculture, experimental physics and mathematics. Politics and science competed for his attention, but the latter looked likely to win: a career in science, the discipline which had appealed to him from his schooldays, seemed fairly secure when he sat an exam for a science scholarship at the South Kensington Museum, with a promise of a post as his assistant from a friendly analytical chemist. But at the last minute his health broke down under the strain of overwork. There was another ignominious return to Lossiemouth for several months, when he was nursed by Bella and Annie. He was unable to complete the scholarship exam, and his hopes of a scientific career ended forever. He was to be neither a scientist nor a ploughman.

Some have suggested that MacDonald was hypochondriac. He may have been. There certainly was a morbid streak in his character. He was convinced that he would die young. He suffered from depression, quite serious depression at times, and he was burdened by a sense that he was jinxed, sometimes by minor strokes of ill fortune, sometimes by very real tragic blows, and always by a sense that fate was not on his side. He *was* frequently ill, towards the end of his life seriously as well as often, and in these early days he pushed himself to the limits, still taking no care to ensure that he was properly fed or rested. He does seem not to have noticed how spartan was the regime to which he submitted himself.

*

For the moment, however, fate was good to him, and very soon indeed after his health broke he was back in London, taken on as private secretary to Thomas Lough, a substantial merchant who was also a radical politician and at this time the organising secretary of the Home Rule Union. The four years he spent as Lough's private secretary were critical. Lough was described as 'Liberal and radical', and through him MacDonald came to know those on the left of liberalism. Lough's financial resources also catapulted Ramsay into a level of society which he would not otherwise have reached for many years. He acquired a social confidence, a knowledge of practical politics and an acquaintance with important and influential people. Lough had stood for parliament unsuccessfully in 1886 and was now the prospective Liberal candidate for West Islington. By 1888 more than sixty Liberal Associations were affiliated to the Home Rule Union, which Lough had founded.

MacDonald's salary started at £75 a year, rising to £100. Comparing Victorian salaries with those of the present day is almost impossible because of the lack of correlation between salaries and living costs. But the average male salary at this time was £56 a year, which meant that MacDonald's income was pretty close to that of a professional man at the start of his career. In a purely financial sense, the young Scot on the way up was doing well.

But MacDonald's ambitions were not financial ones. Before he even left Lossie, he had been precociously advocating the formation of a Socialist Union of Young Men and engaging in debate in the

Christian Socialist with professional economists. The move to London did not end these interests but fed them. He was involved in CL Fitzgerald's Socialist Union. Interestingly, the position of the Socialist Union was to participate in the parliamentary system, making use of its machinery to advance the cause of the working classes. This remained a crucial element of MacDonald's philosophy: existing democratic devices were not to be destroyed; on the contrary, they were to be the means of advance. This principle was always at the heart of his policy. It informed his approach to the formation of the first Labour government. It was inherent in his decision to remain at the helm when the bulk of the Labour Party declined to take part in the National Government in 1931.

MacDonald was a member of the managing and editing committee of *The Socialist*, a publication launched by the Socialist Union in 1886. He advocated the Socialist Union case in meetings of the Woolwich Labour League and the Kilburn Liberal Club. It is important to remember that these organisations were at this stage not remotely political parties. They were pressure groups which existed in and around existing political parties. Membership of one of these groups was no bar to being a member of another or, indeed, of a political party, the only vaguely radical political party available being the Liberal Party.

In the circles in which MacDonald moved there was an exciting buzz of interest in how progressive interests could best be served. He wrote in 1887 to a Lossie friend that 'the spirit of Socialism is abroad, not only stirring the lower ranks of Labour to discontent, but moving those whose physical wants are all provided for and whose education and intellectual training are such as to preclude every idea of their being led away by any mere sentimental fad or impracticable scheme'.[5] Thus MacDonald was present at the 'Bloody Sunday' demonstration in Trafalgar Square on 13 November 1887, when a crowd that had gathered to defend the right of free speech was broken up by soldiers and mounted police.

*

Employment by Thomas Lough at the cutting edge of progressive politics was thus a very significant step forward in MacDonald's political career. He now moved in the world of the National Liberal Club and the newspapers that mattered. He met politicians who were building up the Progressive Party in the London County Council, and he helped to organise his employer's campaign in Islington. He was enjoying an early and very important introduction to the real world of politics: his practical experience would distinguish him from contemporaries who had to be content with theory.

Lough sent him to Scotland in the autumn of 1889 to help Seymour Keay, an 'advanced Liberal' candidate at a by-election in Elginshire and Nairnshire. Keay's platform was indeed distinctly radical and went further than what MacDonald had been advocating when he talked in Lossiemouth about land ownership. Keay wanted state aid for fisheries, and free education to cover university as well as school, and his pitch appealed to the electorate. He was elected by a comfortable majority. There were those who considered that the victory was more MacDonald's than Keay's.[6]

Keay's principal interest was Home Rule, and MacDonald himself became involved in pressing for Scottish Home Rule. Two years after a Scottish Home Rule Association had been set up in Edinburgh, MacDonald successfully proposed that there should be a distinct London general committee of the Scottish Home Rule Association. He became its honorary secretary, the first of what would be innumerable positions which he was to hold in these early days. There were even suggestions that he would stand as a Home Rule candidate in Aberdeen, but his commitment to the Home Rule cause was a sideline which narrowed and finally stopped altogether.

He had no shortage of other commitments. He helped run a boys' club; he joined the 'St Pancras Parliament', one of those innumerable bodies that existed throughout Britain, helping aspiring politicians hone their debating skills and master parliamentary procedure. This sort of activity was common enough for earnest young men in those days, but MacDonald was beginning also to enter the more elevated levels of the radical hierarchy. He joined the Fabian Society and in 1890 was actually invited to take George Bernard Shaw's place as its lecturer on 'The New Politics'. He met, too, that other eminent Fabian, Sidney Webb, who, with his wife, Beatrice, would be hugely significant in the development of left-wing British politics in the early twentieth century.

Sidney and Beatrice Webb were untiringly omnipresent in progressive politics in the first half of the twentieth century. They were active in almost every radical institution of the times and, indeed, had founded most of them, including the London School of Economics and the *New Statesman* magazine. They were a slightly unlikely couple, he small, bearded and intense, she much taller, beautiful and passionate. Before marrying Sidney, she wooed and was wooed by the great Joe Chamberlain for four years after the death of his second wife. Ultimately her feminist views were too much for Joe. They would have made a lovely couple, the imposing and elegant Chamberlain and his tall and distinguished bride. But it beggars belief to imagine the couple: the leader of the Liberal Unionists with his grand visions of a forward policy for the empire and the earnest, driven social engineer. In 1892 Beatrice settled for Sidney, a much less prepossessing figure, about as great a contrast as can be imagined with the magnificent Chamberlain. The relationship wasn't based on passion so much as shared causes. Their honeymoon was spent in Dublin and Glasgow, researching trade union records. As a partnership their contribution to social and political progress was enormous, vital and humourless. Sidney's speeches in the Commons were interrupted by catcalls of 'Nanny'. This wasn't an early reference to the nanny state but a comment on the fact that with his little goatee Sidney looked distinctly like a goat. Beatrice, a vinegary lady with shrewish style, considered herself the cleverest member of one of the cleverest families in the cleverest class of the cleverest nation in the world.[7] MacDonald's relationship with the Webbs was not always easy, but being part of their group was very important.

Few institutions were as significant in the development of British labour politics as the Fabian Society. It had been founded in 1884 by Sidney Webb, Bernard Shaw, Sydney Olivier and Graham Wallas, a breakaway group of dissenting members of a body called the Fellowship of the New Life.* The Fellowship was 'an organisation

---

* The Fabian Society took its name from Quintus Fabius Maximus Verrucosus Cunctator, the third-century BC Roman general. In command of the Roman forces against

designed to reform society "in accordance with the highest moral principles" by a woolly minded American named Thomas Davidson'.[8] After the Fabians broke away, the Fellowship continued without them. It had been founded in 1883 to encourage the 'cultivation of a perfect character in each and all' by means of the 'subordination of material things to spiritual'. Although it was notionally socialist, it was preoccupied with a very other-worldly form of socialism, which looked to the betterment of the individual character rather than the betterment of society. But this abstract ideal was, and remained to the end, at the heart of what MacDonald sought for, and this almost religious spiritual commitment lay at the heart of his appeal as a speaker. It was consistent with his participation in the ethical movement, where he attended services and preached.

Membership of the Fellowship of the New Life expanded MacDonald's range of acquaintance and the reach of his activities. Edith Lees, its secretary, who was soon to marry Havelock Ellis,* had heard him on women's emancipation and at her request he repeated his lecture for the Fellowship. A communal home for Fellowship members was acquired at 29 Doughty Street in Bloomsbury. MacDonald was its first secretary. A year later, MacDonald took over as secretary of the Fellowship itself from Edith Lees. Edith advised him not to keep the secretaryship for more than two years or otherwise 'it will make you a mellow humbug & ... I'd be sorry

---

Hannibal during the Second Punic War, he avoided conflicts with Hannibal's much larger forces and instead deployed guerrilla tactics, combining attacks in the rear with minor opportunistic engagements. His tactics were successful. He was described as a man who, by delaying, restored the state. The honorific name 'Cunctator' means the delayer. His other honorific name, 'Verrucosus', meaning 'warty', referred to a wart on his upper lip and was meant to distinguish him from other family members.

* Havelock Ellis was an extraordinary man with a wholly improbable range of interests. Apart from concern for progressive politics and social reform, they are extraneous to this book. He was Anglo-French, a eugenicist (he resigned as a fellow of the Eugenics Society over the issue of sterilisation), and an early writer on what were then very advanced notions of sexuality, including transgender issues. His marriage to Edith Lees was not entirely satisfactory, as she was openly bisexual. His friends were amused by his apparent expertise in sexual matters, as it was understood that he was impotent until the age of sixty, only liberated by a bizarre discovery he made at that age.

to see that'. She also cautioned him facetiously against the approaches of the 'new women' who were numerous in the circles in which MacDonald and Lees moved. The good-looking young Scotsman had a number of admirers, but at this stage he was too occupied by other matters to respond to their advances.

What is fascinating about this period in his life is the chasm that MacDonald crossed in the six brief years that he had been in London. He was no tongue-tied provincial hobbledehoy. The man who had left school at fourteen was now moving among high-flying progressives like Shaw and the Webbs, working alongside practical politicians many years his senior, and mixing on terms of easy intimacy with the sophisticates of the Fellowship.

5

THE TESSELLATED PAVEMENT
OF RADICAL POLITICS

MacDonald arrived in London at just the right time. In 1885 the total membership of all the socialist societies in the United Kingdom had been only about a thousand,[1] and even future leaders of the movement, like Keir Hardie, remained members of the Liberal Party. But things were changing fast. The trade union movement, formerly the domain of skilled workers only, was being opened up to unskilled workers. They came to form the 'new unions' mostly run by the socialists, who, rather than Liberals, were also gaining ground within the Trades Union Congress (TUC) itself.

This opening up of the trade union movement was a hugely important development. The significance is difficult to understand today. Until then the working classes were divided, with skilled workers, relatively comfortably off, recognised almost as members of the medieval crafts, established and contemptuous of the masses of unskilled workers, on whom they looked down. In many pubs there were separate rooms to make sure that the skilled did not have to rub shoulders with the inferior unskilled. A bricklayer would be in one room, separated by a huge chasm as well as by a brick wall from a bricklayer's labourer. They were separated in their politics too. The miners, for example, tended to be Liberals. They didn't affiliate with the Labour Representation Committee (discussed below) until 1905. The skilled workers were trade union members; unskilled workers were not.

The recruitment of casual, unskilled workers into the 'new unions' owed much to the great London dock strike of 1889, when the public quite suddenly became aware of the plight of people like the dockers, half-clothed, ill-paid and overworked. The dockers' conduct was dignified and peaceful, and highlighted the plight of the unskilled worker, winning support from figures such as Cardinal Manning and from middle classes who had been unaware of their conditions. Ben Tillett emerged as the strikers' leader and formed the Dock, Wharf, Riverside and General Labourers' Union. He was not the only leader to emerge: John Burns, Tom Mann and Joseph Havelock Wilson were also propelled onto the national stage.

With the unionisation of the unskilled workers, labour relations underwent a revolution. The coming together of the two bodies of working people resulted in dynamic growth of the labour movement, led to a large extent by socialists. But, as I have noted, socialism was not a system or theory. Keir Hardie made that very clear: 'Socialism, I say again, is not a system of economics. It is life for the dying people.' Robert Blatchford, the author of a book published in 1893 that sold two million copies, *Merrie England*, popularised a similar view of undogmatic socialism: 'English Socialism is not Marxian, it is humanitarian. It does not depend upon any theory of "economic justice", but upon humanity and common-sense.'[2] Nineteenth-century dictionaries struggled to define socialism: 'The range of application of the term is broad. It is typically understood to involve the elevation of the social position and interests of the working class, esp. through redistribution of land or wealth ...'[3] Given the vague and disparate foundations of British socialism, a tessellated pavement without cement, it is legitimate to wonder again what the tradition was to which MacDonald was untrue in 1931.

*

Those who had hoped for revolution turned to evolution. In 1886 the Trades Union Congress set up a Labour Electoral Committee, soon to be the Labour Electoral Association, to increase union representation in the House of Commons. The great issue with which socialists had to engage was whether to enter parliament through the portal of the Liberal Party or through a separate, explicitly socialist organisation. The Labour Electoral Committee favoured the use of the existing Liberal organisation. It seemed obvious that it would be foolish to neglect a mechanism which was already available.

The Fabian Society, which was becoming increasingly influential—the collection of essays they published in 1889 had been well received in progressive circles—was strongly in favour of using, infiltrating and influencing the Liberal Party. MacDonald was with the Fabians. Then and always he saw the need for party discipline, and he was unimpressed by the efforts of independent socialists. His approach was always infiltrationist.

*

MacDonald was increasingly his own man. He had left the employment and security of working for Lough, and was supporting himself—only just—by freelance journalism. In July 1892 he went to Dover to help the Labour Electoral Association's candidate, a Major Edwards, in the general election. Even in a straight run with the Conservatives—there was no Liberal candidate—Edwards was soundly beaten. He did not endear himself to the Liberal Association, describing some of the local party members as 'a set of old Tory grandmothers'. MacDonald, on the other hand, made a good impression, and the local association unanimously selected him, at the age of just twenty-five, as the next candidate. His oratory in support of Edwards had been admired; but when he tried to speak on his own behalf he was subjected to a great deal of drunken barracking. MacDonald coped with this quite well, but the ousted major did not. At one meeting, when the chairman, the Bishop of Manchester, rose to speak, Edwards started singing the music hall song 'Ta-ra-ra-boom-de-ay' and had to be ejected.* As a result he brought an action for assault against the stewards and further divided potential supporters.

---

* The song came from the United States but became hugely popular in London in 1892, largely because of the performances by Lottie Collins. The song began quietly enough ('A smart and stylish girl you see / Belle of good society / Not too strict but rather free / Yet as right as right can be!'). It came to life in the chorus, when Lottie launched into a sort of can-can, particularly on the word 'boom' when her high kick exposed her bare thighs and stockings held up by sparkling garters.

MacDonald said that he was fighting Dover as a Labour candidate. This didn't mean that he wasn't a Liberal, simply that he was part of the Labour wing of the Liberal Party. He was feeling his way forward, looking for a formula, a formula that he never quite found. He said that the Liberal and Labour parties had yet to be united to create a new progressive party. He wrote a series of articles for the *Dover Express* which were reprinted as *The New Charter*, his first published pamphlet. His proposals included the land nationalisation which he had been advocating since he read Henry George, along with proposals to deal with poverty and the establishment of an eight-hour day. He did argue for a set of specific policies, but truly he was simply asking for representation of the working classes by their own representatives. He wasn't hugely radical. The Labour wing of the Liberal Party was not to be identified with a class. 'In politics it is frankly democratic, in economics it is co-operative, in social theory it has thrown aside the metaphysical individualism of the Old Radicals, which is so unreal that it has never been experimentally tried.' Socialism was an attitude of mind rather than any kind of dogmatic theory for MacDonald at this time—and later. He was very much still a Liberal, even if on the left of the party.

Whether these complicated formulations would appeal to the electors of Dover was never put to the test, because MacDonald's attentions now moved westwards, along the coast to Southampton. Southampton was a two-member constituency. The Liberals had one representative and the Conservatives the other. The Liberals sought to find a Labour candidate to run alongside their sitting member. They managed to bungle the selection process spectacularly, and as a result of a series of chaotic manoeuvres, MacDonald's name was not put forward as a candidate. He decided to stand against the Liberals as an independent Labour candidate. But he still wanted the best of both worlds, and he asked the Liberals for their support. When the election took place in 1895 the result was a bad one for the progressive cause. The two Conservatives won the seats, the two Liberals came third and fourth, and MacDonald came a very bad fifth.

What was much more significant was that MacDonald repositioned himself. He had come to the conclusion that the Labour

THE TESSELLATED PAVEMENT OF RADICAL POLITICS

Electoral Association (formerly Committee) was in terminal decline. He wrote to Keir Hardie on 15 July 1894, applying to join the Independent Labour Party (ILP). He said he'd stuck to the Liberals up till then, but now found it impossible to maintain his position as a Liberal: 'Liberalism, and more particularly local Liberal associations, have definitely declared against Labour ... The time for conciliation has gone by and those of us who are in earnest ... must definitely declare ourselves ... I shall place part of my spare time at the disposal of the Party, to do what work may seem good to you.'[4] Joining the ILP didn't imply severing all contact with the Liberals, but it was an important move.

*

The ILP had been founded in 1893, largely because of the same frustration that MacDonald felt over the Liberals' reluctance to embrace the working classes and the policies that radical politicians wanted. The Marxists, revolutionary rather than evolutionary, looked to class conflict as both inevitable and desirable, and had no time for parleying with the bourgeoisie. They founded their own Marxist Party, the SDF, already referred to in connection with HM Hyndman, in 1881.* One of the features of the SDF that was much criticised was their quasi-military organisations. Some of these were, however, taken over by the ILP, which organised demonstrations of the unemployed, who marched to the uplifting beat of 'The Starving Poor of Old England'.†

At the first ILP conference in January 1893, Keir Hardie was elected chairman. Others at the meeting who would dominate the early Labour years included Ben Tillett and George Bernard Shaw. MacDonald's pragmatism and freedom from dogma was evident now, as always. He was hostile to the idea of 'a left-wing purist section' in the ILP.

At the 1895 general election, when MacDonald did so badly, the ILP generally disappointed. There were initially twenty-eight ILP

---

* Although Marx's son-in-law, Edward Aveling, was a founder member of the ILP.
† Presumably a parody of 'The Roast Beef of Old England'.

candidates, though in the event the party supported also the four SDF candidates. Even Keir Hardie failed to be elected.

The ILP seemed an ideal home for MacDonald at this stage. The party had neither programme nor constitution, as Keir Hardie pointed out at the inaugural meeting. It was infinitely flexible. It was a wide umbrella which sheltered pretty well everyone who wanted to march below it towards economic freedom and reform. The rules of democracy were to be respected, but subject to that there was a welcome for members who could be trade unionists, Marxists, Fabians or pretty well anything else. Many of its members came from the churches, particularly Methodism, and there was a warm, familial feeling about the movement, in some ways akin to the ethos of the New Life. The tolerant, embracing spirit of the ILP was an expression of what MacDonald had been stumbling over at Dover. He now belonged to a crusade.

That's not to say that there weren't practical problems. While the party's decisions were made at annual conferences, to keep it going on a day-to-day basis a National Administrative Council (NAC) was formed. It consisted of regional delegates acting under the authority of local conferences. Inevitably, particularly after the disappointments of 1895, the NAC came to assume a level of authority which conflicted to a degree with the central notion of federal democracy. It was dominated by Keir Hardie; Bruce Glasier, a Scot and close friend of MacDonald who would succeed Hardie as chairman in 1900; Philip Snowden, an effective advocate of socialism who was no great friend of MacDonald; and MacDonald himself. Improbably Glasier, Hardie and Snowden—who were, with MacDonald, known as the 'Big Four'—were all illegitimate.

Like the party itself, MacDonald was subject to inner tensions. After the Southampton result, the local Liberals made overtures to him, to which he responded despite discouragement from the ILP secretary, Tom Mann. He always enjoyed the wheeling and dealing of electioneering more than pure theory. Moreover, the break from the Liberals he had talked about with Keir Hardie was not a true rupture, but rather a matter of relative proximity.

Equally, membership of the ILP did not end his relationship with the Fabian Society, nor was there any reason that it should have done. Active progressives continued to be involved in a multiplicity of forward-looking bodies. He was elected to the executive of the Fabian Society in 1894 and in March of the following year he was appointed chairman of a Fresh Activities Committee. Beatrice Webb recorded in her diary that he was 'one of a certain set of young people, all more or less devoted to the Fabian Junta'.[5] Her patrician detachment is interesting. Beatrice did not long remain an unqualified admirer of MacDonald. He attacked her and Sidney over a legacy left to the society. She thought there was a personal element to this: his application to be a lecturer for the society had been rejected. He wanted the society to organise branches in the provinces. Beatrice thought that his real aim was to use Fabian money to create what would actually be ILP branches. Another diary note from Beatrice a year later: 'Do we want to organise the unthinking persons into Socialistic Societies or to make the thinking person socialistic? We believe in the latter process.'[6]

Beatrice had described MacDonald as one of the Fabians' 'lower middle class followers,[7] and ILP candidates were not viewed with enthusiasm. In a Fabian Society report drafted by Shaw for the London Congress of the Second International in July 1896, the ILP was described as 'frivolous'. MacDonald tried to secure the deletion of parts of the report which he regarded as likely to be offensive to Continental socialists. He was not successful.

He was never averse to becoming an office-bearer of the numerous societies he frequented, and he was for a time the secretary of a discussion group which promoted radical and socialist theory. He was keen on a monthly publication, the *Progressive Review*, and became secretary of the company that was set up to publish it. It was not a success and folded within the year.

6

THE STEPS OF THE BRITISH MUSEUM

In May 1896, MacDonald was unwell and in St Thomas's Hospital. There he received a letter enclosing a cheque for a pound as a contribution to his election campaign at Southampton. The letter and the cheque were signed 'ME Gladstone'.

He would marry Margaret Gladstone. When he did so, he entered the happiest part of his life. Indeed, his marriage to Margaret Gladstone was perhaps the only truly happy period of his life. He existed before her and he existed after her death, but it was only during the brief years of their marriage that he truly lived.

He loved his mother. He loved his children, of whom there were six. When his third son, David, died of diphtheria as an infant—just eight days before MacDonald's mother's death—he was hit very hard. But he loved Margaret more than anyone else. He depended on her; their lives were intertwined. Tragically this hugely important union lasted just fifteen years. Margaret died on 8 September 1911 at the age of forty-one. Ramsay never recovered from her death.

*

MacDonald had grown up without the presence of male family members in a household which consisted of two very strong women. He was always happier in the company of women. He had male friends, and in those days the political world was largely populated by men; but he found the company of women much more congenial, and there was a notable lack of stiffness in his relationship with his female friends. We have briefly met Bruce Glasier, who was to succeed Keir Hardie as chairman of the ILP. Glasier was the illegitimate son of a farmer from Irvine in Ayrshire. His background and views were remarkably close to MacDonald's. He attended the inaugural meeting under Henry George of the Scottish Land Restoration League in 1884 and was a founder member of the SDF in the same year. He died at the age of just sixty-one in 1920, not living to see Labour in power. He was about as close as any of MacDonald's male friends, but it is noticeable that MacDonald corresponded much more freely and frankly with Glasier's wife, Katharine, than with Glasier himself. Just as Glasier came from a similar mould to MacDonald, so Katharine was in some ways similar to Margaret, the daughter of a Congregationalist minister, educated at Cambridge and the editor of *Labour Leader*. She was a beautiful, intelligent and talented woman, who deserves to be remembered as more than her husband's wife.

*

In the courtship which followed the receipt of Margaret's cheque, *she* made the going. MacDonald's fate was determined before they even met. David Marquand says that Margaret had already heard quite a lot about MacDonald from neighbours who employed a friend of his from Lossiemouth as a governess, and that she had marked him out as a potential husband before she even met him. She opened a special notebook to record his acknowledgement of the cheque: 'First letter from JR MacDonald: May 29, 1895', to be followed by 'First saw him, Pioneer Club, June 13, 1895'. What she saw wasn't perfect. His red tie and curly hair were 'horribly affected'. But that impression wore off quickly when she was properly introduced to MacDonald at a party given by the friends who employed the Lossiemouth governess.

Thereafter the relationship moved quite fast. They met at suitably serious venues such as the Socialist Club in Bride Street and the British Museum. By June 1896 Margaret was writing to Ramsay about the financial practicalities of marriage. She crossed out the sentence that amounted to an overt proposal, but did so lightly enough to allow it to be read, going on to say that 'I think I hardly had any business to write that last sentence'. She sent him her journal of the previous eight or nine years, although she said that she had 'never expected anyone to see it—unless I am married'.[1]

THE STEPS OF THE BRITISH MUSEUM

MacDonald was aware of the social distance which separated them. It was a real enough gap. The Gladstones lived at Pembridge Square, in Bayswater, in a property of some distinction. Margaret's father, one of the founders of the YMCA, was professor of chemistry at the Royal Institution and a fellow of the Royal Society. And yet the Gladstones, like MacDonald, were originally Scottish, serious, and devoted to worthy causes. Professor Gladstone was a Liberal who had stood for parliament in 1868.

Margaret could be light-hearted, and in her correspondence with MacDonald she teases him; but she was far from frivolous, distinctly a new woman. She was the granddaughter of a Presbyterian minister and niece of Lord Kelvin. She had been educated in Bayswater and then at the women's department of King's College, where she studied political economy under Millicent Fawcett, the hugely influential leader of the Constitutional Women's Suffrage Movement. She taught at a weekly class for servant girls at the Nassau Senior Training Home when she was seventeen. She was a Sunday school teacher in Kensington, where she was also involved in a boys' club connected with the church. By the time she met Ramsay she was the manager of several board schools, the secretary of the Hoxton and Haggerston Nursing Association, and a charity visitor. In all, a formidable young woman. Coming from this purposeful background, and seeing the grim realities of working-class life in Edwardian London as she did in the course of her work, it is hardly surprising that she embraced socialism.

Margaret was an attractive young woman and had no shortage of admirers. She had turned down four proposals before she met MacDonald. In him she saw exactly the person with whom she wanted to share her life.

> When I think how lonely you have been, I want with all my heart to make up to you one tiny little bit for that. I have been lonely too—I have envied the veriest drunken tramps I have seen dragging about the streets as if they were man & woman because they had each other ... This is truly a love letter: I don't know when I shall show it to you: it may be that I never shall. But I shall never forget that I have had the blessing of writing it.

She had no hesitation in describing her financial circumstances. They were comfortable. Her mother's marriage settlement brought in about £160 a year. Her father had provided for a legacy of £10,000 in her favour in his will. During his lifetime he paid her £300 a year. Margaret thus had a total income of about £460 a year. She toyed with the idea of renouncing her trust fund, but MacDonald encouraged her to dismiss what he called this 'Quixotic notion … Reduce your cost of life to a moral minimum, do service to society, hold the rest as a trustee to the community … [Real immorality consisted in] neglecting to use the opportunities you have in life.'[2] But it would be an absurdly facile error to think that he was interested in her for her money. He was far too other-worldly a man for that. When he did worry about the difference in their circumstances, Margaret chided him and breezily swept the issue aside.

When they became engaged—on the steps of the British Museum, which was appropriate—her family took the news well, 'all so kindly—not nasty & cantankerous & unsocialistic like you', she joked to MacDonald. Her father, cautious Scot as he was, made some discreet enquiries through an economist friend, who reported that the prospective son-in-law was acceptable, a 'quiet bookwormy sort of person'.

*

Margaret couldn't visit Annie Ramsay in Lossiemouth to convey the news of the engagement, as her own grandmother was ill. Instead she wrote a charming letter:

> My Dear Mrs MacDonald,
>
> Your son tells me that he has told you that we love one another, and that you send me kind thoughts and words. I thank you for them from the bottom of my heart. I never knew my mother, and I always hoped that if I ever married, my husband's mother would be living and would like me …
>
> There is one thing that I should be very glad if you would tell me, and that is by what name I am to call your son. I only know him as Mr. MacDonald & really don't know what Christian name he uses. Mine is Margaret.

THE STEPS OF THE BRITISH MUSEUM

He tells me that you asked him if I could cook and keep a house clean, & that he did not know. I have done a little both of cooking & of housework, but I have not had much practice, & I am afraid you would not think much of my performances, though I liked what I did of both. I often make butter when I am staying at a farmhouse which my grandmother goes to every summer & I always long to milk the cows there, but I have never screwed up the courage to ask if I may ...

I am, if you will let me be, yours affectionately

MARGARET GLADSTONE

Annie Ramsay's reply is interesting, not only because it reveals the limits of her education:

My Dear Margaret

my Dear gural you ask me for my Young Mans christian name it is Jamie Ramsay Macdonald we call him Ramsay My own name is Annie Ramsay My son is a good son to me and i trust if it please God that you and Ramsay be happy i trust god will go with you in all your ups and downs in life and I shall be verry glad to sea you in Lossiemouth My Dear Gural you spoke of milking cows i have Milked cows and made Butter and all that work but for the last 29 years i have been doing little but sowing in my dear little home Now my dear i will not forget to pray god for you as i have done for him in the past that god may be with you both and that you may be happy Ramsay will soon be Back to London and i will be all alone again with Much Love and I hopes you will writ me soon

from your frind
MRS A RAMSAY[3]

MacDonald was always 'Jamie' in Lossie.

Shortly afterwards, when Margaret's grandmother had died, she was able to visit Lossiemouth, and from there she wrote a teasing letter, addressed to him as 'Person', from his desk and using his ink. It says something about Margaret's character that she went off alone to see Ramsay's mother, someone with whom she clearly could have had little in common either in background or in educational attainments.

*

THE CANCELLED PRIME MINISTER

Ramsay and Margaret were married in November 1896 and set up house at 3 Lincoln's Inn Fields.* MacDonald had wanted a respectable home in the suburbs; Margaret said that if he went to any such place, she would move out and pitch a tent in the slums of the East End. The flat attracted a wide range of visitors, from family friends to Labour politicians to eminent European socialists like Jean Jaurès. There were regular At Homes that drew in a Bohemian mix. Margaret was involved in MacDonald's political activities, as well as continuing to do her social work. She was on innumerable committees, an unconventional figure with no interest in her clothes or appearance. On one occasion she was prevailed on to wear a new blouse for an important event. She knuckled under, but appeared with the blouse on back to front. The domestic arrangements were chaotic. One of MacDonald's secretaries described the confusion—largely Margaret's: MacDonald's inclination was to be tidier than she. Committee meetings took place with children crawling around the floor and a little girl sitting on her potty.

It was a busy, messy house, and a happy one. Whenever possible MacDonald and Margaret spent their evenings together. He would read aloud from Thackeray, Dickens, Scott, Carlyle or Ruskin. Later they bought a weekend cottage in Buckinghamshire, where MacDonald grew vegetables and standard roses. The family went for long walks, which MacDonald used as an opportunity to educate the children on the beauties of nature and the historical associations of their surroundings.

When the family was in Lossiemouth they went to the Free Kirk every Sunday. In England they did not attend church, but on Sundays, instead of reading the usual adventure stories to the children, MacDonald read from the Bible or from popular science. Before their marriage, MacDonald and Margaret thought that they might have differing views on religion. In fact their views were very similar. Margaret believed very strongly in a God, but adhered to no single creed. She thought there was spiritual value in the writings of anyone, even atheists, who looked beyond the banalities

---

* The flat is part of a block described by Nikolaus Pevsner in *The Buildings of England* as 'a six-storeyed monstrosity overshadowing London's oldest square'.

of daily life. After her death, MacDonald wrote that she saw spirit in everything.

The readings from popular science are instructive. MacDonald never jettisoned his commitment to spirituality—far from it. But he sought to reconcile the religious tradition with Darwinian science. To some extent the reconciliation was expressed in his commitment to the ethical movement in which he was increasingly involved.

*

Margaret was direct, uncomplicated and confident. MacDonald later described how at ease she was in company, 'chatting, cheering, introducing, … a perfect hostess'. He learned from her, became more socially at ease. He increasingly adopted the bearing and confidence that enabled him to move easily in aristocratic and even royal circles, and during the short years of their marriage, under Margaret's influence, MacDonald's prickly self-doubt and aloofness were not evident. They remained, however, very real—and they became more evident again after Margaret's death and particularly in the years that followed his first term as Prime Minister in 1924. Harold Macmillan never saw MacDonald's diaries, filled with self-pity and complaint. All the same he could see 'a natural tendency towards martyrdom', which MacDonald did not in fact find uncongenial. 'He almost seemed to me to even enjoy and even exploit the troubles and worries of a Prime Minister. He would go about complaining that he felt like "a weary titan".'[4]* Macmillan, the old showman, would have known that he could have been talking of himself as he wrote those words.

Margaret's importance for the support, companionship and confidence she gave to her husband was enormous. But that was not all she did. She made a great personal contribution to the labour movement and in particular to the lives of female industrial workers. She joined the Women's Industrial Council in 1894, became secretary of its Legal and Statistical Committee and a member of its

---

* Macmillan described MacDonald's stance as 'only part of the histrionic side of his temperament. He was a good actor and like all good actors he threw himself completely into his part.'

Investigations and Education committees. She carried out research on its behalf and the results were published. She gave evidence to the House of Commons Select Committee on Home Work. She played a critical role in the establishment of municipal workrooms for clothing workers. In 1905 she organised a march of unemployed women in Whitehall. She was also chairman of the Industrial Committee and secretary of the Legislation Committee of the National Union of Women Workers. In the year of her death she lobbied Lloyd George to extend the benefits of the National Insurance Act of 1911 to include non-working wives and married home workers.

These are no more than a hint of the extraordinarily numerous ways in which this remarkable woman poured out her energies. She would be commemorated by a bronze statue designed by Ramsay in Lincoln's Inn Fields, and a new ward named after her in Leicester Children's Hospital.

7

REFINING HIS PHILOSOPHY

When his children were young and the family was on holiday in Lossie, MacDonald made a point of taking them for a walk through the property of the laird, the local landowner. The incursion was deliberate and symbolic, and involved cutting the barbed wire. This little ritual is revealing. It was symbolic, but largely a joke; and MacDonald and the laird subsequently became very good friends. His detached attitude to the singing of 'The Red Flag' and the Marseillaise at the Albert Hall just before he became Prime Minister—of which the King so disapproved—is part of the same civilised amusement.*

This detachment is essential to an understanding of MacDonald. He was not wholly part of either of the worlds in which he existed, his political world or his increasingly rarefied social surroundings. It was in his retreat into his thoughts and speculations, or when spending long hard days alone on the hills, testing his endurance and reflecting on nature, that he was really himself.

The earnest and humourless Beatrice Webb failed to recognise that MacDonald was so often at a slight remove from his surroundings, observing them with flippant detachment. She recorded meeting MacDonald after the 1926 TUC conference at Bournemouth:

> What interested me was JRM's conversation. He was particularly gracious to us; came to our table and took us into his private sitting-room. But he was evidently absorbed in the social prestige of his

---

* 'The Red Flag', incidentally, wasn't exclusively the communist anthem, but was also the official song of the Labour Party.

ex-premiership enhanced by a romantic personality. Immaculately groomed and perfectly tailored—too deliberately so for artistic effect—it made him look commonplace—he went out of his way to tell me that he was going on to stay with Mrs Biddulph near Cirencester—'the Hon. Mrs Biddulph', he added, and then described her as a patron of good English craftsmanship in furniture. Once again he spoke of the difficulty of getting old pieces of furniture ... and described his adventures with this dealer or that ... His thoughts and his emotions are concentrated on his agreeable relations with the men and women—especially the women—of the enemies camp ... He is becoming impatient with the troublesomeness of the working class.[1]

As well as being snobbish, Beatrice Webb was imperceptive. For Ramsay, studying the upper classes was all part of the game, just like cutting the laird's barbed wire. To be fair to Beatrice, which is not something one instinctively wishes to be, it was and still is very difficult to pin down the essence of MacDonald. Beatrice herself fluctuated between calling him the 'greatest artist of British politics' and 'a magnificent substitute for a leader'. His admirer Molly Hamilton hinted at his abstract charisma: 'the whole is more than the sum of its parts'. Lord Francis-Williams said: 'the more one knows of MacDonald the less one knows him'.[2]

Another observer, the journalist Sir Alexander Mackintosh, said: 'This or that man claimed to know him. They came in contact with him as a lover of books or an enthusiast for art or a perfervid Scot, but there was a realm to which he invited no man's company. He retired to thoughts among which he dwelt alone. The result was that he seemed a mass of contradictions.'[3]

Suggesting that MacDonald was 'impatient with the troublesomeness of the working class' is another imperceptive judgement. MacDonald believed always and strongly in the need for discipline if Labour politics were to achieve anything. The tension between the insistence on discipline and the party's inherent aversion to being controlled is at the heart of 1931—as well as of more recent Labour crises. Over-excited talk—and there was frequently over-excited talk at TUC conferences—would lead to confrontations

REFINING HIS PHILOSOPHY

from which extremists on one side or the other might gain but from which steady incremental social progress would certainly not emerge. Others might deplore the slow, boring doctrine of gradualism, but MacDonald never wavered in his evolutionary approach. His economic theories were uncomplicated. He was not necessarily wedded to free trade, as Philip Snowden was, and he was vaguely sympathetic to the idea of the expansionist economics advocated by Maynard Keynes, John Strachey and Oswald Mosley while still a member of the Labour Party, but their theories did not excite him, and for him they were certainly not revelatory.

*

Marriage, and the confidence and connections it brought, moved MacDonald up a gear in his political life. He had been involved with a political discussion group known as the Rainbow Circle* for some years. Indeed, it has been suggested that at this time MacDonald was more at home in the Rainbow Circle than among the Fabians.† The Circle decided to publish a monthly review. The ambitions for the review were extensive. It was to be the mouthpiece of all aspects of the progressive movement. It was to be for that movement what the *Edinburgh Review* had been for the Whigs. Its aspirations reflected the distinction of its members. MacDonald was now moving among pretty solid people, like Graham Wallace, who had become professor of political science at the London School of Economics; Herbert Samuel, who would have a distinguished career in the Liberal Party, indeed leading the party from 1931 to 1935; and William Clarke, one of the founders of the Fellowship of the New Life, and then a Fabian who contributed to the influential 1889 *Fabian Essays in Socialism*.† Some of the Rainbow Circle were Liberals and others Independent Socialists. What united them was a belief in collectivism rather than individualism.

*

---

* So called because its meetings initially took place in the Rainbow Tavern in Fleet Street.
† His early promise was sadly unfulfilled. Latterly, physically and emotionally weakened, he lost faith in socialism: 'the masses are such fools', he wrote four years before his death.

THE CANCELLED PRIME MINISTER

The extent of MacDonald's travels in these years is interesting. It not only reflects his vision of socialism as an international force but also foreshadows the international concerns which occupied his mind when Prime Minister. Sometimes with Margaret and sometimes on his own, he not only visited Europe repeatedly, but also travelled to North America, Australia and South Africa. How different from seclusion in Lossie. He visited India in 1910 and again, after Margaret's death, with a royal commission in 1912–13. India was to be a particular concern of his as Prime Minister. The internationalism that was reflected in his diplomacy when in power was deep-rooted.

One of Ramsay's jaunts with Margaret—they both loved travel—was a voyage to the United States in August 1897. Although their sensitivity was disturbed by the elaborate class division on the ship and by the conditions in which the crew worked, MacDonald was impressed that the customs officials at New York were 'prepared to discuss Bryanism while they counted my shirts'.* The visit was purposeful and established a sound basis for a knowledge of American politics, which served him well in his later career.

At the April 1896 ILP conference he stood for the National Administrative Council (NAC) and just failed to get elected. Three months later, on the death of a council member, it was MacDonald who took the vacant place. He was re-elected at the April 1897 conference.

Keir Hardie had been one of the co-founders of the ILP in 1893 and remained its chairman until 1900. Initially MacDonald viewed the beloved father of the party with some suspicion. MacDonald was one of the Fabian delegates to the 1896 London Congress of the Socialist International when Hardie and Tom Mann voted to allow anarchists to be represented. MacDonald was strongly against the idea. He had no time for anarchism, which he dismissed contemptuously as simplistic and impractical. So even at this time he was for safety first: an incrementalist, conservative and reassuring approach.

---

* William Jennings Bryan was an American Democratic politician who ran for president in 1896, 1900 and 1908. Bryanism was the rejection of Imperialism as being contrary to the spirit of the United States.

REFINING HIS PHILOSOPHY

The defensive philosophy that took him into the National Government can already be discerned.

*

In the summer of 1904 MacDonald went on holiday to Italy to convalesce after an appendix operation. He was accompanied by Keir Hardie, who could give confident medical reassurance, having had a similar operation a year earlier. Hardie complained to Bruce Glasier, 'Mac is not an ideal travelling companion ... he wanted to see everything not so much I think for any real interest as to be able afterwards to talk at dinner tables about what he has seen'.[5] That sounds a rather contrived slight, but MacDonald's complaint to his wife seems equally improbable: whenever MacDonald wanted to rest, Hardie wanted to 'go on the spree'—an intriguing vision. MacDonald never had much time for Hardie. When he lost the seat at Southampton in 1895 he wrote to Herbert Samuel, 'Hardie by his own incapacity lost his seat and none of us—being scapegoats—got in ... The party of progressive ideas is so badly led that it is almost suicide to join it.'[6]* Detachment again.

The distance between the two men narrowed over time. It was largely to do with the fact that Hardie had a more or less absolute distaste for what was to him a discredited Liberal Party. MacDonald's approach was more nuanced. The Liberal Party might be doomed in the long term, but for the moment, and indeed for quite some time, he could see a use for it, and some Liberals were better than others. He was always more interested in making things work than in doctrinal purity. In March 1897 he wrote a long letter to the *Bradford Observer*, prompted by hostility of the Halifax Liberals to the ILP. 'No one hates Toryism more than I do and yet no one distrusts Liberalism more.' But that uncompromising declaration was followed by the more positive view that the ILP could continue to work with 'the genuine radicals' within the Liberal Party. 'I have never given up hopes that a limited and temporary trial might be given to an electoral

---

* John Burns referred to the ILP campaign of that year and the money that had been devoted to fighting it as 'the most costly funeral since Napoleon'.

co-operation in certain favoured constituencies.'[7] Similarly he emphasised that the ILP could not afford to frighten the horses but must reassure moderate progressives.

8

SOUTH AFRICA AND BEYOND

The First World War and MacDonald's attitude to it were to cause him problems which came to shape the way he was defined. The South African War hinted at what these problems would be.

The First Boer War, which lasted just three months, from December 1880 to 1881, had resulted in an uneasy relationship between the Dutch and the British in southern Africa, which rumbled into the Boer War proper, what is now known as the South African War. This confrontation caused anxieties in the left which tended to throw the radical Liberals and the ILP closer together.

MacDonald's attitude to war was simple, consistent and strongly held: he hated the very idea of it. It was cruel, violent, pointless and antithetical to all that he believed in. In addition to that intrinsic gut position, he had a profound distaste for the arrogant assertion of the imperialists in both the main parties who took it for granted that they were exporting the values of civilisation. These reactions to the South African War would inform his response to the world conflict in 1914.

The ILP saw the South African War as a product of capitalism and something that had to be opposed. The Fabians on the other hand were not unequivocally against the war, and MacDonald's outright condemnation of the conflict separated him from the Fabian mainstream. The Fabians refused to condemn the war for a variety of reasons. Bernard Shaw had no time for MacDonald's sensitivity. He wrote to him: 'Democratic sentiment be blowed! Do you want to go back to the old Radicalism that always had a foaming bowl of virtuous indignation on tap, and never a practical suggestion.'[1]

THE CANCELLED PRIME MINISTER

MacDonald resigned from the Fabian Society: the war marked the end of his Fabian period.

*

The early history of the labour movement is confusing with its fluid range of overlapping institutions and the alphabet soup of acronyms. It's worth saying again that on the whole these organisations didn't consider themselves to be exclusive or in competition with each other. It was as perfectly possible to be simultaneously a member of the Liberal Party, a socialist, a Fabian and a member of the SDF in 1890 as it would now to be a member of the Labour Party, the European Movement, the Fabian Society (still around) and Amnesty International. They were all means to the same end.

This book is not meant to be a history of the Labour Party or a guide to the birth of progressive politics in Britain, but a rough outline of the political landscape may be helpful. To sketch that outline we must wind back by some twenty years.

*

At the start of the last decade of the nineteenth century there were three main socialist organisations, the SDF, led by Hyndman and the Marxists; the Fabians, scarcely socialists at all; and the ILP. The trade unions were not really part of the mainstream of socialism at this stage, trade unionists being mostly Liberals and not particularly political. But beneath the surface the Trades Union Congress (TUC) was warming towards socialism. A resolution at the 1898 conference hinted at this move, and in the following year the railway servants proposed that a conference be called to secure an increase in the number of Labour members. The conference took place in March 1900. Although there were only 129 delegates, the proceedings were described by Marquand as being 'as dramatic as any in recent British history'.[2] The momentum was provided by the ILP representatives under Keir Hardie and the outcome was the establishment of the Labour Representative Committee (LRC), a permanent body tasked with implementing the railway servants' proposal. The ILP might in theory have become subsumed in the LRC, but MacDonald particularly considered that the ILP had an independent and essential role in pressing the LRC towards progressive aims.

SOUTH AFRICA AND BEYOND

The LRC was founded at a meeting in the Memorial Hall, London, on 27 and 28 February 1900. The conference had been convened by the TUC and the intention was to ensure that trade union interests would be promoted and defended in the Commons. The executive committee was to consist of twelve trade unionists, ten people from the cooperative societies, and two each from the ILP, the Fabians and the SDF. The cooperative movement, however, declined to send representatives and, accordingly, the unions had a two-to-one majority.

There were various important provisions. Labour candidates were not to be exclusively from the working class, something which MacDonald thought very important. An SDF resolution committing the organisation to a class war was rejected, as was a suggestion that the new body should be committed to trade unionism rather than to politics. The secretary of the new organisation was JR MacDonald. Keir Hardie recalled the 1900 meeting when MacDonald became the LRC's first secretary:

> I remember the anxious hours spent before the first conference was called, trying to find someone who had the necessary qualities and abilities to undertake the most responsible of all tasks at that period—to act as Secretary to the Party. Those who had known MacDonald's work in the ILP felt that he was the one man above all others who, if he could be induced to take the position, would give our then nascent movement its best chance of coming to fruition.[3]

MacDonald was now very visible, one of the leaders of the progressive movement. It was now that the *Labour Leader* described him as one of the two best-looking men in the ILP,[4*] and the *Leicester Mercury* referred to him as 'a tall, strong, vigorous young man [who] has evidently got a lot of fight in him. He appears to have a great deal of nervous electric energy as well as abundant muscular force. He stands upright with every inch of his measurement—with conscious power.'[5]

---

* The other man was Frederick Brocklehurst, who was initially proposed as secretary of the LRC, but withdrew as he was unwilling to move to London. He later moved directly from the ILP to the Conservative Party and in 1917 he founded an anti-Semitic group, 'Britain for the British'.

The LRC was to be hugely important in the growth of the labour movement, and that was pretty clear from the start even if in its infancy it was a tiny and delicate creature. It had no premises of its own. The committee met in MacDonald's flat. One committee member had to spend a meeting sitting on the coal scuttle.[6] MacDonald remained unpaid until 1901, despite a proposal by Hardie a year earlier that he should receive a (very modest) fee. The original affiliated membership was just 187,000, but it was growing. The committee was tasked with an essential purpose, and it was the only agency that could achieve that purpose.

*

This summary of progressive political history brings us back to the challenge of the South African War. The LRC's first great test came too soon: at a general election as early as September 1900. It fielded fifteen candidates, of whom two were returned, one of them Keir Hardie at Merthyr.

MacDonald stood in Leicester. In the patriotic mood of the 'khaki election' and the context of the South African War, he had no chance of winning; in any event he faced two Liberal candidates in this two-member constituency. He made it clear at the outset that he was not in favour of the war but, prefiguring his approach to the First World War, he treated South Africa as 'too sacred a matter for the platform'. He dwelt on domestic matters. He was inevitably charged with splitting the anti-Conservative vote. He responded by attacking the quality of the Liberal Party MPs. But he may indeed have split the Liberal vote: only one of the Liberal candidates was elected. He had done nothing to endear himself to the Liberal Party. The fifty-seven Labour MPs in the Liberal Party, of whom MacDonald was not one, were not an impressive collection. MacDonald said disparagingly that they had tasted the fleshpots—just what his enemies would later say of him. They were largely elderly and trade unionists, and they lacked leaders with real political skills.

*

MacDonald returned to working for the LRC. But he kept his mind on his parliamentary prospects. To this end, despite the difficulties he

SOUTH AFRICA AND BEYOND

had had with the Leicester Liberals, he cultivated sympathetic members of their party, notably Jesse Herbert, the private secretary of the Liberal Chief Whip, Herbert Gladstone, son of the Grand Old Man.

In the summer of 1901 the House of Lords delivered its judgment in the *Taff Vale* case,* the effect of which was to make it possible for a trade union to be sued for damages caused by its members. This was a massive setback to the trade union cause, and MacDonald made much of it in the column he wrote for *The Echo*, a periodical edited by the politician and suffragist Frederick Pethick-Lawrence. He positioned the LRC to attack the judgment. The result was that membership of the LRC rose from 350,000 at the beginning of 1901 to more than 700,000 by September 1902. He also addressed the need for funds, advocating a trade union levy.

In June 1902 the war ended and in August Ramsay and Margaret went to South Africa to investigate conditions in the country. It was a very thorough investigation. They spent four months in South Africa and their visit included crossing the veld in a three-day wagon-and-mule journey followed by four days in a Cape cart. This was hardly casual tourism. MacDonald was able to interview politicians, soldiers and newspapermen. He and Margaret became friendly in particular with General Jan Smuts and his wife. Smuts had recently fought Britain but was now engaged in peace-making and reconciliation. MacDonald's distaste for war was intensified by sight of the cemeteries, the stench of rotting flesh still hanging over the veld, the trenches scarring the ground. He was affronted by the pointlessness and destruction. He arrived in the small town of Lindley one evening and woke to look on the ruins of the town, burned to the ground almost in its entirety. He took away from South Africa a sense of desolation coupled with a conviction that the war had changed nothing.

*

---

* The Taff Vale Railway Company sued the Amalgamated Society of Railway Servants for loss of income as a result of an industrial strike. The House of Lords, on appeal, awarded substantial damages against the union. There had long been debate about whether unions could be liable in damages. The decision that they could be struck at the whole notion of strikes as an instrument of industrial policy.

On his return from South Africa, MacDonald capitalised on his friendship with Jesse Herbert and embarked on serious discussions on creating a firm arrangement between the LRC and the Liberal Party. He emphasised that the LRC was now a substantial force in politics, with a membership of a million and a political fund with an income of £5,000 a year. He negotiated well, and meetings with Herbert were followed by meetings with his boss, the Liberal Chief Whip, Herbert Gladstone. In the meantime three more LRC candidates were elected to parliament at by-elections, the election of Arthur Henderson in July 1903 for Barnard Castle being important for the future.

The MacDonald–Gladstone pact was a result of negotiations that were kept very secret. It was MacDonald's personal achievement. Keir Hardie was aware of what was going on, but the LRC committee was not. The pact was not binding on either party and no formal concessions were made. Effectively, what was agreed was that the Liberal Party and the LRC would not run in opposition to each other. By the end of January 1904, the LRC had adopted thirty-eight candidates in addition to its sitting members. Twenty-seven of the thirty-eight were in single-member constituencies, in seventeen of which there was no Liberal opponent. The remainder stood in two-member constituencies, and in only one of them was there more than one Liberal candidate. Of the twenty-nine LRC members elected at the 1906 election, all but five had Liberal support.*

As well as national negotiations there were local ones. In Leicester the Liberal Association elected a new president, Edward Wood, whose aim was to bring the Liberals and the ILP together. He wanted MacDonald to be the approved candidate for Leicester and have an open run against the Conservatives. Wood was not without opponents. There were many who wanted to see two Liberal candidates, but he worked hard on MacDonald's behalf, genuinely believing that Labour was under-represented, and his efforts ended in success. MacDonald reciprocated, declaring that it was not inconceivable that Labour could support a Liberal govern-

---

* There were fifty LRC candidates in the election, of whom thirty-one had no Liberal support.

ment in the House of Commons. He did this in the face of opposition from the German Social Democrats at the Amsterdam Congress of the Second International in 1904 and locally from his friend Bruce Glasier. It was easy to claim that in working *with* the Liberals, MacDonald was truly working *for* them, but that was very far from his intention. He was very clear that Labour had to be a distinct force with its own ideology. He set out his views in a 1905 pamphlet, *Socialism and Society*, in which he argued that society was not 'a mere collection of individuals like a heap of sand [but a] unified and organised system of relationships, in which certain people and classes perform certain functions and others perform other functions'.[7]

MacDonald did tend to articulate his views by remote analogies which may have sounded well in speech but look over-elaborate in print. The 'boot and shoe operative of today [was] as different from the boot and shoe operative of fifty years ago as the stomach of the bell animalcule is different from that of man'. The barons of the Middle Ages were the 'nerve fibres and ganglia' of the body politic. The response to a law of mutual aid was compared to the 'law which determines that the bee must pack its cells as octahedrons and not as cubes'. Bell animalcule, ganglia, octahedrons ...

*

The Conservative government had been hit below the waterline by Joe Chamberlain's adoption of tariff reform in 1903. Arthur Balfour, at the party's helm, scarcely had the inclination to keep the ship afloat. When he went to the country in 1906, his party was returned with 157 seats against 401 for the Liberals.

It was a great victory for the Liberal Party. But it was a great victory too for MacDonald. We have noted that as a result of his vigorous commitment to the LRC and to his deal with Herbert Gladstone, the LRC had seen twenty-nine candidates elected. In Leicester, Edward Wood said that the Liberals were only going to run one candidate and they were going to take their coats and hats off to work for the return of Ramsay MacDonald in the second seat. In the two-member constituency the Conservative candidate polled 7,504 votes and MacDonald 14,685, just 60 votes behind the Liberal candidate. These two men won their seats with an enormous majority. Jamie MacDonald had moved from the cottage in Lossie to the House of Commons.

9

WESTMINSTER

So Ramsay MacDonald was in the House of Commons. It's worth thinking for a moment just what that meant, just how foreign these surroundings were for the 'Lossie loon' and the other working-class Labour members.

Roy Jenkins has analysed the social composition of the 1906 parliament. Excluding the Lib-Labs, the Liberal Party had 377 members, of which 64 were practising barristers, 22 were service officers, and 69 were simply described as 'gentleman'. There were 154 businessmen, mostly from distinctly well-to-do backgrounds. There were 21 solicitors, 25 writers and journalists, 9 teachers (mostly university teachers), 5 doctors of medicine and just 8 trade unionists. A third of the Liberal members, 125 men, had been to a public school, 32 to Eton, while 135 had gone to Oxford or Cambridge. The social composition of the Conservative and Liberal Unionist parties was even more different from that of MacDonald and his colleagues.[1]

So MacDonald was not part of the traditional Westminster scene. But he was one of a historically significant group of Labour representatives, the spearhead as it was hoped of a great new force in British politics. Even if their achievement was slightly over-hung by the scale of the Liberal landslide, it was still a historic moment. Not that they looked like revolutionaries. Lord Elton said of a photograph of the twenty-nine men taken on the terrace of the House of Commons in 1906, 'They look less like a set of revolutionary malcontents, than an excursion of non-conformist lay-preachers.'[2]

Equally, with just a few exceptions—MacDonald, Hardie, Henderson and Snowden—they were not remarkably able or

71

dynamic. They were not, either, particularly cohesive politically. Only six were nominees of the ILP, and the SDF considered that even *they* were not true socialists. The trade unionists on the other hand regarded the ILP members as extreme and dangerous. The trade unionists were themselves cautious and conservative and preoccupied by the concerns of the unions they represented. In MacDonald's view the conservative trade unionists were a drag on the other representatives. But the unions mattered. When the LRC had been formed, the affiliated trade union membership was 187,000. By 1912 it was 1.9 million.

It was now in 1906 that the LRC formally adopted the name of the Labour Party, with Hardie as its first leader. The essential characteristic of the Labour Party as opposed to the SDF was that it was not doctrinaire or dogmatic. People could enter it without subscribing to any narrow creed, and the breadth of the church meant that there was little inclination towards schism. The SDF had always been fissiparous. It was because of this characteristic that the LRC itself had come into being, and members of the continuing SDF went off to join the Socialist Labour Party in 1903 and the Socialist Party of Great Britain in 1904. In 1911 what was left of it joined the British Socialist Party, which after further splits became part of the Communist Party of Great Britain in 1920.

MacDonald's vision and aspiration as he and his colleagues entered the parliamentary arena reflected his unthreatening vision of progressive politics: 'A united democratic party appealing to the people on behalf of a simple, comprehensive belief in social reconstruction, it will be as far ahead of Liberalism as Liberalism itself was of its progressive predecessor Whiggism.'[3]

Manny Shinwell pointed out in his history of the Labour Party that when MacDonald won the 1906 election he 'had not been a socialist candidate, but an LRC nominee'. He went on: 'There was no evidence that MacDonald believed in the genuine socialist concept of political life even if on other occasions he found it convenient to preach it.'[4]

Organic evolution was very different from revolutionary cataclysm. MacDonald rejected Marx totally, though he might be 'the father of modern socialism', locked as he was to Hegel's commitment to dialectical clash. MacDonald had no time for the idea of class war and class interests.

The election of Keir Hardie as the leader of the Labour MPs sounds inevitable, but it wasn't. There were no less than three votes before a winner emerged. MacDonald didn't vote until the third one. In the event he voted not for Hardie but for David Shackleton.[5] MacDonald and Hardie got on well enough at this time, but they were very different. Hardie had clear aims and ideals but had no interest in the practical matter of achieving them; MacDonald was practical, political, and a tactician. His aims were vaguer.

In 1906 he succeeded Snowden as chairman of the ILP. But while he was very much at the centre of events, he was frustrated. Labour wasn't able to do very much in parliament. And he was hurt by attacks from his own side. In negotiations with other parties he was pliant and ready to compromise; he did not expect attacks from his own side, and his response to them was to fight back.

*

Arthur Henderson, formerly a Liberal agent and still at heart more Liberal than Labour, worked well with MacDonald. He was content to be subordinate to MacDonald and was not his rival. 'Uncle Arthur' Henderson was a sensible, moderate and reassuring man with a gift for organisation. While he could seem slow-witted and unremarkable, his unthreatening appearance was in itself reassuring and respectable.

Philip Snowden on the other hand was ambitious and much more steely than the homely Henderson. He and MacDonald worked together, but without any affection: though they were long in harness together, their outlooks were as different as could be. The Clydesider Davie Kirkwood said that they would have been divorced for incompatibility of temper. 'Instead they continued their association for the sake of the family.'[6] Harold Macmillan could never understand why Snowden was in the Labour Party. He seemed essentially a Liberal. He was born in Yorkshire, where his parents were weavers. He was badly injured in a cycling accident at the age of twenty-seven, initially paralysed from the waist down. He spent two years learning to walk again, and it was the reading which he carried out during this period that moved him from the Liberal Party to socialism. For the rest of his life he walked with a limp, supported by two sticks. He was in constant pain. He never complained, but an element of bitterness entered his character. That was hardly surprising. Although his reading matter during his convalescence had converted him intellectually, his cast of mind was said to be as conservative as that of a member of the Junior Carlton Club, and his views on the nature of society, and in particular on the sanctity of free trade, were inflexible.

*

From the start, it was MacDonald, and not Hardie, who was politically dominant. He fitted easily into the House of Commons, not in the least over-awed. Just eight days after the new parliament met, he asked his first question, followed by a second six days later. He made his maiden speech three weeks into the parliament in a debate on the civil service estimates. He spoke about the men from Balliol College, Oxford, whom he had met in Johannesburg, and described them as a Balliol kindergarten and a failure. In his view administrators should receive a technical education rather than a general one. His speech was business-like and not remotely spectacular. His intention was to show that Labour was responsible and could contribute to the practical matter of government. He got on with this task, speaking twice on the day of his maiden speech. As time went on, he continued in this quiet, reflective way, eschewing socialist rhetoric and even the word 'socialist' itself in his speeches. Arthur Balfour paid particular attention to MacDonald's contributions, and his later description of him as 'a born parliamentarian' is fair.

In July of his first session, MacDonald moved for leave to introduce an Unemployed Workmen Bill. It is interesting to note that he was already setting out a very no-nonsense, unsentimental position: 'The Bill provided that the habitual shirker should be compelled to perform reasonable work under the Unemployed Authority. He hoped it would not again be said that the Labour Party had any sympathy with the loafer and shirker or worker, who tried to batten and fatten on the public funds.'

The fact that Labour was constructive and participatory rather than threatening meant that they gained traction as they would otherwise have not, even if their impact on the House was underwhelming. For instance, when the Liberal government brought in a Trade Disputes Bill to reverse the *Taff Vale* decision, Labour succeeded in amending it considerably. It was a mark of Labour's influence that this bill—legislation not wholly congenial to all wings of Liberal sentiment—went through as it did. Labour also introduced motions on old age pensions and trade union matters, and a bill for the provision of meals for children.

MacDonald had little difficulty in working with the Liberals in general. Some Liberal policies, like Irish Home Rule, were his party's policies too. Salaries for members of parliament, a Liberal innovation in 1911, were welcome to Labour. In that same year, MacDonald was happy to work with the Liberals in supporting the National Insurance Bill. Labour members sometimes disapproved of this fraternisation. But what was much more important was that, remarkably quickly, the Labour members were seen as practical, workmanlike people rather than dangerous revolutionaries. It was MacDonald who was behind the constructive tactics that created this impression. It was he, rather than Hardie, who ensured that at the start of each session the group agreed what they would do and not do, and where its contributions would be made.

In May 1911, Lloyd George introduced his National Insurance Bill, a system of compulsory state insurance against sickness and unemployment. It was financed by premiums paid by the state, employers and employees. It was sellable to the capitalist establishment, including, essentially, the Liberal Party, because employees and employers made part of the contribution to funding the scheme. It was not one-sided state bounty.

But what made it acceptable to the capitalists made it unacceptable to socialists. Beatrice Webb attacked the contributory principle in her minority report on the Poor Law, and the ILP found it equally abominable. The scheme was a tax on the poor. MacDonald didn't agree. He had reservations on some of the mechanics of the scheme, but he recognised the essence of the matter, which was that the state was indeed accepting its responsibilities. Unlike Beatrice Webb, he welcomed the 'insurance' aspect of the whole scheme. He did so in unsocialist language. Without some contributory element 'the whole scheme would degenerate into a national charity of the most vicious kind, which would adversely affect wages and would not help the Socialist spirit'.[7]

The ILP were against the bill. So was the *Labour Leader*. So were Beatrice Webb and the Fabians. So was George Lansbury. But MacDonald told the Commons that they need not 'have the least doubt but that the Labour Party stands for a contributory scheme'.[8] MacDonald's limited commitment to theoretical socialism is reflected in the fact that throughout the debates he always favoured insurance and contribution and did not expect a 'free gift' from the state to those who needed support: no question of 'to each according to his needs'. An amendment opposing the contributory principle was defeated overwhelmingly, although Snowden and Keir Hardie voted for it. Snowden said, 'If the ILP will stand that, it will stand anything.'[9]

MacDonald carried the party with him, but at some cost. People like Snowden and Lansbury wanted something much more like Aneurin Bevan's National Health Service, costly and comprehensive and not earned by contributions. Lansbury was always a bit of a nuisance to MacDonald. Later, Harold Nicolson described 'Mr George Lansbury, who at that date [1924] exercised much influence on the [national] Executive, [as] a man of quick emotions and a slow sense of reality: in a voice throbbing with tortured idealism he would reprove Ministers for their deviations from strict Socialist doctrine … The Prime Minister [MacDonald] was irritated by these interruptions: it seemed incredible to him that any man could be so unrealistic as not to recognise that in domestic matters the Labour Government were not their own masters.'[10]

While most of the parliamentary party voted with MacDonald and the Liberal government, not all did, and not all forgot. MacDonald did not flinch. He talked of unity, menacingly hinting that the liberty of party members might need to be curtailed. This was leadership, and brave leadership. It was pragmatic. In the meantime he continued with important technical improvements which he wanted to see reflected in the legislation. He contrasted this practical approach with pointless 'irregular guerrilla warfare without plan'.

In these practical ways MacDonald worked with and not against the Liberal government. Indeed he worked so closely with the government at this time that the Chief Whip, Alexander Murray, the Master of Elibank, sent him an advance copy of a government guillotine motion. For MacDonald, practicality and material achievement were what mattered, and he was exasperated by those who allowed their doctrinal consciences to get in the way of the march of progress.

All the same the internal, self-destructive complaints continued. Among those in the rank and file who wanted revolutionary pyrotechnics rather than permeation there was a feeling that not enough was being done. This was in part because the government itself was unable to do as much as it wanted. The Liberals might have a huge majority in the Commons, but they had become bogged down in the famous conflict with the Lords, which dominated politics in these years. Keir Hardie was also worried. He felt that the party's collaborative approach was resulting in its disappearing from public sight. Even 'the comic papers and the cartoonists are ignoring us. A fatal sign!'[11] He was concerned that this was the consequence of too much support for the Liberals. Consequently he resigned from the leadership of the ILP in order to be able to speak out more. His successor appeared likely to be David Shackleton, but in the event Bruce Glasier was elected to succeed him.

*

One particularly divisive issue for the Labour Party was women's suffrage. There were differences over many aspects of suffragism, but the biggest problem was militancy. Before he resigned, Hardie had sent a telegram of sympathy to imprisoned militant suffragettes and in 1912 George Lansbury resigned his seat of Bow and Bromley to contest it as a defender of militancy. MacDonald viewed all this with detached amusement. He wrote to Bruce Glasier on 1 November 1911 to say that the 'Lansbury antics are becoming so comical that, in the House of Commons at any rate they have ceased to be serious'. As would be expected of such an unrevolutionary man, he was strongly opposed to militancy. While this is reflective of his hatred of violence of any sort, it also underlines his desire for stability and an ordered society.

MacDonald was professionally gregarious—unusually so for a man of the left. He breakfasted and dined frequently with Liberals—Lloyd George, the Master of Elibank,* and Jack Seely.† His relationship with Herbert Asquith was cooler: there was little warmth in their friendship even then, and soon there would be little friendship either. They played golf together in Morayshire in 1913, and Violet, Asquith's daughter, was alleged to have fallen in love with MacDonald, though platonically rather than romantically. MacDonald's relationship with Lloyd George was more ambivalent. Lloyd George could appear to be everyone's friend and often courted MacDonald, but certainly after the outbreak of the First World War and perhaps before, there was some friction between the two men. All the same, Lloyd George invited MacDonald for breakfast at 11 Downing Street, addressed him as 'my dear Ramsay' and referred to his children as 'my little friends'.

*

---

* Alexander William Charles Oliphant Murray, known as the Master of Elibank, was a prominent Liberal politician until he was obliged to resign in 1912 after having been implicated in the Marconi scandal. When that happened and he moved to the House of Lords, he wrote a warm letter to MacDonald. Murray had been Liberal Chief Whip and he told MacDonald that *his* 'whips, in fact all your party, treated me with a consideration which went far beyond the ordinary courtesies of parliamentary life'.

† Jack Seely, largely forgotten now, was a politician of some importance and a fascinating figure in his time, dashing, adventurous and larger-than-life. He was a Conservative MP from 1900 to 1904, and a Liberal MP from 1904 to 1922 and again from 1923 to 1924. He distinguished himself in the South African War by his courage, for which he was mentioned in despatches and awarded the DSO, and by his indifference to authority. Although a senior politician and a former Secretary of State for War, he volunteered to fight on the Western Front in the Great War and remained there from 1914 to 1918, when he was gassed. He led the last great cavalry charge in British military history on his warhorse, Warrior, at the Battle of Moreuil Wood. His career wasn't without setbacks. He came out of the Curragh Incident badly and had to resign office. He was an unrepentant appeaser and a (finally repentant) admirer of Hitler. He was not modest: he is said to have recommended his batman for a Victoria Cross on the grounds that throughout an engagement the man had never been less than twenty yards behind him. For most of his life Seely was the coxswain of the Brook lifeboat.

Despite his parliamentary duties Ramsay continued to be exceptionally involved in world affairs. Every year from 1907 to 1910 he was on the Continent, three times as a delegate to a Congress of the Socialist International. In 1909 he was part of a Labour delegation to Germany, where, to the distress of the German socialists, the British delegates junketed with many who were not part of the socialist clan. MacDonald met Bethmann Hollweg, Chancellor of Germany from 1909 to 1917 and emphatically not a man of the left: MacDonald took the view that he was in Germany to look at Germany rather than at fellow socialists.

The extent of his interest in the international field was very unusual by the standards of parliamentarians of those times. It wasn't parliamentary free-loading; he knew and engaged with Continental political leaders. He understood them and they understood him. He networked, and his pretty much unique list of contacts was the basis of his diplomatic bravura when he became Prime Minister and Foreign Secretary. He did not confine himself to Europe. He and Margaret visited Canada, Australia and India in these years. These weren't holidays, although they valued the expeditions as times when they could see more of each other than they did at home. In Canada they mixed with political leaders and government officials. India resulted in a book, *The Awakening of India* (1910), which is a perceptive analysis of the subcontinent and of the strengths and weaknesses of both the rulers and the ruled. Addressing India's aspirations would be an important preoccupation when he was Prime Minister.

*

The MacDonalds had to accelerate their return from India. In November 1909, the Lords rejected Lloyd George's budget. A general election was held in January 1910. The Labour Party approached the election in a spirit of righteous radical indignation. The obstructionism of the House of Lords was not the only animating issue. In 1909 the Law Lords unanimously upheld the High Court judgment in the *Osborne* case and held that a compulsory levy on trade union members to raise funds for political purposes was illegal, reversing a practice that was fifty years old.* This decision threatened to destroy the Labour Party. It was four years before the Liberal government, with of course Labour support, reversed the effect of the judgment by passing the Trade Union Act of 1913.

Despite the apparently propitious circumstances of the election, the Labour Party lost five seats. The importance of the Gladstone–MacDonald pact was underlined by the fact that in those seats where it was not applied and there was a Liberal candidate, the Labour candidates lost. MacDonald himself was elected, but that was small consolation for other blows that now fell on him.

---

* *Amalgamated Society of Railway Servants v Osborne* [1910] AC 87 was brought to court by Mr Osborne, who had been a member of the Amalgamated Society for sixteen years. He argued that the union's financial support of the Labour Representation Committee was *ultra vires* because the society's rules did not provide for promoting parliamentary representation. The House of Lords agreed with him. The society expelled Osborne for bringing the action, but he had no hesitation about turning to litigation and the court held that he could not be lawfully expelled.

10

FAMILY LIFE IN LOSSIEMOUTH

Ramsay's birthplace still stands in Gregory Place, Lossiemouth. So does the house in which he spent his youth. It was slightly bigger than the Gregory Place house but still very small. In 1908 MacDonald and Margaret decided to build a bigger house where his mother could live, together with the children when he and Margaret were away from home.

This house, The Hillocks, was designed to be built on the hill at the top of the town, with exciting views out to sea, but MacDonald was quickly told that 'bastards don't build up here'; he should build his house in 'the slums' in the fisherfolk community.

In the event the house was indeed built near the fishing community on Moray Street. It doesn't have the dramatic view that the hilltop site would have given it, but the rugged, whin-covered ground in front of the house, which obscures the view of the sea, gives an impression of seclusion and isolation. It cost £400 to build, about the same as MacDonald's annual salary; the Gladstone trust fund helped out.

Beside the harbour in Lossiemouth, the Lossiemouth Fisheries and Community Museum has recreated MacDonald's study and filled it with MacDonald memorabilia. It's an interesting part of a museum, which contains much more MacDonald material. But the Hillocks—in its entirety—is a MacDonald time capsule. It's a private residence, but those invited to visit it find it almost exactly as it was in MacDonald's time, full of MacDonald's papers and mementos, all in tantalising disarray, as if its former occupant had briefly stepped outside. His bedroom must be exactly as he left it.

THE CANCELLED PRIME MINISTER

The side of the house which faces away from the street and across the undulating whins is dominated by a large veranda. Life in MacDonald's time was largely lived here. Meals were eaten al fresco. The immediate impression of the house is of a building of some substance, but it is more modest and much smaller than it initially appears. There were not enough rooms in the house for all the children. A London policeman and a secretary needed bedrooms. MacDonald's daughter Joan usually slept on the veranda, and other children in outhouses.

*

Ramsay and Margaret had six children, Alister born in 1898, Malcolm in 1901, Ishbel in 1903, David in 1904, Joan in 1908 and Sheila in 1910. David was the son who died so tragically young. Alister and Malcolm, the two other boys, went to Bedales School in Hampshire (Malcolm was head boy). Bedales is a public school. The education of Labour politicians' children is always a problem, but what can be said about Bedales is that from its start in 1893 it was a consciously distinct break with the atmosphere of the conventional public school. Co-educational from 1898, it deliberately rejected the conventional public-school culture. The list of its alumni shows that they didn't emerge from a determinist mould, ranging from Lily Allen to the left-wing Labour MP Konni Zilliacus, taking in on the way Daniel and Tamasin Day-Lewis, Alan Jay Lerner and Michael Sadler of the SAS.

Alister spent three years with the Society of Friends' Medical Corps during the First World War. After the end of the war he trained as an architect; he was the architect who worked on MacDonald's Hampstead home. Malcolm, who went on to Queen's College, Oxford, stood for Bassetlaw in Nottinghamshire in 1923 and 1924 while still a student. He became a London County Councillor and entered parliament. He was Minister of Health in Churchill's war-time government, and went on to be High Commissioner in a number of Commonwealth countries, and Governor of Kenya. He was a member of the Order of Merit. He was an able and interesting man, a poet and, perhaps more than any other person, the architect of decolonisation. When Malcolm

FAMILY LIFE IN LOSSIEMOUTH

MacDonald died, there was a memorial service in Westminster Abbey. But his memory was tainted by descent. Labour attendance at the service was minimal. Old animosities were evident too long after MacDonald's death when the Labour Party refused to supply a memento to place in the replica of his study which was being created in Lossiemouth. It was left for the Tory MP for Moray and Nairn to approach the Tory Speaker, who magnanimously arranged for a special reprint of MacDonald's maiden speech. Cancellation in practice.[1]

Ishbel was even better known than Malcolm during Ramsay's life, because of her role as MacDonald's hostess at Number Ten. She studied domestic science and took part in local politics, and she bought and ran Ye Olde Plow Inn near Chequers. Ramsay took an interest in the business of the pub, which employed a number of former staff from Chequers.[*] Her first husband was the captain of the darts team of Ye Olde Plow. After he died in 1950, she married a Scots widower, James Peterkin, and when he died in 1955 she moved back to the Hillocks, where she lived until her death in June 1982. Her ashes were scattered in the Lairig Ghru in the Cairngorms.

Joan was educated at Edinburgh University and became a doctor, practising as a general practitioner in Leeds. In 2007 her daughter, Iona Kielhorn, moved into the Hillocks, where all her Augusts had been spent[†] and which has been occupied by the MacDonald family continuously since it was built. Interestingly, Iona Kielhorn did not grow up in the shadow of her grandfather's memory. Her father, like her mother, was a doctor, and MacDonald was never a topic of conversation in their busy house. All she knows of MacDonald she has learned since she moved to the Hillocks.

---

[*] The Plough, as it now spells its name, was the pub to which David Cameron took Chinese President Xi Jinping for a pint of India Pale Ale and fish and chips in 2015. A year later it was acquired by a Chinese investment company.

[†] Her mother did all her patient visits on foot during the war, saving up her petrol coupons for the annual visit to Scotland.

11

TRAGEDY

The Awakening of India was dedicated to 'the two who took much interest in the journey but who never saw this book'. They were Annie and Margaret. But there was a third death. On 3 February 1910 David MacDonald died at the age of five of diphtheria.

MacDonald was affected in a complicated way. 'There are', he wrote, 'strange, mysteriously spun bonds of affection that entwine us to the dead and draw us away. We live in the companionship of memories and ghosts. The world changes, the things of substance dissolve, the unseen claims us and we go, and nothing can keep us back.'

Five months later, on 4 July 1910, he wrote in his diary:

> My little David's birthday but no little people were calling when I awoke 'happy birthday'. Sometimes I feel like a lone dog in the desert howling from pain of heart. Constantly since he died my little boy has been my companion. He comes and sits with me especially on my railway journeys & I feel his warm little hand in mine. That awful morning when I was awakened by the telephone bell, & everything within me shrunk in fear for I knew I was summoned to see him die, comes back often too.

Margaret's reaction was slightly similar:

> Last night, when over in the sitting room, I left the door open as I always do when the children are at home, so as to hear them if they waken. I pretended he was there, and though I laughed at myself I humoured the fancy. I always say 'good-morning' to his little spirit, too, in case he wants me.[1]

THE CANCELLED PRIME MINISTER

In Lossie, Annie now became seriously ill. A few days after David's death, MacDonald cancelled his attendance at a Labour special conference on the *Osborne* judgment and hastened to Lossiemouth to find his mother delirious. He wrote to Margaret:

> This is the most heart-breaking experience I have yet had. I am sitting with mother & the poor thing is glaring at me with wild eyes telling me of the terrible things that have been done to her. They have ill-used her and beaten her and there are now evil persons about and holes in the walls through which light is coming. Death is terrible but oh nothing like this.

She died on 11 February. At this time MacDonald was considering taking on the chairmanship of the party, but he was so shaken by David's death that he began to doubt if he could accept the job.

David's death and Annie's were each terrible in their different ways, but neither had anything like the impact of the next tragedy MacDonald had to bear, the death of the woman who had come to mean so much to him, on whom his whole existence depended. Did she die of her grief for David? Many said that she never recovered from the shock of his death. We can never know. She drove herself hard and did not allow herself the luxury of pouring out her thoughts and concerns on paper, as Ramsay did. Something has been seen of her industry and activities, and they were carried out in addition to bearing and raising a large family with limited domestic assistance. Even before David's death, she had been shaken by the news on her return from India that her close friend Mary Middleton, the wife of MacDonald's assistant, JS Middleton, was dying. After David died she made a journey of one and a half hours pretty well every day to see Mary until her death in April 1911. MacDonald thought that the deaths of Mary and David seemed to have drawn the will to live out of his wife. As Lord Elton put it, 'From now on she herself seemed to walk constantly in the shadow of death.'[2]*

Towards the end of July 1911 Margaret developed blood poisoning. She continued with her duties all the same. She and MacDonald went to their country cottage for a weekend's rest. He wrote later:

---

* Ramsay and James Middleton were to establish the Mary Middleton and Margaret MacDonald Baby Clinic and Hospital in memory of the two women.

TRAGEDY

> She complained of being stiff, and jokingly showed me the finger carrying her marriage and engagement rings. It was badly swollen and discoloured and I expressed concern. She laughed away my fears: 'it is only protesting against its burdens!' On Saturday she was so stiff that she could not do her hair, and she was greatly amused by my attempts to help her. On Sunday she had to admit that she was ill and we returned to town. Then she took to bed.

Margaret remained in bed for six weeks. She was unafraid, confident that death would reunite her with David, Mary Middleton and her father. She declined a visit from a clergyman. 'That would be a waste of time. I'm ready. Let's speak of what has gone past. God has been very good to me.'[3]

At the end some of his friends rang MacDonald to tell him that they had hired a car and would take him out for a drive to cheer him up. When they came to the house, MacDonald came out in evident distress. 'I'm afraid Margaret's dying.' On 8 September 1911 she died.

*

Four days before Margaret's death, MacDonald had written to his old friend Bruce Glasier:

> Since last Sunday when she had a serious relapse my wife has been losing ground slowly but steadily, and the source of all the trouble has never ceased its virulence ... Such a slender thread supports her life now that the least strain may snap it in an instant. My way has been dark and hard. But do not think of coming up. We are both of those unfortunate people who sorrow alone. I know I have your most earnest thoughts. But there are some places we have to cross without the help of a hand except those we feel to be stretched out from afar.

After a cremation at Golders Green, Margaret's ashes were taken north to Spynie churchyard.

*

MacDonald was in shock. He received many moving letters from those who had known Margaret and who understood something of the closeness of their marriage. But they did nothing to relieve his suffering. Margaret had foreseen how difficult life would be for him without her support. She asked him to write a memoir: 'The writing will help you, and perhaps you will turn to it sometimes and find me dwelling in it.' He wrote it as she had asked, but the exercise provided no therapeutic benefit. Katharine Glasier understood Margaret's thinking: 'I felt myself hearing *her* approval of it, so much so that I seemed to see her hand on your shoulder as you wrote—& grew foolishly weakly blind with tears for the pain that was there.'[4]

In 1912, he followed the memoir with a proper biography which ended:

> I have just returned from a walk she loved to take at nightfall. The vast expanse of the black sky was glittering with stars as when she and I walked together, and she talked of hope like a gem sparkling upon a background of despair; the sea was moaning as it did when she said, 'do not let us speak: let us walk silently, because then we speak most truly'; the weird call of the curlew, flying away into the night, came out of the darkness as it did when I first brought her here, and she shuddered and told me it made her wonder, and wonder, and wonder what was in the heart of the Unknown and the Infinite.[5]

MacDonald—an artist—wrote beautifully and sensitively, and the memoir and the biography are as fine as anything else he wrote. Composing them might have brought him some sense of closure, but it did not. Perhaps there was too much artistry involved to allow a true emotional release. His grief at the loss of Margaret was never reduced or shared. It remained within him to the end.

From his closest friends he did not hide the extent of his suffering. He described his paralysing despair to Katharine Glasier: 'I cannot write. A horrible reaction has come upon me since I was in London and if work will not give me peace I do not know what I shall do. Oh, if she could only come back and tell me if she knows about us all and cares about us all.'

Throughout his life he continued to visit Margaret's grave at Spynie. His devotion to her continued to the end. He told his friend Lord Elton that he could never have become a Conservative

TRAGEDY

because to do so would have been to trample on all that Margaret had stood for.[6]

In his sixties he wrote in his diary, after another family death, 'These ranks of the dead grow & I live more & more with them.' A few days later: 'As usual I lived much with the days & the people who are gone.'[7] Again in his diary on 12 April 1929 he wrote: 'how often I think of the dead. Oh, had she been here these last years. I wonder if they [the dead] know.'

For such a man with such thoughts it is not surprising that he dabbled in spiritualism. He never found it convincing or reassuring. He never knew 'if they know'. In September 1931, a spiritualist medium, Mrs Grace Cooke, wrote to tell him that she had been in touch with Margaret. She went on to write to him with instalments of news from the spirit world over a period of several years. MacDonald acknowledged her letters courteously, but there is nothing to suggest that they offered him any consolation. He never let go. In 1933, twenty-two years after David's death, MacDonald still felt himself to be wandering 'over Lossie roads holding the hand of my little boy in his dark blue jersey. Very saddening.'

We shall later look at the great society ladies who became MacDonald's friends. There was even a woman whom his children thought he might well marry: Molly Hamilton, Mrs Mary Hamilton, the daughter of a university professor and a graduate of Newnham College, Cambridge. But he never remarried or even came close to doing so. The existence of the unhealed wound that Margaret's death inflicted on him seems all the more poignant because none of these friendships came remotely close to replacing what he had lost.[8]

12

LEADER OF THE LABOUR PARTY

Political life went on. After the first of two elections in 1910 the new parliament had to deal with the veto which the House of Lords had exercised over budget legislation. The Labour Party's ideal solution was to move to a single chamber and abolish the Lords. That was not MacDonald's view. He did not believe that it was the wish of the electorate. He accepted the government's proposals to curtail the powers of the Lords. The alternative approach, favoured by the diehard Tory Lord Hugh Cecil, was that the composition of the Upper House should be altered in some way, but that the power of veto should be retained. MacDonald enjoyed himself by explaining how much more Conservative his policy was than Cecil's. He wanted to preserve the composition of the Upper House but adjust its powers. He made amusing play of this argument, but in truth he was displaying, as he would often do, a romantic veneration for the institutions of the state, a consistent part of his philosophy, if not of a doctrinaire man of the left.

> On the shoulders of our ancient aristocracy tippets hang naturally, and the coronets sit quite properly upon their brows, but on the shoulders of our newer nobility, of those who have just left holiday-making on Blackpool sands, the tippets do not hang naturally. They are not an aristocracy. They have purchased their way into the other House, and whatever respect—and I am bound to say that, as far as I am concerned, I have respect for them—we have for the old aristocracy, we have absolutely none for the new. Therefore, I am not at all in favour of the reform.

His respect, even affection, for the traditional aristocracy is instructive.

> A picturesque House of Lords has a certain value in the Constitution. There are certain ceremonies which are meaningless but nevertheless of considerable picturesque and educational value, which we go through from time to time in connection with our legislative processes, and I would be the last man to suggest a constitutional change that would abolish these picturesque ceremonies. The Second Chamber ought, therefore, to have an historical foundation, and to have its roots deeply dug in the ancient soil which has borne the various products and fruits of our historical achievements.

Admiration for the distinguished parts of the constitution is no part of true socialism, but it was certainly part of the credo to which MacDonald remained consistent.

*

In the new House the Liberals no longer had their huge majority of 1906. This put the Labour Party into a more powerful position, but potentially an invidious one if they too visibly supported the government. The Liberals had 275 seats, only two more than the Conservatives, and Labour with 40 and the Irish Nationalists with 82 held the balance. Labour's dilemma was illustrated in a little episode in March 1910 when MacDonald moved an amendment to the Wages for Government Employees Bill. The Conservatives surprised everyone by supporting the amendment, and in order to avoid bringing down the government, sixteen of the nineteen Labour members had to vote against their own amendment.

*

When Edward VII unexpectedly died on 6 May 1910, the deadlock over the Lords had not been resolved. A constitutional conference in which neither Labour nor the Irish Nationalists were represented made no progress. Lloyd George proposed a coalition. Many Liberals thought that MacDonald should be in the cabinet.[1] There is indeed a suggestion that MacDonald was disposed to accept an office in the coalition.[2] But the notion is improbable given the Labour Party's desire for independence, and is almost certainly without substance. Lord Elton has an anecdote about MacDonald's being offered a cabinet post at about this time and tossing the letter away, declaring, 'I shall never take office till I am head of a Labour government!'[3]

*

In December 1910, Asquith, now armed with George V's agreement to flood the Lords with Liberal peers, went to the country again. This time the Liberals and Conservatives were precisely balanced with 272 seats each. The Irish Nationalists had 84 and Labour 42, a gain of two seats for the party. At this critical constitutional moment Labour and the Irish Nationalists again held the balance of power.

Labour was far from united. Although the party had changed its name from the Labour Representation Committee (LRC) to simply 'the Labour Party', there was no outbreak of unity within the labour movement. The union men didn't think of themselves as socialists, and the socialists had little time for the unionists. While the ex-LRC Labour Party members were ready to work with the Liberals, the ILP were not. In 1907 there had been a real threat of a rupture in the labour alliance, an intimate one: at the 1906 general election, ten of the fifty LRC candidates were sponsored by the ILP. Things got no better, and in 1909 MacDonald and the other three national members of the ILP National Administrative Council (NAC) resigned because of what they described as a 'movement of irresponsibility' within the party.

*

MacDonald had been secretary of the LRC from its birth in 1900. He muttered as early as 1903 about giving up the secretaryship in order to have more time for politics and leisure, but this was never a serious suggestion. He relished the fact that as a permanent secretary of the party he had more real power than a changing chairman had. But the chairman's job became more appealing when there were suggestions that the chairman should be eligible for re-election.

Keir Hardie had been the most powerful member of the LRC since its establishment, largely on his initiative, in 1900. He had immense prestige, being in effect the creator of the labour movement—though

MacDonald thought he was a poor leader, not pulling the party together and not even attending meetings all that regularly.

Hardie was never the chairman of the LRC, but when it adopted the name of the Labour Party in 1906 he did become chairman of the new incarnation. In 1908 he was succeeded by Arthur Henderson. Henderson's aim was to bring the party as close as possible to the Liberals, and he became, as a result, as unacceptable to the ILP as Hardie had been to the trade unions.

On 15 February 1910 the *Daily Telegraph* reported that MacDonald had consented to accept nomination as leader of the Labour Party; but a day later it was announced that George Barnes, a member of the ILP from its outset, trade unionist and a supporter of the cooperative movement, had been unanimously elected. MacDonald had in fact been backed by Barnes to succeed Henderson, but no doubt as a result of David's death, he stood aside. Barnes was not an effective leader, fell ill, and did not stand in 1911.[*] MacDonald had been critical of Barnes. In his diary he said, 'Matters not going well with Labour Party. Barnes' chairmanship is a sad failure. He has no energy and no grasp of policy. Our action in the House itself is consequently feeble.'[4] MacDonald resigned the secretaryship in favour of Henderson[5] and became leader of the party.[†] He would be described at the party conference of 1912 as 'the engineer of the whole movement',[6] and from his arrival in the House, he had been in effect the de facto leader. He was a natural parliamentarian and a natural leader.

On the face of it, MacDonald doesn't seem to have particularly wanted to be chairman. He had written to Bruce Glasier:

> I do not want the chairmanship. Last year I was not keen, after a beastly letter I had from Hardie, for it, but I wrote [David] Shackleton [MP and trade unionist] a letter saying that I would put myself in the hands of the party. It is not true to say I refused to take it. But the events of the year and the continued experience of the party made me become firmer and firmer in my opinion that under present circumstances I should let the whole thing alone.

---

[*] He was party leader for just eleven months and holds the record for the shortest tenure.

[†] Henderson remained secretary for twenty-three years.

LEADER OF THE LABOUR PARTY

One wonders. At any rate, he was elected chairman at the opening of the first session in 1911 and remained chairman until he resigned on the outbreak of war in 1914. Keir Hardie said:

> No words were required from any quarter to testify to his value in connection with the Labour Party. As was written in St Paul's Cathedral regarding Wren, 'if you want his monument, look around ...' Many were the influences which went to the building up of a great Movement, but without the man to rally round no movement recorded in history had ever found its way to success.[7]

Hardie may have had his reservations about MacDonald, but he did not attack his intellect, as MacDonald attacked his. He described MacDonald as the ILP's 'greatest intellectual asset'.[8]

*

MacDonald *may* have meant that he didn't want to be chairman and leader. Lord Elton said that a more reluctant leader had seldom been elected. But for all his disavowals, MacDonald thought about the leadership as early as 1907 though inclined to rule himself out. He certainly thought that there had been more real power available to the secretary hitherto. But with a re-electable leader things had changed.

Under the new rules the chairman could go on forever, as long as he was re-elected each year. This necessity for annual re-election left the leader vulnerable, but MacDonald took steps to consolidate his position. As soon as he was elected chairman, he saw the constitution changed so that he could continue to sit on the executive as party treasurer. Beyond that important structural change, he redefined the nature of the leadership, making it something closer to that of the other parties. The Labour representatives had till now been an inchoate gaggle. Some of the members scarcely saw themselves as separate from the Liberal Party—more a pressure group than a distinct party. Others were more sturdily independent, but the coherence of something that was so fundamentally incohesive was weakened by divisions between those more or less favourable to the Liberal Party. The tradition of party discipline and party loyalty which existed in the other parties was scarcely present in the Labour Party.

THE CANCELLED PRIME MINISTER

MacDonald increasingly emerged as the sort of leader which his predecessors had never been. He had already shown his mastery of procedure and of tactics. Now his de facto practical pre-eminence was coupled with the powers that he brought to the office of leader. In addition he injected into the mix the intangible quality of leadership, abilities matched by a sense of authority and a dignity of bearing.

He had to deal with a party that liked nothing better than factionalism. When 'the Big Four', MacDonald, Hardie, Snowden and Glasier, had resigned from the ILP council, despite a choral plea 'Will ye no' come back again?', they did so to check the extremist element in the party. The ILP's 1910 pamphlet had been called *Let Us Reform the Labour Party* and it argued for warfare against 'both the capitalist parties'—Liberals as well as Conservatives. A number of the extremists were extreme enough to leave the ILP in 1911 to form a British Socialist Party. These views of the farish left were expressed in the *Daily Herald*, promoted by the ILPer George Lansbury, which was more extreme and more fun than the official Labour *Daily Citizen*.

Another deviant strand of the left was to be found in the syndicalist movement and figures like Tom Mann, who had led the 1889 dock strike. He and his supporters wanted to use violent industrial action to take control of the economy. Syndicalism started with the trade unions and had support there, but it was also informed by Marxism and by the writings of the French socialist Georges Sorel.[9]

Syndicalism was not the only manifestation of extreme trade unionism, and MacDonald didn't like it. He thought industrial strife disruptive and unnecessary and that conciliation was the proper way forward. In his book *The Socialist Movement*, he made his position on class conflict very clear: 'The appeal to class interest is an appeal to the existing order, whether the class addressed is the rich or the poor. The motive force of Socialism is therefore not the struggle, but the condemnation of the struggle by the creative imaginative intelligence and by the moral sense.'[10] In 1912 he addressed the extremism of London dockers and said they were 'plunging the whole country into a state of unsettlement'.

*

Facing these unruly and independent-minded factions was a daunting job. It was a job which MacDonald had to perform throughout his political career. He found it difficult and he often despaired, at least in private, of his colleagues' lack of discipline. From most he disguised his irritation. He unconvincingly claimed that 'a demonstration of the virile unity of a party is just as important as the speeches of its members'.[11] But he added a headmasterly admonition, demanding of his pupils 'more loyalty, more work, more participation in debates, better attendance at party meetings and at any speaking opportunities outside the House'.

*

The march of progress and the genial relationship with the Liberals were imperilled in the series of strikes, particularly in the docks and on the railways, in the summer of 1911 already referred to. MacDonald did not react to strikes as a stereotypical socialist would. He saw strikes as the tool of syndicalists, who believed that the withdrawal of labour could remould society. His view was that society would unite against strikers and become all the stronger in its original mould. He referred to the recent strikes in Sweden, where, rather as in the case of Britain's 1926 General Strike, the middle classes had manned the buses and cleaned the streets.

That doesn't mean that his sympathies were with the employers and the capitalist classes. He considered the strikes as a reaction against conspicuous consumption and the political prejudices distilled in the *Taff Vale* and *Osborne* judgments. He attacked Churchill for his robust approach to strikes. 'The people', he wrote in the *Socialist Review* in October 1911, had been 'weeping with poor children during the strike [while] *The Times*, the *Daily Telegraph*, the *Liverpool Post* and suchlike papers have been spewing out a filthy flush of hypocrisy'.[12] 'One way to maintain law and order is not to allow policemen to break a man's head and then say no enquiry is going to be made for three or four months, while the man who retaliates in hot blood is hauled up before the magistrates next morning.'[13]

The railway strike was called off as a result of negotiations in which MacDonald was involved, and a royal commission was set up. Again, his practical, conciliatory approach was criticised in the

Labour ranks, even by his friend Bruce Glasier. Things went worse for MacDonald when the union rejected the commission's recommendations. Once again, practical MacDonaldism succeeded: he pressed for and established negotiations between the unions and the railway companies.

All of this is important. MacDonald was not identifying himself with sectarian labour, but rather with an overarching national interest. Although he formally supported the strikes, he publicly deprecated what he called syndicalist anarchists with their absurd economic and political ideas. He saw the strikes as an unfortunate aberration and not as an intrinsic part of the class dialectic.

*

What MacDonald was doing can be described in a few sentences of reportage, but it was hard, painful work, involving draining advocacy and exhortation—often in the face of bitter recriminations. In July 1912, he wrote:

> I am being persuaded against my will by the actions of the Party itself that it is hopeless to go on. The members see so little ahead & know so little of how to fight that [they] give life to every rumour which disrupts us. My leadership has consisted not in leading the party against an enemy but in shepherding its ranks so that they did not become a disorganised mob.[14]

He often despaired of his party in this way. It was for him a vehicle, not an end in itself. He was facing the ever-repeated Labour conflict between governing and protesting. In the face of this, his health suffered.

*

He was able to escape on a voyage to India in December 1912 as a member of a royal commission on the Indian public services. It took him away from Britain for four months. Not a holiday, of course. The commission took detailed evidence, and in addition to work on their report, MacDonald developed his understanding of Indian politics. Additionally, he assembled materials for a further book on India.

LEADER OF THE LABOUR PARTY

In India he was not being sniped at or stabbed in the back. He returned to Britain bronzed, fitter and healthier. He came back to news of a by-election in Leicester. MacDonald held one of the two seats, and the other had become vacant when the Liberal member resigned after being cited as co-respondent in a divorce case. The question was whether Labour should contest the seat. If it did, it put at risk the arrangements which had allowed MacDonald to be elected for the other seat without contest from the Liberals. Matters got very heated. Many in the ILP thought that the party had a duty to contest the seat. In the event, after long and complicated negotiations, the Labour Party did not field a candidate. But the British Socialist Party did. MacDonald was minded not to contest his own Leicester seat if the ILP or the Labour Party backed the Socialist Party candidate. Even though they said they would not do so, he decided he would still find another seat if Labour electors in the constituency supported the Socialist Party candidate in any numbers. Fortunately they did not do so.

But the shock waves from Leicester spread throughout the whole labour movement. It was a disheartening time for MacDonald and undid much of the good of his Indian trip. It was against this background that he had to decide how to react to overtures from Lloyd George.

The Labour Party had of course emerged to an extent out of the Liberal Party, and the distinction between membership of the two parties was still a fine one, so it is not surprising that the Liberals frequently thought of a formal coalition with Labour. As we have seen, this had been mooted earlier, in 1910 and again in 1911, when he was sounded out separately by Lloyd George and the Master of Elibank. It has even been suggested that MacDonald himself hinted at a coalition involving him, Lloyd George and Balfour, but not Asquith.[15] All of that is cloaked in doubt and seems improbable. Politicians enjoy abstract speculation, and that is probably what this talk consisted of. But in 1912 something more definite happened. Elibank told him he should not join a coalition, for which the time was not yet right, but to come into the cabinet at a high level in his own right. It's interesting that Elibank considered MacDonald as pretty well part of the Liberal Party: 'you are one of *our* best debaters' (my emphasis). MacDonald's response—that he wasn't prepared to support the government through thick and thin, and that his joining the cabinet would damage the Labour Party greatly—gives the lie to the idea that there had been serious coalition negotiations. It also suggests that the appeal of office for its own sake was limited.

In 1914, in the context of the crisis over Ireland, Lloyd George and Percy Illingworth, the Chief Whip, with (he claimed) the approval of Asquith, met MacDonald and Arthur Henderson for Labour and proposed three things: an electoral deal which would allow Labour to increase its membership; an agreed programme; and seats in the cabinet if they were wanted.

MacDonald was attracted. He was concerned by the Curragh mutiny, when senior army officers threatened to resign rather than coerce Ulster into accepting Home Rule, and thought that the Home Rule Bill had to be enacted without delay. But the discussions were kept very secret and ultimately came to nothing. At the ILP conference at Easter 1914, MacDonald denied that there was any agreement with the Liberals. Philip Snowden didn't accept the denial. Keir Hardie intervened to say that no proposal of a formal agreement had been made: the matter had only been mentioned. Snowden pointedly said that he would accept *Hardie's* reassurances. As the Liberals contemplated the implications of Curragh, their appetite for an early election diminished and the prospect of a formal coalition disappeared.

The years of peace were ending, and a war approached, a greater and more awful war than that in South Africa. It would pose a great moral dilemma for MacDonald. More than half his political career was now over.

13

MACDONALD'S LADIES

MacDonald may have disdained them, but other Labour men were more susceptible to the suffragettes. Bruce Glasier once described Mrs Pankhurst as 'the Delilah who has cut our Samson's locks'— 'our Samson' was Keir Hardie. George Lansbury was upset by the forced feeding of suffragette prisoners. On one occasion he shook his fist in Asquith's face and shouted, 'You will go down in history as the man who tortured innocent women!' MacDonald, on the other hand, said that he had no time for childishness masquerading as revolution and dismissed the suffragettes as 'pettifogging middle-class damsels'.[1] When Edith Picton-Turbervill was invited to lunch at Downing Street as a Labour candidate, she was disappointed to find that MacDonald was reluctant to discuss politics with women, candidates or not.[2] He found the suffragettes less appealing than ladies with whom he could discuss his silver collection.

Even those who know very little about Ramsay MacDonald tend to be aware of his duchesses. We might look at them now. He had a large trophy room, and the first head that is mounted on its walls is that of Lady Margaret Sackville, the daughter of Earl De La Warr.* His friendship with her began in 1912, just a year after Margaret died. She considered herself a poetess, and sent him volumes of her poetry. Her political philosophy was simplistic. She approved of social justice but couldn't understand why Ramsay attacked the landed classes, to which she belonged. The friendship lasted for four or five years, but

---

* Lady Margaret's brother, the ninth Earl, would, however, be a member of a MacDonald government.

THE CANCELLED PRIME MINISTER

it never seems to have meant much to MacDonald. It certainly didn't lift his sense of desolation. He was acutely aware of the lack of a close friend with whom to share the satisfaction of success or the disturbance of defeat. He said he felt like a solitary stag.

After his wife's death, Katharine Glasier advised MacDonald to marry again. His children thought that he might well marry Mrs Molly Hamilton. Of course he never did, and there's no evidence that he ever came close to remarrying. Indeed, could they have married even if they wanted to? Molly's husband had left her soon after they were married, and they may never have divorced.[3] At one stage she and MacDonald read aloud to each other, and he kept photographs of her, although no letters. There is room for no more than speculation about the relationship. Initially she considered herself to be a devotee, but later was critical. Her changing views of MacDonald can be traced in two sketches she wrote of him, one in 1923 and one in 1925.[*]

Many widowers remarry to find a housekeeper. MacDonald did not need to. He called on the services of a Dutch housekeeper from Lossie immediately after Margaret's death, and a variety of Lossie lasses came to London 'to cook for Jamie', so there were no practical problems about looking after the children. They came back to Lossie with stories of a very simple, even spartan regime in MacDonald's house. Even when he became Prime Minister, he continued to rely on the girls from Lossiemouth. One was intrigued to come into the dining room and find MacDonald and the whole party sitting on the floor to eat their meal. Gandhi was MacDonald's guest. He had said that he preferred to eat in this way, and MacDonald insisted that everyone else would do so too.[4]

What MacDonald pined for was the support and fellow feeling of a kindred spirit. Some of that he found in the most celebrated of his ladies, a much more significant connection and one who could be used to support the idea that he was seduced by the aristocracy. At a dinner at Buckingham Palace during the 1924 government, MacDonald found himself seated next to the Marchioness of Londonderry, a famous Tory hostess. The initial contact started

---

[*] *The Man of Tomorrow* (1923) and *J. Ramsay MacDonald, 1923–1925* (1925).

badly. She disapproved of his pacifism during the First World War and he disapproved of her politics, despite the fact that she was a Scot—and a Highlander—on her mother's side. On the following day he was warned that she could be dangerous. Despite that, he invited the Londonderrys to stay at Chequers.*

His friendship with Lady Londonderry developed fairly slowly at first, but by 1930 he was writing to her not as 'my dear Lady Londonderry' but as 'My dear Ladye'. Note the medieval conceit. The chivalric tone of the correspondence reflected the romantic, fictional world which they both chose to inhabit. He signed himself 'Hamish', the Gaelic form of the first of his names. She stayed with him at Chequers, and he visited her and her husband in the Highlands. He was also frequently at Londonderry House.

Londonderry House was unique, something left over from a previous century. Lavish receptions took place there, particularly at the start of the parliamentary session. Guests were greeted by powdered footmen and, in a process that could take fifteen minutes, progressed to the top of the great staircase, where Lady Londonderry would await, usually with the current leader of the Conservative Party. Even Conservatives could find it over the top. Baldwin thought it was something left over from 'the golden age of corruption'.

As MacDonald's friendship with Lady Londonderry developed, he was a more and more frequent guest at this venue, so alien, so extraordinarily distant from the socialist imagination, indeed from the cottage in Lossiemouth. By the time he became leader of the National Government, it was he who stood at the top of the stairs with Lady Londonderry. MacDonald's colleagues were horrified and disgusted to see him go native, as it seemed. Even the Conservatives disapproved. Baldwin thought that MacDonald was

---

* The Marquess of Londonderry, a major pit owner, was not a great friend of the miners. He complained that when some of them came to a garden party at his country house they stole the crockery and buried it in the garden. Later he complained about Emanuel Shinwell coming to the family pit and addressing 'the miners from the steps of the pavilion on the recreation field which my family had given to the miners. Not one voice was raised in my defence when he attacked me in his speech' (Quoted in Howell, *MacDonald's Party*, p. 139). This didn't stop MacDonald from seeking to improve the working conditions of the miners in his second administration.

motivated simply by ambition. The Tory FE Smith had described Lord Londonderry as 'catering his way to the cabinet'. Londonderry himself had no qualms. He described himself as 'Ramsay's man' and recognised what he owed to his wife when he was appointed as MacDonald's Secretary of State for Air in 1931.

It was in the period when he headed the National Government that MacDonald became closest to Lady Londonderry. She had never been afraid of scandal. As a girl she had ridden *astride* Highland ponies, to the horror of her family. She had a snake tattooed on one of her legs. During the First World War she had founded a society called the Ark, which met at Londonderry House every Wednesday evening. The members had pet names—Churchill was 'Winston the Warlock', Balfour 'Arthur the Albatross'. In due course MacDonald was 'Hamish the Hart'. Lady Londonderry herself was 'Circe'.

There was almost certainly nothing sexual in the relationship but a good deal of flirtation. On one occasion, MacDonald telephoned her to tell her the outcome of negotiations at Lausanne in 1932. She replied:

> Your telephone message gave me *such* joy—not only for the greatest event, but on the account of the success of your vy dear self ... My whole heart goes out to you in joy and admiration at the manner in which you have pulled it off—Bless you—all my love is yours ... To hear it, in your own dear words—was wonderful, I still feel breathless—I always knew you were a great man—so I am not surprised—but I am doubly proud and pleased—All my love dearest H,
>
> From CIRCE

They created a mystical world composed of elements of the Round Table and of medieval romance. He described her as a fairy princess in her castle, their relationship as 'my Isle of Avalon where falls not rainbow nor snow, nor ever wind blows loudly ... my dear, my love'.

The conceit was very elaborate. He wrote to 'My Dearest of Dear Persons' after some debate within himself between the Shy Spirit and the Bold Spirit.

> My Dear you were very beautiful, and I loved you. The dress, dazzling in brilliance & glorious in colour and line, was you, & my dear,

you were the dress. I just touched its hem, & pray for your eternal happiness wondering at the same time what generous hearted archangel ever patted me on the back & arranged that amongst the many great rewards that this poor unwelcome stranger to this world was to receive was that he would be permitted before he returned to his dust to feel devotion to *you*.

The extravagance of the words and their distance from reality show just how much a thing of the imagination the relationship was. But imagination never did more than temporarily relieve reality. The pain of his losses was never relieved. He never stopped wandering over Lossie roads 'holding the hands of my little boy in his dark blue jersey'.

Between Molly Hamilton and the full-on friendship with Lady Londonderry, there was Cecily Gordon-Cumming, daughter of Colonel Sir William Gordon-Cumming, the Laird of Gordonstoun.* MacDonald met Cecily on a cross-Channel steamer in 1928. Despite the fact that she was younger than his daughter Ishbel, he invited her to Lossiemouth for 'golf & gossip'. A bit like Asquith and Venetia Stanley. Soon he was addressing her as 'My Dear Cecily' or 'My Dear C'. She stayed with him at Chequers. He read aloud to her. He walked with her as he had walked with Margaret. He held her hand under the rug while they rode together in the back of his car.

---

* Gordon-Cumming traced his descent through Charlemagne to the fourth century AD. Although he suffered from asthma and was blind in his right eye, he had some remarkable adventures, which included stalking tigers on foot in India and being shipwrecked off Cape Town. He swore in both English and Hindustani. He boasted of 'perforating' large numbers of aristocratic ladies, including Lady Randolph Churchill. In 1890 he was accused of cheating at baccarat in a game in which the Prince of Wales had taken part. The matter was meant to be hushed up so as not the involve the Prince of Wales, and Gordon-Cumming, though protesting his innocence, signed a pledge saying he would never play cards again. Despite that, the matter came to court when Gordon-Cumming raised an action for slander against his accusers. The Prince had after all to appear in the witness box and as a result went through a period of great unpopularity. Gordon-Cumming lost the action. On the following day he was dismissed from the army and married an American heiress. He was ostracised for the remainder of an unhappy life. The famous game of baccarat was played at Tranby Croft, and the episode is remembered as the Tranby Croft affair.

She married in the summer of 1931, and he continued to write to her for the rest of his life.

What was all this about? Much less than it sounds like. She was not in love with him, although she conceded that he might have been 'in a small, far-away way slightly in love with me'. He never said so and never made any moves. She said that he never 'pounced'.[5] All he said, by way of hint, was that some things could never be. He even advised her not to fall in love with old men. When she got married, MacDonald wrote a jovial letter to her, full of tomfoolery and ending with words from an old song: 'We'll kiss no more / By sea or shore / Ahint a door; / For noo she's mairrit / Happy & pairrit / Her auld jos maun bair it'.

Next up was no mere Lady, but a full-blown princess, Marthe Bibesco, sometimes known as La Nymphe Europe. She was the wife of a Romanian diplomat and an old friend of Lord Thomson (of whom we shall hear more). She was introduced to MacDonald by Thomson during the second Labour government when she was having tea on the terrace of the House of Lords. She had read MacDonald's memoir of his wife only the night before, had been moved by it, and told him so. She, like Cecily Gordon-Cumming, was much younger than MacDonald. She was also beautiful and sensitive. She was asked to Chequers, and after Lord Thomson's death in an air accident, MacDonald suggested they should write to each other 'when the spirit moved them'. He wrote to her almost every week for the rest of his life. The tone of his letters to her was less flirtatious than his letters to Cecily, but in correspondence with her he was able to find solace for burdens he found increasingly heavy. After he resigned as Prime Minister he wrote to her, 'When I get some rest & sleep I have no doubt but that I shall be much fitter again, but meantime I am traversing weary country.' He told her that when her last letter had reached him, 'the clouds scudded across the sky. I was no longer without friends, no longer solitary in a dreary world.'[6]

The final head isn't on the wall at all. If he had an affair with a notorious 'cocotte' during visits to central Europe in the 1920s, she was certainly not part of the harem and was far removed from his London seraglio. There was an allegation that he had some contacts with this lady, that he was blackmailed, that she was paid off with secret service funds and that the letters were destroyed. A variation which is more fun is that JH Thomas, whom we shall meet properly later, was sent to Paris to pay her off with Labour Party funds but lost the money. There is always gossip about powerful people, and the right was keen to discredit Labour. The story is wildly improbable at every level—not least because MacDonald would have run a mile if confronted by a Mata Hari figure—and can be dismissed without much thought.

*

What are we to make of MacDonald and the ladies? Not an awful lot. When he effectively abandoned Labour to head the National Government—to save the nation, as he saw it—he was immediately reviled by his old colleagues. We shall see in due course just how much he was regarded as a traitor and turncoat. There had been those before then who regarded participation in the ceremonial, theatrical part of constitutional life as foreign to the spirit of the Labour Party. MacDonald did not see things that way. He did not want to end tradition and form but simply to nudge the institutions of the state in a progressive direction. Many took a different view and, even prior to 1931, complained about his consorting with high society. After 1931, the criticism turned into hatred.

The charge against MacDonald in relation to society and the duchesses was no doubt based partly on jealousy. There were two theories. One was that he was vain and contemptible, that his interest was never with the working classes, that he may or may not have used social advancement as a means of fostering his ambitions but that in any event he was simply intoxicated by the glitter of society. The other theory was that the Establishment had deliberately seduced him, pandering to his weaknesses in order to destroy the threat which he posed. Sidney Webb wrote in the *Political Quarterly* that the political right was well used to 'the weapon of seduction'. 'It took some time to make Disraeli the beloved of Duchesses ... On more recent cases, it is needless to dwell.'[7]

Webb's account was developed by Harold Laski:

> Timid, indecisive, vain of applause, [MacDonald] shrank from the price of unpopularity among the society he had growingly come

to esteem. Its self confidence nourished his lack of it. Its own faith in its standards gave him standards he could not otherwise attain ... The ribbon is in his coat; and he will not live to read the verdict of history.[8]

There are several possible responses. First, there is nothing surprising about the fact that MacDonald liked female company. He was not a man's man. He had very few male friends. Lord Thomson, whom I have just mentioned, was one of them. There are not many more. MacDonald was a physical, outdoor person. He enjoyed his golf. He particularly enjoyed long and testing walks, in which he pushed himself to the limits of endurance, but he was not interested in taking part in or watching team sports. He had no interest in relatively gregarious blood sports like shooting or fishing. His other interests were in books, in conversation, in romantic fantasy. In these areas he found women more congenial companions than men.

He was thin-skinned and sensitive, and he suffered. He suffered most from the deaths of David and Margaret and the continuing sense of loss that their deaths engendered. He was also hurt by the buffets of politics. Again and again he felt that he was unappreciated by his party, that he had to fight on without its support and despite its attacks. He needed to unburden himself. Others might find release in other ways, but he found it in the company of sensitive women. The stress from which he suffered built up to bring him regularly to the point of breakdown. Without a spouse his only way of unwinding was with trusted confidantes.

Thus women. But did they have to be aristocrats? Why should they not be? That brings me to my second point. We have seen that MacDonald, perhaps fancifully, subscribed to the idea that nobility could be found in any class of society. The notion may seem strange, but it is one in which he genuinely believed. He was not sophisticated or cynical. In some ways he was quite simple. If he found a woman congenial company, it would not have occurred to him that friendship was precluded by the social distance or by his Lossiemouth origins. Some of his confidantes were indeed not aristocrats. Molly Hamilton was not. Katharine Glasier was not.

MACDONALD'S LADIES

To the pure all things are pure, and MacDonald was at the upper end of the purity index. He was pure in a number of senses, including the belief that social rank was of no significance.

*

Even at a material level he could feel that the distance that had separated him from the aristocracy and as a young man had reduced dramatically. In 1916 he moved from Lincoln's Inn Fields to Hampstead and a terraced house on Howitt Road. It is understood that there was a degree of ostracism by his well-heeled neighbours. In 1925 he received a legacy that allowed him to move from Howitt Road to Upper Frognal Lodge, a twenty-roomed Georgian house still in Hampstead. The legacy came in fact from Mary Middleton, the second wife of James Middleton, whose first wife, also Mary, was the friend of Margaret, who had died in 1911, causing her such distress. Her husband, who had been MacDonald's assistant, had become a successful businessman in Newcastle, and Mary came greatly to admire MacDonald.

Upper Frognal Lodge was a distinguished Georgian house dating from about 1745. Some alterations were made in the early nineteenth century and others have been made since MacDonald's time. It was a very suitable house for a former Prime Minister, if not perhaps for a socialist leader. He sold Howitt Road to his son Alister below market value at £1,200. He paid £6,000 for Upper Frognal Lodge. Converting 1924 pounds to the present-day value is inaccurate at the best of times, but when we are dealing with residential property prices in Hampstead, the process becomes meaningless. It was, however, a huge sum for a fairly poor man, and despite Mary Middleton's legacy, MacDonald had to sell some of his possessions to complete the purchase. It was a substantial property, and even though all the family apart from Alister moved in with him, the scale of the place must have seemed excessive. Nowadays it has been divided into two houses. Alister, by then a young architect, supervised repair work and the landscaping of the garden.

From the grandeur of Upper Frognal Lodge he could write to Lord Londonderry, 'If ever you or your Lady Londonderry want a walk on Hampstead Heath on a Saturday or Sunday afternoon when

I am in town, come and pick me up and return with me to tea. I am just on the edge of the Heath in a nice old Georgian house.'⁹

In the year that he wrote that letter to Lord Londonderry, he spent lengthy holidays in Ceylon (Sri Lanka) and in the Sahara: from every point of view he felt able to write to his noble friend on terms of easy equality. That would not be the way society saw the relationship between the two men, but MacDonald was an innocent, and his innocence is reflected in the fact that he did not impute to others the sort of slurs which they imputed to him.

*

Thirdly, there is no evidence to suggest that his weakness for aristocratic female company ever affected his judgement. He may or may not have said when he consented to lead the National Government, 'Tomorrow every duchess in London will want to kiss me', but if he did, the evidence of all that he said and wrote would show that he used the words in a spirit of weary resignation and not of triumph.

While MacDonald's conduct can be exonerated and explained, that's not to say it was wise. It clearly weakened his authority with the mainstream of Labour supporters that he should be perceived to be intimate with those who were, at the end of the day, his political enemies. It made it very easy to accuse him of hypocrisy, vanity and social climbing. It would have been better for his reputation if he had remained close to his origins and to the values of his supporters, in the same way as Clement Attlee never departed from the norms of *his* background. MacDonald was led astray by his otherworldliness, the same simplicity of spirit that would ignore the arguments against joining the Conservatives in the National Government.

14

1914

CRISIS

Like other intelligent observers, MacDonald worried about what seemed to be approaching inexorably in the years running up to 1914. Events appeared to be moving towards international breakdown, and governments were failing to address the threat. With Hardie and others he formed the Union of Democratic Control (UDC), which sought to campaign against war and to bring the conduct of international relations generally under a more democratic system of control. As early as 1910 he had spoken in the German Reichstag,* impressing the Chancellor, Bethmann Hollweg. In the following year he counselled his party against hostility to Germany, recognising that German trade and competition were bound to continue to increase.¹ The party was not particularly receptive, and when the Kaiser lunched with Viscount Haldane in London in 1911 and MacDonald was one of the guests, there were protests. The Dumfries branch of the ILP, for example, censured him for 'lunching with the Kaiser'. MacDonald said they should mind their own business.

But he was a patriot, and the idea that he was fawning on the German warlord was absurd. When Germany sent the gunboat *Panther* to Agadir in July 1911 to confront France and her interests in Morocco, MacDonald warned in Palmerstonian tones that if Germany were to ignore Britain's concerns and her responsibilities

---

* Another badge of internationalism which few other politicians of the day could wear.

as an ally of France, that would be 'a humiliation intolerable for a great country like ours'.[2] As he would do in 1914, he said that while Labour might be unable to support a war, it would not seek to 'weaken the national spirit or national unity'. War was to be deprecated, but Britain must win any war in which it was involved.

*

MacDonald's attitude to the First World War was, then, complicated, nuanced and misunderstood. He was an internationalist. His close links to foreign socialists, in particular the German Social Democratic Party, distinguished him from simplistic jingoism. He liked being abroad and he liked many of the people he met there. He frequently pointed out that the German socialists had done nothing to help the Kaiser build up the German Navy, the weapon with which Wilhelm sought to match Britain's power. He distinguished between Germany and German militarism. Long before 1914 he had consistently attacked the policy of the Foreign Office under Sir Edward Grey in what he saw as a seriously mistaken failure to distinguish the different elements in Germany.

He was realistic. He could see before July 1914 had ended that war was inevitable. When his Chief Whip said it would be unpopular, MacDonald laughed and told him that no war started as being unpopular.

On 2 August 1914 MacDonald was summoned to a meeting at Downing Street. On his way there he bumped into the elderly Liberal radical Lord Morley, who asked him what his position would be in the event of war. MacDonald said he would have nothing to do with it. Neither would Morley, who resigned from the cabinet twenty-four hours later. When he got to Downing Street he found ministers worried that there would be no popular support for war. MacDonald assured them that there would, that this would be the most popular war in which Britain had ever fought. He was right and all the more courageous in dissociating himself from that war.

Later that day he dined with a number of Liberal grandees. He could see that they were searching for ways to support a war, whatever their position had been in the past. His position was different. He felt at home with many of the leading political figures on mainland Europe. He was comfortable in the international community. Part of that community with which he did not sympathise, however, was Russia. Like most socialists he found Tsarist absolutism and the nature of Russian society hugely distasteful, and he deprecated the government's alliance with the Romanovs. The Social Democrats in Germany, by contrast, were much more congenial company. Like him, they were opposed to militarism, and at this stage he could still hope that they would stand against it.

MacDonald was against war in general, but not all wars. What that meant was that he didn't think that the war against Germany in which Britain took part in 1914 was necessary. When Grey rose in the Commons on 3 August to make the famous speech which would set out for the first time where Britain stood in a dispute to which it was arguably not a party, MacDonald was already biased against the Foreign Secretary and his policy and unlikely to be impressed by anything he had to say. Overtures from the Liberals had dried up as his distaste for Grey became more evident. Grey's speech was momentous. It won over important elements of the Liberal Party, which had had reservations very similar to MacDonald's. Grey quoted from Gladstone, arguing that it was profoundly against Britain's interests to stand back and watch the unchecked aggrandisement of any one Continental power. It was this traditional element of British policy rather than a legalistic insistence on Britain's obligation to Belgium under a treaty of 1839—the 'scrap of paper', as the Kaiser described it—that swung the House: the treaty obligation, the requirement to defend Belgium's independence, was no more than the pretext for entering the war. The real argument was preserving the balance of power, and that argument carried the House.

MacDonald recognised that Grey had delivered a speech 'the echoes of which will go down in history'. He said that if Grey's analysis had been correct, the Labour Party would have voted money to the government and given their lives to the cause. MacDonald's speech is a very well-argued one, 'the greatest single speech in the political life of MacDonald', as MacNeill Weir described it.[3] But he failed to accept Grey's premise—that the unchecked aggrandisement of one European power was an attack on Britain just as much as a direct physical attack would have been. He rejected that analysis entirely. He did not see that the country was in danger, that Britain's safety, let alone her existence, was challenged. He found Grey's invocations of Gladstonian principles spurious. Grey, he said, had not shown that there was a need for war: 'I want to say to this House, and to say it without equivocation, that if the right hon. Gentleman had come here today and told us that our country is in danger, I do not care what party he appealed to, or to what class he appealed; we would be with him and behind him ... but he has not persuaded me that it is.' He turned to the issue of Belgian integrity, the technical *casus belli*, and said that if the government were confining the conflict to the defence of Belgium, the Labour Party would support it, but that the sort of conflict now envisaged was going to go far further than the matter of Belgium.

This was one of those rare parliamentary occasions when no one truly knew what the outcome would be, and when one speech—Grey's—created that outcome. There were strong arguments against participation in the war. Britain was not directly part of the quarrel between the two opposed alliances on the Continental mainland. She had a vast and powerful navy, but she had only a very small army available to form an expeditionary force: initially just six divisions as opposed to the sixty that would be in Europe by the end of the war. It had been the British tradition to avoid substantial military commitment on the Continent, relying instead on her fleet and subventions to allies. There were many in the Liberal Party who were and long had been declaredly anti-militaristic. But Grey carried the day.

He was not necessarily going to do so. As it was, John Morley, the senior and distinguished member of the cabinet whom MacDonald had met on 2 August, resigned rather than go to war. Even Lloyd George, the 'Welsh Wizard' who would be celebrated as 'the man who won the war', wobbled. We tend to see the First World War as such a central feature in British history that we look at its outbreak only with the distortion of hindsight. Britain might well have stood aside. Some historians argue indeed that if Britain had done so and had watched her commercial rivals on the Continent tear themselves to bits, she would have emerged as the dominant creditor nation, which the United States became. At a moral as well as a political level, there were those who opposed Britain's entry. The Bishop of Hereford declared, 'I feel that our government is in duty bound to keep England strictly neutral.' The Bishop of Lincoln said, 'For England to join in the hideous war would be *treason* to civilisation and *disaster* to our people. God save us from the war fever!'[4]

There were others in the Labour Party who were much more against the war than MacDonald. Snowden was one. In his memoirs he described MacDonald's position as a 'facility in dancing around the mulberry bush'.[5] ED Morel also referred to MacDonald's delicately nuanced position: 'He has a hundred little subtleties which keep me in a constant state of vigilance all the time.'[6]

*

On 5 August the executive in the parliamentary party condemned Grey: 'We condemn the policy which has produced the war. We do not obstruct the war effort, but our duty is to secure peace at the earliest possible moment.' That was pretty much MacDonald's position. But a few hours later, when he sought to follow through by arguing against the Prime Minister's demand for a war credit, he was not allowed to speak. He resigned as leader of the party. Only five Labour members, all ILPers, were with him. The Parliamentary Labour Party voted for war credits.

MacDonald was succeeded as party leader by Henderson, who continued as secretary. His colleagues didn't necessarily want him to go. A deputation of members of parliament urged him to stay on. Even Henderson urged him to come back.

Why did he resign? His position regarding the war is always said to be complex. It was impractical too. He wanted Britain to win, he thought Britain would win, and he knew that his opposition to the war was not going to weaken support for the government. Was it necessary therefore to make himself as unpopular as he did? He didn't enjoy unpopularity. Long before he was (as we shall see) expelled from the Lossiemouth Golf Club, he was being cut on the course by members. That upset him. It was simply the case that this was a war he couldn't conscientiously support. It could be argued that he did neither himself nor anyone else much good by parading his conscience, as Lansbury was to do between the wars. On the other hand, so far as the ILP was concerned, he improved his credentials by his detachment from the mainstream of the national mood. It was, however, a risky calculation to stand apart from that mood. In the early months and years of the war those who stood apart from the patriotic frenzy were as unpopular as they would be among bereaved widows and parents in the final years.

There has been speculation about his motives. Fenner Brockway thought that he was bidding for the leadership of radical opinion. The historian AJP Taylor went along with this, suggesting that he was preserving his political purity as part of a long game. Nothing about MacDonald ties in with these ideas. The truth is what he said it was. He hated war and did not see that his country need participate in a war which did not directly touch its interests. In making that appreciation, he failed to see the extent to which Britain's interests would be affected by the outcome of the war; but his decision, his mistake, was not based on self-interest.

Even in the midst of his concerns over the war, other matters were in his thoughts. On 8 September 1914: 'We made a pilgrimage to Spynie and stood by her ashes. This is the anniversary of her death. We all said "blessie, mammie: blessie, David".'

*

His thoughts were, as always, introspective rather than Machiavellian, and as Snowden said, there was a bit too much of the mulberry bush. It was perfectly arguable that Grey was wrong and that Britain should not have gone to war in August 1914. But once that decision was taken, the situation immediately changed. Britain's interests were now challenged. If Germany had won the war, Britain, her navy and her empire would have been at enormous risk. Within a month or two of the outbreak of war it was clear that Britain was engaged in a battle for her survival and the survival of liberal values throughout the Continent. It was self-indulgent and illogical for MacDonald to go on opposing a war which was no longer the one he had opposed at the beginning of August. It was also unacceptable for him to leave his position so blurred and paradoxical, against war but against conscientious objectors, wanting victory but not wanting to encourage recruitment. As far back as August 1914 he had said, 'Whatever our views may be of the origins of the war, we must go through with it', but he gave little impression of encouraging that process.

He was clear that he wasn't a pacifist. Most people thought he was. His attitude to recruitment, for example, was complicated. The ILP was in principle against recruitment. The official Labour Party was not. MacDonald was not prepared to appear on a 'pro-war platform', by which he meant a recruiting meeting, although he was prepared to allow others to use their own judgement. He wrote a celebrated reply to an invitation from the mayor of Leicester to appear at a recruiting meeting, in which he declined to attend, but in language filled with patriotism: 'Might and spirit will win, and incalculable political and social consequences will follow upon victory. Victory therefore must be ours. England is not played out.' He would be delighted to appeal to 'the pure love of country—which I know is the precious sentiment in all our hearts, keeping it clear of thoughts which are believed to be alien of real patriotism'. All the same he would not attend. His reasons were clouded by dense verbiage which could be described, using words of his own from his letter to the mayor, as 'the mists of a plague and the shadows of a pestilence'.[7]

What was the reaction to his opaque evasiveness? Lord Elton summarised MacDonald's position in three assertions. First, Britain had been wrong to enter the war. Second, if Britain was in the war, the war had to be won. Third, even at war, the voice of moderation must speak: militarism was to be defeated, not adopted.[8] It was an enlightened but politically opaque position. Only those with a mind to analyse his words forensically would understand that he was not a pacifist.

MacDonald's position was more than anything else an emotional one. He was instinctively averse to violence and could never have associated himself with the inhumanity of war. To support that gut reaction, he had recourse to a number of fairly unimpressive arguments. He attacked the policy of maintaining the balance of power through alliances. He pointed out that Gladstone himself had recognised that in a general conflict formal neutrality might be violated, and he saw the sanctity of Belgian independence as a fraudulent concept.

He dismissed suggestions that he should resume the leadership. He affected not to be overly concerned to be away from the centre. On 12 October 1914 he wrote: 'Another birthday of very unexpected circumstances ... Friends urge a return to the stream of public life. Little do they know how happy I am where I am, the world against me, a spectator only ...' He seemed to need time and space in which to consider where his political inclinations would lead him. And if he was less popular than he had been with the Labour Party, the ILP was pleased with his stance. MacDonald was so touched by the messages of ILP support which poured in that he thought the ILP had recovered its old spirit of 'comradeship and confidence'.⁹

I have some doubt about the argument that MacDonald's wilderness war years gave him important credentials with the left, building up within the ILP a reputation of incorruptibility, and emerging as the obvious successor to Keir Hardie, who was to die in 1915. His evasiveness, his complications—favouring enlistment but not recruitment, for example—confused many.

*

His position certainly alienated public opinion generally. As the nation suffered shock after shock on the battlefield, as volunteers flocked to the colours, to be followed by conscripts, as the roll of honour filled the pages of the newspapers day after day, MacDonald was seen as an egregious traitor. As early as 1 October 1914, *The Times* said in a leading article that 'no paid agent of Germany had served her better' than MacDonald. On 3 October *The Spectator* asked, 'Is it right that Mr Ramsay MacDonald should be drawing £400 a year from the British taxpayer when so far as we can judge by his correspondence in the Press, the chief work he is doing for the country at the moment is heartening the enemy?' And these reactions came at a point when the awful nature of the war and the real risk that Britain might lose it were not yet evident.

He was no coward. At the end of 1914 he crossed to France to help organise volunteer ambulance corps. The visit ended in confusion, with MacDonald arrested, perhaps on the orders of the British government, perhaps on the orders of the Belgian government, and sent back to England. He returned to the front as an official visitor just a few days later and drove through Ypres. His car moved forward through occasional shellfire and then under heavy rifle and machine-gun fire, which hit the bonnet, windscreen and mudguards of the vehicle. Four hundred yards from the French frontline, he and his party, including the daredevil Jack Seely, took cover in a ditch. Seely and MacDonald rushed towards the fighting and into a French support trench. MacDonald wanted to go forward with the French assault force and was only dissuaded by Seely. They returned to headquarters with shells falling around. Seely recorded that MacDonald had thoroughly enjoyed himself and had 'behaved with the utmost coolness, and, indeed, suggested that we might go forward ... instead of endeavouring to return to a place of safety'.[10]

He enjoyed this brief visit to the front and he wanted to return as part of an ambulance unit. His elder son spent these years in the Friends' Medical Corps, and MacDonald could have been there too if he had been allowed. How different his image might have been. All of this is consistent with the outdoor man, who drove himself to the limits on the hills, tested himself by rough sleeping on the bracken, who enjoyed fast driving and flying and who, indeed, exposed himself to opprobrium and personal danger by expressing his complex thought processes when he could more safely have remained silent.

Becoming aware of how the man in the street saw him did not change his position, but it pained him. He wrote to Charles Trevelyan, a Liberal MP who would join the Labour Party in 1918, 'The opposition to us is tremendous. So soon as one goes outside one's own immediate personal circle one meets it in the most cruelly oppressive way. People do believe we are selling our country & that we are tainted as with leprosy.'[11]*

While there were narrow arguments and qualifications which separated MacDonald from pacifism for those who were prepared

---

* Charles, later Sir Charles, Trevelyan, 'a damned serious gowk' according to his future father-in-law, belonged to the same earnest progressive groups as MacDonald, the Rainbow Circle, the Union of Democratic Control and so on. He was President of the Board of Education in both MacDonald's administrations, although no friend after 1931.

to examine them, his opponents, and indeed the uncommitted observer, would see him as a straightforward enemy of the national effort. It was not a comfortable position to be in at any point in the First World War, particularly in the early years. Indeed, as late as 1918 there was a celebrated meeting on Plumstead Common, Woolwich, when there was an attempt to silence him. A reward was offered for anyone who 'brought in MacDonald dead or alive'. Some Scottish soldiers on leave chose to act as his bodyguards. In the same year Maitland Hardyman, MC, the youngest colonel in the army at the age of twenty-three, was another soldier who publicly sided with MacDonald. He prepared to resign his commission like Siegfried Sassoon but, after consulting MacDonald, decided he should go back to France and be with his men.

Despite the endorsement of the Scotsmen on leave and of Colonel Hardyman, MacDonald was perhaps the most unpopular politician in Britain. There was not always a bodyguard for him. He was stoned when speaking at an ILP gathering. He thought that the police were disrupting meetings. In Lossiemouth people he knew sent postcards addressed to 'Herr' Ramsay MacDonald. The word 'Traitor' was scrawled on the garden wall of his Lossiemouth house.

It was an uncomfortable time. There were anti-German riots. The police seized UDC pamphlets. Conscientious objectors had a difficult time. Clifford Allen almost died as a result of violent attacks.* MacDonald was often shadowed by the police. ILP meetings were broken up. While the stones flew, he stood his ground.

*

Most of the social circles that he had frequented were closed to him. He was, however, frequently received at Garsington Manor by Lady

---

* Clifford Allen, the chairman of the ILP in 1923, was an idealistic pacifist during the war, publishing a speech with the provocative title, *Is German Right and Britain Wrong?* He would have been exempted from war work on health grounds, but he chose to resist conscription on the grounds that as leader of the No-Conscription Fellowship, he was carrying out essential war work. In addition to being beaten up, he was arrested, court-martialled and jailed. He took what was known as an absolutist position, refusing to carry out non-military work as well as military work. He was sentenced to two years' hard labour, but released from prison as a result of his deteriorating health, which left him with severely damaged lungs for the rest of his life.

Ottoline Morrell, a cousin of Elizabeth Bowes-Lyon, later Queen Elizabeth, the Queen Mother. Her house was a famous sanctuary for conscientious objectors as well as the Bloomsbury group. Molly Hamilton said that Bertrand Russell was Garsington's 'god' whereas MacDonald was at most a minor prophet. Russell quite liked MacDonald but did think that his long, boring Scottish stories never came to a point. Despite his histrionic style, Ottoline enjoyed hearing him read aloud. She was moved by hearing him read Whitman's 'Good-Bye My Fancy'.[12]

Attending Garsington was a dangerous activity for a man of the people. The Bloomsbury intellectuals, the avant-garde artists and the whole precious atmosphere of these weekends were far from the realities of a nation at war, and mixing with such people in such surroundings did not enhance MacDonald's reputation as a tribune of the people. The morals of Garsington, where both his host and hostess entertained their lovers, were very far from the domestic virtues of the working class. If MacDonald had wished to make himself a target for Horatio Bottomley and his reactionary populist magazine *John Bull*, he could scarcely have gone about the job better. He even expressed some scepticism about the widely believed atrocities of the German army in Belgium. In *John Bull* the Australian writer AG Hales started by enumerating such atrocity stories as matters of fact: 'Dear, sweet-faced old dames, trembling on the edge of the grave dishonoured ... Girls of tender age ... have been ravaged ... Vestals have been shamed in front of older relatives.'

Two days later *John Bull* made the first of its attacks on the 'high priests' of 'Damnable Treason'. The first high priest was Hardie, but the more dreadful one was MacDonald: 'We call him Traitor, Coward, Cur. We demand his trial by Court Martial, his condemnation as an aider and abetter of the King's enemies, and that he be taken to the Tower and shot at dawn.'[13]

15

HUMILIATIONS

It is telling that the two episodes that affected MacDonald most during the war were not pro-war demonstrations or bullets from the German trenches in 1914. What bothered him was not *John Bull*'s nonsense about being shot at dawn but the issue of 4 September 1915 in which an article began:

> For months past—ever since the man who calls himself James Ramsay McDonald, but whose real name is James McDonald Ramsay, has stood aloof from the almost unanimous response of the nation to the call of the King—we have persistently labelled him as a traitor and a coward ... We knew that this man was living under an adopted name—and that he was registered as *James McDonald Ramsay*—and that, therefore, he had obtained admission to the House of Commons in false colours, and was probably liable to heavy penalties to have his election declared void. But to have disclosed this state of things would have imposed upon us a very painful and unsavoury duty. *We should have been compelled to produce the man's birth certificate.* And that would have revealed what today we are justified in revealing—for the reason we will state in a moment. It would have revealed 'James Ramsay MacDonald', MP for Leicester, late 'leader' of the Labour Party; late member of a Royal Commission, under the seal of His Majesty: the leading light of the 'Union of Democratic Control'—libeller and slanderer of his country—it would have revealed him as the illegitimate son of a *Scottish servant girl!*

A facsimile reproduction of MacDonald's birth certificate followed, revealing that his name at birth had of course been registered as 'James McDonald Ramsay'.

THE CANCELLED PRIME MINISTER

MacDonald was hugely upset. In his diary on 12 September 1915 he wrote,

> On the day when the paper with the attack was published, I was travelling from Lossiemouth to London in the company as far as Edinburgh with the dowager Countess De La Warr, Lady Margaret Sackville and their maid. Breaking the journey in Aberdeen, I saw the Contents Bill of the paper announcing some amazing revelations about myself and when I rejoined the ladies at the station, I saw the maid had *John Bull* in her hand. Sitting on the train, I took it from her and read the disgusting article. From Aberdeen to Edinburgh, I spent hours with the most terrible mental pain. Letters of sympathy began to pour in upon me. The first time I had ever seen my registration certificate was when I opened the paper at Aberdeen. Never before did I know that I had been registered under the name of Ramsay, and cannot understand it now.

Bottomley ('that leprous person')[1] did not achieve exactly the response he expected. MacDonald received many letters of support, some of them quite moving. Katharine Glasier expressed her horror that anyone could have done as Bottomley did, and went on, 'For you—I can't think of anything for the moment but the glowing light of your wife's smile as once I was privileged to see it, into your dear mother's eyes. She was so proud of her. And so was Lossiemouth.'

Manny Shinwell said that life was even harder for MacDonald than for other Scottish boys of his generation 'because he constantly sensed the stigma of his birth even when among people who were unaware of his illegitimacy'. I doubt that, but Shinwell was certainly correct when he went on to say that 'the sense of martyrdom which he carefully nurtured was an effective goad to better himself as well as a means of keeping constantly in his mind the inequalities of his class among people who had everything they wanted'.[2] Shinwell never thought that MacDonald's privations were sufficient to make a revolutionary of him: he recalled that MacDonald's modest declaration was simply that 'at one end of the scale people were a little too poor; at the other a little too rich'. This, Shinwell said, was 'the tolerant disquiet of the typical Liberal: things were wrong, but not so wrong but a little compromise could put them right'.[3]

HUMILIATIONS

The other episode, which possibly hurt him even more, related to his golf club in Lossiemouth, Moray Golf Club. He loved his golf and played there with his sons whenever he was at Lossiemouth. In August 1915 a motion was submitted demanding that his name be removed from the roll of members because his membership endangered the reputation of the club. MacDonald wrote a rather good letter to the club secretary, saying that the council was not there to make political judgements but 'to preserve sobriety in the clubhouse, to see that gentlemen do not insult ladies—or Radicals—on the course and to put appropriate penalties on rabbit scrapes, ditches and people who play too well'.

Nothing happened for exactly a year, when a further motion was submitted. This time it was alleged that MacDonald's membership had caused other people to resign. A special meeting was held in the Burgh courthouse in Elgin, which nearly one hundred members attended. The motion was carried by seventy-three votes to twenty-four. MacDonald had consulted the Lord Advocate and considered taking court action to prevent a meeting from taking place. In the event, the radical Glasgow solicitor Rosslyn Mitchell advised him that he would have to take the case to the House of Lords before he would get a decision in his favour.* He wrote a dignified letter to the secretary and never played on the course again.

Golf—and walking (and they come indeed to much the same thing)—were the two recreations which MacDonald listed in *Who's Who*. Golf in Scotland was a very much more democratic activity in the early years of the twentieth century than it was to become. It meant a lot to MacDonald. When he was about to marry Margaret, he wrote to her that he would have 'nothing whatever to do with a girl who cannot swing a golf club'. He was pleased to tell her that

---

* Rosslyn Mitchell was a famous politician in his day. He had stood at the 1910 general election as a Liberal and represented Paisley as a Labour MP from 1924 to 1929. He was teetotal and a pacifist. At the 1924 election he defeated Asquith by 2,200 votes. Asquith had a rough time at the election and had been silenced by the singing of 'The Red Flag'. Mitchell showed more distress at the way Asquith was treated than Asquith himself. Mitchell came from an evangelical background and his speeches in the prayerbook debate on the revision of the Book of Common Prayer were regarded as among the most powerful parliamentary occasions of the twentieth century.

he was writing to her between rounds with 'a dignified dean and a professor of church history'. MacDonald told a story of losing a game against his old schoolmaster. They had played to the end, despite pouring rain. 'The dear old man when we left the last hole put his hand in mine and with a lump in his throat said, "MacDonald, when I saw you first as a fat little boy I said you are either doomed to be hanged or something worth doing." I am telling you that because I really think he was right.'[4] The course and the club were a sacred crucible. When thereafter he played at Spey Bay, that was a second best which reminded him of his expulsion.

Many years later, during MacDonald's second term as Prime Minister, the club unanimously voted to allow him back in. He wrote to an old Lossie friend:

> The members have had any number of opportunities to put things right within the last few years—and once they definitely declined to do so. Now, everybody laughs at them, and the existence of a resolution humiliates them—not me.
>
> I enjoy the Spey Bay course, and so do my friends. It came to my rescue in 1916 and I am not a man to treat any friends of mine as a mere convenience. Therefore I stick to Spey Bay.[5]

But Moray Golf Club could do even worse than that. In 2020 a twenty-one-year-old single malt whisky was bottled for the club, presumably to make money. One hundred bottles were produced. The marketing material declares, 'This bottle is titled Exclusion and has been produced to celebrate Moray Golf Club member Ramsay MacDonald. MacDonald was a British statesman who was the first Labour Party politician to become Prime Minister of the United Kingdom.' Pretty crass even for a golf club.

Beatrice Webb hadn't approved of MacDonald's bourgeois sport. When she heard that he played with Liberal cabinet ministers, she scornfully imagined the improbability of a German Social Democrat playing golf with the German Chancellor: 'The British governing class is extraordinarily clever in winning over the abler revolutionary elements.'[6] But Beatrice was frightfully petty and she wouldn't understand the democratic ethos of a Scottish course.

16

POLITICAL CHANGE

When the war broke out in August 1914, Herbert Asquith presided over a Liberal government, and the great Liberal Party looked likely to dominate British politics for the rest of the century. The war changed all that, as it changed so much else. In May 1915 Asquith was obliged to form a coalition containing an important Conservative element. Labour was invited to join the government. This was a historic step on the journey from peripheral existence to a potential party of government. Or, from a left-wing perspective, 'the Labour Party became a prisoner of the war lords, unable to resist the conscription of workers into the munitions industry or military service'.[1]

But Labour didn't leap into the arms of the capitalists. The other parties to the coalition were asked to agree that there would be no conscription. That undertaking was not given, and the Labour Parliamentary Party rejected the invitation. But the National Executive took the opposite view, and a subsequent joint meeting of the parliamentary party and the executive allowed members freedom of action. Arthur Henderson became the first Labour cabinet minister as President of the Board of Education. Remarkably the party allowed him to make whatever terms he wanted in regard to his membership of the cabinet. It goes without saying that there were many in the party who were unhappy with the situation. Accepting the possibility—indeed the likelihood—of conscription was anathema for many, including MacDonald. He could imagine joining a coalition to defeat an opposition demand for conscription, but not joining a coalition which didn't rule conscription out. More generally he felt that with Labour in government there wasn't now a party campaigning for an early peace. No party, he said, could be in the cabinet and not of it.

MacDonald was always ready to criticise his party. He described its leaders as 'poor dear flattered and innocent things'.[2] He had no doubt that he was in the right. He rarely had such doubts. He looked down on his colleagues from a position of detached, superior judgement. There was condescension in his attitude. It did not endear him to the pygmies. The Labour members of the government were, in his view, putty in the hands of their opponents.

He was right to think that conscription was becoming a real and critical issue. The Tories, now within government, were agitating for it. Labour, egged on in particular by the trade unions, met with the government to press them not to go down the conscription route. They said that the army could find the men that Asquith and Lord Kitchener, the Secretary of State for War, needed by voluntary methods. They were wrong as well as misguided, and by December the government decided on conscription. Even before the National Executive allowed individual freedom, Henderson had declared that he would vote for conscription whatever the consequences. At a conference on 6 January 1916 MacDonald stuck to his principles and was the star of the meeting. The National Executive's decision in his view meant 'You can win the war', he said, 'and in winning it pay such a price that the nation will have lost'.

Labour got itself into an enormous muddle at this conference. A resolution was carried pledging support for the voluntary system, but before the day was out the National Executive resolved by sixteen votes to eleven that the Labour Party could no longer remain in government. The 'Red Flag' was sung and delegates left the meeting, according to the *Labour Leader* still cheering about their triumph over 'British Prussians'. Six days later, after some assurances from Asquith, the National Executive reversed its decision, and Henderson and the other Labour ministers withdrew their resignations. MacDonald wondered about the future of the party.

Three months later the government decided to extend the Military Service Act. The parliamentary party rejected this proposal. Despite speeches from Asquith, Kitchener and the Conservative leader, Bonar Law, at a meeting where the Labour

POLITICAL CHANGE

Parliamentary Party and the National Executive were present together with representatives of the major industries, the executive proposed to put the matter to a national conference. That never happened. By the following day the unions had chosen to support the government.

That support was critical. In 1915 the unions had been resisting conscription, and in the face of that the government had compromised by introducing Lord Derby's scheme under which men between the ages of eighteen and forty-one 'attested' that they were ready to be called up on the understanding that single men would be called up before married men or widowers with children. But by 1916 the unions were prepared to accept compulsion. MacDonald had always been critical of them, and the fact that most of them increasingly supported the war heightened his contempt. Trade unionism was in any event changing. Not least, its scale had changed. Between 1914 and 1919 the total affiliated membership of the TUC rose from 2.5 million to more than 4.5 million (which wasn't necessarily bad for the Labour Party, whose membership in the same period rose from 1.6 million to 3 million). But as well as increasing the number of union members, the economic effect of the war was to put far more money into the pockets of the working classes. To an extent the interests of the unions and the Labour Party began to diverge at the very time when the influence of the unions, and Labour's dependency on them, increased.

*

Lloyd George had been Chancellor of the Exchequer until 1915. Then he became a dynamic Minister for Munitions and next an equally dynamic Secretary of State for War. Increasingly it was he who dominated the government, changing the nature of the war, bending the whole resources of the state to prosecution of the conflict, applying the country's industrial resources to the furtherance of war aims. In a managed economy of this sort, the participation of the unions was essential. Industrial workers were aware of their strength and importance. In 1915 engineering workers on the Clyde went on strike for a wage increase and, thereafter, against dilution of the skilled cadres. In 1917 there would be an unofficial national strike of munitions workers at a critical stage in the war, when the country faced starvation and the army prepared for the Third Battle of Ypres.

*

In December 1916 Lloyd George's manoeuvrings culminated in his deposing Asquith and succeeding him at the head of a second coalition. Though Lloyd George was now leader of the Liberal Party, he diluted Liberal membership of the government. The War Cabinet was dominated by the Conservatives. They had abominated Lloyd George when he brought in his People's Budget and attacked the powers of the dukes, but they were now delighted to serve him and support him. Labour too did not resist his charms. Arthur Henderson became a member of a tight little War Cabinet. John Hodge became Minister of Labour (a new office) with a seat in the wider cabinet, and George Barnes became Minister for Pensions (and ultimately a member of the War Cabinet). There were other appointments outside the cabinet. MacDonald was particularly disappointed that Labour was joining the War Cabinet and thus intimately binding itself into the war effort. It is surprising that the Labour Party came through the war without breaking apart, in view of its members' dramatically different views on the war and support for it.

MacDonald, of course, continued on the back benches, fighting his nuanced and personal battles: against the war and conscription—but also against industrial action, critical of the Clydeside militancy and the support it received from the ILP. At the same time he continued to support his country at war. Though he was strongly against conscription, he did not discourage enlistment. As far back as August 1914 he had said, 'Whatever our views may be of the origins of the war, we must go through with it.'

*

MacDonald's response to the first Russian Revolution, which led to the fall of the Tsar though not yet to the coming to power of the Bolsheviks, was entirely enthusiastic. 'A sort of spring-tide had broken out all over the world.'[3] In March 1917 a provisional government was formed under Kerensky. Later in the month the Petrograd Soviet decided to withdraw from war with Germany. MacDonald was excited and alarmed: excited by the idea of a negotiated peace which could bring an end to the war but alarmed by the idea that Russia might make a separate peace. He wasn't alone: Labour in general shared the idea that Russia had to stick with the Allies. The British government sent Henderson to Petrograd to rally the new government.

Overall, MacDonald saw the revolution very much as something to be welcomed. He wanted the ILP to welcome it too. The Russian revolutionaries he found rather like the ILP, if perhaps just a little bit more extreme. His main worry about the revolution was that it would be neutralised. He allowed himself to entertain the notion that somehow Kerensky's Russia could link up with social democracy in Germany and elsewhere. This idea of a brotherhood of socialism was the sort of dream which idealists had believed in 1914 might stop the war at its outset. It was hardly a tenable view in 1917.

MacDonald set about telling Kerensky how to conduct himself. He drafted one letter which wasn't sent and a second one which was. Socialist parties all over Europe took it upon themselves to organise events in Russia. The Dutch socialists decided to convene a special meeting at Stockholm. The British Labour Party decided that it would be better for a conference to take place in London. The Soviets thought that if there were to be an international conference, it should be held in Russia.

MacDonald came to believe that the British government would grant him a passport to go to Russia. Indeed, Lord Robert Cecil confirmed that he would be given one. So MacDonald made his way to Aberdeen, arriving there on 10 June 1917. He found that the Seamen's and Firemen's Union regarded him and the ILP as unpatriotic traitors. They weren't allowed to board their ship, which sailed without them. MacDonald's naive attempt to influence world events in this way came to nothing; but in any event Kerensky's supporters were losing control and the tide of events was with Lenin and the Bolsheviks. MacDonald's support for Kerensky was not forgotten and was frequently quoted against him.

At the centre of British politics, and in particular among the Conservatives in the coalition, there was none of this excitement about jumping on boats in Aberdeen harbour or talking to Marxists and quasi-Marxists in places like Stockholm or Moscow. Whatever Lord Robert Cecil might have said to MacDonald, the government refused passports to would-be delegates, and in all this turbulence Henderson resigned from the War Cabinet (his place was taken by Barnes), and the Bolsheviks seized power, agreed to an armistice and signed a humiliating peace at Brest-Litovsk. The Soviets did not trouble to read the ignominious treaty which they signed.

*

This was a turning point for Labour and its attitude to the war. Although Labour remained in the government, the left of the party was drawing away from commitment to the coalition. In January 1917, MacDonald had already elaborated on his complex attitude to the war in *National Defence: A Study in Militarism*. Now he was one of the authors of a *Memorandum on War Aims*, which looked to international arbitration and something like the League of Nations as the guarantor of peace. His own preference, when the establishment of the League of Nations was still no more than a subject for discussion, was for the kind of open diplomacy which President Woodrow Wilson advocated. The old diplomacy, he told the House of Commons, was a 'corrupting system [which] should be swept away. It stands like a dirty old slum area, full of vermin and disease.'

I referred to MacDonald's idea for international governance as being 'something like the League of Nations' because the League itself as it was originally envisaged did not appeal to him. He dismissed it as 'quackery' and said that national armies did not constitute an international police force.[4] When Sir Eric Drummond was appointed Secretary-General of the new League, MacDonald saw him as the embodiment of the old system:

> He has been brought up in the ways of the Foreign Office, trained in the methods of discredited diplomacy, with no Democratic vision and no conception of what World Democracy means, and it is beyond reason to expect from him any inspiration which would

make the league anything more than it is now—the organ of the victors to dominate the world.⁵

In the long run, events vindicated MacDonald's early misgivings, but before then he warmed to the League till he became its brightest star.

*

So in November 1917, Russia came out of the war long before America, which had joined the Allies in April, was able to make any contribution. A vast deal had to happen in military terms between then and November 1918, when the Germans signed the armistice. In the same period there were political changes. The new Representation of the People Act gave the vote to all men over twenty-one and to women over thirty with an occupancy qualification.

*

At the start of 1918, at the seventeenth annual conference Labour agreed on a new constitution. The high-water mark of doctrinaire socialism is usually regarded as clause 4 of this new constitution, the Labour Party Rule Book. Clause 4, which had been drafted by the Webbs, committed the party 'to secure for the workers by hand or by brain the full fruits of their industry ... upon the basis of the common ownership of the means of production, distribution and exchange'. The watermark was not in truth very high. What was envisaged was no wholesale nationalisation of the state, simply a more efficient operation on the basis of whatever common ownership meant. There was no talk at this stage of nationalisation of the 'commanding heights of the economy'. The adoption of the 1918 new constitution was the outcome of horse-dealing and compromise. MacDonald's primary aim in the smoke-filled rooms in which the Labour Party executive met was to protect the interests and traditions of the ILP members of the party and to preserve the essence of federalism. As a matter of practical necessity, he accepted the changes, but he certainly didn't embrace them. He had described Arthur Henderson's proposals, made in response to his own, as 'very badly drafted in form & in spirit & grasp. Just an election agent's document.'⁶ The Webbs' proposal, *Labour and the New Social*

Order, was ambitious—guaranteed employment, nationalisation, social welfare and popular education—but the detail was much more limited and practical. MacDonald moved a resolution on 'increased production', then, as now, an attractive if vague alternative to anything more concrete.

*

The war came to an end in November 1918. Lloyd George's Liberals would continue in coalition with the Conservatives; Asquith's Liberals would not. The Labour Party went to the polls in December 1918 independent of the coalition.

MacDonald's position was interesting. His shaky commitment to the Labour Party as the vehicle for change is reflected in his idea of the possibility of the emergence of 'a new democratic party'.[7] It was pretty clear what he did not want. He had no interest in the theories of Webb and his friends. In his pamphlet *Socialism after the War*, published by the ILP in 1917, he had condemned state socialism and trade union domination through the block votes. In the debate on the 1918 constitution, he did his best to limit the power of the unions, whereas Webb and Henderson worked to limit the power of local branches of the Labour Party. Yet again, MacDonald's interest had nothing much to do with doctrinaire socialism or union power. What he wanted was a representative progressive party. Apart perhaps from his views on the war, there was never really anything to mark him out as a Labour man. His views were those of many Liberals.

17

ABROAD AND IN THE WILDERNESS

The 1918 general election took place in the glow of victory in the Great War. For most people Lloyd George was the man who had won that war. At this time the Conservative leader, Bonar Law, 'honest to the point of simplicity', according to Lloyd George, said that if he wanted to, Lloyd George could be a dictator for the rest of his life. The coalition government—now just the Conservatives and Liberals—gave a coupon to their approved candidates. These candidates, their coupons stamped by those who delivered victory, were almost guaranteed election. Their opponents, those Liberals who had followed Asquith rather than Lloyd George and the Labour Party, were out of tune with the music of the times.

MacDonald, as one of the Labour members who had opposed the war, had a particularly difficult task. He stood for Leicester West. In Leicester East the coupon candidate Sir Gordon Hewart, Solicitor General in the coalition and later Lord Chief Justice, focused his attack on MacDonald and the war. MacDonald had 'put an odious stain and stigma upon the fair name of Leicester'. His views were echoed by the *Leicester Mercury*: 'Elected as its representative [MacDonald] became its misrepresentative.'[1] MacDonald expected to lose by about 500 votes. In the event he lost by over 14,000 votes. On New Year's Eve he declined invitations to go out: he could think of nothing except the fact that Margaret seemed further away from him than ever.

*

At fifty-two and after twelve years in the Commons, his career was in ruins. The future seemed bleak. The parliamentary salary which he lost when he left parliament had amounted to £400. The income from Margaret's estate had reduced considerably.

> The end of the old song has come. I am out as I expected but much more thoroughly than I expected ... The people are afraid of revolution and are vengeful ... I did not feel my defeat till I got home to feel the disappointment of my children. Their little sad faces made a tightening in my throat and a swelling of something in my eyes.

On the following day, Sunday, 29 December, he wrote,

> How lonely one feels at a time like this. I sit in my room [too ill] to write to keep myself doing something, but there seems to be a log in the way of the free flow of thoughts and words and they come in trickles ... How reputation makes us up for this stage of life and how grotesque is the closing and general garb in which—often without our own knowledge—we play our parts.

Ramsay found some comfort among his friends, though among them, too, he was reminded of mortality. His old friend Bruce Glasier died. His political friends were less important than those outside politics like Alexander Grant, another Lossiemouth man, who had made a fortune in biscuits (we shall hear more of him later), and Alec Martin, who worked with the auctioneers Christie's. His family mattered too, though their growing up reminded him of the brevity of life. When Ishbel was sixteen he wrote in his diary, 'Oh, Time, Time why do you go so fast.' When Alister was twenty-one, his father's diary reflection was, 'Yesterday he was a toddling babe. So we drive on like mad flies to our graves.' At the birthday party he was aware of two who were missing. Of one of them he said, 'I saw the little boy lying in that mortuary behind the glass.' He was unsparing in the pain which he imposed on himself.

He continued to travel, visiting the Middle East in 1922 for example. He read voraciously the demanding literature of the previous centuries, Gibbon, Boswell, Sir Walter Scott, and less voraciously in more recent writers. He thought about writing a biography of John Knox. He contrasted the rigorous minds of the past with 'the mediocrity of this Parliament ... I read for consolation Gibbon's *Decline and Fall* [and] the minor prophets.' Above all, he found peace in the exhaustion of rugged walking. 'It soothes me & being able to tramp over miles of wet heather & to sleep in a bed of wet stuff & get up as fresh as a daisy to see the sun & wash in the roaring torrents of icy water makes me feel that there may be some kick left yet.'[2] He described an expedition in the Cairngorms with his children in *Wanderings and Excursions:*

> I lay down that night under a shelter of a great granite boulder, which, in times when the poor earth was convulsed with pain, came down like an angel from the heights to minister to the comforts of men. The wind moaned like a wild beast prowling around; I could hear the drip, drip of the rain in the little pools round the stone. At eight o'clock we stretched ourselves out to sleep without a dry square inch of clothing on us and with the brittle stalks of heather, which had mercifully been left by whoever had last taken a night's lodging in this free 'hotel for travellers', pricking us.
>
> When we did sleep—a happy, dreamless sleep. Now and again the bed became too hard, or the heather too sharp, or the wind puffs too cold, but the dark moments of wakefulness only added to the pleasure. No king in his feather bed was happier. We were alone amidst the clouds, the companions of the storm and the rushing waters. We were to have started again at four; we slept till six. Fifteen well measured miles on the map were before us ...[3]

The reality of hard physical challenge and the tough rigour of the intellectual past threw into contrast the artificiality of political life.

*

At this bleak moment in Labour's history, MacDonald remained capable of big thinking. The ILP, which continued to grow steadily, considered affiliation to the Third International.* MacDonald's posi-

---

* The Internationals, now largely forgotten, were a series of ongoing conferences that marked the birth and development of international labour politics. The First International (correctly the International Working Men's Association) was set up in London in 1864, largely on an Anglo-French basis. Marx was a member of the provisional General Council and came to dominate it. Splits and schisms were inherent among the Internationals. The First International split at The Hague congress in 1872

tion was not one of unqualified opposition to the Third International and communist expansion or of unqualified approval. He deprecated Allied military intervention in Russia, but he was never blind, as many of his more gullible colleagues were, to the violence to which the communists had recourse. He hated that violence and rejected fanaticism. He identified, as Marx had done, the paradox that communism, in theory, belonged to a pre-capitalist stage and not to the industrial stage of economic evolution. He worked to keep the ILP from going down the Leninist route.

He was in a very different position from George Lansbury, who had formed an unrealistically benevolent view of communism and of Lenin's intentions. Lansbury entered parliament in 1910 as the Labour member for Bow and Bromley. He was a purist who disapproved of MacDonald's cooperation with the Liberals. He was passionately in favour of the suffragettes and was suspended from the Commons after the clash with Asquith over forcible feeding. He was the editor-proprietor of the *Daily Herald* and presided over its pacifist line. He also published *Lansbury's Labour Weekly* along with Raymond Postgate, who in addition to his political activities created the *Good Food Guide*. As MacDonald's First Commissioner of Works in the 1929 government, he created 'Lansbury's Lido' on the Serpentine. When MacDonald formed the National Government, Lansbury became leader of the Labour Party. His innocent, pacifist line prompted a famous attack from Ernest Bevin for 'hawking your conscience from body to body asking to be told what to do with it'. AJP Taylor described him as 'the most loveable figure in modern politics'.

---

between supporters of Marx's socialism and Bakunin's anarchism. The Second International, sometimes called the Socialist International, was formed in 1889. Its main difference from the first International was that it eschewed anarcho-syndicalism. It substantially foundered in the face of the First World War and the patriotism which it engendered. The Third International, also the Communist International or Comintern, was founded in 1919, the Second International having been substantially dissolved in 1916. It held seven world conferences and conducted thirteen Enlarged Plenums (even pedants didn't use the plural 'plena'). An Enlarged Plenum was not a medical complaint but a mini-congress involving the Comintern executive committee. The Comintern continued until 1943. The Internationale was the official anthem for all three Internationals.

ABROAD AND IN THE WILDERNESS

An ILP delegation attended the Third International but came back convinced that there could be no compromise with the communist movement. MacDonald agreed. He was utterly opposed to communist participation in Labour institutions: the communists came into the Labour Party to wage war. His instincts were largely those of the anti-communist unions, but battles had to be fought, as at the 1925 Labour conference at Liverpool.

In July 1920 MacDonald went to Berlin for the first time since the war. He was horrified by the deprivation he met and the ongoing effects of the Allied food blockade. Equally he was dismayed by the negativism of the German socialists who had failed to throw themselves into the fight to improve politics and the conditions of the poor. What he saw in Berlin contrasted with what he found in Georgia a few weeks later. Georgia was Menshevik as opposed to Bolshevik,[*] and in Georgia he could see the practical results of social democracy.

MacDonald's purpose was to make politics work. He had a minor wobble after the 1918 election, when he was briefly attracted to direct action and the use of the strike as a political weapon,[4] but it was no more than momentary. Increasingly he warned against the use of organised labour, as in the rail strikes of September 1919 and in 1920. Collective action would only provoke the right and play into its hands. He warned that, attractive though it was to deploy the strength of the workers, nothing must be done to give Lloyd George the excuse for another election and another majority. There was 'an unlimited supply of bogeys. Mr Lloyd George can extract them as a magician takes rabbits out of a hat.'

He made this sort of point again and again in relation to the strikes, actual and proposed at this time, even a possible general strike. His position was far from that of most Labour leaders, including the young radical ones, with whom he was careful to keep in touch. His caution and inherent moderation were a continuous feature of his political position, and a distinctive one.

*

---

[*] In the Russian Social Democratic Labour Party the majority faction was the Mensheviks and the minority faction the Bolsheviks. Mensheviks eschewed violence and the Bolsheviks embraced it. The Bolsheviks won.

THE CANCELLED PRIME MINISTER

In January 1921, a by-election was required in East Woolwich. East Woolwich had evolved from the seat of Woolwich itself. The two seats had been held by Labour from 1903. MacDonald was invited to stand. He had his doubts: he was already a prospective candidate for Aberavon. He was persuaded to go for Woolwich. It was a mistake. Even his Woolwich agent, Councillor Barefoot, a good Shakespearean name, warned him about the likelihood of personal attacks. Woolwich had in its time been the chief dockyard of the British Navy and was thereafter the home of the Royal Arsenal. It was hardly a congenial seat for the great denouncer of the war. Trams in town carried placards: 'A Traitor for Parliament?' To make matters worse, his opponent, Captain Robert Gee, was a man of the people, the son of a frame-maker who served in the ranks for twenty-three years before being commissioned, *and* a hero. He had won the Victoria Cross at the Battle of Cambrai. Woolwich was invaded by Tory canvassers peddling an astonishing array of improbable allegations. MacDonald was an atheist and a revolutionary. He had drunk toasts after the war to the European revolution and its German friends. He was against pensions for soldiers and in favour of sinking hospital ships. He was against marriage and applauded married women who had children while their husbands were at the front. And of course Gee had his coupon. MacDonald lost and was hurt by the viciousness of the fight. 'I miss my dear dead companion at such times. Lonely, lonely.'

But the remarkable thing was that despite all the circumstances, he lost by only 683 votes. He had really done extraordinarily well, and more sophisticated political observers realised that. Horatio Bottomley had been very active in the campaign, supporting the heroic Gee and attacking MacDonald and his very different war. His intervention was resented in the constituency and attracted some post-election sympathy for MacDonald.

*

Sensing a turn in the tide, MacDonald stood for the ILP administrative council in 1921. He was moderate by ILP standards, and his support for the Second as opposed to the more extreme Third International was not reflective of mainstream ILP opinion. Despite that, he emerged top of the poll with 471 votes. His nearest rival had 270. His stock was on the rise again.

*

The debate about whether the ILP should affiliate to the Third International continued. Affiliation would certainly work to promote the cause of communism in Britain. MacDonald had been disappointed and deceived by the fact that the social democratic movement in Germany had been far from robust and had not been prepared to oppose the war. An injection of views from the left might be a good thing. On the other hand, he had no illusions about the nature of Bolshevism and the essentially undemocratic nature of the Third International.

His views were not universally shared. George Lansbury came back from a brief visit to Russia with a rosy appreciation of Lenin's views, and he carried the 1920 ILP conference with him. It decided by a substantial majority to disaffiliate from the Second International, although it had its doubts about affiliating to the Third. An ILP deputation went off to Moscow but came back disenchanted. In February 1921 the first conference of what became jokingly known as the Two and a Half International took place in Vienna. In the meantime the Second International, eschewing the politics of the Third, remained in session. Its headquarters moved to London. The Labour Party executive backtracked on disaffiliation, and MacDonald and Harry Gosling, the dockers' leader, became its joint secretaries in November 1920. MacDonald was doubtful but accepted the appointment, to the displeasure of the ILP council. There were tentative negotiations for a rapprochement between the two Internationals. Finally they came to nothing. The separation between the Internationals became final. The Third International was discredited as a democratic force, and MacDonald was able to withdraw from his secretaryship of the Second International, his job done.

18

THE APPROACH TO POWER

At the general election in 1922 MacDonald stood for Aberavon in South Wales, as he had wanted. He fitted into the constituency naturally. Keir Hardie had been the member for the neighbouring seat of Merthyr, and MacDonald sensed that he was treated as an adopted son in the constituency. He recognised that his Scottish identity, far from excluding him, ensured his welcome. He was treated like Gladstone in the previous century. In 1924 he was accompanied by a journalist, Henry Nevinson, who described how the working classes looked to MacDonald as someone who had come to deliver them from their wretchedness. 'The car could hardly move. We had to shut off the engine and allow the crowds to push us along. The crowds swarmed on every inch of it, and clung to every bit of MacDonald they could touch.'[1]

Descriptions of his platform style at this stage talk of his expressiveness, how he could move from a flowing melody line to the crack of a whip. Others speak about the beauty of his voice and admired its flexibility, as it rose from a whisper to the great bass notes of an organ.[2] The effect was not achieved by accident. He was aware of the power of his oratory. MacNeill Weir, who saw him closely, if through a critical prism, as his parliamentary private secretary in 1924, said that MacDonald thought himself one of the great orators of history.[3] His oratory had something of the qualities of an Impressionist painting. Although he took enormous trouble with his speeches, what he was looking for was the whole effect rather than the detailed content. His speeches were, he said, 'a mere channel for oratory'. Thus, particularly in his declining days, people said of MacDonald that before he spoke they had no idea what he was going to say; while he was speaking they had no idea what he was saying; and afterwards they had no idea what he had said. Something similar was said of Arthur Balfour: 'He says nothing so beautifully, I could listen to him for hours.'[4] The evidence of the quality of MacDonald's speeches lies in what people thought of them at the time rather than how they read now.

MacDonald's charismatic appeal was of an order unknown in politics today. His mesmerism meant that many ILPers could not withdraw their support for him, however much they disapproved of his policies. Henderson warned Davie Kirkwood that in a few years he would be trying to put him out,[5] but Kirkwood, hard-boiled as he was, was smitten:

> His head was a thing of beauty. Black hair waved and rolled over a fine brow ... his voice was ragged but soft, and as he spoke there came into it a throb ... Standing upright he was a splendid figure of a man and his appearance of height and strength was increased by his habit of rising on his toes and throwing back his head.[6]

The broadcast recordings which we can hear today don't do him justice. Baldwin took the trouble to be taught how to use the radio technique and, like Franklin D Roosevelt in the States, used his broadcasts as fireside chats with his audience. To begin with at least, MacDonald's broadcast speeches were recordings from the platform and not the studio, so that his voice came and went as he moved nearer to and further from the microphone.

*

Wales was the home of Lloyd George; and in 1918 Aberavon had been won by a national Liberal—another war hero, Major Edwards—with a majority of 6,000. But things had changed a great deal from 1918. Lloyd George had tried to take the country—and indeed the empire—into a war with Turkey over the Chanak crisis. The Conservatives rebelled at the famous meeting in the Carlton Club in 1922. Despite Bonar Law's prediction that Lloyd George could be in power for the rest of his life if he wanted, the wizard was turned out of Downing Street and it was Bonar Law who called

THE APPROACH TO POWER

the election. The great Liberal Party, successors of the Whigs, never took office again except in coalition. Equally, Lloyd George, 'the man who won the war', never held office again.*

The constituency was propitious for MacDonald. He was a Celt among Celts and his potential constituents were working class. He was supported by a skilful and industrious agent, Ivor Thomas. MacDonald's evangelical style appealed to people brought up in the chapel tradition. In the local Labour Party broadsheet, the *Afan Sentinel*, he asked, 'Is the Christian, the moral state, never to be anything but a dream? No, my Labour friends, through the darkness of the days we must keep our faith and continue striving to the light.' He was returned with a majority of 3,207 over his nearest opponent.†

The Conservatives were the chief beneficiaries of the collapse of the coalition, winning 347 seats, a majority of 88 over the other parties combined. But for the longer term, Labour's achievement was more significant. They had 142 seats, while the two separate and hostile Liberal parties, the followers of Asquith and the followers of Lloyd George, had a total of only 117 between them. Labour was now the second party in the House. To be only 205 seats short of the Conservatives in what had been a Conservative landslide was pretty remarkable.

The Scottish components of the new parliamentary party set off for Westminster on Sunday, 20 November. A huge crowd in St Enoch's Square in Glasgow sang 'Jerusalem' and the Internationale, and saw them off on their train southwards. 'When we come back,' said Davie Kirkwood, 'this station, this railway will belong to the people.'[7]

*

The new Labour Party was very different from what it had been before. In 1918 the party had been very much the creature of the trade unions, with only three ILP members. Now the trade union

---

* Although to understand the politics of the inter-war years, one has to remember that no one knew that then. Right up to 1940, Lloyd George was thought to have the potential to return. The Liberal breaches might heal, or he might preside over the coalition. His potential was regarded as immense.
† In the course of his campaign he found time to speak for the Labour candidate in Neath, William Jenkins, father of Roy Jenkins.

element was much less significant and about a hundred members belonged to the ILP, led by Clifford Allen, a powerful chairman— committed, as the ILP itself was, to socialist purity. MacDonald, Snowden and others like Fenner Brockway were moderate and not doctrinaire. They had their hands full, controlling a party which continued to grow, opening many new branches between 1923 and 1925. In April 1923 ILP members interrupted the proceedings of the Commons by singing 'The Red Flag'. MacDonald didn't approve. When James Maxton fulminated about Tory frugality ('In the interests of economy they condemned hundreds of children to death, and I call it murder'), *The Times* said that MacDonald 'sat on the front bench white with anger at the folly of his own supporters'.[8]

David Marquand points out that in 1918 the Labour parliamentarians were not highly educated. No members had been to public schools and only one to a university. This time nine had gone to public school and twenty-one to university. The Parliamentary Labour Party reflected ideas rather than class—what MacDonald had always argued for.[9] It was now a serious party, capable of government. It included fiery Scots such as Jimmy Maxton with his skeletal body, cadaverous face and jug ears, surmounted by an oversized bowler hat,* Davie Kirkwood and John Wheatley. Alongside the theorist Sidney Webb, there were practical politicians who would dominate the party for the next fifty years: Clement Attlee, Manny Shinwell and Herbert Morrison.†

But the lack of cohesion of the Labour Party has to be stressed. The trade unions were the most disciplined element, and the political levy meant that they dominated party finance. At a political level they were also dominant: the block voting system meant that their millions of votes prevailed. The unionists who were at the top of the Labour Party saw their role as chiefly pressing for workers' rights. One was Arthur Henderson, a good organiser, a

---

* Later Maxton tended to become a 'character', an unlikely friend of Churchill and John Buchan, but he was always an orator and he could be a dangerous enemy. He was a purist and a fierce critic of gradualism. By urging its disaffiliation from the Labour Party he accelerated the decline of the ILP.
† The relationship between the working-class socialists and the intellectuals was always fraught. The former laughed at Sidney Webb. 'Sit down, Nanny.'

veteran of Lloyd George's War Cabinet, loyal and patient but stolid. The railwaymen's leader was JH Thomas, a dapper man with a carefully trimmed moustache who played up his Cockney character role splendidly and was not averse to the contact with upper-class life which he now enjoyed.* JR Clynes was a much more colourless unionist, but a man of loyalty, quite happy to serve under MacDonald.

Part of MacDonald's success in his contribution to the creation of modern Labour was to take the trade unions, not essentially political in nature, impose a political ethos on them and create for them a more truly political function. The ILP, although less numerous than the unions, had a lot of influence. The most prominent of MacDonald's colleagues in the ILP was the testy and crippled Philip Snowden. Alongside his physical handicaps was his wife, Ethel, outspoken and unpopular.

'To the social gospel of the ILP the Fabians responded with social engineering.'[10] It is impossible to dissent from the caricature. They were earnest, humourless vegetarians. Their children were likely to be enlisted in the Woodcraft Folk movement. They were enthusiastic followers of 'Fletcherizing'. Horace Fletcher, 'The Great Masticator', advocated chewing food at least a hundred times until it was completely liquefied before swallowing it. 'Nature will castigate those who don't masticate'. Other eminent Fabian Fletcherizers were the Webbs, Shaw and Wells. Sidney Webb was possibly the most eminent of the Fabians. He took himself seriously and Beatrice did so too, but they were an unappealing couple, much less influential than they thought themselves to be, and Sidney spoke too quietly in the House of Commons to be heard.

---

* There are lots of stories about him. One of the nicest is of his coming down to breakfast after a heavy night at a country house. 'I've got an 'orrible 'eadache,' he said. His fellow guest Lord Birkenhead said, 'You should try a couple of aspirates.' Another Birkenhead remark about Thomas deserves to be remembered. 'There is not a man in the present Labour Party, with the possible exception of Mr JH Thomas, whom I would entrust to let out push bicycles.' That deserves to be remembered alongside a comment in Beatrice Webb's diary on 21 December 1929: 'Jimmy [Thomas] is a boozer, his language is foul, he is a Stock Exchange gambler, he is also a social climber. He is, in fact, *our* Birkenhead.'

THE CANCELLED PRIME MINISTER

And then there were the Red Clydesiders, State Socialists and Guild Socialists, prohibitionists and jolly beer drinkers, academics, pacifists and splendid nonconformists, like Colonel Josiah Wedgwood who belonged to a tradition going back to the seventeenth century. The diversity of the membership of the party was reflected in the divergence of its aims. In 1923 'seven members of the Labour Party' published a booklet called *The Labour Party's Aim*. They warned that there shouldn't be too much concern about 'the palliatives of present misery; we should always take care lest they should hamper our progress towards our final aims, and still more, lest they themselves should become our objectives'.[11] The lack of a single shared aim goes at least a little way to explaining that there was no single commitment for MacDonald to abandon in 1931.*

*

Clynes occupied the chair of the parliamentary party before the general election, but it was felt that the new and invigorated party needed a new and vigorous chairman. Maxton nominated Wheatley. Wheatley was to prove an outstandingly able member of the party, but he was a Scotsman, not well known in England, who had only just arrived in Westminster. Most money was on MacDonald, particularly ILP money. He was nominated by Shinwell, opposed predictably by Snowden, but safely elected. The major caesura in his political career, the First World War, was over. Whenever he touched success, though, MacDonald was conscious of withered garlands: 'I am lonely though. All my people are dead. The victory has come when there is no one to cheer.' On 1 January 1917 he had written:

> This is the first new year for some years I have spent away from Lossiemouth. But my heart is there at Spynie. Do my dead ever know? I wonder. I see the grey gravestone on the top of the hill where they lie. I'm sitting by its side asking them to help me to keep the faith ...[12]

---

* For a detailed analysis of the make-up of the Labour Party at this time, see Lyman, *The First Labour Government*, Chapter 1.

THE APPROACH TO POWER

The mechanics of replacing Clynes are interesting. The parliamentary party had to decide on tactics after the election result. The ILPers met in advance of the parliamentary party meeting. Shinwell proposed that MacDonald should contest the leadership with Clynes. James Maxton and Philip Snowden disagreed. The parliamentary party meeting was held on 21 November 1922, and much turned on 'the Battle of the Bench': Clynes had been in discussions with the Speaker but had been unable to persuade him that Labour should be entitled to occupy the whole opposition front bench. The Speaker was prepared to give Labour speakers precedence over the Liberals, but that was all. These things matter, and it was thought that Clynes hadn't fought hard enough. MacDonald sensed the mood of the meeting and arranged that a letter be sent to the Speaker demanding exclusive use of the front bench—and indeed of the seats immediately behind it. The meeting went on to consider the proposal that those in office at the end of the last session should continue in their positions. MacDonald's supporters required new elections on the spot, and MacDonald defeated Clynes by sixty-one votes to fifty-six.

Behind these brief facts there is a hint of planning and plotting. The ILP at an earlier meeting had already agreed on a contest. Fortunately, twenty-two trade union MPs were absent: they would largely have voted for Clynes. There are allegations about canvassing and negotiations ahead of the meeting and in particular of approaches to the new Clydeside MPs. This is one of the more obvious of those occasions when MacDonald can be seen to be playing politics and jockeying for personal position.[13] It was an important event not only for MacDonald's personal career but also because the Battle of the Bench resulted in a clear demonstration that the Labour Party had now emerged as an official opposition, ready to assume the responsibilities of government.

*

MacDonald was aware of difficulties, particularly in creating a continuing sense of purpose and achievement for the new recruits, who had still to learn about the hard slog of political life. He knew that parliamentary life called for discipline and long, dull days and nights;

many of the new men looked for poetry rather than prose, for the storming of barricades and dramatic headlines. They viewed the necessary contact, even friendship, with their class enemies as collusion and betrayal. The Clydesiders were particularly undisciplined and disruptive.

MacDonald did not share the assumption that politics had necessarily changed for ever and that the Labour Party had replaced the Liberals for all time. He had seen Labour thrown back before and he was afraid that it might be thrown back again, that the Liberals could repair their differences and return as the natural representatives of progressive causes. That was not unreasonable: the Liberals had a history which the Labour Party did not have, and they had an organisation in the country which the Labour Party lacked, as well as secure financial backing. He had no delusions that Hegelian dialectics had irrevocably and permanently thrown the Labour Party up to challenge and defeat capitalism. He did believe that the British political system was binary and would favour a two-party structure: the position of the Labour Party as part of that structure could only be achieved by work and discipline.

*

It was a relief to MacDonald that he had other matters to deal with than his fractious back benches. I would argue that foreign policy always interested him more than domestic politics, and the grand strategy of international affairs rather than dreary logistics. He could see that the Versailles settlement of 1919 was unfair, irrational and no basis for a stable European future. His contribution to international relations from this time till he withdrew from government was an attempt to create a long-term settlement.

Germany had already defaulted in the delivery of timber to the Allies, part of the reparations system imposed by the Versailles treaties. Bonar Law proposed a four-year standstill on reparations. That was rejected by the European Allies. In January 1923, Germany defaulted again, this time in respect of deliveries of coal. Britain and France reacted in very different ways. France, with Belgian support, occupied the Ruhr. Within months they controlled all but the British zone. Germany's response was to resort to passive resistance while her economy degenerated as a result of the invasion. There was a formal *rupture diplomatique* between Britain and France, only one step short of open hostility. The mark fell; and German politics became violent and dangerous.

These developments alarmed MacDonald. He could speak with more authority than most of his Conservative opponents: his earlier criticisms of Versailles were vindicated, and his standing was enhanced by the long years of almost solitary opposition to wartime foreign policy.

The wartime allies had separated. The armies of France and Belgium faced German civilians in the Ruhr Valley. Europe appeared to be drifting back to war, and the British Foreign Secretary, Lord Curzon, that remote and aristocratic figure, made little mark on popular opinion. At MacDonald's instigation a conference of socialists was called. Finally the Germans declared that they would accept independent arbitration. MacDonald, who had been active at the Paris conference where the negotiations took place, represented the outcome as a Labour achievement, which to an extent it was.

*

In May 1923 the Conservative Prime Minister, Bonar Law, resigned. A throat problem had already caused a temporary absence from politics, but it had returned, diagnosed as inoperable cancer. He was succeeded by Stanley Baldwin. In some ways the two Conservative leaders seemed to have some things in common. The Canadian Scot Bonar Law had been an iron and steel merchant in Glasgow, a member of 'the Iron Ring' at the Glasgow Royal Exchange. 'All the ironmongers thought he was a great politician, and all the politicians thought he was a great ironmonger.'[14] Baldwin's family were iron and steel makers in Worcestershire. Indeed Baldwin was frequently referred to as a businessman by his supporters to emphasise his practical common sense. That down-to-earth personality was contrasted with what Baldwin had described as Lloyd George's 'dynamic force' when he destroyed him at a famous meeting of Conservative MPs at the Carlton Club.

In fact the two men were very different. Baldwin looked *away* from the chimneys, the smelters and the cooling towers towards an idyllic rural England which had never truly existed and which had certainly disappeared long before he wrote his romanticised pictures of it in a series of speeches published in book form as *On England*. He may have had considerable political skills. His imperturbable, semi-somnolent demeanour was certainly reassuring in difficult times. How far his style was conscious and how far reflective of lethargy and inanition is difficult to say. He spent much time taking the cure at Aix and other Continental spas, and at times of crisis, such as the abdication of Edward VIII, he returned from them at a pace that was slower not only than the railways' but indeed that of well-organised horse-drawn transport in the nineteenth century. His failure to address the problem of Germany's rearmament is now regarded as amounting to culpable deceit, though at the time the public were prepared to collude in the deception. No doubt any man who becomes Prime Minister has a degree of icy ambition in him, but it was not obvious in the case of Baldwin. When, later, he became MacDonald's deputy in the National Government, he made no effort to push him aside. Leo Amery said: 'Thinking, with him, was not a definite process, but rather the gradual subconscious maturing of vague impressions towards some sudden and instinctive conclusion.' For Harold Nicolson, 'He regarded logical processes as un-English: he preferred to rely upon instinct, and would sniff and snuff at problems like an elderly spaniel.'[15]

Having become Prime Minister, Baldwin felt ready for a holiday and went off for one of his usual long cures at Aix-les-Bains. On his way back he stopped for a meeting with the French prime minister, Raymond Poincaré, who had ordered the occupation of the Ruhr in the previous year. There was now a remarkable change of policy. Baldwin and Poincaré became firm friends and Britain stopped insisting on support for Germany. Germany ended passive resistance and resumed deliveries of materials. Peace had broken out, although not the kind of peace that MacDonald had been arguing for.

*

This was not Baldwin's only volte-face. In the turbulent economic post-war circumstances the Conservative Party had come to the conclusion that the doctrine of free trade, a semi-sacred creed that

THE APPROACH TO POWER

had stood unchallenged from the 1840s, had to be replaced by protective tariffs. This was the proposal which Joseph Chamberlain had made at the turn of the century, putting the Conservative Party out of power for seventeen years, and it was a dangerous idea to rerun. Since Bonar Law had pledged that protective tariffs would not be introduced in the life of the current parliament, Baldwin brought that parliament to an end and declared a general election. This, the election of 1923, taken together with the election of the previous year, was critical for Labour.

The 1923 election threatened to do what MacDonald had feared all along, and bring back the Liberal Party as the true opponents of the Conservatives. The Liberals historically *were* free trade. They had championed the doctrine and credited it with being more than the way to cheap food. It was also the route to progress, enlightenment and, above all, peace. Lloyd George, with impeccably bad timing, had declared just before the outbreak of the First World War that world peace was ensured as the happy product of the worldwide adoption of free trade. Free trade was regarded as the political expression of moderation, decency and civilisation.

But now, in 1923, the abolition of free trade was the declared policy of the Conservatives. Faced by that, the divided Liberals reunited to protect what was almost the reason for their existence. All the circumstances were there to end Labour's displacement of the Liberals as the party of opposition. It was MacDonald's great success that he was able to neutralise the effects of tariffs as a divisive issue, depicting it as an extraneous sideshow. The fight was not between protection and free trade.

Labour claimed that it was the only party which could sort out unemployment. It would do so by a programme of public works funded by a capital levy or what was called in the manifesto 'a non-recurring, graduated War Debt Redemption levy'. The policy contrasted with Tory inaction. William Joynson-Hicks, 'Jix', then the Conservative Minister of Health, asserted that it was better to do nothing than to do something wrong. The capital levy alarmed the electorate, and MacDonald is said to have privately blamed it for the loss of fifty winnable seats. He and Snowden later quietly abandoned the levy.

It is to MacDonald's credit that the election worked to Labour's advantage. It's astonishing to reflect that this election, from which Labour would emerge as a party of government, came just five years after the end of a war in which MacDonald had been execrated for pacifism. Untainted by involvement in that war, MacDonald could present himself as the man with clean hands who would work for peace, rather than get involved in disputes between the relative rights of Germany and the Ruhr-occupying French. He looked like a sensible, responsible statesman as he arbitrated and adjudicated on the European scene. *The Times* put it well: he had risen to big occasions in a big way.[16] And, despite the Red Clydesiders, MacDonald did not alarm the bourgeoisie. In the course of the campaign the *New Leader*, admittedly not the bedside reading of ordinary members of the Conservative Party, described him as being 'head and shoulders above his competitors [in] knowledge, tact, ability and judgement … kindliness and geniality'.[17] And Beatrice Webb, usually so critical of MacDonald, used almost the same words to her husband.

In the event the Conservatives lost their overall majority, keeping 259 seats. Labour, with 191 seats, were 32 seats ahead of the combined Liberals at 159. The Labour Party was, then, confirmed as the voice of progressive politics and the established second party of the state in its own right, not merely by reason of divisions in the Liberal Party.

*

What were the immediate practical effects of the vote? MacDonald returned from Aberavon to reports that Baldwin would resign and send for him. This didn't happen. MacDonald was in no doubt about what he should do. At a meeting in the Albert Hall on 8 January 1924 he delighted his audience with a speech which was repeatedly punctuated with cheers:

> We are a party that away in the dreamland of imagination dwells in a social organization fairer and more perfect than any organization that mankind has ever known. (Cheers.) That is true, but we are not to jump there. We are going to walk there … 'one step enough for me.' (Laughter.) One step! Yes, my friends, on one

THE APPROACH TO POWER

condition—that it leads to the next step. (Cheers.) ... We accept our responsibilities.[18]

There was a significant pause between the announcement of the election results and a decision on what was to happen next. MacDonald seems to have foreseen from the start that Labour might form a minority government. The Tories had lost 115,845 votes and Labour had gained 121,310. The Liberals, however, gained 186,109, so it was very much a Conservative defeat; indeed it would have been much greater if the Conservatives hadn't contested sixty-four more seats in 1923 than in 1922.[19]

Jimmy Maxton and others were for throwing down a gauntlet, introducing a socialist programme which would be rejected, going back to the country and, in an inflamed, adversarial contest, seeking a strong national mandate. Others argued, more sensibly, that Labour should decline to take office rather than rule impotently as a minority. MacDonald's vision was less dramatic. Labour would enter government not as firebrands or revolutionaries, but rather as a quiet element of continuity and constructiveness. This unrevolutionary approach was revolutionary in its way. It meant that a Labour government was not seen as a challenge to the Establishment, but rather as part of the Establishment.

⁂

The fact was that the big parties were exhausted and had almost lost the will to govern. The war years, and indeed the constitutional crises of the years before the war, had involved politicians in a huge expenditure of nervous and physical energy. Post-war events, the break-up of the Conservative–Liberal coalition and the electoral blows to the Liberal Party, had sucked the air out of the political world.

That's not to say that there weren't those who were shocked by the prospect of a socialist government. According to the *English Review*:

> We stand now at a moment when the sun of England seems menaced with final eclipse. For the first time in her history the party of revolution approach their hands to the helm of state, not only, as in the 17th Century, for the purpose of overthrowing the Crown, or

of altering the Constitution, but with the design of destroying the very bases of civilised life.[20]

When Labour tabled a motion of censure on the Baldwin government, before the government had thrown in its hand, Churchill, never one to under-react, proposed that the Commons should send an address to the Crown that would include both the motion of censure and a motion repudiating socialism. The King could decline to 'enthrone' a Labour government because he was following the recommendation of parliament.

There was fear, alarm, even panic. Establishment figures argued for desperate remedies to avert red revolution. It was Asquith's duty, as leader of the Liberal Party, to keep Labour out of power. It was the Conservatives' duty to put Asquith in power. There should be a government of the good and great, some of them not even currently members of the House of Commons.

Even within the Labour Party there were those who counselled against taking power if it were offered, as a minority government which would be bound to fail. Many meetings took place. The Labour Party National Executive met. It met again along with the TUC General Council. MacDonald's inclination was constant, always to govern, despite the risks. His fear was that if they did not do so, they would become irrelevant and politics would revert to the usual Tory–Liberal Punch and Judy show. Ultimately, to his credit, and disdaining the hysteria of the Conservatives, it was the Liberal leader, Asquith, who displayed a measure of statesmanship and rose to the level of events. A less kindly view might be that he didn't have a lot of choice. Supporting the Conservatives and revisiting the shameful days of the coalition and the 'coupon election' was unthinkable. On 18 December he told the Parliamentary Liberal Party that the Liberals would neither keep the Conservatives in office nor exclude the Labour Party. A Labour government 'could hardly be tried under safer conditions … It is we, if we really understand our business, who really control the situation.'

At this period Asquith briefly returned to his best form, speaking well and wittily and in a statesmanlike way. He said that whatever people had voted for, it was not for the continuation of the Conservative government. When parliament met, Baldwin's government would go and the King would presumably then send Ramsay MacDonald to form a Labour minority government. The import of what he was saying was that petty manoeuvring should not stand in the way of history.

The result was that although Baldwin chose to remain in office, and to present the King's speech to the new parliament, the vote on the address was lost. On 22 January 1924 Baldwin left office.* The result of what Asquith had said to the Parliamentary Liberal Party was that at noon on that day, MacDonald went to Buckingham Palace to be sworn of the Privy Council. In the afternoon he returned, kissed hands, and was appointed as Prime Minister.

---

* MacDonald described the Conservatives as being like a corpse waiting for a coffin.

19

GEORGE V

As the crow flies, the distance from George V's fifty thousand acres at Balmoral was only fifty miles from Lossiemouth. The metaphorical distance between the two men may seem much greater, but in a sense it was not. For all the King's hidebound conservatism, he was a practical man who wanted to make things work. On 22 January 1924 he asked MacDonald to form a government. 'He impressed me very much; he wishes to do the right thing ... Today twenty-three years ago dear Grandmama died. I wonder what she would have thought of a Labour Government!'[1] But he reflected that he was his own man and in different circumstances. MacDonald wished to do the right thing, and so did the King. Ahead of his meeting on 22 January he wrote, 'There are really no precedents for the present situation. I must use my own judgment as each case arises.'[2]

It was the achievement of the two men that the radical move from a semi-aristocratic if paternalistic system of government to popular social democracy in Britain took place so quietly that the change was hardly noticed. The point is that it was a deliberate achievement. It didn't happen by accident. Both men very much wanted it to go that way. While this is a book about MacDonald and focuses on his role in the governmental revolution, George V's role must not be underestimated.

He—and his private secretaries—played an essential part in easing the formation of the first Labour government in 1924. If it had not been for his insistence—pretty much his orders—MacDonald would not have consented to lead the National Government in

THE CANCELLED PRIME MINISTER

1931. The King and MacDonald are closely bound together in the history of these years.

*

When Ramsay MacDonald arrived at the Palace at midday on 22 January for the meeting to be sworn of the Privy Council, he met with a minor royal reprimand. The King took it very badly that at the Labour Party meeting in the Albert Hall a few days earlier 'The Red Flag' and the Marseillaise had been sung.

MacDonald never lacked self-confidence. His self-assurance was inoffensive but impermeable. He had never felt socially disadvantaged. He was never in the least overwhelmed by the very grand aristocrats with whom he increasingly consorted. He felt at no loss in the presence of foreign dignitaries on the world stage. He was not in the least in awe of patrician intellectuals like Beatrice Webb. Equally there is no hint in his diaries of nervousness about his first formal meeting with his sovereign. He reassured the King that the Labour Party had rather got into the habit of singing the 'Red Flag'; he hoped to break them from the habit. He had indeed managed to induce them not to sing the song in the House of Commons when the Baldwin government fell. This brief divergence in musical tastes was quickly put aside, and the Lossie Loon was entirely satisfied by his sovereign's friendliness. 'He talked so steadily that I could hardly thank him.'

When MacDonald kissed hands he agreed to the King's request to form an administration but not to the suggestion that the name of the party, the Labour Party, was provocative and should be changed. The Prime Minister said that he himself had engaged in hard manual labour in his time.[3]

The King was worried about Russia and hoped that he would not be compelled to shake hands with the murderers of his relatives. Of the two men, it seems that the King was the more nervous. 'King plays the game straight, though I feel he is apprehensive. It wd. be a miracle were he not.' The King arranged for MacDonald to be given a memorandum summarising the essentials of the relationship between King and Prime Minister.[4] JR Clynes said that the King

> gave us invaluable guidance from his deep experience, to help us in the difficult time before us, when we should become his principal

ministers. I had expected to find him unbending; instead he was kindness and sympathy itself. Before he gave us leave to go, he made an appeal to us that I have never forgotten: 'The immediate future of my people, and their whole happiness, is in your hands, gentlemen. They depend upon your prudence and sagacity.'[5]

From this time onwards a special bond developed, so that the King would say at the end of his life that MacDonald was his favourite Prime Minister. The relationship between the two is so important—and indeed goes so far to explain why MacDonald took the most controversial decision in his political career—that the King's character and the friendship that developed between him and MacDonald require some exploration.

*

George was born in 1865. He was in every sense a Victorian. At his birth he was the third in line to the throne, coming behind his father, the future Edward VII, and his elder brother, Albert Victor. Very much the spare, he was never truly prepared for monarchy. His career was to be in the Navy, and he trained for that, pretty much like a middle-class naval recruit, starting as a midshipman. It's important, when we think of him in the 1920s, to remember that his career had begun under sail in the wooden ships of Victoria's Navy. In them he sailed around the world, putting in at the many ports of his grandmother's empire. In the course of his voyaging he acquired a tattoo. It is pleasing to imagine the Tattooed Sailor and Lady Londonderry, the Tattooed Duchess, comparing their artwork.

When his elder brother died in January 1892, George was twenty-six; not a lot changed in his way of life. Princess Mary of Teck, his brother's fiancée, was recycled to become his. The marriage was an outstandingly happy and successful one—save that, as George acknowledged, he was quite incapable of showing his feelings. The genuinely tender relationship between him and Mary was only revealed, as far as he was concerned, in sentiments which he could express only on paper.

When he left the Navy, he pretty well withdrew into private life and a quiet, almost reclusive existence in York Cottage, a small residence at Sandringham. He was, like Nancy Mitford's fictional

THE CANCELLED PRIME MINISTER

Uncle Matthew, almost a caricature of a withdrawn countryman with a dislike of foreigners and made-up dishes. His first biographer, Harold Nicolson, despaired of his time as Duke of York when for twenty years he did nothing other than 'kill animals and stick in stamps'. The stamp collection was an extraordinarily large one and, as stamp collections go, ultimately a very valuable one. The killing was also on an enormous scale. In ten days in Nepal in the course of his Durbar celebrations in 1911 he killed twenty-one tigers, eight rhinoceroses and a bear. At a shoot in 1913 he killed over a thousand pheasants at the rate of a bird every twenty seconds.[*]

So the first thing to note about George V is how limited and boring he was. The courtiers who had known his father commented on his limited intellectual power. Lord Esher, for instance, a huge admirer of Edward VII, remained staunchly monarchist, but increasingly found George commonplace, stupid and, worst of all, bourgeois. Courtiers might be expected to be critical of their new boss and compare him with the old boy, but they weren't the only ones who reacted in this way. Pretty well everyone did. HG Wells said that the King was boring and an alien. To his credit, George V conceded that while he might be boring, he did object to being described as an alien.

He was also, like others of the House of Windsor, bad-tempered. He was insistent on punctuality to a ludicrous degree. All the clocks in royal residences were kept half an hour ahead of the real time. There would be appalling outbursts for anyone who was late in terms of this artificial timetable. As adults his children quailed before these rebukes. Only his daughter-in-law, Elizabeth, Duchess of York, could get away with unpunctuality. When she apologised for appearing late for one meal, he sweetly said that she couldn't have been late and that they must have been early. Others received a very different treatment. He spoke very loudly and often shouted. His language was that of the quarterdeck, and he was inclined to dirty jokes.

His prejudices were many. They were directed against evidence of modernism[6] and in particular against any deviation from an

---

[*] At the end of the day he wrote to his son David, later King Edward, who had been with him that day: 'Perhaps we went a little too far today, David.'

extraordinarily formalised dress code. If a button should have been buttoned and wasn't, that would be remarked on. If a button was buttoned that shouldn't have been, that would also be regarded as a crime against humanity. No errant collar, no inappropriate touch of braid would go uncastigated. The King of Great Britain, Ireland and the British dominions beyond the seas, the Emperor of India, was intimately involved in devising a uniform for the Royal Corps of Commissionaires, a civilian body originally founded at the time of the Crimean War to provide employment for ex-servicemen as uniformed doorkeepers and guards. It is all the more surprising, against all this punctilio, that he chose to have his trousers ironed at the sides, rather than fore and aft.*

*

And yet, while he had none of the acumen that Lord Esher had noticed in his father, George had common sense. He needed to deploy it. Very few reigns have seen challenge and the speed of change that George V's did. He saw Europe convulsed by the most terrible of wars, in the course of which ancient dynasties disappeared in Germany, Russia and Austria-Hungary. He was related to all of them. He saw the birth and growth of socialism and of communism. He saw the social certainties and the assumptions of the institutions of the country challenged and destroyed. The enormous wealth of the richest ten per cent was dispersed—though not, as it turned out, for ever. A limited franchise was extended to men— and to women, who were substantially liberated by the First World War. The powers of the hereditary peerage were curtailed. The unity of his kingdom was broken by the partition of Ireland. A sense of danger and impermanence threatened his country. Before he died he saw and worried about the growth of fascism and the likelihood of another war, perhaps more awful than the Great War.

---

* The Great Trouser Problem has strangely fascinated generations of historians. One distinguished scholar argues that it was a habit he had learned as a midshipman. Another has suggested less respectfully that it was done because he had very distinct knock knees, arguing in support of his theory that the King was known in Scotland as 'nell-kneed (Scottish for knock-kneed) Geordie', to distinguish him from his son George VI, 'stammering Geordie'.

This limited, unimaginative monarch did not face all this passively. Indeed, the stolid countryman took personal initiatives in a way that no monarch before him had done for hundreds of years and no monarch has done since, to try to address great political problems and avert disaster.

The first was at the very outset of his reign, when he was a youngish man of forty-five. The constitution was threatened by the great conflict between the Lords and the Commons over Lloyd George's budget and over which House, the elected Commons or the hereditary Lords, should ultimately prevail. Shortly before his death, Edward VII had agreed to the wholesale creation of new peers, so that the political control of the Upper House would lie with the Liberals and not with the huge Conservative majority. George V renewed that undertaking. It was not entirely without parallel. Something similar had been done by William IV to ensure the passage of the Great Reform Bill in 1832. But it was a big thing for a monarch to do. It involved something like breaking faith with the Conservative Party, which was much more the party of the monarchy in 1910 than it had been in 1832. In any event it was a hugely radical step from which a far from radical king might have shied away.

He took a very personal role in the negotiations. In the same way he intervened in the crisis over Ireland by calling a conference of the parties at Buckingham Palace in July 1914 to try to thrash out the difficulties. In this and in other ways, he, this most conservative of monarchs, was prepared to exceed his constitutional rights, and he did so because he was truly concerned about the stability of his country.

The next great constitutional challenge was in 1931, when the cohesion of the country was threatened by a great economic crisis. Here too he personally intervened and, I argue, was the man who was truly responsible for MacDonald's decision to preside over a National Government at the expense of his own party career.

*

So we have stupidity or, at least, lack of imagination counterbalanced by pragmatism, a sense of duty and an element of practical common sense. His bad temper was also balanced by a decent ordinariness.

GEORGE V

Intellectuals sneered at the King's bourgeois little ways, his lack of interest in the arts,* his enthusiasm for killing birds and sticking in stamps, the story that when it was suggested to him that he should send a message of congratulation to Thomas Hardy on reaching his eightieth birthday, he sent, as he assumed he was being asked to, congratulations to his fishing-rod maker, Mr Hardy of Alnwick. There are some elements of affinity between the traditionalism of the uneducated King and the reflections of the mature MacDonald who finished reading Lytton Strachey's *Eminent Victorians* and 'felt the virtues of the Victorian times so condemned by Mr Strachey'.

George's ordinariness was the ordinariness of most of his people. If his reign hadn't been so long it might not have worked, but in the event they saw him as very much like themselves, his values their values. Towards the end he was seriously ill, and he was astounded and touched to find that his people actually loved him. 'I cannot understand it,' he said. 'After all I'm only a very ordinary sort of fellow.' That very way of putting it explains exactly why his people loved him. He put it rather more beautifully, but perhaps no more movingly, when he spoke on the night of his Silver Jubilee: he sincerely expressed how moved he had been by the crowds that attended the procession to St Paul's. He went on, 'I can only say to you, my very dear people, that the Queen and I thank you from the depths of our hearts for all the loyalty and, may I say, the love with which this day and always you have surrounded us.'

*

So these strands, common sense, pragmatism, a desire to make things work and keep the country going, and a fundamental ordinary decency, come together in his handling of the accession to power of Labour.

We have seen that the King reflected on how differently his father or indeed Queen Victoria would have greeted the approach of socialism. He was clear, however, that he was living in different circumstances and had to move with the times. That's not to say that he and

---

* In an art gallery, confronted by an Impressionist piece, he called Queen Mary over, 'Come and look at this. You'll laugh.'

165

his advisers didn't give a great deal of thought in advance to what was happening. Lord Stamfordham, the King's private secretary, engaged in a wide correspondence, sounding out the views of Conservative and Liberal leaders. The royal establishment didn't embrace MacDonald without extensive research and a degree of trepidation. But the personal element was very important. George V was reassured by MacDonald's moderation, considerateness and the combination of 'cosmopolitan distinction and Scottish sense'.[7] The King was always clear that there was a great deal of difference between Ramsay MacDonald and the more extreme members of his party.

*

Clynes recorded in his memoirs 'the strange turn in Fortune's wheel which had brought MacDonald the starveling clerk, Thomas the engine-driver, Henderson the foundry labourer and Clynes the millhand to Buckingham Palace'.[8] MacDonald could never have written these words. In his own thoughts, he had already migrated from the world of the starveling clerk. On the other hand he was aware of the huge accommodation between the party of working men and a few working women and the Establishment. In his diary of 23 January 1924 he said, 'Without fuss, the firing of guns, the flying of new flags, the Labour govt. has come in … At noon there was a Privy Council at Buck. Pal; the seals were handed to us—and there we were ministers of state.'

How would the King, this martinet, this stickler for protocol, receive the people's tribunes? Till then cabinet ministers wore court dress, a tailcoat with matching waistcoat and breeches, lace cuffs and jabot, silk stockings, buckled shoes, cocked hat, white gloves, and often gold and silver embroidery. The King wanted continuity but was understanding. Lord Stamfordham wrote to the Labour Chief Whip to say that the uniform could be obtained from 'Messrs. Moss Bros' for thirty pounds. There was flexibility on the Labour side, at least as far as MacDonald was concerned. It was proposed to Stamfordham that the required dress could simply be black evening dress and knee breeches and that a cadre of ministers who were willing to wear this fancy dress could attend formal functions, other less compliant radicals being excused. MacDonald was motivated partly by respect for the King, but he quite enjoyed dressing up. In any event, he was quite clear that some things mattered and some things didn't:

> I suppose the anti-gold lace people will be at me again. They're a dull witted lot ... These braids & uniforms are but part of an official pageantry & as my conscience is not on my back, a gold coat means nothing to me but a form of dress to be worn or rejected as a hat would be ... If royalty had given the labour government the cold shoulder, we should have returned the call. It has not. It has been considerate, cordially correct, human & friendly. The king has never seen me as a Minister without making me feel that he was also seeing me as a friend.*

Ishbel MacDonald confirmed that MacDonald did 'fancy' himself in court dress. Even his Conservative adversaries admitted that he was 'very distinguished', with 'a fine profile, like a Roman coin'. The King was delighted when Jimmy Thomas told him that Sidney Webb wouldn't be able to wear breeches. 'His wife wears 'em.'⁹

Not all Labour supporters agreed with MacDonald. At one meeting someone shouted, 'A workers' government, ye ca' it! It's a bloody lum hat government like a' the rest.'¹¹ The picture in the papers of MacDonald wearing his gold-braided court dress and sword was distasteful to the left-wing members of the party. There was some patronising concern about his daughter, too, and aristocratic ladies offered to help her. She said she had no need of any help. 'I have already chosen my frocks and I think I know how to behave at Court.'¹¹†

The officious Beatrice Webb established what she called the Half-Circle Club to teach Labour wives how to behave. Ishbel thought it

---

* Similarly, he told one of his children that they should stand up for the national anthem not for the sake of the monarchy, but out of respect for society and its conventions. Good reasons but not revolutionary zeal.
† It's interesting that in his very hostile appraisal of MacDonald, MacNeill Weir, who had been his parliamentary private secretary in 1924, described the people who complained about MacDonald's appearance at court as his 'Socialist followers', acknowledging that the party as a whole could not be characterised with that adjective.

was an 'awful' idea and would have nothing to do with it. She did institute a weekly At Home for Labour wives. MacDonald was hugely pleased with Ishbel's performance as his housekeeper, the 'College Girl Hostess of No. 10' as the *Evening News* called her.

Ishbel was twenty-one on 2 March 1924, and MacDonald wrote in his diary, 'How happy I am with her. Daily she grows more like her mother. Neither of us like the social side, but she shows how it can be done without vanity or vulgarity of swollen head. I see my ideals of democratic dignity carried out.' On 5 May 1924: 'I am very happy that Ishbel has shown … simple dignity.'

*

The spirit and friendliness continued. There were many differences between the King and Prime Minister, but there were real points of similarity. Both were sincere, both were ordinary, both were pragmatists. When MacDonald resigned as Prime Minister, the King said to him,

> I hoped you might have seen me through, but I now know it isn't possible … I wonder how you have stood it—especially the loss of your friends and their beastly behaviour … You have been the Prime Minister I have liked best: you have so many qualities, you have kept up the dignity of the office without using it to give you dignity … You will see me as often as you like and of course you will come this year to Balmoral and as you now have nothing to do will not merely stay a weekend.

As George V's life was coming to an end, a meeting of the Privy Council took place so that he could appoint a Council of State to act on his behalf. The King was only just conscious. The privy counsellors filed out in tears. MacDonald wrote, 'I was the last out and I shall never forget the look illuminated by tension … my final farewell to a gracious and kingly friend and a master whom I have served with all my heart.' 'A kingly friend': this was the essence of the relationship.

Very soon after that Council of State the King died, his death hastened by a lethal injection from his doctor, Lord Dawson of Penn, given partly so that the King's death could be announced not

GEORGE V

in the sensational evening press, but in the more decorous morning newspapers. His successor, Edward VIII, immediately had the royal clocks adjusted. In John Betjeman's quietly poignant words,

> In that red house in a red mahogany bookcase
> The stamp collection waits with mounts long dry
> The big blue eyes are shut which saw wrong clothing
> And favourite fields and coverts from a horse.

*

Paris was well worth a Mass, and MacDonald had no difficulty in accommodating to the conventions of being the King's First Minister. Westminster was worth a visit to Moss Bros. The new Labour cabinet was the first at which members smoked, but in most ways it continued very much as its predecessors had done. Lord Haldane, Asquith's seasoned Lord Chancellor, returned to the Woolsack and was able to brief his colleagues on practice and protocol at the first Labour cabinet meeting.* Haldane had been in on things as early as 11 December, when MacDonald phoned to arrange an urgent meeting. 'In the evening he offered me anything I chose if I would help him; the leadership of the House of Lords, the Chancellorship, Defence, Education.' Soon afterwards Baldwin 'begged' Haldane to join the Labour government and help them out, an interesting example of a cross-party desire for peaceful change. Baldwin genuinely wanted to ensure that Labour were peacefully assimilated into the current political system. On 23 December, MacDonald was back with more offers, Education again, Admiralty, India. Haldane invited MacDonald to his house in Perthshire, Cloan, where MacDonald agreed that Haldane would come in as Lord Chancellor.[12] He gave advice on etiquette, including the need to address MacDonald as 'Prime Minister' and other ministers by their surnames or their ministerial titles. The headmasterly MacDonald pressed his colleagues to ensure that they turned up on time to cabinet meetings.

---

* Haldane was quite busy at the time. On 14 January he held a dinner for leaders of the party. He wrote to his mother saying that he had followed his sister's suggestion and provided lemonade and orangeade in place of wine.

20

REFLECTIONS FROM THE PINNACLE

MacDonald was confident in himself. He never doubted that he had it in him to reach the top, and he had the ambition to want to get there. But it was not a coarse or vulgar ambition. He looked at himself from a distance and dispassionately. Now, despite all the factors that had made such an achievement so wildly improbable, he had reached the very top of political and national life.

There was no rejoicing. On the contrary, his achievements seemed empty and trivial compared with his tragedies. He had spent his Christmas holidays in Lossiemouth just two weeks before he became the King's First Minister. When he got back to London he wrote of 'times of sad reflections & gloomy thoughts. The people of my heart are dead; their faces on my walls; they do not share with me. Had much difficulty in returning. How vain is honour now.'[1] A few days later, as his future became increasingly obvious and he was in touch with the Palace about taking office:

> Queer unreal feeling about it all. Sometimes feel should like to run away home to Lossie to return to reality & flee from these unreal dreams. I am a Socialist because I prize above all things the simple life & here I am in this, encountering it on the way to Socialism ... so I swing between my two beings & go on.

None of the worldliness of Harold Macmillan, when he celebrated becoming Prime Minister by taking his Chief Whip, Edward Heath, out to dine on oysters. Indeed, no worldliness at all.

MacDonald seems almost to be expressing the disillusionment of old age through these routines. But he wasn't old. Macmillan was sixty-four when he became Prime Minister. MacDonald was just fifty-eight in 1924. He was not only fairly young as party leaders went in those days, but outstandingly active. He had boasted a year or two earlier that he could outwalk Gladstone at the same age, and his recreation was still to walk over the hills and moors at great length. In 1925 he took his first flight and wrote to thank Sir Hugh Trenchard for arranging it: he had become 'a keen convert to your ways of getting about'.

He could bear these physical burdens well. Indeed he was inspirited by physical challenge and the stimulation of solitary endeavour in natural surroundings. What he found much more wearing was the effort of day-to-day living and the tedium of attending to prosaic necessities. He had very little money. Until he became Prime Minister, his salary as a member of parliament was £400 a year, and there was nothing on top of that for being Leader of the Opposition. The income from his wife's trust fund continued to reduce. The party reluctantly agreed to pay him £800 a year to cover secretarial expenses, but that was barely enough: in the year to November 1925 he paid out just over £720.[2] Like Churchill he relied on freelance journalism, but while Churchill did it to finance an elevated lifestyle, MacDonald did it simply to survive. He was not realistic enough to see that he could have made much more by capitalising on his fame. He turned down the offer of an advance of £50,000 for his memoirs simply because he disliked self-publicity. Where Churchill negotiated hard and with great skill to get paid as much as he could and to be paid in ways that were fiscally advantageous, MacDonald was an innocent, taking whatever he was offered, sometimes very little indeed. Impractical to the point of negligence, he struggled even to complete his tax return both because of the time it took and because such matters were so remote from his mindset.

What is now often disdainfully referred to as 'administration', the necessity of dealing with the tiresome practicalities of everyday life, he found a heavy burden. He constantly complained about the effort and strain. As leader of the party, a lot of the political life in which he was involved was not the big-event grandstand moments when the adrenaline pumped and the faithful cheered. He had to energise a party that fed on division and to hold together the broader movement on which the party depended. 'You imagine', he said in response to a request to help with a campaign, 'that we have got nothing to do except come on platforms and talk—no House of Commons work that requires preparation, no work required for bread and cheese, no rest and no recreation.'³

The nervous cost of being Ramsay MacDonald was a price which more typically urbane and sociable politicians did not have to pay. 'This terrible weariness of brain that is upon me is like the malignant ill will of the devil.'⁴ 'Friends will send invitations & thank goodness they do, but some lame excuse from me for not going is a bad way of showing my pleasure at having been invited.'⁵ 'To keep up with the business of the House of Commons & *to think about it* & work at it; to speak in the country & even faintly satisfy the exacting demands of the Party; to write every weekend enough to keep the house going—it is impossible almost & means incessant drudgery with no rest, no gaiety, no lilt in life.'⁶

There are many more complaints of this sort, but they crystallise in a diary entry of 20 January 1928 which can be taken as typical of innumerable others:

> How tired I am. My brain is fagged, work is difficult, & there is a darkness on the face of the land. I am ashamed of some speeches I have made, but what can I do? I have no time to prepare anything. It looks as though it will be harder to make my necessary income this year ... To be the paid servant of the State is objectionable; to begin making an income on Friday afternoon & going hard at it till Sunday night, taking meetings in the interval, is too wearing for human flesh & blood. On the other hand, to live on £400 pounds a year is impossible. If it killed one in a clean, efficient business-like way why should one object, but it cripples & tortures first by lowering the quality of work done & then by pushing one into long months of slowly ebbing vitality & mental paralysis.

*

Distilling these concerns into the privacy of his diary was one way of coping with his burdens. He rarely expressed these thoughts to others. If Margaret had still been alive he would have talked to her—or, perhaps more therapeutically still, she would have sensed his concerns without his needing to utter them. Again, had he not been the shy and solitary man he was, he might not have suffered from burdens which other Labour leaders bore more easily. But he was who he was, and the burdens were real and remained on his shoulders throughout his political life.

Long arduous expeditions in remote countryside were the most effective method for recharging his batteries. Another effective way for finding peace was in sea voyages and foreign travel. He even made a visit to the Sahara in 1926. Music meant nothing to him. Harry Lauder, the Orpheus Choir and what he asked for of Lord Reith, the director general of the BBC, 'simple and sincere singing', were about his limit. Reading and collecting of an antiquarian sort were more important. He haunted art galleries and salerooms, threw himself into negotiations to acquire works for the Scottish National Gallery, and was proud to be a trustee of the National Gallery in London. He collected rare books and furniture. He admired craftsmanship and understood the tradition of William Morris—admiration for a vanished world in which the honesty of beautiful things stood in contrast to the cheapening effects of nineteenth-century industrialisation. Another example of his rootedness in a romantic lost world.

Not many British prime ministers of the twentieth century were intellectuals, and MacDonald was certainly not one. Most of those who were not intellectuals tended to be highly intelligent. Mrs Thatcher is a good example of the intelligent non-intellectual. It is interesting to speculate on who is more dangerous—the dim intellectual or the intelligent non-intellectual. MacDonald was certainly intelligent, though his mind was not as quick as Mrs Thatcher's. But what he did have in an enormous degree was imagination. He adopted some elements of an Anglo-Saxon carapace, but what was within it was essentially Celtic.

He had not attended university, which deprived him of one of the veneers of political life. Equally, he had not the institutional background of the army or the professions, which would have enabled him to move with ease in varied circles and settings. His warmest praise was for people he found 'homely'. There were not many such people in politics. He saw the importance of the socialist academics and intellectuals and was encouraging to John Strachey, GDH Cole, Harold Laski and RH Tawney; but he felt threatened by them and uncomfortable with them, and they knew it. He was too embarrassed by his shortcomings to admit that the specialities of others were not his, and he tried unconvincingly to suggest that he knew as much of their special subjects as they did. The net effect was that he was not greatly liked by those with whom he worked most closely. They found him inconsiderate and impersonal, inaccessible, touchy and vain. Molly Hamilton talked of going into his room and being 'looked at, if looked at at all, as though not there', and described the experience as chilling.[7] He could dominate his party, but, however much the rank and file might idolise him, the equals among whom he was first did not love him.

1. The railway comes to Lossiemouth in 1852. Fourteen years later, MacDonald was born there. He was brought up in the town and formed by its influences. He never truly left.

2. MacDonald's childhood home in Lossiemouth. There has been no 'log cabin to White House' journey in British history to match this.

3. Ramsay MacDonald, his two elder children, Ishbel and Joan, and his beloved Margaret. The picture conveys something of her strength of character. She was a remarkable woman in her own right.

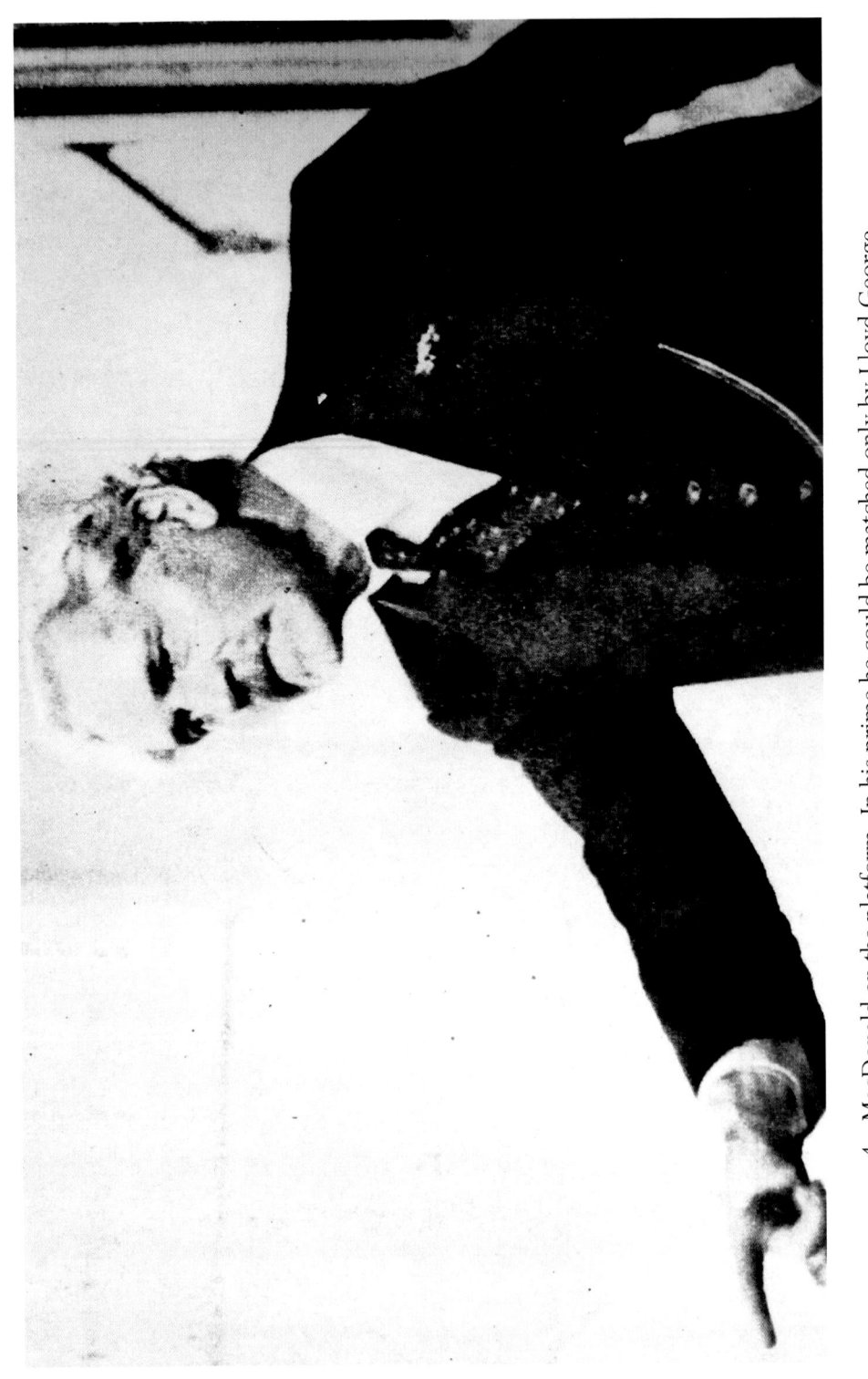

4. MacDonald on the platform. In his prime he could be matched only by Lloyd George.

5. In 1910, Ramsay and Margaret built The Hillocks in Lossiemouth to accommodate their growing family; she died very soon afterwards. It is not as large as it looks. Some of the children slept in outbuildings.

6. Ramsay MacDonald's spartan single bedroom in The Hillocks.

7. Ramsay MacDonald's sitting room in The Hillocks, pretty much as it was in his day.

8. The first Labour Government. In an early example of photo editing, Stephen Walsh has been slipped in as the second figure from the left in the second row. Haldane on MacDonald's right. Arthur Henderson in a casual suit, first on right, first row.

9. *Punch* 18 June 1924 contrasts the docility of the Liberals with the fiery Clydesiders.

10. With no wife, MacDonald relied on Ishbel to act as his hostess at Number 10. She never put a foot wrong, and charmed all she met.

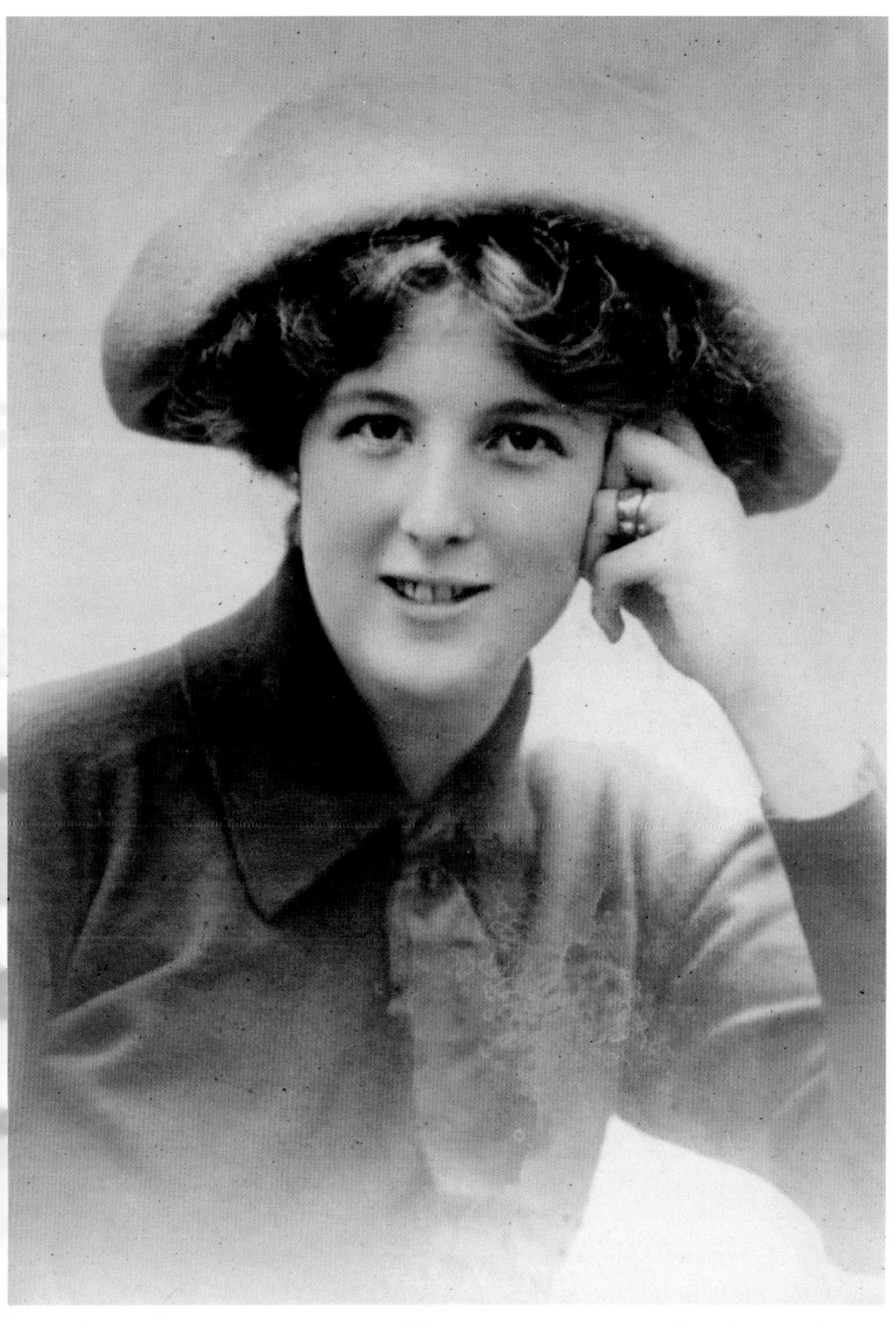
11. Lady Londonderry was MacDonald's favourite aristocrat, though a marchioness rather than one of the duchesses whose company he was said to enjoy.

12. David Low shows John Maynard Keynes at rest. He rarely *was* at rest. To many he was the most revolutionary economist of his age.

13. It's difficult not to warm to Jimmy Thomas. Here he is telling a fairy story to his grandchildren.

On August 24 the Labour Government resigned and a new administration, headed by Mr. Ramsay Macdonald, took office. The new Cabinet (seen here) consisted of ten members only: Front row, reading from left to right: Lord Snowden, Mr. Ramsay Macdonald and Mr. Stanley Baldwin. Second row: Sir P. Cunliffe-Lister, Mr. J. H. Thomas, and Lord Reading. Third row: Sir Herbert Samuel and Lord Sankey. Fourth row: Mr. Neville Chamberlain and Sir Samuel Hoare. On September 20 a fresh crisis arose. A General Election took place in October and a "National Government" with an economy policy was returned by a large majority.

14. The core of the National Government. First row from left, Snowden, MacDonald, Stanley Baldwin. Splendid attitude by Jimmy Thomas in the middle of the second row. Precariously on top, Neville Chamberlain and Sir Samuel Hoare.

15. The historic Labour government of 1945. It was MacDonald's legacy. Two members were not in the Commons during his administrations and of the others, only two did not have some experience of government under him.

16. The graveyard at Spynie. Here Margaret and Ramsay's infant son David was buried. It was in MacDonald's thoughts throughout his life, and here his ashes were interred.

21

LABOUR IN POWER

In the lead-up to the 1924 election, the more respectable newspapers had been fairly measured in their reporting of the Labour campaign. Even *The Times* and *The Spectator* were as critical of the other parties as they were of Labour. Others, like the *Saturday Review*, were less moderate. The *Sunday Pictorial* foresaw 'a financial panic within 24 hours'.

There was some apprehension about the arrival of the first ostensibly socialist government. There were apocryphal stories about countesses fleeing the capital to avoid having their throats cut. But given events on the Continent, the surprising thing was how little fear there was of red revolution. Asquith and Baldwin helped, because they felt that the rules of fair play should be respected—even if they hoped and half expected that Labour would fail. The Liberals in particular were not averse to letting Labour have a go. They would prove to be the victims of their own generosity. There was also a creditable measure of Conservative goodwill. The Clydesiders were amazed to receive social invitations from their class enemies. Davie Kirkwood, about as far to the left as any, was taken aback by how welcome he was made to feel: 'I had to shake myself occasionally, as I find myself moving about and talking with men whose names were household words. More strange was it to find them also simple and unaffected and friendly.'[1] The Labour Party itself was not so expressive of genial goodwill.

Although the newspapers had not been unkind to Labour as it approached government, the party had no substantial media backing of its own. The *Daily Herald* did support the government, but its real sympathy was with the extreme left. Similarly, the ILP *New Leader* tried to shape Labour policy rather than to applaud it.

*

MacDonald was well aware of the enormous difficulties that faced a minority Labour government. He considered that Labour had got to this situation as a result of what he called an 'insane miracle', and he regarded the task the government faced as being of an 'almost incalculable magnitude'. He was determined to take the opportunity that presented itself. He wanted to demonstrate that Labour could work, that it could legislate responsibly and exercise the functions of a mature political party. So at the outset there was this conflict: MacDonald wanted to show that Labour was fit to be a progressive party; his more fervid followers wanted radical policies and had no time for moderation.

When Sir Keir Starmer made his speech on the steps of 10 Downing Street on becoming Prime Minister in 2024, he said that he would govern 'unburdened by doctrine'. On the face of it, that was a pretty remarkable declaration for a socialist Prime Minister, and in a way he could never have said those words if Ramsay MacDonald had not demonstrated that there was a concept of socialism which had nothing to do with abstract theories. When Roy Jenkins, as a successful Labour cabinet minister, was asked what socialism meant to him, he replied that he hadn't used that word for many many years. Slightly more elliptically, when Starmer was elected leader of the Labour Party, he was asked what his position was. He said he stood for 'moral socialism'. MacDonald could have used exactly these words. No one knew what Keir Starmer meant, and most people had great difficulty in knowing what MacDonald stood for.

The importance of the fitness for government idea is emphasised in MacDonald's report to the King on 8 August 1924: 'So the first stage of the Session comes to an end. From more than one point of view the Session has been historical. The Prime Minister may perhaps justly claim that he has shown the Country that the Labour Party is fit to govern, and that the system of minority government, although accompanied by inconveniences, is a feasible proposition.'[2]

MacDonald's role as leader of the party and Prime Minister was very different from Attlee's in 1945. The party and its institutions were immature, and the leader had far less authority than the leaders of the other parties then or the leaders of the Labour Party later. Consequently, MacDonald didn't have a free hand in appointing his ministers. There's a good deal of inconclusive talk of who may have advised MacDonald about the composition of his cabinet. MacDonald's old friend and golfing companion General CB Thomson, who became Lord Thomson as Secretary for Air, may have been involved.

Christopher Birdwood Thomson had become one of MacDonald's closest friends and confidants, and deserves a few biographical words for that reason and also as an illustration of how MacDonald could find friends with very different backgrounds from his own. Thomson was the son of a major-general in the Royal Engineers. He was educated at Cheltenham College and the Royal Military Academy, Woolwich. He had a distinguished military career: fighting in the South African War, teaching at the staff college and taking part in the advance through Palestine. He became a brigadier-general and attended the 1919 Peace Conference. He had displayed no particular interest in politics, but equally was not a blinkered military man. He read widely, spoke a number of languages, was interested in painting and sculpture, and had a wide circle of friends. It was he who introduced Princess Marthe Bibesco to MacDonald.

In 1924, as Secretary of State for Air, Thomson entered the House of Lords as Lord Thomson of Cardington, the town in Bedfordshire where the government airship works were situated. He was a popular and effective speaker in the House of Lords, where he more or less led for Labour: if he had lived longer he would no doubt have become the leader of the Labour peers. Before that could happen, however, he died for the sake of politics. On the formation of the second Labour government, Thomson returned to the Air Ministry.

There he championed not only the Royal Air Force as Britain's primary defence, but in particular the R101 airship. Two airships were being developed in competition, the 'Capitalist' R100 built by Vickers and fuelled by petrol, and the 'Socialist' R101, constructed by the state-owned airship works and fuelled by heavy oil. Heavy oil was a good fuel in the tropics, but the airship was unstable, with inadequate fins and rudders. Thomson pressed for an early inaugural flight so that he could make a dramatic return to the Imperial Conference in London. The R101 took off on 4 October 1930 with Thomson and his staff, Sir Sefton Brancker, director of Civil Aviation, and ten other passengers with a crew of forty-two. The airship crashed near Beauvais in France at two o'clock on the following morning. There were only six survivors. Thomson was among those killed, and he was buried with the other members of the expedition at Cardington. The subsequent inquiry exonerated Thomson from taking an unjustifiable risk, though the novelist Nevil Shute, who was working as an engineer on the Capitalist project, described R101 as 'the plaything of a politician'.

In 1930, just before the opening of the Labour Party conference at Llandudno, MacDonald heard that the Airship R101 had crashed near Beauvais.

> A little after 6am today my bedside telephone rang. The R101 had crashed and Thomson was not amongst the living! ... So when I bade him goodbye on Friday and looked down upon him descending the stairs at Number 10, that was to be the last glimpse of my friend, gallant, gay and loyal. No one was like him and there will be none.[3]

When he heard of Thomson's death, he had wanted to cancel his speech. He was obviously under great strain and he admitted that he would not have been there if it hadn't been his duty. He linked the risks which the crew of the R101 had taken with those of his 'old friends, the miners', for whom death was 'an ever-present companion'. He ended this section of his speech with words of gratitude for the support of the French government, above whose soil the tragedy had taken place. 'France knows how to stand by the side of the mourner.' Having won his audience to his side, he built on that structure an appeal to ideals to which he urged his audience, telling them not to allow their socialist faith to be eroded by pettifogging issues. The reception was tumultuous. His opponents were silenced, and when James Maxton moved to criticise the government, his resolution was defeated by 1,800,000 votes to 330,000.

Beatrice Webb and, indeed, Sidney took it upon themselves to proffer advice on cabinet appointments via Haldane. Gratifyingly, none of Mrs Webb's protégés was rewarded.[4] However, MacDonald didn't go out of his way to consult on cabinet-making. He even went off to Lossiemouth at one stage in the process. He did have to make compromises all the same.[5] Snowden was a fairly obvious choice as Chancellor of the Exchequer. Apart from Beatrice Webb, who wrote him off as 'chicken-hearted' and timid, Snowden was at the moment well regarded in the party, and not just out of sympathy for his handicap.

When Beatrice Webb described Snowden as being chicken-hearted, she meant that he would never question the Treasury's desire for rectitude. He never did. Churchill memorably described Snowden's arrival at the Treasury as 'the High Priest entering the sanctuary. The Treasury mind and the Snowden mind embraced each other with the fervour of two long-separated kindred lizards, and the reign of joy began.'[6]* Roy Jenkins, like Churchill and Snowden a Chancellor of the Exchequer in his own time, extended the idea of the reign of joy by saying that Snowden fell in love with the Governor of the Bank of England, Montagu Norman. It was often said that Snowden pretended to be a socialist. Certainly, his first budget, for which he had researched Gladstone's speeches, was designed to resist demands for expenditure as strongly as the Grand Old Man himself would have done. There was no mention of the capital levy. Tax reductions were centred on food. Prunes became cheap, and Snowden talked about the idea of a free breakfast table. No red Bolshevism, and MacDonald was delighted by the Chancellor's moderation. Snowden's budget in April 1924 was orthodox, liberal and for free trade. It cut both indirect and direct taxation, and there was a significant if temporary reduction in unemployment. The budget was on the whole well received.

The budget was indeed bound to be well received by orthodox observers. Snowden's notions were pre-Gladstonian. He was unin-

---

* Churchill liked his metaphor. In *Great Contemporaries* he recalled seeing Snowden and MacDonald together again after a long estrangement. He wrote that they looked like 'two venomous old lizards, very suspicious, very polite, very deadly'.

fluenced by Keynes or expansionist economists, let alone any taint of socialism. Quite why he was in the Labour Party is not clear. He would have been a very orthodox Liberal Chancellor. Even in the second Labour government, in the shadow of the Depression, he regarded borrowing as evil, threatened to resign rather than agree to a revenue tariff which would relieve 'the well to do at the expense of the poor', and contributed £50 million to the Sinking Fund designed to pay off the national debt.

And yet, and yet, Sir Charles Trevelyan, President of the Board of Education in 1924 and again in MacDonald's second administration, considered Snowden, when he looked back, as the outstanding member of the government, and JS Middleton, a party secretary, called him 'the greatest propagandist Labour ever had'.[7]

Trevelyan, 'the best-dressed man in the House of Commons', was the son of the famous Liberal MP Sir George Otto Trevelyan. He had been groomed for politics. After Harrow and Trinity College, Cambridge, he was secretary to the Earl of Crewe, Viceroy of Ireland. He entered parliament as a Liberal and was appointed to the Board of Education in 1908, but he opposed the First World War and, with MacDonald, helped to found the Union of Democratic Control. His appointment to Education acknowledged the fact that he had been involved in education since the start of his political career. He was no revolutionary, and although he wanted to increase the number of children in secondary education, there was no question of abolishing the competitive entry principle.

JR Clynes was deputy leader of the party and became Lord Privy Seal and Leader of the House of Commons.

These were fairly easy appointments. What to do with Arthur Henderson was more difficult. He was better equipped for office than most, having been a cabinet minister under Asquith and Lloyd George and a chairman of the Parliamentary Labour Party. He had, however, lost his seat at the general election, and MacDonald's initial instinct was not to parachute him into government, but to use his accepted administrative qualities to organise the party from outside parliament.

There is some doubt about precisely what MacDonald was up to here. Henderson certainly had a claim to high office. Indeed,

MacDonald considered him for the War Office and the Ministry of Health, and finally did indeed allow him to be parachuted into the House of Commons by way of a by-election, after which he became Home Secretary. On the other hand he hadn't rushed to assure Henderson about his prospects, and suggested he might be happy to be chairman of the Ways and Means Committee and Deputy Speaker, outside the cabinet, until the next election, which MacDonald thought wouldn't be very far away. The dyspeptic Sidney Webb accused MacDonald of treating Henderson with no great respect. The charge may be based on the fact that MacDonald tended to look down on Henderson as pedestrian and his social inferior. Henderson, conversely, disapproved of MacDonald's fondness for high society.[8]

At any rate, Henderson finally got the Home Office. It is a major challenge for any politician. Its responsibilities are so extensive that it is difficult to spot problems in advance. Henderson had little opportunity to innovate or to devise and apply challenging policies, and had instead to address different practical problems as they arose. The mindset of Home Office civil servants then, as now, tended to be narrow and illiberal, and Henderson's reputation suffered accordingly. He was involved at the very start with two important strikes.

There was a national dock strike in February 1924 and a month later a dispute with the Transport and General Workers' Union, with a strike by redundant tram workers. The government was anxious to show that it wasn't afraid of the unions. In March the cabinet approved a draft Proclamation of Emergency. The coalition's old Emergency Powers Act of 1920 was dusted down and activated. Under it the government exercised extensive powers between 28 March and 1 April. That put an end to strikes for the remainder of the first Labour administration. Use of the Act, however, made it very clear that MacDonald's government was not a radical one. Labour had attacked the Act bitterly when it was passed by Lloyd George in 1920, and many in the party deprecated its implementation now. Even right-wing sections of the trade union movement were aghast. The National Executive of the party minuted their disapproval. From this time an immense animosity developed between MacDonald and the TUC's Ernest Bevin. When it was reported to Bevin that MacDonald had called him a 'swine',

Bevin's response was that everyone found out sooner or later the sort of man MacDonald was.⁹

The public, if not the party, liked this robustness, and when Arthur Henderson's parachute landed at the by-election in Burnley in March, he had a majority of 7,000 over the Conservatives against a Labour majority of 2,000 in the general election just three months earlier.

The foreign secretaryship was difficult. MacDonald's first choice was JH Thomas, but the ILP was unhappy with the idea that foreign policy should not be in the hands of one of their members. The ILPers were numerically less important than the unions, but politically they continued to dominate. MacDonald was pressed to take the office himself in addition to being Prime Minister. There was still a lot to do in repairing the damage of Versailles, and he was far from unwilling to accept a role for which he was not only well qualified, but in which he had a particular interest. The international stage appealed to his histrionic side. Some thought that Arthur Henderson might have been a good appointment, but MacDonald believed that conditions in Europe were so grave that a Foreign Secretary with the added authority of being Prime Minister was almost essential. In the event his appointment to both positions was a sound move, and not just because, as the frugal Snowden pointed out, there was a saving of a ministerial salary.

The House of Lords was also a problem. Labour was not significantly represented there. It was suggested that the government might have to take in some Liberal peers. The fact that in the event there were five peers in the cabinet, where Lloyd George had only had three, reflects perhaps a desire to dilute the left. MacDonald was wise to embrace Haldane. With his long experience in government, including a crucial spell as Secretary of State for War, his contacts were everywhere, his antennae sensitive. He warned his old friend Asquith that the armed forces might be difficult about a Labour government.¹⁰ He had been one of the crucial pillars of the Liberal Party when it came to power in 1906 and particularly after Asquith replaced Campbell-Bannerman in 1908. In those early days he became far and away the most important Secretary of State for War in the twentieth century. Without him and the far-reaching reforms which he introduced, Britain would have been hard put to it to send an expeditionary force to France in 1914, let alone the outstandingly professional divisions that composed it. He subsequently became a very distinguished Lord Chancellor until most unfairly pushed out of office, largely as a result of a xenophobic attack on him by the Northcliffe press, based on a reference he had made to his days at Heidelberg University and the fact that the lecture hall there had seemed to him to be his spiritual home. On the basis of that trifling remark allegations, including the suggestion that he was the Kaiser's brother, were erected. Since then he had assumed a non-partisan identity. MacDonald's initial plan had been to appoint Sir John Sankey* as Lord Chancellor with Haldane in a powerful executive ministry—the Admiralty, the India Office or the Board of Education. Dignified and statesmanlike as always, Haldane concluded that the management of the House of Lords would be 'very delicate' and that he could best serve Labour by carrying out that role as Lord Chancellor. He stipulated that he should not be required to sit on the judicial committee of the House of Lords routinely. Instead, he continued in his interest in military matters by chairing the Committee of Imperial Defence.

Also from the Lords came Lord Parmoor, a distinguished lawyer who had been a Conservative MP but had joined the Labour Party after the First World War, and who was Stafford Cripps's father. He became Lord President of the Council. Another peer with a Conservative background, Lord Chelmsford, a former Viceroy of India, became First Lord of the Admiralty.

*

When parliament met on 12 February 1924, MacDonald set out his stall. He said that the House had to adapt to the fact that there was

---

* Sankey did eventually become Lord Chancellor in 1929 and continued in office in the National Government. When Baldwin replaced him in 1935 with Hailsham, Sankey dissolved in tears and refused to sit as a judge for several years. He was spinsterish, something of a figure of fun, living with his sister and taking his atlas into cabinet meetings so he could find the places his colleagues were talking about. But he was high-minded and a good lawyer and he devised a metaphor that defence lawyers, including Rumpole of the Bailey, have loved: the presumption of innocence is 'one golden thread [that runs through] the web of the English common law'.

a minority government. He was not interested in the tradition of snap votes forcing a dissolution. His government would go if it were defeated in a vote of confidence; otherwise it accepted the responsibilities of a minority government and claimed the privileges of such a government. It was a quiet, dignified speech in which, at a time when national confidence was low, he appealed for 'security and confidence based on goodwill'. It was an appeal that few could have made so effectively, and on the whole the minority government was treated in a civilised way.

The new government in the Commons, as in the Lords, was scarcely proletarian. A number of trade union leaders declined to take office, the well-regarded Robert Smillie, for instance. It was difficult to combine full-time politics with full-time union work. The Liberal MP Charles Masterman* complained that there were too few working-class people in the government—it had 'no claim to call itself Labour'.[11]

*

MacDonald was quietly and understandably proud of what he achieved. His mother's younger sister, Aunt Bella, was a nanny in Sussex. She came to see him in Downing Street:

> Aunt Bella came. To see her was worth everything else. She was as proud as punch—in a dignified way. 'Eh. Never did we think this was to come.' That was all. We are a great lot & hide our hearts well. Had there been others to share with Aunt Bella, who is the last, it would have been good.

A barrier across Downing Street which had been erected by Bonar Law to keep out the unemployed was removed. Life within Number Ten was fairly spartan. Although he had a salary of £5,000 a year as

---

* Masterman was far from working class himself, but he had a very real interest in the working classes. He was related to Elizabeth Fry. As well as his well-known *The Condition of England*, he wrote *From the Abyss: A Picture of the Reality of Life at the Edge*, which he published anonymously after living for some time in London slums. During the First World War he was head of the War Propaganda Bureau and employed among others John Buchan and HG Wells. He was responsible for the famous film *The Battle of the Somme*, which was shown in cinemas in Britain while the battle was still being waged.

Prime Minister, he had no entertainment allowance. His purchases were made from the Co-operative Society and delivered in a Co-op van.[12] Sometimes staff were dispatched to Covent Garden market to pick up cheap left-over vegetables.[13] The family dined in the official banqueting rooms and not in their private quarters, which they would have had to heat at their own expense. Porridge was eaten at breakfast, though more generous hospitality was offered on Sunday afternoons, when there was open house for Lossie exiles. MacDonald was not teetotal, but he drank very little

He adapted to the new life and to the business of government, and recognised the value of civil servants. Haldane compared MacDonald's chairmanship of the cabinet favourably with that of Campbell-Bannerman and Asquith. Even Sidney Webb was complimentary. MacDonald's conduct in the House was also impressive. An inexperienced team inevitably has teething problems, but MacDonald addressed lack of coordination by establishing a weekly meeting of an inner group of senior ministers to direct and control. By-election results showed that the country, far from being frightened by Labour, thought it was doing a good job.

*

There were difficulties with the service departments, as Haldane had predicted. The government wanted to re-examine the question of establishing a new naval base at Singapore, and a long battle took place between MacDonald and Admiral Beatty, First Sea Lord, veteran of the Battle of Jutland. The Foreign Office favoured going ahead with the base, but MacDonald, describing himself rather oddly as 'a non-party Secretary of State for Foreign Affairs', thought that it would be best to give up the base in the interests of international agreement on disarmament. MacDonald prevailed, but not without difficulties. He went on to face more opposition from the services over fresh proposals for a Channel tunnel. This issue, remarkably, went to a full-scale meeting of the Committee of Imperial Defence, to which all living prime ministers were invited. The Little Englanders won the day, like, MacDonald said, an 'old woman who seals doors & windows to keep her from shivering'.

In the previous government, Sir Samuel Hoare had been building up the Air Force. Lord Thomson wanted to continue the process. He said that while the party was opposed to the use of force, the aircraft were essentially for defensive and peace-keeping purposes. Backbenchers thought this a departure from the purity of Labour's pacific idealism, and amendments to the army estimates were proposed. The government successfully saw them off. One amendment, to reduce the army by 150,000 men, received just eleven votes. Lansbury, the old pacifist, proposed that soldiers could contract out of any obligations connected with the suppression of industrial disputes. He lost by 236 votes to 67. Jimmy Maxton sought to allow appeals from courts martial to the Court of Criminal Appeal, but that too was defeated.

There was more serious opposition to what were called 'the five cruisers'. The previous government had embarked on some gentle expansion of the fleet. Now Lord Chelmsford, at the Admiralty, wanted to continue with the policy. Snowden, for economic reasons and because of the party distaste for armaments, did not. In the event, partly because of unemployment implications, the government decided to go ahead with five cruisers and two destroyers, as opposed to the eight cruisers that the Conservative government had planned. Ernest Thurtle, a veteran of Cambrai, where he had been badly wounded, and husband of Dorothy Lansbury, George Lansbury's daughter, asked whether the decision to proceed with the five cruisers was 'to be taken as a great moral gesture to the world'.* It wasn't an easy task to demonstrate that the cruisers were particularly needed or that their construction would help alleviate unemployment, and in the navy estimates vote, though the government won, fourteen of their own party voted against them.

The Labour government's orthodoxy on defence issues was overwhelmingly the result of the influence of Lord Haldane. Few politicians have demonstrated such a long, serious and disinterested

---

* If Thurtle is remembered today it is because it was he who was responsible for the abolition of the death penalty for cowardice or desertion. He introduced the measure in 1924 and it finally passed in 1930. Controversy continues today in regard to the execution of British soldiers during the First World War.

concern for their country's defence. He made the first statement on behalf of the government in relation to defence policy. He saw it as his role to protect the Committee of Imperial Defence from any pacifist prejudice. It is surprising, then, that it was Haldane rather than anyone else who took the decision not to continue with defence construction at Singapore, but he did so to concentrate on what he regarded as the more immediate problem of European defence and air strength. The Labour government's defence policy was Haldane's defence policy. Haldane was an intellectual warrior, though his appearance was far from martial. He was latterly more or less spherical, although one of his caricaturists always showed him as a rhetorical penguin. Leo Amery described him as an old-fashioned family butler, but the description that captures his gravitas and dignity best is that when he entered a room, he did so like a procession of one man.

*

The rank and file of the party in parliament were more difficult than voters at by-elections. There were complaints in *Forward* that 'Comrade Chelmsford and Lord Beatty and Admiral Tyrwhitt are in a position to make the policy of the Labour Government'. Forty-five Labour MPs abstained from voting on the Trade Facilities Bill, which was only carried with Conservative and Liberal votes. Between the independence of his backbenchers and the lack of any clear understanding with the Liberal Party, the fact that the government stayed in office as long as it did is pretty remarkable. Asquith had crucially allowed the government to take office, but relations between him and MacDonald continued to be poor. MacDonald had never been impressed by Asquith and his patronising manner—and indeed, by this time, very few people did think highly of him.

*

The most remarkable thing about MacDonald in this strange situation, as the first socialist Prime Minister of Great Britain—still one of the greatest powers in the world—and on a stage so different from the world in which he had been brought up in Moray, is that from the very outset he behaved with extraordinary assurance, as if he had been at the centre of political and social power for decades. He was conscious of what was required from him, and was appalled when Labour backbenchers failed to react in a similar way to their changed circumstances. He wanted to govern unencumbered by dogma, and he didn't understand why his comrades couldn't do so too. He was not concerned by traditional class attitudes. He recognised that he could work more easily with the Conservatives than with the Liberals. Asquith's patrician manners alienated him, and he had nothing but contempt for the Lloyd Georgians. He disapproved of Lloyd George's manoeuvres at the Versailles negotiations and his sale of honours. More than anything else, he was aware that while the Liberal Party might seem closer to Labour in policy terms, both parties were fighting for the same position, to be the dominant progressive force in politics.

*

MacDonald's perception of political life and obligations was exceptional, and his position was lonely. His burdens as Prime Minister were physically and emotionally draining. He had to perform a virtuoso solo. And to his burdens as Prime Minister were added the burdens of office as Foreign Secretary. He had none of the phlegmatic reserves of Baldwin, and clubbable opportunities for relaxation had no appeal for him. He lived on his nerves and expended nervous energy, but his reserves were not those enjoyed by Lloyd George, in some ways a similar solo performer. After some months he was showing signs of exhaustion, sleeping badly and feeling under stress. One of his private secretaries, Gower, reported to the Palace in August 1924 that 'the strain upon the Prime Minister during the last few weeks has been terrible'.[14] Others spoke of his exhaustion and pallor. Even his holiday in Lossiemouth didn't much help. The weather was bad. 'Not once did I lie out in my whins & sun myself.'

But at great cost he had achieved a lot. A working-class government had come to power and Winston Churchill had got it wrong when he said that 'the enthronement in office of a Socialist Government will be a serious national misfortune such as has usually befallen great States only on the morrow of defeat in war'.[15] What had happened in Continental Europe as a result of violence and revolution had arrived in London with scarcely a stir. There were no barricades. There was no guillotine. The government had achievements of which to be proud. The King still had his head on his shoulders—and, indeed, was rather enjoying working with his Labour Prime Minister. George had been advised by his private secretary, Lord Stamfordham, that he 'should do his utmost not to hamper in any way Mr Ramsay MacDonald',[16] but he had no need for Stamfordham's advice.

*

The first Labour government didn't do much at an imperial level. Labour wasn't, of course, an 'imperial' party: they criticised the Tories for being just that. But, in any case, in their short ten months in office MacDonald and his colleagues had very many other matters to deal with. Additionally, their lack of experience particularly unsuited them for planning on an imperial scale. When Labour came into power, the previous government had been using air attacks to control the unrest in Iraq. This had very much been Churchill's policy as Colonial Secretary. Lord Thomson, the Secretary of State for Air, retained this policy, pointing out that bombing Iraqi villages was proving to be very humane. It was done with advance warning, and no British or Iraqi lives were lost, whereas formerly raids by armoured cars and machine guns had meant many losses on both sides. All the same, dropping bombs on villages, even empty villages, was not calculated to appeal to Labour backbenchers.

There was a lack of political balance between the back and front benches. The left was under-represented in the cabinet. Jimmy Maxton and Tom Johnston, for instance, were not members. Even John Wheatley, who was to be a great success in the first Labour government, was only to have been an under-secretary until he insisted successfully on being in the cabinet, at Health, where he was one of the most effective ministers.

Wheatley had been born in Ireland but was brought up in Lanarkshire. Like his father, he became a miner, but he left the mines at the age of twenty-four and after various enterprises set up a publishing company which was successful enough to enable him to send his children to fee-paying schools. He was involved in local government and campaigned for affordable housing. He was genial but forceful, the leader of the Clydesiders who went to Westminster in 1922. MacDonald had his reservations about Wheatley and his exuberant colleagues, but his abilities couldn't be ignored. In any event, he was not particularly extreme: Tom Jones, the civil service supremo, thought he was 'Pale Pink' rather than 'Turkey Red'. He was ready to accommodate to court etiquette and, indeed, became quite friendly with the King. When he told the King about the circumstances in which his parents and eight children had lived in a cottage without drainage or running water, George V responded, 'Is it possible that my people live in such awful conditions? ... I tell you, Mr Wheatley, that, if I had to live in conditions like that, I would be a revolutionary myself.'

Wheatley was very popular in the House and in the party. He could have challenged MacDonald, whom he did not regard highly, but he refused to stand against him. At that time, Housing was part of the responsibility of the Ministry of Health, and it was in Housing that Wheatley was hugely successful. As a result of his Housing Act, the government subsidised the building of a vast number of council houses. He successfully rescinded what was called the 'Poplar Order'. The Poplar Order had been issued in 1921 and put restrictions on the granting of rates relief by Poplar Council, which was thought to have been irresponsible in spending local authority money. Before parliament even met, Wheatley rescinded the order and, in doing so, put the future of the Labour government at risk at the very outset: on the second day of the new parliament, Asquith pretty well promised that Labour would fall unless they cancelled the rescission. In a brilliant speech, Wheatley said that the order had meant nothing and that existing and wider legislation already applied to Poplar. Asquith himself told Snowden that 'in all his parliamentary experience he had never heard a minister make a more convincing defence of his action'.[17] The Liberals scarcely bothered to vote on the matter and Wheatley became a star—an unlikely overweight star. Although a Clydesider—the only one in the cabinet—and politically well to the left, he had an engaging and courteous manner and found practical solutions to practical problems.

His Housing Act formed the basis of housing reforms under Neville Chamberlain in the Tory administration that succeeded the first Labour government. What Wheatley did resulted therefore in a revolution in the housing of the poor in the years running up to the Second World War. His civil servants thought that he was an even better Minister of Health than Chamberlain. In 1923–4, 86,210 houses were built. By 1927–8 there were 238,914. The quality of the houses as well as the volume was important. No longer could it be said that a single nail supported two pictures, one on either side of a common wall.

All that was good. However, evictions continued to increase, to the dismay of backbenchers. One of them introduced a private members' bill which, with Liberal support, got as far as a second reading. Without government support it died in committee, and perhaps the reddest of the Red Clydesiders, Davie Kirkwood, attacked MacDonald. Wheatley proposed that where non-payment of rent was due to unemployment, evictions should be prohibited except in limited circumstances. The whole thing ended in technical and procedural confusion. Wheatley's reputation suffered to an extent, but not fatally, as a result of this and his stance on birth control.

Wheatley saw the need for compromise between socialism and capitalism. He was aware that in his Housing Bill he was putting forward something that was less than socialist. He was frustrated. He said that the country was not ready for socialism. 'Meantime I have to take the materials which are available and use them, however much I may disagree with them, in order to contribute, however slightly, to the betterment of my fellow men.'[18] MacDonald had no such sense of tension. The betterment of his fellow men was the sum of his political philosophy. Wheatley could see that. He said that if the Tories were wise, they would make MacDonald their leader.[19] That, of course, they went on to do.

22

A MATINÉE IDOL ON THE WORLD STAGE

It was in foreign policy that the government's principal achievements—and MacDonald's own greatest success—lay. He was a natural diplomat, one of the most successful foreign secretaries Britain has had. Not only did he look like an international statesman, but he was truly interested in international relations and felt that he had a contribution to make. In the years before he came into office he had travelled widely and moved among foreign statesmen. He entered the world of diplomacy knowing many of the people with whom he would deal.

He approached the crisis in Europe from the standpoint of someone who had always disavowed the Versailles settlement, and saw the rift between France and Germany as an entirely predictable result of that settlement. He devoted a great deal of time and effort to persuading the French that they should back down from that hostile approach to the Germans, of which the occupation of the Ruhr had been the most traumatic example.

At American instigation, two committees had been set up, one to address the problem of the German economy and one to look separately at the reparations issue. The first of these was the committee known as the Dawes Committee, after its American chairman, General Dawes. The committee met just a week before MacDonald became Prime Minister. He immediately took steps to advance reconciliation in a conference in London from 16 July to 16 August.

He was now engaged with the very aspect of foreign policy which had absorbed him since the end of the war: the unfair burden imposed on Germany by the victors and its consequences. From the outset he had little sympathy with the French position at Versailles, which was that the German economy should be so crippled that she could never again threaten France's security. France had sought a neutral zone on the right bank of the Rhine and the detachment of the left bank from Germany. Britain and the United States had vetoed such an outright rejection of Wilsonian self-determination. But they had not provided an effective alternative, and France was left to rely on crippling reparations.

Reparations and war debts were seen differently by the different nations. France had of course suffered horribly at the hands of the Germans—far worse than her western allies—and the state of her economy reflected that. It was inevitable that she wanted every penny she could get from Germany. Apart from the reparative aspect of the exercise, the weaker the German economy was, the less danger Germany posed to France. Britain, which had not suffered the same economic consequences of the war, could afford to take a more liberal view. In Britain there was a good deal of sympathy for Germany—and indeed a desire that Germany should recover as an important constituent of Europe. Europe dominated by France was a prospect that worried Britain then as it had done in earlier centuries. France did not seem Britain's most obvious ally or Germany her most obvious enemy.

Britain's approach was to favour an all-round cancellation of debts. When in 1922 Arthur Balfour suggested this in 'one great transaction', President Calvin Coolidge disposed of the matter briskly: 'They hired the money didn't they?' The Americans' unconstructive response meant that *her* debtors could not let *their* debtors off the hook. Latterly France had found the Conservative government easy to deal with: now they found MacDonald much firmer in resisting the imposition of penalties on Germany. He would have no part in proposals for the 'occupation' (to use a word that was being adopted from the French at this time) of new parts of Germany. And yet, despite French perception that the new Labour government was going to be much more difficult to deal with than Baldwin and Curzon had been, the relationships between MacDonald and the French prime minister and former president, Raymond *Poincaré*, turned out to be cordial and constructive.

A MATINÉE IDOL ON THE WORLD STAGE

MacDonald had no wish to see the continuation of a *rupture diplomatique*. He sought to make the Dawes Report workable. His initial approach to Poincaré, very soon after coming into office, was a personal letter, a diplomatic irregularity which shocked the Foreign Office but to which the usually prickly Frenchman gave an unusually cordial response. MacDonald's position was delicate. The conventional spirit of mutual distrust, which had displaced the close wartime relationship, informed Foreign Office attitudes, and France's legitimate concerns about a strengthening Germany were dismissed as unreasonable and aggressive. Much of the Labour Party agreed and saw France as bent on a militaristic mission that would see the destruction of Germany. MacDonald's conciliatory line was not matched by Henderson, who continued to irritate the French by talking about a need for revisiting Versailles. MacDonald had to induce the French to buy into the Dawes Report, which recommended that the German economy should be stabilised. This could not happen while French troops were interfering in Germany. MacDonald had to win France over, and France responded to his approach. They could not indeed afford to be over-aggressive: the franc was falling.

MacDonald continued in this way. His approach was a combination of isolation and reassurance. He told France and Belgium that Britain would not stand by passively if they did not accept Dawes, but equally warned Germany that sanctions would be deployed if there were any more reparations failures. The Belgian prime minister and foreign minister visited MacDonald at Chequers and accepted his solution.

Poincaré was to be the next to visit Chequers. Again MacDonald was pragmatic, prepared to be friendly to someone he had formerly called the wrecker of European civilisation. He knew precisely what he was doing, and his approach was measured and deliberate. He said he had to see if he could break the deadlock by making a dramatic gesture. In the event Poincaré's party lost the French elections, and it was his successor, Édouard Herriot, who came to Chequers. Herriot was a weaker negotiator than Poincaré, but a man of the left and of a conciliatory disposition. It helped that Herriot had not been involved in the occupation of the Ruhr.

*

When the Dawes Report was debated at the conference in London in August 1924, MacDonald dominated. He was ubiquitous, approachable and informal. While he particularly reached out to the French, he also took pains to treat the Germans respectfully and as equals. The Dawes Plan was accepted. It was agreed that some of the Ruhr would be evacuated immediately and the rest within the year. In his concluding speech to the conference MacDonald said:

> We are now offering [Europe] the first renegotiated agreements since the war; every party here represented is morally bound to do its best to carry it out, because it is not the result of an ultimatum … This agreement may be regarded as a first Peace Treaty, because we signed it with a feeling that we have turned our backs on the terrible years of war and war mentality.[1]

What was to prove a tragic over-expression of hope was a judgement that was widely shared. David Marquand has described this time as 'the high point of [MacDonald's] Government—perhaps of his career'.[2] Without his emollient intervention, what was bound to be a difficult conference might have ended in failure.

When he went to a session of the League of Nations in Geneva a month later, he went with the reputation of the statesman who had rewritten the Versailles treaties and purged them of their imperfections. His reception in Switzerland reflected this. He was seen as a far-seeing visionary. Again he worked very closely with the French and with them arrived at what was called the Geneva Protocol, a promising plan for reconciliation between the victors and the defeated in the First World War and for a mechanism for the future on which peace would rest. The protocol—compulsory arbitration, disarmament, sanctions—was the epitome of the hopes, finally false hopes, of these years. It was never implemented.

The failure of the League was in the future; at the time it was the focus of hope for the future, and MacDonald's foreign policy was widely regarded as successful,[3] a success achieved by vigour and determination. He had put the Dawes Plan into operation, renewed contact with an isolationist United States, reduced tension between France and Germany, and established a possible relationship with Russia.

A MATINÉE IDOL ON THE WORLD STAGE

In August 1924, the *Observer* editor, JL Garvin, no friend of Labour, summed up MacDonald's performance in relation to France and Germany: 'Mr MacDonald has largely succeeded in restoring confidence to Anglo-French relations; he has brought Germany into negotiation on an equality; he has helped to bring the reparations question within sight of a genuine solution for the first time ... Labour can claim that it has made a mark upon the foreign policy of the country.'

On the international stage MacDonald was an impressive figure. He was respected by other diplomats. He looked the part, distinguished, elegant and formally dressed. There was none of the dithering, Mr Pastryish image of his later years;*none of the effete qualities that were part of Arthur Balfour's charm when he became the Foreign Secretary. He was vigorous and he engaged with his interlocutor. A Liberal journalist described him at this time as transforming the 'whole atmosphere of European relations' by the friendliness of his demeanour.[4] He brought to foreign policy, at a critical moment, an essential element of urgency. It had already been said that 'before the First World War his reputation in international Labour circles brooked no comparison ... There is no doubt that his international prestige equalled that of such men as Jaurès and [the Austrian socialist Friedrich] Adler.'[5] Now his prestige was immeasurably greater.

Even if his proposals for the Geneva Protocol came to nothing, his speeches to the League generated excitement as no other speaker did. He was described not as a diplomat but as a prophet.[6] The League of Nations was at the heart of his vision; his early reservations had been forgotten. He was the first British Prime Minister to address it, and there he was regarded as a visionary in his commitment to peaceful ways, such as arbitration, to avoid conflict. His aims were to re-establish good relations with France and to secure a French evacuation of the Ruhr, resolve the reparations question, bring Germany back into the mainstream of world politics, and have a closer relationship with Soviet Russia. He suc-

---

* 'Mr Pastry' was a television character played by the actor Richard Hearne: an old vague man with a walrus moustache, flyaway hair and pince-nez glasses.

ceeded in almost all of these aims in the few months that were available to him.

*

By then it was very clear that a Soviet Russia was going to stay. MacDonald was hardly any keener on it than the Conservatives had been, but from a practical point of view an accommodation was needed. He lost no time in recognising the Soviet Union. Britain wanted a trade agreement and some money for British bondholders whose debts to the Romanov government had been repudiated. Russia wanted a loan.

A diplomatic note recognising Russia invited representatives to a conference in London to discuss a variety of outstanding issues. The conference opened on 14 April 1924 and went on for four months. George Glasgow described the meetings with Russia quaintly as 'a series of conferences and congresses, which in the charming Russian manner talked much more than was necessary and did much less than was necessary'.[7] MacDonald took the chair at the start but then left his parliamentary under-secretary, Arthur Ponsonby, in charge.* Russia's desire for money and trade credits was very much part of the agenda. Negotiations were far from easy, not least because of difficulties from Snowden. After a tense meeting with him, Ponsonby found a solution. He rushed up to MacDonald's flat and, while choking on an apple tart, got MacDonald's agreement to the idea that there should be two treaties, a commercial treaty and a general treaty. The general treaty would, however, come to nothing unless further negotiations between the bondholders and the Soviet government won general approval. If that happened, a third treaty would be signed which would contain what the Soviets really wanted, a British government guarantee to a loan.

The Conservatives took little interest in all this. They didn't seriously challenge the treaties. The Liberal response was more complicated. Lloyd George wanted the treaties rejected out of hand.

---

* Arthur Ponsonby was another unlikely Labour politician. His father was Queen Victoria's private secretary, and Ponsonby was brought up at Windsor, going on to Eton and Balliol College, Oxford.

Asquith accepted the principle of the guaranteed loan but attacked the lack of an identified quantum and of tight conditions.

MacDonald thought that the Liberal approach to the treaties was 'mean and unscrupulous, the tactics of pettifogging & disgruntled partisans—a combination of vanity & sulks—not a pleasant judgment to write but a true one. A contemptible coterie with a lazy old man at their head whom I have always tried to respect but have failed.'[8]

The Liberals identified the treaties as the means of bringing the government down. They conflated the treaties with a more general anti-Bolshevik rhetoric. In the election that followed the collapse of this first Labour government, there was much play on the loans. One poster showed John Bull displaying his empty pockets while a Russian filled *his* pockets with money. Another had a British workman saying 'I need work', with a Russian beside him saying 'I wantski £40 million'.

*

When Ponsonby, choking on the apple tart, had met MacDonald in the flat, the Prime Minister was discussing his holidays with Ishbel. By the time he got to Lossiemouth he was starting to worry. He asked Ponsonby to send him the text of the treaties so that he could study them again, because by then it was clear that the Conservatives would join the Lloyd George and Asquithian Liberals in opposing them. Asquith was haughtily disdainful: the treaties were 'crude experiments in nursery diplomacy'. Ratification was postponed.

23

PROBLEMS CROWD IN

The first six months of the Labour government had gone well. Now it started to stumble from crisis to crisis. Some of the problems were just the sort of events which all governments face. They could have been better handled, but their real significance arose from the parliamentary arithmetic. No one had expected the Labour government to last long. From the start the opposition parties waited for Labour to fail—with luck, to fail so spectacularly that the party would disappear for ever. In those days before remotely accurate opinion polls, and when opposition parties lacked hard data on which to base the timing of an election, the instinct was simply to seize on any major slip-up to force the government's defeat at a time when its fortunes were assumed to be at a low point.

The first problem was an old friend of MacDonald's, Alexander Grant. Grant's father had lived near MacDonald's uncle in Morayshire. They were both guards on the Highland Railway. Grant did very well. After completing an apprenticeship as a baker in Forres, he moved to Edinburgh and started working for the established bakery firm of McVitie & Price. It was he who devised the still secret recipe for the eponymous 'digestive biscuit'. McVitie's flourished and Grant with them. He became general manager, and when Robert McVitie died in 1910 he acquired control of the business. McVitie's benefited from important contracts with the Ministry of Defence during the First World War, and Grant was spectacularly generous with his money. During his lifetime he gave away the equivalent of £1.5 million in today's money. Part of it was for the establishment of the National Library of Scotland. He handed a blank signed cheque to HP (subsequently Lord) Macmillan, the chairman of the Scottish National Library Committee. Macmillan was left to fill the amount in himself and entered the figure of £100,000. I wonder what Grant had had in mind. Macmillan bathetically declared that to such a benefaction 'the word "magnificent" may well be applied'.[1]

Grant was also well disposed to his old friend MacDonald. He lent him a Daimler car and £40,000 in stocks and shares so that he would not have 'to worry about income [while] absorbed in public duties'.[2] There was some discussion about whether the shares should be invested in MacDonald's own name or in the name of trustees. If the capital had been held by trustees, as MacDonald's solicitor appears to have recommended, all would have been well, but for no very obvious reason MacDonald didn't like that. The oddness of the mechanics of the loan fuelled suspicion. Grant decided that his friend should have a holding of £30,000 in the preference shares of McVitie & Price and £10,000 in trust securities. He didn't, however, buy and transfer the shares. He didn't want the transactions to be known about by his staff: MacDonald was to buy the shares as a private investor.[3] The share certificates were delivered to MacDonald in March 1924.

In April 1924 MacDonald recommended Grant for a baronetcy. There was absolutely no reason why Grant shouldn't have received an honour, and his name had already been on the list of prospective honours. His philanthropy entirely justified it. From all we know of MacDonald and, indeed, from all we know of Grant, the gift and the honour were unconnected. But the timing was unlucky, and the scandal of Lloyd George's honours sales was very fresh in the memory. MacDonald was not unaware of how things might look. In reply to a letter from Grant, thanking him for the baronetcy, MacDonald wrote to say that he was a little bit worried that in the event of his death it would emerge that he had left £40,000. He proposed that when he and Grant had more time, they should do something to put their 'private affairs in order'.[4]

But nothing had been done when on 11 September the *Daily Mail* reported that MacDonald had acquired 30,000 £1 shares in McVitie & Price and had become its second-largest shareholder. MacDonald mishandled the matter badly. He said he only owned the shares in a technical sense. He went on to tell the press that soon after he became Prime Minister, Grant had offered to give him a car but that MacDonald had said he would hire one. Grant had insisted on lending him a car, a Daimler to be precise, and the income from the shares was meant to cover running expenses.

By the end of the year the shares and the car had gone back to Grant. But the damage was done. It consisted not so much of public opprobrium—the public don't seem to have been hugely interested in the matter—as in the hurt to MacDonald's pride. In the days before social media and Sunday morning television grillings, politics were done differently. For most of the rest of his political career, MacDonald could hardly venture into a public meeting without facing a barrage of catcalls, 'Biscuits!' A more sophisticated quip at the time was 'Every man has his price, but not every man has his McVitie & Price'.

*

The next great embarrassment was the Campbell case. On 25 July 1934 an article appeared in the *Workers' Weekly*, a Communist Party periodical written by the well-known communist Harry Pollitt, asking soldiers to declare that in no circumstances would they shoot their fellow workers. The Director of Public Prosecutions, Sir Archibald Bodkin, well known as the scourge of progressive literature, brought the matter to the attention of the Attorney General, Sir Patrick Hastings.* Doing that seems an excessive reaction to a minor political stunt, but this was just a year or two after the Russian Revolution. Hastings decided that the article was an incitement to mutiny. He instructed the DPP to prosecute under the Incitement to Mutiny Act. A warrant for the arrest of the editor of the *Workers'*

---

* Hastings had been a Liberal but, disillusioned by the Asquith–Lloyd George split moved to Labour. He was a brilliant lawyer, dazzlingly effective in cross-examination, but he lacked political sensitivity, disliked politics generally and particularly hated his time as Attorney General. He thought that MacDonald had shamefully abandoned him over the Campbell case. In 1936 he appeared successfully for the editor of the *Radio Times* in the Talking Mongoose case.

Weekly, John Campbell, was issued. Hastings's decision was immediately attacked by the left of the parliamentary party. James Maxton said that Campbell had only been saying what most members of the labour movement would say.

At this stage MacDonald's role in the matter isn't clear. Although the War Office and the Air Ministry had been consulted, MacDonald appears not to have been. He told the Palace that when he heard about the matter, he sent for the Attorney General and the DPP and gave them 'a bit of his mind'. That was in itself an interference with the legal process, even if it had no practical consequences. He thought that Campbell should never have been prosecuted but that once the prosecution had started it would look weak if the government stopped it. The Cabinet Secretary's notes reveal some confusion: ministers blamed each other, and there were downright misunderstandings about where responsibility lay.[5]

By now Hastings was having serious second thoughts. He had discovered that Campbell was only acting editor, that he had fought throughout the war, had lost both feet and been awarded the Military Medal at the Battle of the Somme. He could see what he, had he been a defence advocate, might have done with the prosecution. Moreover, Campbell was now prepared to write a letter of apology. The cabinet decided that the charge against Campbell should be dropped. They resolved that in future no prosecution of a political nature would be taken without prior cabinet approval. About-turns are always politically embarrassing, but up to that point the incident had been unfortunate and badly handled, but not more serious than that.

Matters became more complicated as they came under more scrutiny. Although the Attorney General was entitled to seek the cabinet's views, he had a quasi-judicial function to discharge and could not be told what to do by the cabinet. The cabinet minute was badly framed and it gave the distinct impression that the decision not to prosecute had been taken by the cabinet. Secondly, Treasury counsel, telling the magistrates that the charge was being dropped, referred to 'representations' that the article had not been designed to incite mutiny. What were these 'representations'? It looked as if they had been made by the government, again an unconstitutional interference in the judicial process. The Communist Party then said they were sorry that the prosecution was being dropped, as they would have called MacDonald and other ministers as witnesses for the defence. The suggestion was that the government had something to hide and that the prosecution had been dropped to keep it hidden. To add to the government's problems, Campbell had still not written his apologetic letter, which was a precondition for Hastings's decision to abandon the prosecution.

MacDonald blundered all the way. When the Conservative Sir Kingsley Wood put the crucial question to him about whether he had given directions for the prosecution to be dropped, MacDonald said that he had not been consulted about the institution of the proceedings or their abandonment. Tom Jones, the Deputy Cabinet Secretary, who had been present at the cabinet meeting, said that he felt a shiver go down his spine. Maurice Hankey, the Cabinet Secretary, described MacDonald's reply as a 'bloody lie'.[6]*

MacDonald's health wasn't good at the time. He was still getting over the affair of Grant's Daimler. He felt hunted and vulnerable. He claimed that he hadn't understood Sir Kingsley Wood's question. That wasn't good enough. Hastings had faced a similar question and, by a studiously careful reply, managed to get out of danger. MacDonald either lied deliberately or was woefully negligent in preparing for a question of which private notice had been given.

The opposition parties sensed an opportunity, and the Conservatives lodged a censure motion. The Liberal Party went further and wanted a select committee to investigate the whole matter.

In the run-up to the debate MacDonald continued to act foolishly. The Lord Advocate had told him that his reply to Sir Kingsley Wood had been inaccurate. MacDonald told Hankey to alter the cabinet minutes to say that he had questioned the accuracy of the earlier minute, which dealt with the dropping of the prosecution.

---

* Hankey and Sankey. It's easy to get confused between two similar names. Both men were on the face of it slightly colourless, but they had very different careers and rose to the top of their different professions. Sankey ended up as Lord Chancellor, though admittedly not the most interesting holder of that position. Hankey was Cabinet Secretary and much else, at the centre of affairs for a long time, and in truth the man who created the modern British system of cabinet government.

He had indeed questioned its accuracy, although very belatedly. Tom Jones, who had drafted the minute, was unhappy that doubt was being cast on the accuracy of his record.

The debate began on 8 October 1924. MacDonald was strangely insouciant in the run-up to the debate. He thought that the Liberal Party had to some extent let him off the hook by not concentrating on the censure debate. They had also widened their attack on the government by coupling it with rejection of a Russian trade treaty. He misjudged the gravity of the situation. On 1 October 1924: 'The end is definitely in sight ... Had the fall come upon the Attorney alone, and had his mistake been isolated from other issues, a dissolution would have been an awkward thing to ask for ... Asquith's blunder in giving notice of the resolution to reject the Russian Treaty gives a general political significance to the vote of censure.' He seemed strangely satisfied with the way things were going.

MacDonald was not at his best when he appeared at the House.

> The accusation [that I was personally interfering] was one of those things that made one feel most resentful, and in concentrating my ideas about a personal approach, on account of personal reasons, I used an expression which, when my attention was drawn to it two days afterwards, I had to admit went a little further than I ought to have gone, because it implied not merely that I, as a person, was either approached by the Attorney General or approached the Attorney General for personal reasons—a thing I had repudiated hotly—but it also implied that I had no cognisance of what was going on. I am very sorry. I did not mean to imply that. It was simply the concentration of my personal resentment at that gross imputation which made me for a moment forget that officially, and in conjunction with colleagues, the matter was talked about when no personal considerations were in our minds at all. If I have misled any hon. Members, I apologise for having done so.[7]

The Conservatives now changed their position and said they would vote against their own motion of censure and in favour of the Liberal amendment, requesting a select committee. The amended motion was carried easily. MacDonald refused to accept that a select committee inquiry could be impartial, and was curiously determined not to face the indignity, as he saw it, of being subjected to inquiry. On the following morning he went to Buckingham Palace to ask for a dissolution.

So that was the end of the first Labour government. It had never been going to last for long, but the Campbell case was an odd way for it to fall. The case was in its way a fairly trivial issue. Sir Patrick Hastings had been overworked and was carrying a load which would normally have been shared with three or four others. The Campbell article was fairly innocent and there should never have been a prosecution. There was a lot of counterfeit indignation on the opposition benches and there were even those on the Labour benches who used the issue to further their own interests. James Maxton, for instance, was glad to see the end of a government which was not working for the kind of socialism that he wanted. MacDonald was exhausted, and the 'biscuits' controversy had been particularly wearing. His handling of the Campbell case was sloppy and incompetent. He became far too personally involved and he compromised others. In what was to be his last speech to parliament, Asquith pointed out that there had been many select inquiries before and said that his party would not seek to pack the committee. As he left the House, he said that 'he had never known a case where the government had so wantonly and unnecessarily committed suicide'.[8] MacDonald erred in thinking that a select inquiry would be hugely damaging. There is a sense that an overworked and exhausted government had lost the will to continue.

MacDonald's statements in the House had been equivocal. Baldwin had been astute in withdrawing his vote of censure, which wouldn't have been supported by the Liberals, and moving instead to support the Liberal proposal, but MacDonald had exacerbated the position by an unconvincing performance and a failure to rebut the claim that the prosecution of Campbell was abandoned in the face of pressure from the left of the Labour Party. The idea of buckling under left-wing pressure chimed in with the handling of the Russian treaty, in which MacDonald had first refused a loan to Russia, only to reverse his position under pressure from the left.

The King was friendly and sympathetic. He said he would protect MacDonald by sending him a memorandum saying that he granted the election with great reluctance, and hinted that MacDonald could say so. MacDonald said that that would bring the monarch into politics and that he would not make anything public—though he would be happy if the King sent him such a memorandum merely for historical purposes. They talked nostalgically 'about a variety of things from the *Red Flag*, the *Marseillaise* and other revolutionary songs. He [the King] remarked: "You have found me an ordinary man haven't you?" ... And tonight I go into a new world and the dead come to me and in companionship I have spent an hour with them.'

*

The election campaign which followed the dissolution was marked by the third great embarrassment of the first Labour government, the publication of the Zinoviev letter. Northcliffe's *Daily Mail* broke the story on 25 October: 'Civil War Plot by Socialists. Moscow Order to Our Reds ... A secret letter of instruction from Moscow to the British Communist Party.'

The Zinoviev letter is now known to have been a forgery, probably written by White Russian opponents of Bolshevism. It was dated 15 September and ostensibly it was signed by Zinoviev, the president of the Communist International. The *Mail* said that MacDonald had been aware of it for some weeks. In reality the Foreign Office had made it public on 22 October, together with a letter of protest drafted by the Foreign Office and substantially written by MacDonald. But the matter had scarcely been noticed until the *Mail* intervened. That altered everything.

The letter purported to be an instruction from the Comintern, as the Third International was now known, to the British Communist Party and the British proletariat in general to campaign for ratification of the Russian treaties in order to 'assist in the revolutionizing of the international and British proletariat [and] make it possible for us to extend and develop the ideas of Leninism in England and the colonies'. It went on at some length, ordering the British Communist Party to prepare for military action. The government thought the letter was genuine and accepted it as such, although MacDonald personally had his doubts. What was damaging was the idea that the government had apparently sat on the letter until it was aware of the possibility of publication. That, and the weakness of the fairly half-baked government protest, created a disastrous impression. There was no significant threat to break off diplomatic relations with Russia. The *Daily Mail* had 'expected our Socialist Ministers immediately to reply by expelling every Bolshevik in Britain'. The Northcliffe press specifically linked the 'Red Letter' to the McVitie & Price affair and the Campbell case. It was a combination of bungles, an omnishambles, always more damaging than a series of discrete ones.

The Labour government was particularly sensitive about security issues. From the start, MacDonald found that he was refused access to his own security file. Indeed, Scotland Yard suggested that the Prime Minister would not want to see the routine weekly reports on revolutionary organisations which his predecessors had seen! When MacDonald said the security services should pay as much attention to the right as to the left, he was told that 'constitutional organisations' were not subject to scrutiny.[9] He was as suspicious of Foreign Office officials as of the Home Office's. He denounced 'their winks and their smiles, and their little nudges'.[10] The ILP journalist ED Morel thought that in the Zinoviev affair, MacDonald had been imprisoned by the Foreign Office officials, as Grey had been before him. The episode revealed 'the powerlessness of a Labour Government to control the permanent officials of the Foreign Office and to protect itself against their incapacity or worse'.[11]*

MacDonald started off the election campaign with enormous vigour. On Monday, 13 October, he left Euston Station, where he addressed a crowd. He spoke again on his way north at Rugby and Crewe, and held a mass meeting in Glasgow, where he is said to have raised his audience to 'white heat'. Leaving Glasgow at nine o'clock on the following morning, he spoke before lunch at Bishopbriggs, Kirkintilloch, Kilsyth, Stirling, Alloa, Bannockburn, Larbert, Falkirk and Linlithgow. After lunch he addressed three

---

* Although Morel joined the ILP in 1918 and had been moving towards socialism for some time, he made the point that 'of course there is Socialism and Socialism, and mine is of the reasonable unmoderated kind', a positioning which reflects MacDonald's own commitment to socialism. Morel, who looked very like MacDonald, very much deserves to be remembered for much more than that. Among many other things he was responsible for exposing the evils of Leopold II's Congo.

thousand people at the Waverley Market in Edinburgh. Then on to Portobello, Musselburgh, Dalkeith, Lauder and Jedburgh. That night he spoke to four thousand people in Newcastle with another twelve thousand outside the hall listening to loudspeakers. He kept this pace up at the cost of losing his voice at stages. After the Zinoviev letter, however, he and the other Labour candidates were too preoccupied in firefighting to campaign effectively.

*

At the general election, the Conservatives increased their vote and gained 413 seats. But Labour increased their representation, too, to 151 seats. The real losers were the Liberals, who had only 40 seats. David Butler's analysis of the 1924 result shows that the Tory landslide was the result of a Liberal collapse, which suggests, although it may not prove, that the Zinoviev letter had little effect on Labour supporters.[12]

The real significance of the general election was not that Labour lost it, but that they were now, more than ever, established as the opposition to the Conservatives, the only progressive party. But the personal toll on MacDonald was evident. At one of the last meetings of the Labour cabinet, on 31 October, he was ill, anxious and exhausted. He told the cabinet that when he had heard about the Zinoviev letter, he 'felt like a man sewn in a sack and thrown into the sea'. At the last cabinet meeting, on 4 November, it was formally agreed that resignations should be placed in the hands of the King. Haldane asked the cabinet to record its 'warm appreciation of the invariable kindness and courtesy with which the Prime Minister had presided over their Meetings and conducted the business of the Cabinet'. At half past five MacDonald went to the Palace and handed in his resignation. The first Labour government was at an end.

*

How had MacDonald performed as Prime Minister? Haldane had observed Asquith in cabinet for many years and concluded that MacDonald was a better chairman. But getting government done is not the same thing as reaching decisions. His powers of delegation and organisation were not of the same quality as his chairmanship. It's difficult to assess the performance of MacDonald's government in domestic policy, its freedom of movement being limited by its minority status, in power because of the toleration of the opposition parties. Criticism of the government for its limited achievements fails to acknowledge the extent to which it was hobbled. There were certain measures that could have been taken and weren't, such as abolishing the discriminatory age difference for women voters, but most of what Labour did not do in its first period of office was due to its minority position, to MacDonald's partiality for gentle incrementalism or to a desire to avoid the appearance of undue radicalism.

Spending time analysing why the first Labour government was brought down would be pointless: the more surprising fact is that it lasted as long as it did or, indeed, that it ever came into power. It was not only a minority government, but a very inexperienced government. Only MacDonald and Wheatley enhanced their reputations, Wheatley's to the extent that for a while Beatrice Webb thought he might take over the leadership. Some did very badly, like Clynes, Sidney Webb and Colonel Wedgwood. The trade unionists did not emerge with any medals. The civil service generally went out of their way to make government work as well as it could, and relations between ministers and officials were satisfactory.*

But the lack of experience showed. It was evident in the case of MacDonald himself. He insisted on personally opening any mail that was marked as private or personal, and he installed a telephone in his room, which he answered himself. It is hardly surprising that the business of government left him exhausted.

Some of the new members of parliament had been very callow. One of them asked Sir Patrick Hastings if he would be paid if he were suspended. Parliamentary conventions were not always followed. Four members were suspended for calling another member of parliament a murderer. Another called Leo Amery 'a swine and a guttersnipe'. Amery was tough though small,† and responded with

---

* Colonel Wedgwood commented disapprovingly on the dependence of the government on the civil service. Haldane, on the other hand, thought that the dependence had been fruitful.

† It was famously said that he could have become Prime Minister if he had been six inches taller and his speeches thirty minutes shorter.

a punch to the jaw. MacDonald deprecated indiscipline. In 1926 he wrote in his diary about '[a] terrible week of strain when a row might break out at every moment ... Two of the most worthless characters in our Party caused trouble on Tuesday night.'[13] The more unsophisticated members of the party tended to feel a chasm opening up between them and the more professional people who became successful ministers. Davie Kirkwood said of John Wheatley, 'he was a magnificent success as Minister of Health, but we felt that he had left us'.[14]

24

OUT OF OFFICE

MacDonald was blamed for defeat by the usual people—Beatrice Webb, Snowden and others. Snowden talked about MacDonald's incapacity and colossal conceit, and Snowden's wife said that the party had been the victim 'of the worst political leadership of modern times'.[1] MacDonald's response was typically testy and disdainful: 'The Left Wing were out for my blood and had not the sense to restrain itself. Some members do no work but much talking and wish to turn floor of House into a sort of national street corner soap box.'[2]

The party's reluctant submission to discipline gave way. The moderate Clifford Allen, very much a MacDonald man, resigned as ILP chairman in 1925: the party had moved to the left under the influence of the Red Clydesiders at the same time as the trade unions became increasingly militant. The coup which ousted Allen put control of the ILP squarely in the hands of the Clydesiders—Maxton, Wheatley, Kirkwood, Buchanan, Campbell Stephen.

But although MacDonald was blamed for defeat by the mainstream critics and by the Clydesiders, on the whole he enjoyed the respect of the parliamentary party, and there was a feeling that party leaders shouldn't be dismissed frivolously. Accordingly, at a meeting of the parliamentary party on 24 December to elect its officers, no candidate was put up against MacDonald. But at the ILP conference in Gloucester in April 1925, Campbell Stephen moved an amendment to a congratulatory motion from the Yorkshire Divisional Council on the performance of the Labour government at home and abroad.* MacDonald was furious and was seen to grip the table with white knuckles, expostulating, 'That damned little swine—Campbell Stephen.' In his subsequent speech, MacDonald said that governing the country was a much easier business than handling the ILP conference.³

*

Apart from incidents like that there was no major threat to his leadership. The rank and file were supportive. Philip Snowden and some others, including Wheatley and Ernest Bevin, did have reservations about MacDonald's leadership, and asked Arthur Henderson to stand against MacDonald. Henderson's loyalty and decency were reinforced by his knowledge as party secretary that opinion within the party generally was behind MacDonald, and he did not join the conspiracy. By the following year, however, there was a distinct swing to the left with support for George Lansbury. In the same year the TUC began to adopt the militant rhetoric that MacDonald so disliked. He didn't regard his position as secure. In December 1927, for instance, he thought that Jimmy Maxton might be elected as a member of the executive of the Parliamentary Labour Party and that he himself would be put off it, something which he claimed not to find distressing. Later he unconvincingly talked about resignation, and complained about losing his self-respect, about being treated as if he were a worm.⁴ In June 1925 he had told a local ILP branch to 'mind its own business and regard Socialism not as the creed of a lot of blithering easie-oosie asses, who are prepared to pass any resolution without knowing its meaning, and on any subject without understanding it, but as something which requires rectitude of thought and consideration of action'.⁵

He got away with this kind of thing, but it was dangerous to leave so many enemies behind. He remained at the top of the leadership not because he was loved, but because of his evident ability. 'He was

---

* Campbell Stephen was a minister in the United Free Church of Scotland and a member of the ILP. He was a member of the House of Commons from 1922 until 1931 and again from 1935 until 1947.

the nearest to a Gladstone British Labour has had.'⁶* That ability set him apart from his colleagues, rather than bonding him to them. His relationship with Henderson and Snowden was distant. He disliked Snowden. He said he was no orator and no socialist but a Liberal in thought and action. He enjoyed sharing his dislike of Snowden with his colleagues. Snowden did much the same thing in relation to MacDonald.⁷ The cadaverous Maxton was disruptive, always hostile to MacDonald. JH Thomas was a good knockabout performer. They were individuals rather than a team.

MacDonald was not loved, but needed. In 1929, when he returned to Number Ten, it was said of him that he was more firmly in the saddle than ever. The same writer, however, referred also to his 'deliberate isolation', 'schoolmasterly' condescension, and the fact that 'he moves today in a personal vacuum that is almost painful to behold'.⁸ That said, the constituency parties were tending to adopt middle-class parliamentary candidates. *They* owed no particular allegiance to the unions or the ILP: they were the element of the party most likely to support MacDonald. At the 1929 election nearly two-thirds of the candidates were sponsored by constituencies, and union nominees were a minority in the parliamentary party for the first time.

In contrast with excitable firebrands on the left—and, indeed, in contrast with some of the flashier and meretricious figures in the Conservative front bench like FE Smith and Churchill—MacDonald was now an impressive and authoritative figure. At the beginning of the century, as has been noted, the *Labour Leader* had described him as one of the two best-looking men in the ILP. 'A quarter of a century later the dashing, *matinée* idol good looks of his early manhood had given way to a statesmanlike, yet still romantic *gravitas*, accentuated by greying hair and deeply etched lines on an expressive face. A similar combination of gravitas and romanticism marked the stirring yet elusive platform style.'⁹ The elusiveness is important. The very fact that he appeared to inhabit, and speak of, a world of abstraction, of distant and imprecise ideals, placed him above and protected him from the prosaic and sometimes squalid

---

* Until Tony Blair.

world of day-to-day politics. PD Dolan, a Glasgow ILP member, was not alone in calling him the 'Gladstone of Labour'.[10] His audiences at his set-piece speeches at Labour conferences and elsewhere were spellbound.

> He was the most handsome man I have ever known, and his face and bearing can best be described by the conventional term 'princely'. Partly this was due to the spiritual qualities which are so often found in the real Northern Scottish strain, with its admixture of Celtic and Norse blood. Some of it probably came from the paternal ancestry which gave him aristocratic characteristics and marked him as a leader of men.[11]

*

Union power had been weak during the brief post-war boom, but as the economy began to stall, the unions found more to complain about and more to do. In the face of wage cuts in the mines, the unions rallied, and in the summer of 1925 the Conservative government gave way to a threat to embargo movements of coal. The industry was given a six-month subsidy, and a royal commission was set up to look into the matter. This was the background to the General Strike of 1926.

The General Strike followed a series of other industrial crises. MacDonald viewed them as undisciplined and an irresponsible folly, created largely by the miners' leader, Arthur Cook. 'It really looks tonight as though there was [sic] to be a general strike to save Mr Cook's face ... The election of this fool as miners' secretary looks as though it would be the most calamitous thing that ever happened to the TU movement.'[12] Cook's response was that the party shouldn't be attacking union representatives who were just doing their job.

As seen from the present day, MacDonald seems remarkably detached from, as well as hostile to, the General Strike, this great demonstration of the power of working people. The strike brought Ernest Bevin into a more prominent position in the party. He had already been critical of MacDonald's lack of doctrinaire conviction. During the strike he found MacDonald's disengaged stance unacceptable, and in its aftermath he said he could not work with the party as long as MacDonald remained critical of the Miners' Federation of Great Britain. Bevin was another illegitimate Labour leader who moved to Bristol for his first job. He was general secretary of the Transport and General Workers' Union and a member of the General Council of the TUC during the strike.

MacDonald's attitude to the General Strike reflects his concept of what the Labour Party was about. He had always been against industrial action, certainly as a political device, but even as an instrument in industrial negotiation. After the strike was over, he wrote an article in the *Socialist Review*. He declared emphatically that the General Strike was clumsy and inappropriate for industrial purposes. He recommended that the unity and discipline which had been shown in the strike should be shown in politics and directed through the ballot box.

He had some sympathy for the miners at an emotional level, but he could see that their problems were a reflection of the state of the mining industry rather than the action of the owners. He was aware, too, that public opinion was far from solidly behind the strikers, and he did not wish to damage Labour by associating it with an unpopular cause. So although he attended meetings of the General Council of the TUC, he said very little. His approach was obviously not that of the union leaders. Ernest Bevin, who led the Transport Workers, complained to the National Executive Committee of the Labour Party. There was inevitable criticism of MacDonald and his role or lack of role in the industrial conflict. At the ILP's Scottish divisional conference in January 1927 a resolution was lodged criticising him and recommending a change in the leadership. An attempt to block discussion of the resolution failed, but his opponents were treated dismissively in the debate, and MacDonald's record in the war was described as heroic. All the same, the resolution was defeated by just four votes. The attempted Scottish coup prompted a second round of attacks on MacDonald in relation to his membership of the ILP delegation to the Labour Party conference, and to his nomination as the party treasurer. A majority of the National Administrative Council (NAC) was against MacDonald. The outcome was a rallying of the wider membership of the ILP. An address was signed by sixty-nine MPs who were members of the ILP, as well as ILP members who were not in parliament. The left of the ILP, John Wheatley and Jimmy Maxton among them, continued to attack the leader. Snowden was entirely against the NAC, and MacDonald was too impressed by Snowden's economic expertise to separate from him. Snowden left the ILP in 1927; MacDonald didn't. He wanted the ILP to return to his way of thinking. He did, however, give up writing his column in the ILP *Socialist Review*, and he failed to renew his membership for 1930.

A major split between MacDonald and the TUC was only just avoided. After the strike had ended, MacDonald made efforts to obtain redress for some of the strikers' grievances, and the TUC and the parliamentary party were brought together in their impotent opposition to the Trade Disputes Act.

The Trade Disputes and Trade Unions Act of 1927 was enacted by the Tories with the use of a guillotine. It consisted of a scatter of provisions that reversed advances made by the pre-war Liberal government. It made sympathetic strikes illegal; attempts to coerce the government were also illegal; civil servants were not allowed to join unions that were affiliated to the TUC; and trade union members had to 'contract in' and commit themselves to the payment of political levies, which were no longer automatic.

Labour could not stop the passage of the Act, and militancy was by now subdued, with unemployment above ten per cent. The number of days lost to strikes in 1927 was the lowest since records had been begun in 1906.

*

It's worth analysing MacDonald's position a little further. As has been seen, he had long been opposed to direct action. It was the antithesis of the conciliatory and evolutionary approach that he favoured. But he was in a difficult position. He relied on the unions, however much he disapproved of their tactics and the grandstanding of the miners' general secretary, Arthur Cook. He argued eloquently for moderation and for negotiations, but he generally refrained from saying publicly what he thought of the strikers. When the strike had failed and the government passed the Trade Disputes Act, the steam for the moment went out of unionism. His tactics had paid off. He was still there and in charge of a chastened and more united party.

Increasingly he dominated the party conferences. At the 1926 conference, for example, he spoke on twenty occasions. He could be unnecessarily provocative. He said that the leadership would not take instructions from any outside body. The ILP were the sort of outside body he had in mind, and they bridled at such language. There was already a view of MacDonald that contained much of the criticism that he faced after 1931. The left considered that he had not protected the interests of the working class. The General Strike showed that. It was said that he was leading the party to destruction. He was not conciliatory in response. He complained about the 'whirlpool' of class-conscious trade unionists. It was clear that he felt in many ways that he had more in common with moderate Conservatives than with the more extreme members of the workers' party. Churchill said that Baldwin and MacDonald were more alike than any other two men who had held the office of Prime Minister.[13]

MacDonald's standing with the ILP became weaker in the years following the General Strike, as the ILP continued to move to the left. They had supported MacDonald from 1916 till 1922. Now in April 1926, James Maxton was elected chairman and the ILP became more than a think tank. It was at the vanguard of socialist revolutionary thought. The split between parliamentary socialism and class war was distilled into the difference between those who believed in 'pure' socialism and those who wanted to see prosperity and growth. This split was reflected in attacks on MacDonald by the NAC.

In September 1926, a 'commission of enquiry' by Clifford Allen advocated a variety of doctrinaire socialist measures, all aimed at establishing a national minimum wage and an industrial commission to ensure that it was paid. All of this would be funded not from taxation but from the increased production which would be the inevitable result of higher wages. The theory was JA Hobson's 'pressure of higher consumption'. Its validity is questionable, but the practical concept of a managed economy, whatever its supposed benefits, became very generally accepted in the longer term. In the shorter term it caused problems. MacDonald knew all about Hobson's theories and had argued them in his time, but he had reservations. He was an old friend of Hobson, and well disposed to him, but what the NAC was advocating, a living wage and the apparatus which surrounded it, was very different from MacDonald's approach. In a letter to Hobson, he described the political theories that were now being wrapped around the living wage as cranky.

At the 1927 conference the ILP refused to renominate MacDonald as the party treasurer, which he had been since 1912. As a party within a party, the ILP was a peculiar institution. Two-thirds of the parliamentary party were, formally at least, members of the ILP, but the tension between the two wings was huge. Jimmy Maxton, as chairman of the ILP, presided over the production of *Socialism in Our Time* in 1926, which incorporated the living wage proposal. *Labour and the Nation* was the Labour Party programme in 1928. *Socialism in Our Time* and *Labour and the Nation* were manifestos for incompatible programmes. With hindsight, what is surprising is that the split of 1931 had not occurred earlier: here already in 1927–8 the fissure in the party is very evident. Beatrice Webb reflected this in a diary note of 1926: 'My general impression is that JRM feels himself to be the indispensable leader of a new political party which is bound to come into office within his lifetime—a correct forecast, I think.'[14]

*

In 1926, Asquith resigned as leader of the Liberal Party. Lloyd George became again leader of what had become a reunited but almost defunct version of the great party which he had led ten years earlier. He was still a youngish man of sixty-three, still possessed of enormous charm and dynamism, and unhindered by any qualms about ethics or consistency. He presided over the generation of new and dynamic policies in the 'Yellow Books' of 1928 and subsequent years. He argued for the application of the power of the state to economic regeneration in the same way as the state had taken over control of national life to win the war. Both the Conservatives and the Labour Party rightly feared a reanimation of the Liberal Party by its mercurial leader.

MacDonald had most to fear from a resurgence of Liberal progressivism. He chose, unlike the Conservative Party, to refrain from engaging in any way with Lloyd George. Lloyd George's image was seriously tarnished. The sale of honours and his political cynicism meant that he had lost that aura of nonconformist virtue which he had formerly enjoyed. It was best to keep a distance.

What MacDonald did do in these opposition years was to focus on the international level, concentrating on lofty matters of disarmament and foreign policy. So far as he noticed Lloyd George, his approach was dismissive: 'An old performer at familiar tricks.' He compared Lloyd George's promise to conquer unemployment to his promise to build homes for heroes in 1918. Lloyd George's campaign document of 1929, *We Can Conquer Unemployment*, was more than matched by MacDonald's election programme, *Labour and the Nation*. He got his tactics right.

25

STOCKTAKE

Here we are at the centre of the sandwich, with MacDonald on the way to his second government. That government ended in the most controversial events of MacDonald's political career—indeed, of his life. He moved from being the leader of a Labour government to presiding over a coalition dominated by the Conservatives. It may have been an act of sublime self-sacrifice for the national good. It may have been a self-serving betrayal of all he stood for.

Before we look at the events themselves, what do we know about MacDonald? In 1929, when he formed his second government, he was, after all, sixty-two years old. He was not emerging from nothing. He was an experienced politician and a settled personality. What have we seen of that personality that can shed light on the way he would behave during his second period in office? Was it probable that

> Just for a handful of silver he left us,
> Just for a riband to stick in his coat?*

We've learned quite a bit about MacDonald, where he came from, what he was like, what he could be expected to do. Let's try to pull it together so that it informs our understanding of what comes next.

*

---

* The lines from Browning's 'The Lost Leader' were much quoted in 1931. They have also been much parodied. The decision of the women of Girton College, Cambridge, to disband their Browning Society and spend the society's funds on chocolates produced 'They just for a handful of chocolate left us / Just for some sweetmeats to put in their throats'.

THE CANCELLED PRIME MINISTER

What do we learn from MacDonald's voluminous diaries and jottings? They are marked with a warning: 'These notes must not be presented as they stand. They are jottings to present for any future use feelings put down as I felt them at the moment and not final or considered conclusions.' That's got to be disingenuous. The disclaimer is meaningless. The notes *were* put down, clearly intended to be read in the future. There was no instruction that they should be destroyed. There must have been a therapeutic function in the huge daily outpouring, a detailed narrative which mixes political events and personal observations, repeatedly punctuated with reflections on his sense of loss.

His life was packed with lunches and dinners and much cross-party hospitality. He was not remotely in awe of personages of dignity and importance. MacDonald's wide and serious readings are punctuated with occasional odd entries—a lady from Cardiff 'writes in warm friendship: I suppose another agent Delilah'.[1] In addition to the mainstream diary, he uses, appropriately, the 'premier' diary manufactured by Smythson, for whom much later Samantha Cameron was the creative director. This diary is used not so much for the daily record but for less formal jottings, personal observations and quotations. What emerges from his diaries and his letters is a pretty remarkable man. His personal papers are extraordinary—there is nothing remotely similar for any other Prime Minister. They are full of surprises.

The long, revealing, self-absorbed tone of the diaries doesn't show him in a heroic light. Observations on serious subjects alternate with 'poems', pieces of doggerel that this most literary man would know to be pretty dreadful, on the maudlin side of sentimental, full of 'Doric' touches, the ordinary patois of north-east Scotland, the currency of the music hall or the cheap greeting card rather than the salon. It's all very odd. Most studies of MacDonald narrate the oddness but then move on without trying to assess how far that oddness informs the nature of the man. But it needs to be addressed. The easy conclusion, that he was pretty well bonkers, doesn't bear serious scrutiny. Affectation? No: MacDonald's differentness is too all-enveloping, too much of a piece. It permeates his diaries, his utterances and his behaviour, and this specialness needs

STOCKTAKE

to be accepted as being as relevant to a study of MacDonald as his views on socialism or the economy or world peace. It cannot just be referred to and then left aside.

Ramsay MacDonald lived in a world of his own more than any other Prime Minister. Disraeli had his gothic fantasies, his romantic addresses to his Faerie Queen; but compared with MacDonald, he was Charles Pooter. Harold Macmillan was a wonderful actor, but it was an act which he slipped into as consciously as the ancient cardigan he was wont to affect. He could snap out of his act, too. When he thought no one was watching, he was observed on a number of occasions discarding his Edwardian languor and running for a bus in days when former prime ministers were happy to use public transport.

*

The amazing thing is that someone who lived so much in a world of his own, of his own imaginings, a man who had so little engagement with the real world and with the real people who lived in it, could achieve the political success he did. It is usually only worldly politicians who succeed, and the desire to succeed is rarely hidden. How did MacDonald do what he did—and, equally, why did he fail when he failed? The explanations are more than two sides of the same coin.

*

He was very able. That's evident from where he got to despite his social and educational background and the lack of those influences that moulded his peers. He had great charm. It was not just a meretricious, intoxicating charisma that enchanted his huge audiences. Some elements of oratory can be learned. That was what Evelyn Waugh was hinting at when he said that Churchill had degenerated into being a mere personality. That was unfair; but something similar could be said, more fairly, of Lloyd George's skills. MacDonald's spell-binding was not artificial or learned. It was an expression of inherent personality. Beyond his platform skills there was an intimate charm which disarmed not only his domestic political contemporaries, but others from the King to foreign statesmen.

He had a vision of something more sublime than day-to-day politics. That was evident when he spoke on great issues—particularly perhaps when he addressed the League of Nations. He could be vague and nebulous, but that in itself made his idealism easier to buy into. His audience wanted to be won over. A lack of specificity made it easier: there was less to object to.

Of course, the other side to the vagueness was vulnerability, when there was *not* a desire to buy into what he was saying. And when the old man had run out of magic, what had formerly enchanted became vacuous, foolish, without real meaning. But that was in the evening of his days. In his prime he was the best speaker Labour has had—greater than Aneurin Bevan or Michael Foot.

Initially there was lots of substance to MacDonald. In his preparliamentary career he was a practical man of action. It was he who brought together the disparate and fissile elements of the Labour Party to make it credible and capable of forming a government. He saw the dangers of too great an adherence to theoretical purity. He was pragmatic, a necessary political quality as Harold Wilson knew, though not the most popular among Labour supporters of a purist disposition.

He could see that the voters in the classes he wanted to win over needed moderate and practical measures. At the end of the day, in the evolution of the Labour Party, pragmatism overcame theory. Morgan Phillips, a hugely influential general secretary of the Labour Party, said that the British labour movement drew heavily on the religious communities. 'Marxism as a philosophy of materialism, as an economic theory and as a form of political organisation and revolutionary intention and aim is historically an aberrant tendency in the development of British socialism.'[2] Harold Wilson told Bernard Donoughue that in his speeches he didn't want 'too many of these Guardian-isms, Environmentalism, Genderism … I want my speeches always to include what working people are concerned with: jobs, pay, prices, pensions, homes, kids, school, health.'[3]

Without MacDonald, things could have gone in a different direction. When looking at the early years of the Labour Party, British students of history should contrast the development of social democracy in Britain with the turbulent and dangerous transition in

France and Germany, both of which threatened to dissolve into civil war. In the case of Germany there was great violence on the streets.

In his early days, what impressed people was MacDonald's political grip and intuition, his avoidance of grandstanding or grandiose gestures in favour of a grasp of procedure and detail. This is what distinguished him from the left of the ILP—and what so angered them. Though there was plotting and talk of displacing him, what is remarkable is the extent to which he was *not* challenged.

He was not without his personal faults as a leader. He didn't think much of his colleagues; many of them were indeed not hugely impressive: it was very different in the 1945 Labour Parliamentary Party. He did not hide his disdain. An essentially lonely and self-centred man, it was predictable that he was prickly and sorry for himself. He had no hinterland of close political friends. His duchesses were no real source of support—a diversion, rather. His children mattered to him, and if Margaret had survived and continued to provide the support that she had done, his personality and career might have been very different. Among his faults could be mentioned the obverse implication of his lack of commitment to political theory. That lack of commitment allowed flexibility and pragmatism; but it also meant that there was not an item of faith round which he could ask his followers to rally. All he had to sell was himself and his success.

Other Labour leaders have clearly loved their party. MacDonald certainly didn't. From his diary on 2 March 1924: 'I hear a grumbling and I give up time to this. The fools. They have neither sense nor vision. Sometimes I think a new Party must arise.' MacDonald was at the top of a party he didn't much like, committed to a purpose which was obscure. It was a vulnerable position. But it reflected the man, a peculiar man, a man with faults as well as virtues. What he did in 1931 was the result of his faults and virtues and his settled political outlook, and not of conspiracy or betrayal. That outlook was long established before the start of his second ministry, and what followed did so inevitably, almost predictably, and needs no sinister explanation.

*

Finally, it is a great mistake to think that MacDonald's Labour Party was remotely the same as the Labour Party of 1945. The Labour Party of 1945 was not the party he had led, but the party he had allowed to exist by drawing the criticism of the events of 1931 on himself rather than on 'Continuity Labour'. The Labour Party which he left and which supplied Attlee's government was still in 1931 a vulnerable, amorphous concept. After 1945, as the distinguished political journalist Alan Watkins often observed, conference speakers routinely and regularly referred to 'this-great-party-of-ours'. That loved and lovable entity didn't exist in MacDonald's time. MacDonald and his contemporaries never romanticised and venerated the Labour Party in this way. It was, when he left it to lead the National Government, an uncompleted artefact.

The fact that Labour was respectable, electable and capable of being a great government in 1945 was the achievement of a number of individuals. Not least among them was Ramsay MacDonald, who saved the party from the taint of coalition.

26

THE SECOND GOVERNMENT

MacDonald had been nervous for a time about the strength of his political base in Aberavon. His position wasn't helped by the fact that in 1928 his agent was looking for another job. Simultaneously, Sidney Webb decided not to stand again at Seaham in County Durham.

Seaham sought to entice MacDonald with the promise that he need only visit the constituency once a year; even at general elections three or four speeches would be enough. They also told him that as member for the constituency he would not be asked, as was a very common practice, to support local organisations and charities. It's interesting to see how little constituency work a member of parliament could get away with in those days. All the same, MacDonald was reluctant to say goodbye to Aberavon, which had been good to him. Aberavon was equally reluctant to lose him but finally voted to let him go. Despite the sentimentality, MacDonald took the practical step of writing to Seaham to obtain confirmation that he wasn't to be responsible for any of the expense of the local party or the expense of the election and that he was not expected to subscribe to 'any of the score of things that in my present constituency I have to support'. His new agent told him that what he was proposing was exactly what had happened in Webb's time. 'We ought to be able to do our work here and allow you to do yours in larger issues.'

*

As the 1929 general election approached, it was clear that the Conservatives would lose their majority; but MacDonald still worried about the Liberals. Lloyd George continued to set out an appetising programme of public works. MacDonald was dubious about such Keynesian schemes but could see their appeal. He was much less worried by Baldwin, who was going to the country on the famously bathetic slogan 'Safety First'. Lloyd George still had charisma, the vigour of a young radical and of the man who had won the war; and in contrast to Baldwin and MacDonald, both distinctly staid, his magic and vigour suggested he might win the war against unemployment when neither of them could. MacDonald did not have the advantage of youth. He was only three years younger than Lloyd George. He chose to continue to ignore the wizard.

At this 1929 election, the issue, more than ever, was the economy and unemployment. The economist AC Pigou created the phrase 'the intractable million' to describe the ten per cent of the working population that was unemployed in the 1920s—but as the 1920s turned into the 1930s, the number of unemployed was nearly three million. While Keynes's *General Theory* was not published until 1936, there were many, and not all of them professional economists, who rejected Treasury orthodoxy and believed that the solution to economic stasis lay in government intervention and spending. The only political party which subscribed to this abandonment of laissez-faire orthodoxy was the Liberal Party. Conservative doctrine rejected it. The Labour Party was too timid, too committed to constitutionalism to risk a radical departure from orthodoxy. 'It was a parliamentary party with a Utopian ethic', Lord Skidelsky says in his study of the 1929–31 government. 'It was not fit for the kind of power it was called upon to exercise.'[1]

When the election came in May 1929, the Liberals were a poor third with 57 seats. Labour gained 137, to hold 288 seats, and the Conservatives had just 260. This was a real win. This time Baldwin resigned without waiting for parliament to reassemble. The King was at Windsor, recovering from an abscess which had burst, allegedly but apocryphally because of his immoderate laughter at one of JH Thomas's dirtier jokes. Baldwin tendered his resignation on 4 June. MacDonald attended on the following day, when the King was so animated that he forgot to ask him to form a government: 'Went to Windsor. King in Chinese dressing gown with pink edges and ground of yellow with patterns blue and green ... obviously had been very ill. Not always discreet in talk and thundered against two in particular who were to be Ministers. Forgot to ask me to form a government but I had kissed hands.'[2]

On 5 June 1929 MacDonald returned to Downing Street, leading the largest party in parliament. It was an amazing achievement for a new political party, and it was unquestionably a personal achievement for MacDonald.

Ahead of his audience MacDonald had returned from his constituency on 31 May 1929. When he arrived at King's Cross at 11 pm there were twelve thousand people waiting for him. He was literally swept off his feet as the crowd tried to lift him shoulder-high. All he could say before he was submerged in the crowd was, 'I am very grateful, but ...' He was driven off, to begin cabinet-making the following day.

As in 1924, he found the process difficult, but this time he consulted more. MacDonald, Henderson, Snowden, Clynes and Thomas were the 'Big Five'. They had met weekly for lunch during the first government and they had an input into the composition of the second.[3] Eleven of the old cabinet took seats in the new one, and six of them returned to the offices they had formerly held. Wheatley, such a successful member of the old cabinet, was ditched. He had taken a much more pro-striker stance in the General Strike than MacDonald and had approved a fierce anti-capitalist manifesto by Arthur Cook and Jimmy Maxton in June 1928. In a reshuffle in March 1931, some of the key players in the 1945 government would join the cabinet: Attlee, Hugh Dalton and Herbert Morrison.

Making a government involved disappointing many people, and MacDonald's sensitivity is reflected in the pain that this caused him. One man nearly fainted when he discovered he wasn't getting what he wanted. MacDonald talked about broken hearts. 'I have disappointed some good men & offended others. It has been like one of those dreaded nightmares where one meets a malign fate & can do no right.' Snowden returned to the Treasury, Clynes became Home Secretary. Sankey became Lord Chancellor, Haldane having died in 1928. AV Alexander became the First Lord of the Admiralty. He had once been a stoker in the Royal Navy, so he knew the navy from bottom to top. Margaret Bondfield became Minister of Labour and the first woman member of the cabinet. It was a strong team.

There were difficulties about the Foreign Office. A month earlier the others in the Big Five had told MacDonald that he couldn't take this office again and that Henderson wanted the job. MacDonald bridled and said that while he was quite happy to consult, *he* would make the decisions. In the event the matter was not easily resolved.

MacDonald said that Thomas should be Foreign Secretary and Henderson should move from the Home Office to take charge of unemployment policy. The King was rather in favour of Thomas. He suggested that he would be a good appointment in view of his closeness to MacDonald. MacDonald said that whoever was appointed, *he* would retain responsibility for Anglo-American relations because of their importance. The King slipped in the suggestion he had made in 1924: was it perhaps time for MacDonald's party to drop the title 'Labour'. How many of the prospective cabinet members had actually worked with their own hands? MacDonald said that he for one had done so.[4]

Henderson was very angry with the idea that he was not to be Foreign Secretary and threatened that he would take no office at all. Thomas, for his part, was clear that if he wasn't to have the Foreign Office, he wouldn't go back to the Colonial Office. MacDonald tried to resolve the matter by saying that he would indeed take the Foreign Office again, but only for two years. Henderson reiterated his threat to resign. It was Thomas who gave way. On 5 June he backed down and said that he was content to stay put—although in the event he became Lord Privy Seal with special responsibility for employment. Henderson shook him by the hand and said that left *him* the Foreign Office. The detail of the negotiations is complicated and far from certain.* Snowden's autobiography does not agree with MacDonald's diary, and neither of them ties up with a minute of the King's secretary, Lord Stamfordham, who recorded, highly improbably, that MacDonald had offered to stand down as Prime Minister and become Foreign Secretary instead.[5] The detail is not very

---

* If the reader wants to be immersed in the uncertainties, see Bassett, *Nineteen Thirty-One*, p. 28 n.

THE SECOND GOVERNMENT

important. MacDonald certainly wanted Thomas, a man he felt he could work with as Foreign Secretary, rather than Henderson, who was an awkward associate. What was significant about the tiff was a further distancing between MacDonald and Henderson.

What was also clear was MacDonald's own continuing interest in foreign policy. Even if he didn't continue to double the foreign secretaryship with the prime ministership, he did take a central role in foreign affairs. He dominated the sphere of Anglo-American relations and did not confine himself to that. Henderson repeatedly complained that MacDonald interfered in matters which were his responsibility.

MacDonald remained a commanding figure on the world stage. There was no real hint of the exhaustion or failing powers that were perceived a few years later. He was strong, physically and intellectually, with a substantial domestic power base and a considerable reputation in the world at large. In the *New York Times* he was compared to Danton, with a foreign policy 'more spirited' than Palmerston's.[6]

*

A new name was Oswald Mosley, who became Chancellor of the Duchy of Lancaster, with responsibility for assisting Thomas in unemployment. MacNeill Weir is not particularly subtle here:

> Sir Oswald Mosley was one of the wealthy men whose Lucullan hospitality MacDonald often enjoyed. Mosley had other qualities which made him a much-sought-after young man. Fortune had, indeed, been profuse in her gifts to this cultured aristocrat. He belonged to the exclusive inner circle of society. His eloquence, energy and resolution, added to a handsome presence, would have made him a notable individual in any age.[7]*

Mosley had served in the First World War. He had entered parliament in 1918 as one of the younger members of the House. Initially a Conservative, he quickly became an Independent and then joined the Labour Party. As early as 1918 he was describing himself as

---

* Weir's blindness to Mosley's faults reminds us that his criticism of MacDonald need not be taken at face value.

favouring 'socialistic imperialism'. By that he meant he wanted to take practical steps to transform society after the revelatory experience of the Great War. This sense of urgency and frustration would ultimately take him to the excesses of fascism, imprisonment during the Second World War and obloquy; but that lay in the future, and for the moment he seemed a rising star in the Labour firmament, good-looking, vigorous, forward-looking and with a good war record. He replaced Hugh Dalton on the National Executive.

What Mosley identified as the nation's problem was the gap between consumption and production, a gap which led to unemployment. His conclusion was that the state should increase purchasing power through the redistribution of wealth and by participation in a world economy or, at least, the economy of the whole of the British Empire. MacDonald found his powerful advocacy of expansionist economics more congenial than Snowden's orthodoxy. Mosley was supported by John Strachey, who would also flirt with fascist techniques at his meetings, though he never left the Labour Party. They shared a strand of thinking that supported Keynes and disliked the gold standard. MacDonald, though suspicious of the grandiosity of the schemes favoured by Lloyd George and Keynes, could see a continuity between the new thinking and that of his old friend JA Hobson and 'under-consumption'. He was, however, unprepared for the financial turmoil that lay ahead.

The great problem was, of course, the economy. Unemployment had been one of the major issues at the 1929 election and Labour promised a managed reduction in those looking for work. Six months later, Wall Street crashed. Unemployment didn't fall; it doubled to 2.75 million. By the end of 1930 MacDonald referred to an economic blizzard; weather metaphors are irresistible where the economy is concerned. In 1931 it had become a typhoon. Snowden stood for inflexible, unimaginative, financial rectitude. He was not going to reduce unemployment. Nor was it likely to be Thomas and his committee charged with getting unemployment down. Mosley and Lansbury, who were members of the committee, might try in their different ways.

*

THE SECOND GOVERNMENT

MacDonald confessed soon after the election that he had had no idea how bad the economic position was, but he grasped the problem speedily and saw that vigorous action was required. He had already suggested what he called a 'Council of State'. Now he made a formal approach to Baldwin and Lloyd George proposing a conference on agriculture and unemployment. The Liberals were prepared to join in, but Baldwin brusquely dismissed the idea of joining a conference in which the Conservatives would listen to Labour's proposals but would be unable to make any of their own. It was a two-party conference that met in 10 Downing Street on 26 June.

*

MacDonald didn't focus solely on the economy. He was much occupied with other responsibilities. His real and long-established concern for India, for instance, based on visits, research and the books he had written, was important to him. His determination to advance India on the road to something like independence was fixed.

Lloyd George perceived the range of the Prime Minister's concerns. In the debate on the King's Speech he said that MacDonald was simply 'too busy to do his job'.[8] If the government had no single solution to the economy, that was partly due to their different responses to the problem. Vernon Hartshorn, who had been Postmaster General in the first Labour government and had responsibility for employment policy now, tended to the view that fiscal reforms were needed. MacDonald was sympathetic to that; but Snowden would not countenance anything of this sort, and when the question of tariff adjustment came before the cabinet, MacDonald was on holiday in Lossiemouth.[9] The scale of the economic problem required huge questions to be addressed, questions about how far the state should intervene to interfere with economic swings. The idea of borrowing to reduce unemployment was a very new one in the 1920s and 1930s, and how to create a surplus by stimulating growth is one that still eludes governments.

The government did not do nothing. A Pensions Act provided for widows between the ages of fifty-five and seventy. Housing Acts addressed slum clearance and increased rural housing. A Town and Country Planning Act started the process of controlling and shaping planning nationally. There was quite a lot else, even if it were peripheral to bigger, unaddressed issues. By 5 June 1930, the first anniversary of the formation of the government, MacDonald thought that the government had done reasonably well: 'First anniversary of the (or a) Labour govt ... Well, I think, on the whole we have made good, but the state of the country and the Empire has been ominous.'[10]

*

Did MacDonald take a detached interest in domestic affairs both in his first administration and then in his second one? In the period we are looking at, if MacDonald's foreign excursions are added to his holidays in Lossiemouth, he spent about half the year away from London.[11] His interest in foreign policy, so evident during his first period in office, had persisted in opposition. MacDonald had closely followed what was going on at the Locarno Conference in 1925 and elsewhere. Henderson's approach, by contrast, was crude and lacked nuance. He relied on force or the threat of force to maintain the peace: MacDonald very strongly believed in the use of the League of Nations and diplomacy as an alternative to coercion. Thus he considered it to be essential that *he* should frequently attend the meetings of the League in Geneva. The fact that he spoke there to such general satisfaction, including his own, helped. He enjoyed the reception. And he believed what many people throughout the world believed: that the League would create a system which would render war irrelevant.

There were many other international issues which only MacDonald could deal with. There was an Imperial Conference in October–November 1930. And 'I am thinking of nothing but India'. Commissions of inquiry and policy initiatives by viceroys culminated in the Indian Round Table Conference in London of November 1930–January 1931.

MacDonald, very unusually for a Prime Minister, had, as we have seen, visited India and written books about India. He was truly interested in its problems and he wanted very much to move things forward. He supported the idea of dominion status for the subcontinent. He was much more liberal than most British politicians, even if what Britain, MacDonald included, was prepared to give fell short, very short, of what Indian leaders wanted. The Round Table Conference involved detailed, exhaustive work and was ultimately unproductive. The reason for that was a fundamental lack of a meeting of minds, a disengagement that would persist to the end of the Anglo-Indian debate. MacDonald and the Conservatives, particularly Baldwin, worked well together on India. Baldwin, to his credit, because he faced lots of opposition on the matter from his back benches, was determined to see some machinery established that would propel India at least some of the way towards self-government. When the Round Table Conferences failed, he and MacDonald worked together fairly harmoniously to promote the approach which would finally result in the Government of India Act of 1935.

At an imperial level, there was a general and growing feeling among the dominions that their status needed to be reassessed. Lloyd George and his government had fallen in 1922 as a result of the Chanak crisis, when he had proposed war against Turkey by the United Kingdom without consulting the dominion governments. They had entered and left the First World War on Britain's say-so, but they made it clear that times had changed. Negotiations culminated in a conference and the legislation of 1931 known as the Statute of Westminster, which formalised the changed relationship between Britain and her overseas possessions, providing they were white.

*

There was also the problem of the United States. In the years following the First World War, diplomatic relations between Britain and the United States had deteriorated very badly, particularly in relation to naval matters. In the inter-war years the annual US Navy war games proceeded on the assumption that the next war would be between the United States and Great Britain.

At the end of the war, the US Navy Board had recommended that the American Navy should be as strong as the most powerful foreign navy. This was the demand for 'parity'. Britain had worked on the basis of the 'two-power standard', which meant that Britain's navy should be as strong as the next two most powerful navies added together. The detail of the negotiations to reconcile the two positions was very complicated. In the Washington Treaty in 1922 it had been agreed that America should have parity in capital ships—the biggest warships. Whether there should be parity in cruisers was more difficult. Britain argued that because of its far-flung empire it needed a huge fleet of small cruisers. Should parity be defined by the number of ships or their tonnage? Negotiations were tense, and were exacerbated by the fact that the Americans wanted to combine parity with a general reduction in arms, a requirement which flew in the face of British treaty obligations to Japan, France and Italy. Another complication was created when the American delegate at the League of Nations, Hugh Gibson, proposed that parity should take into account factors such as ships' ages and gun calibres.

Nine days after MacDonald came into office, General Dawes, formerly of the Dawes Plan and now American ambassador to Great Britain, steamed into Southampton. Dawes has some unlikely achievements. He was very musical and in 1912 he wrote a composition for piano and violin known as 'Melody in A Major'. Forty years later lyrics were added and it was transformed into the song 'It's All in the Game', which became a number-one hit in America and later in Britain too. It has been recorded by artists ranging from Cliff Richard to Donny and Marie Osmond. Dawes is the only US Vice President who has written a number-one pop hit. He and Bob Dylan are the only people who have written a number-one pop hit *and also* won the Nobel Prize, Dawes for the Dawes Plan.

On 16 June, two days after the musical general arrived, MacDonald met him at Forres, near Lossiemouth. Dawes was a 'cordial & earnest man, spare, thin, in navy stripe & odd-looking pipe'. The meeting seems to have gone well, and at a second meeting, on 25 June, they agreed that a five-power naval conference should be held either in Washington or in London, providing progress was made in the meantime on the methodology of comparison in relation to cruisers.

MacDonald accepted the principle of parity and said that Britain would slow down work on a couple of its cruisers. He hoped that America would do likewise. America said they would do just that. But that was not quite the end of the matter. Before America would agree to a preliminary accord, there was acrimonious disagreement

THE SECOND GOVERNMENT

on big issues, like how many cruisers Britain actually had—as well as on a myriad of very minor ones.

MacDonald, rather than Alexander, the First Lord of the Admiralty, was very much in control of the British negotiations. As always he was a negotiator of great charm whose approach was to win his interlocutor over as a personal friend. He did this very effectively with Dawes, even sending him a copy of his biography of Margaret. He charmed him with little personal touches, telling him that one of his letters was being written 'early in the morning when only the birds are up and even they are sleepy'. Dawes succumbed to the charm, but the Navy Board, back in Washington together with President Hoover and the anglophobe Secretary of State, Harry Stimson, weren't so vulnerable. The American naval establishment was institutionally hostile to Britain even in the months after America's entry into the Second World War.

It says an enormous amount for MacDonald's persistence and his control of detail that he was able to keep the negotiations going: at times they came very close to breaking off. 'Wordy dispatch in bag from America,' said MacDonald on 17 August 1929. 'It insists upon treating us as a potential enemy & is disappointed when we do not do everything it tells us.' To that was added the international implications. The Washington Treaty had provided that the ratio between American, British and Japanese fleets should be 5:5:3. Now the Japanese were demanding their part of the ratio should be 3.5. An explanation to Dawes was typically Ramsayesque: 'There are shadowy entities behind me. A spirit photograph would show you unaccompanied, but round me would be the ghosts of the other nations.'

MacDonald made substantial concessions, but they were very far from all America demanded. It was not clear what the outcome would be when MacDonald, with Ishbel, accepted an invitation from Hoover to visit the United States, and set sail on the *Berengaria* at the end of September. They would not have been on that ship but for the operation of reparations, which so interested MacDonald. The *Berengaria* had begun life as the *Imperator*. She had been a German liner before the war but at its end was allocated to the Allies and, ultimately, the Cunard Line.

This visit to the United States was the first by a British Prime Minister in office. If he did not receive the warmest receptions from

THE CANCELLED PRIME MINISTER

the US Navy Board, he did receive a very warm welcome from Americans generally. He was met in New York by a nineteen-gun salute and a ticker-tape parade. He stayed with the President on his ranch and addressed the Senate. His high moral tone went down very well. He told the Senate that as long as negotiations were conducted

> by correspondence over thousands of miles of sea, we shall never understand each other at all. But in these democratic days, when heart speaks to heart as deep speaks to deep and silence talks to silence, personality, personal contact, exchange of views by the lips, sitting at two sides of a fireplace, as it was my privilege to do this weekend with your President—these things are to be as important as anything else in laying the foundations of an enduring peace all over the world.

This warm, informal approach was very much his own. It seems unremarkable today, but it was groundbreakingly original at the time. The *New York Times* described him as 'unpretentious, unspoiled, with dignity fitting his position, yet with a simple dignity of one who knows how fleeting is fame and by what aid of good fortune men arrive at eminence'.

By the time MacDonald left, the papers had warmed to him even more:

> The British Prime Minister leaves New York today for Canada, with every token and testimony that his American visit has been an overpowering success. Though he modestly puts away the personal aspect of it, it has been a distinct triumph for Ramsay MacDonald, the man. His bearing has been perfect ... his eloquence has been that of elevation of mind and nobility of purpose. On divers strings he has sounded the one clear note of a passion to secure established peace on earth through every reasonable and honorable means. Such speaking as his, coming to a climax as it did in his magnificent address on Friday night, has seldom been heard in any country, from the lips of a citizen of another.

MacDonald went on to Canada, and after two weeks there he returned to London and to the naval conference, the so-called London Conference, on 30 January 1930. The conference went on

THE SECOND GOVERNMENT

till April. It was a difficult, long series of negotiations. Britain, the United States and Japan agreed to a formula between themselves, but the other signatories, France and Italy, were not bound by that. In Washington Britain had effectively conceded parity with America. How were the others to be fitted into that?

US Secretary of State Henry Stimson led the American delegation. The French delegation was led by the prime minister, André Tardieu, accompanied by the foreign minister, Aristide Briand. The Italian were led by their foreign minister, the Japanese by their former prime minister. The British team consisted of MacDonald, Henderson, Alexander and William Wedgwood Benn.* MacDonald was the chairman of the conference.

The negotiations went well. France and Italy were not tied down to a ratio in the way the other three countries were, but the agreement contained hope for the future: there was an understanding that negotiations between Britain, France and Italy were to continue. There was a 'holiday for battleship construction' and various other commitments and undertakings which were intended to lead on to a continuing reduction in armaments. Events put paid to most of these hopes, but the agreement was worth achieving if viewed without the disappointing light of hindsight. 'Of the extremely modest foreign policy achievements of the second Labour government, the 1930 London Naval Treaty was the most notable.'[12] It was very much MacDonald's achievement.

---

* William Wedgwood Benn, First Viscount Stansgate, was a remarkable man, much more than Tony Benn's father. He was a radical of the old nonconformist tradition. He left aside his career as a Liberal minister to fight in the First World War. He saw fierce combat at Suvla Bay in the Gallipoli campaign He declined Lloyd George's request to become Chief Whip and trained as a pilot in the Royal Naval Air Service. He was mentioned in dispatches twice, and awarded the DSO, DFC, Chevalier of the Légion d'Honneur, Croix de Guerre, Italian War Cross and Italian Bronze Medal for Valour. After the war he joined the Labour Party and in MacDonald's second administration he was an able Secretary of State for India, working well with the Tory Viceroy, Irwin, whom he inherited. In 1939, at the age of 62 he interrupted his political career again. He enlisted as a pilot officer in the RAF, ending up as an air commodore. Although he was officially not allowed to fly, he took part in operations. He was again mentioned in dispatches.

27

CRASH

Bad though they may have seemed at the time, the early days of the second Labour government were nothing compared with what was to come. There was a modest trade revival for several months, and in November 1929 unemployment had been reduced by 100,000 from the same time a year earlier. Then the tide turned, and it turned very fast.

By January 1930 unemployment was no longer down by 100,000 against the previous year. It was up by the same amount: the total of those unemployed was now 1,533,000. By June it was 1,946,000, by December 2,725,000 and by June 1931, two years after the election, 2,735,000.[1]

Writing in 1977, David Marquand saw the concurrent calamities of 1930 as arriving at a moment in what he called 'the Keynesian revolution' before the certainties of the new doctrine had prevailed. He conceded that 'the classical system, which Keynes replaced, possessed great intellectual power as well as the weight of tradition and authority'. He implied, though, that the superior qualities of the new theories were evident to those with open minds.

Today we can see that Keynesianism contained some truths, but not all truths and not truths for all problems. There are limits to the extent that one can spend one's way out of trouble, as Keynes knew. Not a lot later than the time that Marquand wrote his book, and after twenty-five or thirty years of broadly Keynesian policies and unparalleled growth in living standards, new concerns arose: worries about inflation, the cost of the Vietnamese war, spikes in oil prices. New political priorities emerged, for which Keynesianism no longer seemed the obvious answer.

THE CANCELLED PRIME MINISTER

Keynes argued that government spending created demand and thus lowered unemployment; and that this and not the specific object of the spending project was what mattered. The alternative view was and is that borrowing is only benign if it generates more direct income than it costs.

In 1930–1, the financial and the political world were as absorbed with trade as with pure economics. We have seen the importance of the debate between the free-traders and the protectionists. In the context of free trade, a country which adopted Keynesian policies would face serious problems when extra spending power had been dissipated in the purchase of foreign imports that did not benefit the domestic economy. Keynes himself favoured a degree of protectionism. It is facile to criticise MacDonald for not introducing measures that would have worked ill for an open, trading economy. Even in the 1970s after the collapse of the Bretton Woods* system, a generation after MacDonald's death, the need for international coordination of economic policies remained unaddressed.

The certainties of one generation do not necessarily pass on to the next. Monetarism, once so enthusiastically advocated by Milton Friedman and others, became so discredited that central bankers ceased at the beginning of the present century to pay any attention to monetary aggregates. It was argued that changes in the money supply didn't appear closely correlated with inflation. The Bank of Scotland economist Charles Goodhart told the European Central Bank's forum in Portugal in September 2021 that there was no longer a general theory of inflation.[2]

In the 1960s and 1970s, when David Marquand was writing his magisterial and on the whole fairly approving biography of

---

* A major international economic conference took place in the Mount Washington Hotel, Bretton Woods, New Hampshire, in 1944. It sought to establish a post-war international economy that would be more stable than that of the inter-war years. The agenda for the conference was immense, but its essential purpose was to avoid the multilateral relationships between individual countries and the price of gold, and this it sought to do by tying currencies to the dollar and the dollar to the price of gold. The system failed when, partly as a result of dollar inflation to meet the cost of the Vietnam War, a dollar shortage turned into a dollar glut and President Nixon suspended convertibility in 1971.

MacDonald, he criticised the National Government's recourse to austerity in the face of the economic crisis of 1931. This is at the heart of the 'intelligent' charge against MacDonald. Marquand was not arguing a case or postulating a novel theory when he suggested that the proper response to the crisis would have been to spend money, to stimulate the economy by having recourse to borrowing or even printing money. Marquand's criticism flowed from a certainty of the rightness of Keynesianism, which was unchallengeable in its day. Economics was seen as divided sharply between pre- and post-Keynes. For example, on 7 November 1957 the economist Roy Harrod wrote to the Prime Minister, Harold Macmillan: 'The idea that you can reduce prices by limiting the quantity of money is pre-Keynesian. Hardly any economist under the age of fifty subscribes to it.'[3] A Canadian-born economist, Harry Johnson, wrote, 'in post-war Cambridge they still talked about "Maynard" as if he might walk into the room at any moment'.[4]

But Keynes's idea of deficit financing was anathema to post-Gladstonian economists and was, putting it very mildly, highly questionable in the 1930s. Indeed, Keynesianism came to be interpreted much more widely than Keynes would have wanted. Before the end of his life he was pointing out that one could not go on deficit financing indefinitely. Lord Skidelsky, writing of the 1950s, said, 'Keynes' "general theory of employment" was not quite as general as he believed.' In the decade of which Skidelsky was writing, the Chancellor of the Exchequer, Peter Thorneycroft, and his entire Treasury front bench team resigned in protest against the allegedly inflationary policies of Keynes's protégé Harold Macmillan. It was 'inconceivable' that Keynes wouldn't have modified his ideas, 'but he was no longer there, and his book was'.[5]

It is undeniable that Labour had no novel solution to the problems of the economy in 1930, any more than the National Government did later, but economic thinking at the time, except at the edges, had no theory available to them. It is facile to say that a Keynesian approach, still a minority concept and much challenged, should have been adopted. Equally, protection, for which Keynes was arguing, was scarcely viable. Political thinking was moving away from free trade, but the process was tentative, involving the rejection of a theory which had been unchallengeable for most of a century. There might be nibbling around the edges, but the wholesale adoption of protectionism was another matter. MacDonald had already talked of a protectionist tariff, but there was still far too much commitment to free trade for that to be a starter as a matter of general application. Snowden, for instance, would never have dreamt of challenging the orthodoxy that held free trade as sacrosanct.

The new ideas about deficit finance were at far too early a stage in their development to have been applied in 1931, but the fact that they were known, the fact that they existed, was enough to undermine some confidence in the old approach. That approach was to react to a downturn with austerity, tax cuts and reductions of benefits.

Snowden represented the old orthodoxy. MacDonald was not unorthodox, but he wasn't quite as blinkered as Snowden. Before he went to the United States and Canada, MacDonald had already hinted to Snowden that the harsh prescriptions of the Governor of the Bank of England, Montagu Norman, might require to be treated with caution. On his return, he presided over a number of lunches in 10 Downing Street with an impressive array of economists, Keynes, Hobson and GDH Cole, businessmen like Lord Weir, Sir Andrew Duncan, speaking for engineering and steel, and Walter Citrine, the general secretary of the TUC. Snowden attended on occasion, as did the permanent secretary at the Treasury. In January 1930 this process crystallised into an Economic Advisory Council: fifteen members supported by a staff of economists and civil servants. MacDonald was not committed to a partisan or dogmatic approach. His reach towards a consensual approach prefigured that of Harold Wilson and in particular Edward Heath, fifty years later. His efforts were not much more popular than those of Heath and Wilson.

*

Margaret Bondfield's Unemployment Insurance Act of 1929 started by annoying the trade unions and then, when concessions were made, ended by giving the impression of weakness. It was followed by a bill to revitalise the coal industry, reducing miners' hours at the cost of concessions to owners. No one was very enthusiastic, and the legislation was opposed by the Conservatives and the Liberals,

Winston Churchill and Lloyd George. 'Winston Churchill conspires against his leader & with Lloyd George ... they are two of the most sinister politicians in our public life today.'

*

This was the background to the Mosley initiative. On 13 December 1929 Mosley went to see MacDonald and told him that he was preparing a memorandum on economic questions. In the middle of January 1930, he sent the final draft to Keynes, who approved it. He sent the memorandum to MacDonald on 23 January 1930. This is the document known as the Mosley Memorandum. The memorandum followed on a book which Mosley had written with John Strachey, his parliamentary private secretary. He advocated Keynesian policies which were not based on Keynesian theories. Mosley, along with George Lansbury and Tom Johnson, was finding it difficult to work with JH Thomas. He sought a new approach; and the memorandum was in some ways a distillation of his developing philosophy, rather than a practical political document. Economics were there: he wanted to see an expansionist public works policy on the lines that Keynes and Lloyd George were arguing for. But he also wanted an overhaul of government and a mobilisation of the nation's resources on something like a wartime basis.

MacDonald was tolerant about this surprising missive from a relatively junior minister. He referred the brash document to a committee under Snowden. There was never any possibility that it would be accepted. It implied a wholesale change in the way in which the country was governed and a radical reorganisation of the machinery of government.

Mosley had shown his memorandum to a number of people, including John Strachey. Strachey in turn had shown it to journalists. An article appeared in the *Manchester Guardian* on 7 February 1930. The government members of the committee which had been set up to examine the memorandum, Snowden, Arthur Greenwood and Margaret Bondfield, were outraged. Thomas raised the question of Mosley's disloyalty at a cabinet meeting on 19 February. The proposals which this fairly junior minister was making to the cabinet were indeed presumptuously ambitious. They involved a reduction in the importance of the role of the Prime Minister, who, under Mosley's proposals, became no more than chairman of an executive committee consisting of senior officers of the government. A diagrammatic representation in an appendix to the memorandum demonstrated the overhaul of the Prime Minister's department.

The impression that Mosley was trying to hijack policy was reinforced by the narrative in the memorandum that what he was advancing was the result of discussions he had had with George Lansbury and Tom Johnson over a period of many months.

Snowden's committee reported on 1 May, saying that the memorandum 'cut at the root of the individual responsibilities of ministers, the special responsibility of the Chancellor of the Exchequer in the sphere of finance, and the collective responsibility of the cabinet to Parliament'. This of course was precisely what it was intended to do. When the cabinet decided to take no further action, Mosley tendered his resignation. He was persuaded to withdraw it for the moment.

*

MacDonald spent a lot of time on Mosley, despite the fact that at this point he was exhausted and alarmed by evidence of lapses of memory. There couldn't be a meeting of minds between an orthodox Prime Minister and a young man who told him that a Napoleon could spend £200 million in three years if he wanted to. MacDonald tended to see the memorandum as a simple attack on Snowden and his policies, but it was really an argument against the current system of cabinet government. Mosley finally resigned on 20 May. In his resignation letter he reminded MacDonald that in the letter that accompanied his memorandum, he made it clear that he had reached 'the very definite conclusion that it is impossible to continue as at present'. He said that the committee which had looked at his memorandum 'presented a report which not only rejects in its entirety the memorandum but also adopts the position which would involve the rejection of any effective alternative for present policy'. He went on:

> In these circumstances, I regret that I hold it to be inconsistent with honour to me to remain a Member of the Government. On the back benches ... I shall claim the right always accorded by our party to its members to ask the party to adopt a policy which I

believed to be more consistent with our programme and pledges at the last election.

It is to me a matter of great regret that as a Minister I have no means of appeal to the judgment of our party except by resignation from the Government.[6]

Two days later he attacked the leadership of the party. In December 1930 an expanded version of the memorandum was published signed by, among others, fifteen MPs. MacDonald's comment in his diary on 22 May 1930 was: 'Heavy day finishing with Party meeting on Mosley. His behaviour crushes one's value of friendship.'

*

In view of the direction in which Mosley was to move and the way in which he is remembered today, it is interesting to note that an economically literate but progressive member of the Conservative Party like Harold Macmillan said that he personally agreed with almost everything in the memorandum. Macmillan recorded in old age how he had been struck by Mosley's acute intelligence and energy. 'Indeed I might have been tempted to join his New Party if I could have seen any practical hope of its success ... Mosley's story is really a sad one, something of a tragedy. Great talents and great strength of character were thrown away in vain. Had he waited, he might have been supreme.'[7]

*

The Mosley Memorandum was an anomalous blip, but the economic problems persisted. The government faced a censure motion from the Conservatives on 28 May but survived. A cabinet reshuffle followed. Attlee replaced Mosley as Chancellor of the Duchy of Lancaster. MacDonald saved Thomas, whose position was very shaky. He kept him in the cabinet, but he was moved from being Lord Privy Seal to the Dominions, which he had refused before.

Thomas was replaced by Vernon Hartshorn, a Welsh trade unionist with a Dickensian name. Hartshorn was provided with strong back-up, including a secretariat of civil servants under the formidable Sir John Anderson. MacDonald himself took charge of a panel of ministers. Superficially, things were being done, but there was little intellectual engagement. 'The machinery, or some of the machinery was there. The will to make use of it was not.'[8] In practice Hartshorn continued to do things much as Thomas had done.

*

MacDonald found the economic problems, which he was not well qualified to deal with, difficult and frustrating. He saw the future in terms of making capitalism work, not in its failure. All sorts of possibilities were discussed. At the end of May, there were even approaches to Lloyd George. The Liberal leader, delighted to be called back to the centre of the stage, agreed to join in discussions if he were allowed access to papers and officials. He got his way and was indeed invited to meet with an ad hoc committee appointed for this purpose. MacDonald was making a big concession here. He was still contemptuous and suspicious of Lloyd George, and probably rightly so: on 9 June, the Liberals moved an amendment to the Finance Bill, arguing that while they were obliged to do so as a matter of principle, they had no wish to bring the government down. In the event, when the division took place Conservatives appeared from hiding holes all around parliament and brought the government to within three votes of defeat.

As the weeks and months passed, the available options seemed more and more limited. There was no appetite for expansion via public works, and the alternative seemed to be to batten down the hatches, using tariffs to discriminate against imports and thus support the domestic economy. The Conservatives were increasingly coming to question free trade, and MacDonald found himself doing so too. Among the Tories, dogmatic supporters of free trade, like Churchill, argued that abolition would put up the price of food. On the other hand agriculture, which was in great difficulties, appeared to need defensive quotas on imports. The Ministry of Agriculture tried to defend the home wheat crop by establishing a marketing board.

These desperate times justified talk of desperate remedies. Tories were attacking the sacred free trade; Lloyd George was advocating a coalition and was talking to the Tories about electoral reform. There was increasing talk about a National Government as 1930 went on. MacDonald saw its attractions, even if not as an immediate possibility. The Round Table Conference on India slightly strengthened the idea of cross-party cooperation that would rise above tribal differences. Baldwin wanted a legacy achievement and was prepared to work on India with MacDonald, ignoring Churchill and the Tory right. As 1930 came to a close and as economic problems steadily increased, talk about a National Government continued in a desultory way and some practical cross-party cooperation took place.

*

There was no reason why 1931 should be any better, and it was not. The government's weakness was emphasised in February when the Trade Disputes Bill was withdrawn after the opposition parties carried an amendment banning general strikes. Another defeat was inflicted on legislation attacking the university seats. Weekly talks continued between MacDonald, Lloyd George and their respective colleagues. There were probably thoughts of a Lib–Lab coalition. The evidence is not conclusive. MacDonald wrote to Passfield,[9] the ennobled Sidney Webb, saying that he was having great difficulty in making ministerial appointments from the House of Lords. 'We have not the material in our Party that we ought to have. The solution will have to come, I am afraid, by moves which will surprise all of you.'[10] He may have meant that he would have to appoint Liberal peers to the government. Lloyd George dictated a memorandum to his secretary, Frances Stevenson, saying that MacDonald wanted a coalition in which he would be Prime Minister and Lloyd George would be Leader of the House, Foreign Secretary or Chancellor of the Exchequer.[11] Lloyd George's observations can never, however, be taken at face value.[12] In the summer of 1931 he was out of action, first undergoing a difficult operation and then convalescing. But for that, the crisis of 1931 might have been very different. He might well have dominated a coalition rather than been left to criticise it.

28

ECONOMIC CRISIS

On 11 May 1931, Creditanstalt, the hugely influential Austrian bank founded by the Rothschilds in 1855, failed. It was an event of momentous significance for Europe. Three weeks later the German Chancellor Heinrich Brüning and foreign minister Julius Curtius came to see MacDonald at Chequers. They told him that Germany's banking system had now been hit by a wave of withdrawals and that they could not continue to pay reparations. MacDonald was sympathetic to the Germans. He had of course always thought that reparations couldn't and wouldn't work. He wrote to the American Secretary of State, Henry Stimson, pressing for a sympathetic approach to Germany. On 20 June President Hoover proposed a year's moratorium on reparation payments and more generally on inter-governmental debts. MacDonald was delighted but France was not. The most that France would agree to was continued reparations from Germany balanced by a loan to Germany.

MacDonald was incensed. Britain and the United States agreed on a conference but the French declined to attend. MacDonald was clear that the French were using this financial crisis to crush Germany. He was suspicious, too, of his own Foreign Secretary, Arthur Henderson, who was indeed conniving with the French to frustrate efforts to resolve the crisis. The Governor of the Bank of England, Montagu Norman, on the other hand, hated France and declined to go to the French health resorts in case he bumped into French bankers. He described French policy in relation to defeated Germany as vindictive. He maintained that France was injecting seized German banknotes into the German economy in order to exacerbate inflation, and he blamed the French for making it difficult for Britain to maintain the sterling rate by hoarding gold. The French were equally unhappy with Norman and remembered that he had declined to help France at the height of her financial crisis in 1926.

A meeting in Paris achieved nothing, and an international conference that opened in London on 20 July fell apart. It had been agreed there would be no discussion of reparations. By the end of the conference on 23 July, it was becoming clear that Britain's financial problems were greater than Germany's. Till then no one had quite understood that what was at stake was not just the German economy. By July it was clear that the crisis was Europe-wide. By 1 August, the Bank of England had lost a quarter of its reserves.

*

The collapse of Creditanstalt, which controlled twenty-seven per cent of the assets of the Austrian banking sector, is usually taken as the start of the Great Depression. The effect of the collapse was felt throughout Europe, but particularly in London, where a high proportion of European banking assets were invested. A run on gold began. The government attempted to redress the situation with the help of loans from France and the United States, but London's credit became increasingly suspect in Paris and New York, and the publication of the May Report, referred to below, exposed the fragility of the City.

*

The strain on the government was immense. In May 1931, at one of the weekly meetings of the Big Five, Henderson announced that he wanted to go to the House of Lords, where he could succeed Lord Parmoor as leader. Snowden too was feeling the strain and was anxious to retire. According to him, Passfield and Beatrice Webb pressed him to give up the Chancellorship, and go to the Lords, where *he* would be leader of the party and Colonial Secretary. Passfield himself begged to be allowed to retire. Snowden, despite pressure from the Webbs, felt it his duty to remain as Chancellor for the moment and try to reduce the national debt, as Gladstone would have done.[1]

*

ECONOMIC CRISIS

Initially it seemed that the economic problem centred on a problem of liquidity rather than confidence. A committee set up under Sir George May, a remarkable man who started out as a clerk with the Prudential Assurance Company at the age of sixteen and who demonstrated great financial acumen as head of the American Dollar Securities Committee during the War, had looked at ways of reducing expenditure. The committee was born of a Liberal amendment to a Conservative motion of censure. Snowden accepted the amendment, stressing the gravity of the economic situation. When the May Report came out at the end of July, it forecast a budget deficit of £120 million and recommended sweeping economies of £96 million, which included a twenty per cent cut in unemployment benefits. The report was not innovative: it said that 'an unduly large proportion of the national income' was already taken in taxation; on the other hand public expenditure had a negative effect on the economy and should be reduced. Importantly, the committee proposed that the bulk of the savings should come from a reduction in unemployment spending of £66.5 million. Those out of work would lose ten per cent of their employment benefit. The essence of the May Report was that austerity in the shape of benefit cuts could not be avoided. The majority report attributed the problem to governmental extravagance; the Labour members said the problem was the burden of fixed debt. They wrote a minority report in which they argued for raising taxes on holders of national debt and other fixed-interest investments. They too accepted cuts, but limited cuts. The leadership accepted the full implications of the May Report. This fissure was what split the Labour Party.

On 31 July, MacDonald headed for Lossiemouth. Once he was there he wrote to Keynes and asked him for his views. Keynes wrote at length. There could be no question of remaining on the gold standard: 'The game is up.' It was a remarkable turn-around. Just a few weeks earlier Keynes had signed the Macmillan Report, the conclusions of the Committee on Finance and Industry, which sought to establish the cause of Britain's economic problems. The committee was chaired by HP (subsequently Lord) Macmillan, the beneficiary of Alexander Grant's largesse to the National Library of Scotland. The report was a cockpit in which Keynes and the

THE CANCELLED PRIME MINISTER

Treasury fought it out. The majority of the committee recommended maintenance of the gold standard, including Keynes, who played the biggest part in writing the report.

Now, in reply to MacDonald, Keynes's prescription was quite different, bold but unworkable. He wanted a committee of all living ex-Chancellors of the Exchequer, followed by adoption of a new currency unit and then by an expansionary programme 'along the boldest possible lines'.[2] Writing in the heyday of Keynesianism, Marquand said, 'There can be no doubt in retrospect that the risks entailed by the pursuit [of a vision of a new expansionist currency bloc] would have been much smaller than those entailed by a forlorn attempt to save a parity which was by now past salvation ... This seems obvious today.'[3] But there was not the slightest possibility of implementing Keynes's proposals in 1931. Even his belief that parity, maintenance of the gold standard, had to be abandoned was not accepted.

*

What was to be done to restore confidence and stop the run on the pound? MacDonald had moved on from Lossiemouth to Rogart in Sutherland, where the US Secretary of State, Stimson, was on holiday. On 8 August he returned to Lossiemouth and found a message from Snowden, who was, unsurprisingly, panicking. He talked of three or perhaps four million unemployed, exhaustion of borrowing powers and the impossibility of raising a loan. He wanted the Economy Committee to meet. 'We cannot allow matters to drift into utter chaos, and we are perilously near that.'[4] MacDonald headed south. On 11 August the Bank of England said that at the rate that the reserves were being used up, the government had only two weeks in which to act. The Economy Committee met almost daily. On 12 and 13 August, Snowden revealed to his colleagues that the budget deficit was likely to amount to no less than £170 million. Keynes's suggestion of devaluation was rejected. Snowden pressed for a tax increase of £90 million and a cut in expenditure of £99 million. There is an interesting little aside in MacDonald's diary ahead of a meeting on 17 August. He had travelled overnight to that meeting by sleeper. He arrived at Downing Street at half past seven, had breakfast and went to work, and in a brief pause before the meeting began

> Slept a little over *John Knox*—a very smart but prejudiced book [by Edwin Muir?] with little critical judgement on the mystery of personality—not an easy matter as regards simple & ordinary men but one requiring some genius and understanding as regards those of great power & at the helm of life. At last four o'clock and the meeting ...

A reflection of the depth of the Prime Minister's hinterland. Tension increased as the meetings succeeded each other. Arthur Henderson adopted the role of protector of the unemployed. MacDonald was angered by his lack of realism and readiness to lapse into 'sulky silence'. Snowden diverged from May and MacDonald. He was for increased taxes as well as reduced expenditure.

The Economy Committee reported to the cabinet on 19 August. It recommended an increase in taxation of £89 million and economies of £78.5 million as against the £99 million which the Treasury had originally proposed. The main change was that unemployment insurance was to be cut by £43.5 million rather than £67 million. Henderson had successfully argued for disguising part of the unemployment benefit reduction as a 'premium', a flat reduction of a shilling a week. The cabinet considered the report on 19 August from eleven in the morning until half past ten in the evening. The government had to reassure the markets, but it also had to get its proposals through the Commons.

*

Harold Nicolson in his life of George V is clear that there was no evidence to suggest that MacDonald had made up his mind by 20 August that he would lead a coalition government. In his view, it was the intransigence of the TUC and 'their overt attempt to dictate terms to an elected government' which 'outraged his political conscience, aroused his personal vindictiveness, and steeled his resolve'.[5]

On that date, MacDonald and Snowden met opposition leaders Neville Chamberlain and Simon Hoare for the Conservatives and

THE CANCELLED PRIME MINISTER

Herbert Samuel and Donald Maclean for the Liberals.* The memories of those involved conflict with each other, sometimes quite markedly, but the minutiae are not relevant for the purpose of an exploration of MacDonald's motives. The Conservatives thought that the unemployment cuts were ludicrously low, and all six thought that the taxation increases were ridiculously high. Later in the day Chamberlain insisted on a further £30 million of cuts. Separately, the Liberals, whose support would be critical, equally insisted on cuts in benefits. The cabinet met again at half past eight on 20 August. Margaret Bondfield reported that a committee which she'd chaired had concluded that Henderson's 'premium' was impractical. She faced recriminations from Snowden, who said that she and her committee had been hopelessly unproductive. The meeting was adjourned till the following morning, 21 August. In the meantime, on the evening of 20 August, a deputation from the TUC General Council said they would not accept unemployment cuts and, indeed, they would not support cuts of any sort. For MacDonald this was the epitome of union irresponsibility, 'practically a declaration of war'.[6] The following day he wrote, 'if we yield now to the TUC we shall never be able to call our bodies, our souls, our intelligences our own'.[7] Henderson reacted in exactly the opposite way. Having gone along with the Economy Committee's proposals in general terms and a sulky manner, he now openly opposed MacDonald and the policy he was attempting to promote. MacDonald was shaken by his meeting with the TUC but strengthened in his resolve to continue with responsible leadership.

It emerged in the course of 21 August that if Britain's reserve continued to haemorrhage, there would be no money left in four days' time. It was essential to obtain loans from New York and Paris. The opposition leaders appeared again. They were told that the government had now been obliged to contemplate reduced cuts in general expenditure and in unemployment insurance. Snowden said that if these reduced measures failed to do the trick, the consequences would be 'the deluge'.

---

* There is a very detailed discussion and record of the negotiations of these tense days in Bassett, *Nineteen Thirty-One*, pp. 85ff.

The opposition leaders withdrew to MacDonald's room, emerging to say that the proposals were unacceptable, that parliament should be recalled and that they would then seek to bring the government down. They also, unusually, asked that the King be brought into the matter.

After a further cabinet meeting at 6.15, the opposition quartet returned. Chamberlain said that the government would be thrown out of office whenever the House met, but that there would be a crash before then. It was MacDonald's duty to avoid a crash and the Tories would support him, 'either with his present or in a reconstructed government'. So the first real proposal of a National Government came not from MacDonald, but from the Conservatives. The diary accounts of those present at this meeting differ in regard to who was keenest that MacDonald should continue as Prime Minister. Unsurprisingly, his account is the one which stresses his availability least. But all present seem to have envisaged, with more or less enthusiasm, that he would remain in position.

When the cabinet met on 22 August, MacDonald proposed that an additional £20 million of cuts should be made and that Paris and New York should then be sounded out on a proposed loan. In the course of the evening Sir Ernest Harvey, the Deputy Governor of the Bank of England, acting in the absence of Norman, who was off sick, reported hopefully about the loan request to the United States.

*

The King, who was at Balmoral, took the night train to London. When MacDonald saw him at half past ten on Sunday, 23 August, he warned him that even if the United States were prepared to make the loan, the government might fall as there was a real possibility that Henderson and others would resign. The King's reaction was to consult the leaders of the other parties. Baldwin had now condescended to return, although at a very leisurely rate, from his cure at Aix-les-Bains, but couldn't be found till after lunch on 23 August. He had gone to see Geoffrey Dawson, the editor of *The Times*, and chatted with him until lunchtime, when they both went to dine at the Travellers Club. Chamberlain and Hoare were irritated, and one result of Baldwin's disappearance was that the King saw the Liberal

THE CANCELLED PRIME MINISTER

Samuel before lunch, when Samuel said that the Liberal Party would support an all-party government, *'formed with a single purpose of overcoming the financial crisis'* (my emphasis: this description of the limited purpose of the National Government conforms to what MacDonald was to say]. Samuel advised that the best chance of getting a broad-based government would be if there were no change of leader. The King was to urge MacDonald to stay on as Prime Minister, and that is what the Liberals and Conservatives wanted. It was not overtly MacDonald's idea.

Sustained by lunch, Baldwin finally reached Buckingham Palace at three o'clock that afternoon. The King asked if he would serve under MacDonald, and he said he would. He also added that if MacDonald resigned he would be quite happy to serve as Prime Minister with Liberal consent. Left to himself, Baldwin wasn't averse to becoming Prime Minister; MacDonald's Tory backer was in fact Chamberlain.

The record made by Sir Clive Wigram, who had succeeded Stamfordham as the King's secretary, suggests that the King didn't decide on a National Government until he had spoken to Samuel and Baldwin, but MacDonald's diary says that at his meeting at 10.30 am on 23 August the King was already in favour of a National Government under him. The King was relieved that MacDonald, if he resigned, would not advise him to send for Henderson. One thing was certain: the King was horrified by the idea of an election. MacDonald seemed far from clear, according to his diary entry, that he would remain in office. He said he had prepared a statement to give to the press at once. 'If I resign ... I commit political suicide to save the crisis. If there is no other way I shall do it as cheerfully as an ancient Jap ... How few people understand the unattractiveness of this place & this office to me.' Sheila MacDonald listed the 'three possibilities for daddy', of which one was 'PM of coalition GOVT. (this is what King wants)'.[8]

The cabinet met at seven on the evening of 23 August. MacDonald asked for the resignations of his colleagues on a provisional basis. The May Committee, which had been nominated equally by the three parties, was in itself an acknowledgement of the need to deal with the crisis on a cross-party basis. When he requested his colleagues' resignations, MacDonald may already have decided on a National Government, but that appears unlikely. Events were tending in that direction, but MacDonald was not controlling them. Indeed, after meeting MacDonald on 23 August, Neville Chamberlain recorded in his diary that it would be impossible for MacDonald on personal as well as political grounds to head a government in which the Conservatives were represented.[9]

The details are elusive, but there is no doubt that there was some attempt to depose MacDonald around this time. Mosley approached Arthur Henderson in the Foreign Secretary's room behind the Speaker's chair and asked him to lead the coup. Henderson declined the invitation. It is hardly surprising that in the circumstances of these dark and difficult days there were stories of plots and conspiracies.[10]

MacDonald told the cabinet that they could expect to hear from New York in the course of the evening. The meeting adjourned at 7.45. At 9.10 ministers were called in from the garden and were read a telegram from the Federal Reserve Bank. It was bad news. There would be no public loan, and at most a short term of credit— and that was not guaranteed and would only be available if the French were prepared to do something similar. The Federal Reserve Bank also wanted to know how far the government had the support of the Bank of England and the City. MacDonald said that the City was supportive. Snowden said that the credits that the Reserve was offering would be enough to avoid catastrophe. MacDonald then turned to politics and asked for a cabinet decision on cuts. He concluded by saying that it had to be admitted 'that the proposals as a whole represented the negation of everything that the Labour Party stood for, and yet he was absolutely satisfied that it was necessary in the national interest to implement them if the country was to be secured'. He said that if there were any important resignations, the government as a whole must resign.

The members of the cabinet then gave their reactions to a ten per cent cut in employment benefit; eleven were in favour and nine against. It was clear that some of those who voted against the proposals would resign, and MacDonald therefore intimated that he would advise the King to convene a meeting at which he, Baldwin and Samuel would be present on 24 August. The cabinet authorised

THE CANCELLED PRIME MINISTER

him to tell the King that they had all placed their resignations in MacDonald's hands. As he left Downing Street, MacDonald passed Harvey, the Deputy Governor, and told him that he was off to the Palace to throw in his hand.

Sir Clive Wigram reported that when MacDonald reached the Palace, he

> looked scared and unbalanced ... The King impressed on the Prime Minister that he was the only man to lead the country through this crisis and hoped he would reconsider [tendering the resignation of the cabinet]. His Majesty told him that the Conservatives and Liberals would support him in restoring the confidence of foreigners in the financial stability of the country.[11]

The Prime Minister asked whether the King would confer with Baldwin, Samuel and himself in the morning, and the King enthusiastically said that he would. MacDonald returned to Downing Street and told his colleagues what had happened.

*

The idea of a National Government did not come from nowhere. Equally, it didn't develop in discussions within the labour movement. JL Garvin, the editor of *The Observer*, had been campaigning for some sort of consensual government since March 1929. Garvin was a remarkable man who had left school at the age of thirteen but went on to edit *The Observer* from 1908 until 1942. He had initially favoured something distinct from the old parties, but he came to see the impracticality of that idea. His first choice for an independent leader standing above everyday politics was Lloyd George, though he acknowledged that the Lloyd George of 1930 was not the Lloyd George of 1918. MacDonald was not his ideal candidate, but he could see that he was 'as little partisan in intellect and heart as any man in Britain'.[12]

MacDonald had discussed the idea with Neville Chamberlain and Sir Samuel Hoare for the Conservatives and with Sir Herbert Samuel and Sir Donald Maclean for the Liberals; but it was some time before he broached the idea with his own cabinet members other than Snowden and Thomas. MacNeill Weir's comment is crude and obvious:

It was not until he had arranged matters with the political opponents of the Labour Party that he had his first meeting with the Cabinet sub-committee. It is significant that those who MacDonald chiefly consulted were Conservatives or Liberals—men who had attacked the Labour Government; men who believed the Labour Government to be driving the country to ruin; men who were determined to overthrow it at the earliest moment.[13]

Even Lord Passfield accepted that MacDonald hadn't plotted to create a National Government. In a letter to Malcolm MacDonald he said that there had been a suggestion of a National Government 'with which nobody can suppose that your father had any connection, if indeed he had ever heard of some of them'.[14]

*

As the cabinet members left Downing Street, Baldwin, Chamberlain and Samuel arrived. Accounts vary slightly about MacDonald's tone at this meeting. His initial position appears to have been that he would resign, not join the new government but support it in the measures it would require to take. Again, it was Chamberlain, rather than Baldwin, who seems to have gone out of his way to try to persuade MacDonald to participate in a National Government, either as a member or as its leader. Baldwin, as before, did not particularly support Chamberlain, and remained silent: after all, if MacDonald did not lead the National Government, it would be he who would do so. The opposition leaders left under the impression that Chamberlain's arguments had not won acceptance;, but MacDonald's diary suggests that that might not be the case.

On Monday, 24 August, MacDonald phoned Ishbel at breakfast time. She then spoke with Malcolm MacDonald. Malcolm was aware of the huge and painful decision that his father had to make.

> To break ... with the Labour Party would be painful in the extreme. Yet JRM knows what the country needs and wants in this crisis, and it is a question whether it is not his duty to form a government representative of all three parties to tide over a few weeks, till the danger of financial crash is past—and damn the consequences to himself after that.[15]

THE CANCELLED PRIME MINISTER

Malcolm described the King as 'imploring' MacDonald to lead the new government. The royal plea was made three times, and in terms which implied that failing to do so would amount to a dereliction of duty.

MacDonald's colleagues in the wider Labour Party thought events indicated that he was about to resign and that Baldwin would preside over a Tory–Liberal coalition. MacDonald had said nothing to them to suggest that this was the case, but he had said nothing to suggest that it was not.

The three party leaders met at Buckingham Palace at ten o'clock that morning. The King said that he hoped that the Prime Minister would remain in place supported by the Conservatives and the Liberals. MacDonald's reputation, he said, would be enhanced by remaining at his post. What was envisaged at this stage was a very temporary National Government, to be followed by a general election in which each party would campaign independently. The King withdrew while the party leaders agreed among themselves on a memorandum which MacDonald took back with him to Downing Street for the last meeting of the Labour cabinet. According to Manny Shinwell, MacDonald 'brusquely' reported the decisions and invited no comment from his colleagues other than an indication of whether or not they would serve under his leadership. The replies replicated the earlier vote. At the end of the meeting, Lord Sankey moved that the cabinet record 'their warm appreciation of the great kindness, consideration and courtesy invariably shown by the Prime Minister when presiding over their meetings'. It would be the last warm appreciation that MacDonald ever received from a united Labour leadership.

Even then it was not all warmth. Snowden said that when the Labour cabinet declined to agree to a reduction of unemployment pay, 'Mr MacDonald assumed too hurriedly that this involved the resignation of his Government. He neither showed nor expressed any grief at this regrettable development. On the contrary, he set about the formation of the National Government with an enthusiasm which showed that the adventure was highly agreeable to him.'[16] Weir simplifies the exchanges: 'MacDonald came in and announced to them that a new government had been formed—in short, *that he was in and they were out.*'[17]

ECONOMIC CRISIS

After the cabinet meeting, MacDonald asked Snowden, Thomas and Sankey to join the new government. They agreed. At 4.10 he went back to the Palace, tendered the resignation of the cabinet and accepted the King's request to form a new government. As HCG Matthew says in the *Oxford Dictionary of National Biography*, 'It is hard to avoid the view that but for royal pressure, MacDonald would have resigned the premiership and the Labour Party would not have split.' In his diary that night, MacDonald wrote of the consternation at the midday cabinet meeting. He was not surprised by Henderson's position, but he was disappointed by evidence of 'weak human nature' which he met on the part of others. 'This is a lonely job.'

But lonely or not, MacDonald was supported by a majority of the cabinet, as was confirmed in an unusual ex-ministers' memorandum drawn up shortly afterwards.[18] It was the existence of a strong minority (eight or nine against ten) that caused the fall of the government.

In the afternoon of 24 August, MacDonald met junior ministers. One of them said that he looked happy and he said he was happy. 'You see I am going out.'[19] He made it clear that he thought that while what he had done was right, it would be the end of his political life. Weir describes this meeting in some detail, and even from his critical perspective, it is clear that MacDonald was taking a practical decision from which he did not expect to benefit and which was designed for national and not party benefit. He had 'decided to form a *personal* government, consisting of a few individuals drawn from various parties, the government being a non-party government, with very few ministers, to carry on until the money situation was alright again, and then it would disperse' (my emphasis).[20] Shinwell asked why MacDonald didn't just stand aside and let the other parties form their own government. MacDonald's reply was, 'Oh, that would not save the country.' He stressed that he did not expect the junior ministers to follow him. They were to think of their careers and avoid the taint which he knew would stain him. He told them that he had safeguarded their positions by saying that there would be no 'coupon' election as in 1918. MacDonald was therefore imposing a higher moral code on himself than on the younger men. Weir described staying on as 'one of those strange lapses that even the cleverest men make', but it was a matter of self-sacrifice rather than a lapse.

THE CANCELLED PRIME MINISTER

By the following day, he had decided he needed Shinwell and asked if he would be prepared to stay at his post as Financial Secretary for Mines. Shinwell did not stay; he tried to persuade MacDonald, whom he admired, not to preside over the National Government. Malcolm MacDonald followed his father and became Under-Secretary of State for Dominion Affairs. The fact that MacDonald thought that a couple of people might be required, because of their abilities, to make the same sacrifice as he had done does not substantiate a charge of hypocrisy, as Weir argues.[21] His general advice was not to stay on, and, said Harold Nicolson, 'Most of the junior Ministers followed, but without much subsequent gratitude, this unselfish advice.'[22]

MacDonald's version of what he had done is expressed well in a letter he wrote to Shinwell on 24 August 1931:

> It is a very painful decision that has to be taken, and I wish you to have no doubt at all about what it was. We were on the verge of a financial crisis which if not dealt with within the space of days, would have meant not cuts of ten per cent, or anything of that kind, in unemployment pay, but would have disorganised the whole of our financial system, with the most dire results to the mass of the working classes. It may take a little time for people to understand what are the issues and the alternatives to what I have done ... The Government that has been formed is not a Coalition but a cooperation between individuals who are banded together to avoid the disaster. No parties are involved in it, and as soon as the country gets on to an even keel again, the Government will cease to exist.[23]

29

REACTION

Whatever members of the Labour Party thought, the public at large was convinced that MacDonald had done the right thing by putting country before party and presiding over a government which would save the nation from disaster. He was still a powerful and seductive figure with an untarnished reputation. Now he was also a national saviour. Against his own inclinations and interests, it could be claimed, he had come together with other men of authority and responsibility, at the personal entreaty of the King-Emperor, to save the economy and the nation. His reputation was never higher than it was at this moment. But his role as a patriotic saviour was short-lived. It was rather like Chamberlain when he came back a few years later with his scrap of paper from meeting Hitler at Munich to bask in adulation that did not last.

Very soon MacDonald would appear to be the prisoner of the Conservatives; but for the moment what was surprising was how prominent Labour was in the new cabinet. MacDonald was joined by Snowden, Thomas and Sankey. The Tories had the same number of seats. Baldwin was Lord President of the Council, Samuel Hoare Secretary for India, Chamberlain Minister of Health and Sir Philip Cunliffe-Lister President of the Board of Trade. There were just two Liberals, Samuel at the Home Office and Lord Reading at the Foreign Office. The lower ranks of the Labour Party were not much represented. MacDonald wrote to the junior ministers and backbenchers, saying that the alternative to a National Government would have been the destruction of Labour, but his letters didn't do much good. Shinwell, Stafford Cripps and Herbert Morrison declined to remain in their ministerial offices, and only four Labour members became junior ministers. MacDonald dangled the prospect of an honour before Henderson, but he resisted the bait. He remained in the Commons and, indeed, became leader of the Labour Party.

The parliamentary party met on 28 August. MacDonald didn't come back from Lossiemouth for it and thus took no part in a historic debate on his future and the future of the party, which resolved to oppose the National Government. The invitation to the meeting had reached MacDonald before he left for Lossiemouth. He could have changed his plans and attended. The fact that he did not do so was the first of various incidents that collectively came to suggest that he had lost interest in the party. It's impossible now to say if things could have turned out differently. There certainly were many individuals who wrote touchingly and sympathetically to him and who only reluctantly followed the party's decision to oppose the government.

MacDonald's own constituency association in Seaham followed that decision and asked him to resign his seat. He didn't do so. On the other hand there were lots of constituents who dissociated themselves from what the local executive had done. MacDonald could have capitalised on the 'thunderous applause' when his name was mentioned and from the shouts of 'good old Ramsay' and made a more personal appeal to the voters. His vanity and aloofness did not allow that.

He had never taken the trouble to cultivate the party and he continued to ignore it. He had got away with this in the past, but now it was fatal. David Kirkwood thought if MacDonald had bothered to turn up at the meeting on 28 August he could have swung the party behind him. In these early days quite a number of Labour MPs told MacDonald, and even the press, that they understood and did not condemn what he had done.

Some distinguished Labour MPs who had not followed him, like Sir Norman Angell and Sir James Sexton, even from the opposition benches spoke of their reluctance to be in opposition. Sexton recorded that he had been in favour of a National Government. The odd Labour opposition MP crossed the floor to join National

REACTION

Labour, including Frank Markham, who became MacDonald's parliamentary private secretary. On 17 September 1931, three Labour peers, Lords Rochester, Marks and Dickinson, soon to be followed by De La Warr and Lord Gorell,* crossed the floor of the House of Lords. But these moves were rare and atypical.

Although MacDonald had initially accepted and assumed that presiding over a National Government would mean the end of his political career, he was taken aback by the extent of the reaction against him. In his diary on 1 September he referred to

> the desertion of colleagues & the flight of the lab: govt. having grievous effect ... Destruction of all we have done. Had the govt. done its duty there would have been little interruption in that work. They ran away & left everything unprotected. If this is the best Labour can do, then it is not fit to govern except in the calmest of good weather.

The disloyalty, the desertion, lay with the ministers who had resigned and not with him. There wasn't much room here for reconciliation.

There is no doubt that initially MacDonald thought that his role in the National Government would be a limited one. He wrote to Molly Hamilton on 1 September saying that if he had not done what he did, the Labour Party would have been swept out of existence and that he was effectively ending his political career for the party's sake.[1] That is consistent with all his actions: he made no effort to stay in the Labour Party, from which he was indeed expelled by the end of September. But there was an element of self-deception. He told Baldwin that he hadn't left his party and had no intention of doing so.

*

And so, very soon after the formation of the National Government, MacDonald's attitude can be seen to be changing. It changed because

---

* Ronald Gorell, who had been Under-Secretary of State for Air under Lloyd George, was the editor of the *Cornhill Magazine* from 1933 to 1939 and co-president with Agatha Christie of the Detection Club in 1956–63. Dorothy L Sayers called him 'Lord Sheep'. All the same, he is said to have been the model for her Lord Peter Wimsey.

he was wounded by the reaction to what he had done. What he had considered a selfless action, the sacrifice of his career for the good of the country to shelter the Labour Party from obloquy, was not recognised as such.

His blindness to how his actions were seen, his conviction that he was right and the mainstream party wrong, his perception that true socialism had been betrayed by the party and not by him, is eloquently articulated in a letter he wrote from Lossiemouth on Boxing Day, 1931, to his old ILP friend Martin Haddow:

> I am afraid that the year is to bring me neither peace nor prosperity, and the worst of it all is what seems to me to be the betrayal by the Labour movement as represented by the majority, at any rate, of the machine of its fundamental socialism and its abandonment of everything except public assistance ... In this way they could keep up the appearance for another twelve months or so of generosity, and in the end the collapse would be so great that nothing but years of revolutionary conditions would be our lot ... A political machine, dominated by trade union officials whose one idea is to make great promises as trade unionists and then ask governments to fulfil them, is not the Labour movement to which I have devoted my life. Man [sic] without vision and with no real courage may be all right for Poor Law Guardians, but not for building up socialism by political means.[2]

*

The violence of the reaction made him feel that the Labour Party was not worthy of his sacrifice. It was the reaction of a self-important man. The consequence of his anger was that he was now ready to contemplate an early election. Such an election could not fail to damage Labour, and he would not have countenanced it if he had not been disillusioned by the party's reaction to what he had done. Initially he had not intended to stay on through an election. Now he changed his mind.

His only worry about an early election, he revealed in a letter to Baldwin on 5 September, was that the Labour Party might win it! To avoid that, the National Government should agree on a fairly long-term timetable. The Labour Party

REACTION

has undoubtedly some rather detestable but nevertheless electorally effective cries, and it must be dealt with very seriously. I have not left my Party and have no intention of doing so, but if it were to have a majority or even form a Government after the next Election, the country would again be faced with a financial crisis ...[3]

*

Both sides became increasingly embittered. As the weeks and months passed, his former colleagues saw how their fortunes were altered by what their leader had done. The violence of the attacks increased. Lord Simon, a member of the National Government, wrote later: 'The denunciations heaped upon MacDonald's head by many who had previously idolised him were the most violent I have ever known in British politics.'[4]

In the course of his long, disdainful relationship with his party, MacDonald had left many hostages to fortune. He had never disguised his semi-detached and critical position, his poor opinion of many of his comrades. It was the public and not the party that he wooed. He regarded the ILP as divisive and irresponsible, and he thought the trade unions took a class and factional view of their responsibilities. He deprecated lack of discipline, failure to subordinate individual aims to a national party which could deliver social progress. That doesn't mean that he plotted to destroy the party. Harold Wilson, who had his own difficulties in keeping the Labour Party together, was convinced that MacDonald never meant to sabotage the party. On the contrary, MacDonald hoped and expected till the very end that it would accept the extreme measures that he and Snowden recommended. But once the split had happened, there was none of the goodwill that would have been needed to mend it.

On the other hand, while MacDonald thought that the cross-party support a National Government would enjoy would enable it to take measures that were essential for the nation, he found little pleasure in association with the Conservative Party. The extent of the Tory vote at the 1931 election caused 'an increase in my anti-Tory instinct ... the oppression of my companionship crushes out every other feeling'. He had a contemptuous disdain for the rank

273

and file of the Tory Party: 'an odd lot of colonels & sycophants, repulsively vulgar'. Even when they were nice to him, he felt apart: 'colleagues loyal & all that, but I am a socialist'.[5]

*

But even at the time there was a widespread view that the formation of the National Government was not an idea that had emerged as a spontaneous reaction to the financial crisis. The fanciful 'plot' theory, promulgated by Sidney Webb and long accepted by many, holds that MacDonald had conceived the idea of a National Government long in advance of its arrival, and had engineered its creation over a significant period. Webb said that the replacement of the Labour administration by the National Government represented 'a single drama, in all its development foreseen in advance ... only by the statesman who was at once its author, producer and principal actor'. He argued that MacDonald had had the idea of a National Government in his mind for months. Later, Webb told Malcolm MacDonald that his accusation had been 'avowedly fanciful and that his father was unconnected with ideas that were circulating of supplanting the labour administration with a national one, even if he had heard of them'.[6]

Snowden said that MacDonald 'set about the formation of the National Government with an enthusiasm which showed that the adventure was highly agreeable to him'. Harold Nicolson, in his biography of King George V, suggests that this was no more than 'one of Mr Snowden's mustard phrases'.[7] Nicolson does not dissent from MacDonald's view that he had taken his decision fully aware that he was committing political suicide; he took the view that MacDonald was acutely aware of what he was doing to his reputation.[8]

The extreme version of what has been called the plot theory is obviously untenable. It is a reflection of the heated reaction by Labour purists to the compromise their leader had made. But a plot theory existed and still exists. Belief in it intensified when MacDonald called the election of October 1931.

*

REACTION

The National Government proved an easy institution to hate. Its Conservative members looked distinctly like the hard-faced men who had done well out of the First World War. The tone of the National Government, a government which would in the event last from 1931 till 1940, was grudging, mean-minded in spirit, reactionary and repressive. It was the National Government which gave to the 1930s the character which WH Auden described, of 'a low dishonest decade'. MacDonald was seen as having turned his back on high-flown imagination and idealism to usher in this sordid decade.

In parliament his old supporters attacked him viciously. 'The hounds were straining at the leash to kill', as one parliamentary reporter described.[9] The press, particularly the *Daily Herald*, was equally immoderate and outspoken. MacDonald did not pretend to be unaffected by it. It upset him to feel that his own people had turned against him. The Labour Party and the progressive ideal that it embodied were part of him, and he suffered from a feeling of exclusion. He never doubted that he had done the right thing, but he lived in a lonely and desolate place.

Clement Attlee described August 1931 as 'the greatest political betrayal in our annals'.[10] Henderson said in a speech at Burnley in the course of the October election campaign that the possibility of a National Government had been on MacDonald's mind for months and had been discussed without ever having been brought before an official meeting of the Labour Party.[11]

At the time, of course, the role of the King was unknown. Having found himself in the middle of the House of Lords crisis immediately on his succession and then having to face the Irish drama, George V, for all his simple diffidence, had been more at the centre of political events than most modern sovereigns. It is true that the delineations of royal competence were less obvious than they are now: even so, George V came close to constitutional excess from time to time. A more proper procedure in the context of the events of 1931 would have been for the King to approach Baldwin, who might or might not have sounded out other parties. MacDonald's reaction to the King's initiative was very simple, typical of his consistent view that if Labour was to be treated as a responsible party, as a permanent element in the political life, it could not run away from crises.[12]

MacDonald was well aware that what he was doing was likely to end his career. The violent attacks of his former colleagues took an emotional and physical toll. He suffered something like a mild stroke. He said that if he died soon, it would be from a broken heart. The idea that he was motivated by personal ambition is not sustainable. At the end of the final Labour cabinet meeting he had, as we have seen, spoken to rising young stars like Shinwell and Morrison and told them that while this would be the end of his political career, they should not join in a National Government which would be their undoing.[13] That is not to say that he was not flattered to be asked—commanded—by his sovereign to save the nation at his personal cost. If it was to be the end of his career, it would at least be a noble end.

30

THE NATIONAL GOVERNMENT

On 10 September 1931 Snowden introduced an emergency budget and on the following day MacDonald himself moved the second reading of the National Economy Bill, the legislative enactment of the economy cuts.

The budget was balanced, but it didn't stem the run on the pound. On 15 September at Invergordon, sailors in the Atlantic fleet 'mutinied', protesting against the pay cuts. On the following day the Bank of England lost £5 million, on the next £10 million, and on 18 September nearly £18 million. A cabinet committee concluded that if Britain were to remain on the gold standard, credits would have to be obtained from abroad. On 18 September, New York and Paris were asked for help. Neither was prepared to do anything. MacDonald, who had gone off to Chequers for the weekend, was summoned back for a meeting by the Deputy Governor to be told that the gold standard could no longer be maintained. 'Did a more solemn conference ever meet in Downing Street?'

In his 1925 budget Churchill as Chancellor of the Exchequer had returned Britain to the gold standard on the advice of Treasury officials and rather against his own instincts. During the Great War the linkage of sterling to the price of gold had been broken. It was a matter of national pride to restore the link, but going back to the old rate of exchange was over-ambitious, and now, on Saturday, 19 September, the Bank made a formal request to be allowed to depart from the standard. On Sunday, 20 September, the cabinet agreed to the request. On Monday, 21 September, the legislation went through all its stages in a single day, 112 opposition Labour

MPs voting to retain the anachronistic link to the precious metal, despite the fact that their colleague Arthur Henderson supported floating the pound.

There was a brief chance of reconciliation despite the vote on 21 September. There were hints that Henderson might support the National Government in return for concessions on unemployment benefit. MacDonald made no attempt to promote a reconciliation.[1] Lord Passfield was amazed at the ease with which the sacred commitment to the gold standard could be disposed of. 'Nobody told us we could do this,' he said.[2]

*

Lots of other countries found they could also abandon gold. Within eight months eighteen countries had abandoned the gold standard and forty adopted protectionist policies. So MacDonald's policy was in line with what other countries did. Lord Skidelsky argued in *Politicians and the Slump* that 'what might loosely be termed Keynesian policies' had been adopted by other countries such as the United States, Germany, France and Sweden, but the prejudice against deficit budgeting was much stronger in Britain than in many countries. It is important to recognise that while Snowden was and is criticised as a very conservative Chancellor, his views were very much in tune with those of the Treasury and the financial establishment. Treasury officials were relieved and delighted when Snowden succeeded Churchill—who himself had not been a radical firebrand as Chancellor of the Exchequer.[3]

MacDonald still hesitated to call an election. From his point of view, it offered nothing except a more formal alienation from his party. But from the point of view of the Conservatives, there was every reason for one. MacDonald's resistance weakened, though he believed that some of his Labour colleagues would not remain within the National Government. In all this agonising, MacDonald's health suffered again and he had to convalesce on the coast.

He had suggested he would not preside over such an election; now he not only called it but said that its purpose was to secure a 'doctor's mandate', an odd phrase at the time. It seems to have implied that the government could do anything it wanted in an

THE NATIONAL GOVERNMENT

emergency situation. At any rate it was not a very socialist idea. The King was all for an election in which he hoped party differences would play no part. This 'doctor's mandate' notion was an expression of that sort of approach: it meant that detailed manifestos were unnecessary.

*

Parliament was dissolved on 7 October. At the election at the end of the month the National Government was returned to power with a huge majority. This was the true break between MacDonald and the labour movement. Having been the leader of a party he didn't much like, MacDonald now found himself the prisoner of a party which he liked even less.

So the idea that the National Government had been a brief and anomalous expedient to repair the economy, after which business would return to the usual, had been abandoned. On the day of the dissolution MacDonald made a broadcast. 'When formed last August the Government contemplated a brief life, finishing by a reestablishment of security and an immediate return to normal political conditions.' That had not been possible and the government was compelled to ask for a mandate which would be unchallenged by 'faction' and 'opposition either organised or disorganised'. There was a token expression of hope that there would be cross-party consensus, but he didn't seriously pretend that he wasn't simply looking for a large electoral majority. Labour's vote fell by 1.5 million. There were 13 National Labour members, 46 official Labour Party members and 6 ILP members. Among the Liberals there were 4 Lloyd George Liberals, 33 Samuelites and 35 Simonites. The Conservatives had 471 seats.

MacDonald, surprisingly, held his Seaham seat with a majority of almost 6,000. 'Surprisingly' because there had been a move to unseat him as the candidate; but unsurprisingly, too, because he was still at this stage a massively popular figure throughout the country. His standing in Labour circles had slumped, but it had been hugely enhanced everywhere else.

It had been an odd election in many ways. MacDonald had been pretty ambivalent about the Labour Party's prospects. There had been an attempt to go to the country with a National Labour slate independent of the Conservatives, but nothing could be agreed, and National Labour was indistinguishable from its Conservative colleagues. He didn't want to see his old party destroyed, but on the other hand he did not respond to a probably futile olive branch from the party.[4] Neville Chamberlain welcomed the single manifesto as an opportunity to crush Labour. That was not precisely what MacDonald wanted. Baldwin behaved generously despite the electoral wind in his sails. When the National Government was formed, he had told MacDonald that if the Tories treated him badly, he, Baldwin, would resign. An essential element in this peculiar election was that the Conservatives were now clearly committed to moving from free trade towards control by tariffs and other means. In the spirit of consensus, nothing about free trade had been said in advance of the election, but on 31 December a cabinet committee advocated a protectionist tariff of ten per cent. MacDonald, as usual not hugely bothered by dogma, did not feel obliged to defend the sanctity of free trade. The Liberals, historically the party of free trade, were not so accommodating. MacDonald had told the King that he couldn't see any way around these difficulties and was inclined to quit the scene. The King would have none of that, and told him that he had to sort things out and that even if he did resign, his resignation wouldn't be accepted. MacDonald responded to his nautical master's admonition and described himself in his election posters at Seaham as 'the captain who stuck to the ship'.

For all Baldwin's friendly geniality, MacDonald didn't think that he and the Conservatives had been playing a magnanimous game. Somehow, he felt that the Labour element had been let down. Conservative Head Office 'played a shady game ... Once again I record that no honest man should trust in too gentlemanly a way the Conservative wire pullers.'[5] That judgement seems difficult to sustain: the Conservatives had a huge majority, National Labour was insignificant, but the Tories got a bare majority of seats in the cabinet, eleven out of twenty.

Ahead of the election MacDonald had repeatedly said that he would not be a 'Tory tool', and when it came to cabinet-making he was equally determined that there should be a 'national touch' in the government. While he didn't get exactly what he had wanted—for instance, he had thought that Chamberlain, though the leading supporter of tariff reform, should remain at Health and the Treasury be occupied by a free-trader—what is surprising is how much he did get.

All the same, he felt real pain over the destruction of the party in whose history he had played such a crucial part. 'Labour I am and Labour I shall remain,' he had declared at Seaham. That was not the declaration of a man who wanted to destroy Labour. But though he still felt part of the party and though he grieved for the party's travails, he blamed the party for throwing him out—and throwing him out in a letter that was authenticated merely by a rubber stamp and some initials. There was talk of a formally organised National Labour Party. Plans were drawn up, but it remained no more than a vehicle for MacDonald's supporters. And that was logical. A formal identity would have implied a break with the Labour opposition of a permanent nature. That wasn't MacDonald's idea at all.

*

The tension in the new government was between those who favoured tariff reform and those who could never countenance the abandonment of the inviolable doctrine of free trade. The National Government itself was not committed to tariff reform, but the Conservatives within it were. The strongest supporters of free trade were the Samuelite Liberals and the Chancellor, Snowden. In general terms, MacDonald saw free trade as a nineteenth-century solution to nineteenth-century problems, but he didn't want the government to split over the issue.

Initially all went well. There was an anomalous and dangerous increase in imports. Without a frontal attack on free trade in general, the cabinet acquiesced in an ad hoc approach to imports in the shape of an Abnormal Importations Act. This was, however, followed by a demand from the Ministry of Agriculture for protection for wheat and various horticultural products. Snowden wrote to MacDonald saying that he could not continue to support this piecemeal attack on a matter of principle. MacDonald complained to Baldwin about remarks by the Conservative Party chairman to the effect that the National Government had a mandate to carry out

THE CANCELLED PRIME MINISTER

Tory policy. The relationship between Baldwin and MacDonald continued to be cordial though not particularly productive, and Baldwin duly reminded his party that the government was indeed a national one and not a party affair.

MacDonald went on to take the first steps on the road to the death of free trade, recommending the imposition of a general tariff. Free-traders, including Snowden, rejected the proposal, as did Samuel. Simon, Thomas and Sankey accepted it. Baldwin spoke emolliently and said that he would be as upset by the fall of the National Government as by that of a Conservative government; all the same, he gently referred to the balance of power between the parties. At the end of the day the potentially disastrous dispute was resolved not through any initiative by MacDonald but rather by the fact that the Conservatives didn't want to fall out with the Samuelite Liberals—or, indeed, with any Liberals. The outcome was the celebrated 'freedom to differ' of 1932—a cop-out of a formula which again proved useful in the run-up to the European Union referendum of 2016.

*

MacDonald's interest in foreign policy, arguably an un-Labour interest, continued. He involved himself in the consequences of Japan's invasion of Manchuria in 1931, and in general he was able to continue to take an independent line on foreign policy, as he had done at the head of the Labour government. In any event foreign affairs were in a sense apolitical, not an issue of tension between the different components of the National Government.

This was not the position in regard to India. The first Round Table Conference had broken up in January 1931, with little achieved. The second conference took place in September of the same year. It looked as if there might be more progress now, as discussions between the Viceroy, Lord Irwin, and Gandhi meant that the latter attended the conference, as also did representatives of the Congress Party. The pact between Irwin and Gandhi had been extremely unpopular with the Tory right. This was the reconciliation which Churchill famously characterised by describing Gandhi as 'a seditious Middle Temple lawyer, now posing as a fakir ... striding half-naked up the steps of the Viceregal palace ... to parley on equal terms with the representative of the king-emperor'. Churchill had quit the Tory front bench over India. He was a dissident backbencher, and he and his hardliners were pretty much disavowed by Baldwin and the party leadership. The Tory element of the government was more sympathetic to Indian aspirations than Conservatives had ever been before, but very little progress was made. The Indians divided on sectarian lines, but both Hindus and Muslims were suspicious of the British, particularly of the Conservatives. MacDonald attempted to make some progress with a federal constitution and by allowing for provincial autonomy. He was unable to get these proposals through cabinet immediately, although they were later fleshed out in the 1935 Government of India Act. He found the Conservative Secretary of State, Samuel Hoare, unimaginative and lacking in understanding. He had to involve himself in the deliberations, and Gandhi congratulated him on driving the conference onward 'with pitilessness worthy of a Scotsman'.[6]

31

HEALTH AND DIPLOMACY

A judgement on MacDonald's decision in 1931 can't be made without looking at the state of his health, as well as his political philosophy. In 1927 he visited the United States, and while he was there he developed bronchitis. After that his ageing was evident. His whole life had required the expenditure of nervous energy in the same way as Baldwin's life consisted of genial relaxation. 'How tired I am. My brain is fagged, work is difficult, and there is a darkness on the face of the land. I am ashamed of some speeches I have made, but what can I do?' He went on to elaborate on the difficulty of trying to add to the salary of £400 a year, on which it was 'impossible' to live, by making an income between Friday afternoon and Sunday night. 'If it killed one in a clean, efficient business-like way why should one object: but it cripples and tortures first by lowering the quality of work done and then by pushing one into long months of slowly ebbing vitality and mental paralysis.'[1]

In the run-up to the 1929 election:

> How often I think of the dead. Oh, had she been here these last years. I wonder if they know. The prospect of death becomes more and more attractive. Have I not done enough? Do I not belong to an old generation? I am convinced that to hang on too long like a dead leaf on a tree is a terrible mistake. The problem is the moment and occasion to fall and let the young leaves expand ... there's the rub.

He collapsed after the National Government was formed and again in the course of the deliberations about coming off the gold standard. His diaries are full of references to his exhaustion and incapacity for work.

THE CANCELLED PRIME MINISTER

His eye problems were well known, as also his other physical and mental health difficulties. It seems surprising that with all his health problems there was no strong suggestion that he was no longer physically fit for office. Some of his problems could be hidden, like his insomnia, his increasing depression and occasional hallucinations. There was also a kindly, collusive ignoring of meaningless patches in his speeches when he effectively blanked out. He still had a good appearance and bearing, and that greatly helped. But there were many, very many, public embarrassments, as when he said in the House that Lloyd George had 'a hawk-like desire for action, without bridle and without saddle, across the Atlantic'.

*

The problem of German reparations had not gone away. We saw that in July 1931 the US President, Herbert Hoover, announced a one-year moratorium, but it was very soon clear that nothing much would change at the end of the year. A conference was convened in Lausanne in June 1932. The conference required Germany to make a final payment by way of an issue of bonds, which would not be redeemable for three years. The effect would have been to reduce Germany's Versailles Treaty obligations by ninety per cent. But the Weimar Republic was on its last legs. The Chancellor, Franz von Papen, was ruling by presidential decree and the parties on the right, including the National Socialists, rejected the Lausanne formula. In any event the treaty would only become effective when agreement had been reached with the United States on settlement of the loans which it had made. No agreement was reached and the treaty was never ratified. Part of the deal was to have been abrogation of the war-guilt clause of the Versailles Treaty. That never happened, and the Nazis were left with a grievance to nourish. In reality reparations had ceased to exist. So had Allied war debts to the United States. Within the year all the Allies—except Finland—had defaulted.* America's inflexible attitude to the money the Allies

---

* Finland's debt was not truly war debt. It represented borrowing in the aftermath of gaining independence in 1917. The sum involved was around $8.3 million. Britain owed $4.3 billion. But repayment was a major effort for Finland, which took pride in its discipline and financial probity.

HEALTH AND DIPLOMACY

had loaned did a lot of damage without ultimately doing the United States much good.

MacDonald took the chair at Lausanne. He was far from well. His eyes continued to trouble him. His exhausted appearance was a matter of comment. He was disheartened by the obduracy of the French and wondered if the Germans for their part really wanted an agreement at all. He cheered up when the conference concluded. No one knew that it would never be ratified. He had from the outset regarded reparations as cruel and unworkable, and he appeared to have succeeded in putting an end to them. 'Tired & pained but it was a new world. The desires of years had been fulfilled & I do not mind much what is to come.' He had a warm reception at Victoria Station when he returned to London, and then joined the King and Queen in the garden at Buckingham Palace. He even had an enthusiastic message from John Maynard Keynes, the great scourge of reparations.

*

Early in 1932 glaucoma was diagnosed. It was operated on, but his convalescence was slow. He spent two weeks in a nursing home followed by three weeks' rest at Newquay. Communiqués were issued to emphasise that although he was making progress, he would have to restrict his activities, particularly reading. His health had made it difficult to deal with the aftermath of Japan's invasion of Manchuria. He had been too ill to take part in the subsequent negotiations at Geneva until April, and when he did get there he had not been the dominating figure of earlier meetings. Now his 'good' eye, his right one, was also playing up, and he had to leave the conference and return to London for a second operation. As before, recovery was slow, and more announcements were made about the need for limiting his activities.

The disarmament conference at Geneva from February 1932 to November 1934, which MacDonald was only intermittently able to be present at, was a huge assembly, attended by the United States and the Soviet Union, not members of the League, along with other countries which were. Hitler came to power in the middle of the conference. He withdrew from the League, and Germany also withdrew from, rejoined and withdrew again from the conference. Hopes of peace in Europe were not thereafter realistically possible.

Anthony Eden had been Britain's representative at the conference. In March 1933 he returned home. Despite opposition from Tory colleagues, MacDonald persuaded the cabinet's Disarmament Committee that he and Simon should go to Geneva to try to save the failing conference. The gestures and the elaborate rhetorical flourishes were still there, but they were no more than memories; he was no longer in full control. He was a sad and weakened figure. In the course of one speech at Geneva he lost consciousness and then, coming back to the present, told his audience to be 'men and not mannequins'. That said, he fought harder than anyone else for disarmament and to stop Germany from abjuring clauses in the Versailles agreement.

He did not of course succeed, but there is some irony in the fact that it was MacDonald, the man who had been vilified for opposing the First World War, that was particularly prescient in recognising the dangers of Hitler, the Reichstag Fire, the Dollfuss takeover in Austria—'slavery willingly accepted because the herd mind as a discipline has taken the place of individual characteristics'.[2] He saw the significance of these things with an intellectual clarity which was denied to most of his colleagues.

By December he was able to make another brief visit to Geneva to try to rescue negotiations. But he was suffering from 'brain fag', and he told a colleague that he had broken down from top to toe. On 27 December he wrote,

> I left Geneva as depressed as though I had got no agreement & ... arrived in London able to do nothing with my head & so physically tired that I could hardly walk. If people only knew! After a week in London I had to throw in my hand and came away [to Lossiemouth], & gave Ll. G. the chance to make a spiteful personal attack ... Were things normal, it would be wise for me to rest now. But if I did, what would happen? ... Who wd. be PM. The govt. wd. be Consvtve. Could Mr Chamberlain run it? As yet, he could not.

*

Hanging on in these circumstances implies a degree of conceit and self-delusion. Although to a degree he seems to have been unaware of the impression he was giving, he was not *wholly* unaware. In his diary for 22 March 1933 he recorded how apprehensive he was about an upcoming speech. On the following day: 'trying to get something clear into my head for the H of C tomorrow. Cannot be done. Like man flying in mist: can fly all right but cannot see the course ... Tomorrow there will be another "vague" speech impossible to follow &c. and as usual with these attacks of head & eyes no sleep tonight'.[3]

By the summer of 1934 his health was giving serious concern. He had a lengthy consultation with Sir Thomas Horder and Dr Stewart Duke-Elder, who told him that he needed three months' rest from close work for the sake of his eyes. After a brief holiday in Lossiemouth, he and his daughter Sheila sailed for Canada. They arrived on 19 July and then spent two and a half months exploring Quebec, Nova Scotia, Newfoundland and Labrador. He enjoyed the holiday and was particularly gratified to find so many people of Scots descent. He may have rested his eyes, but he worried about the political situation at home. He was less and less happy with his association with the Conservatives, but could see no real prospects of any new party grouping. He claimed in his diary to want to retire ('My road is not a Tory one'), but he did nothing about it.

Even while he was still in Canada, he was conscious that his health had not improved; on one occasion for a spell his memory went completely. He was no better when he got to London. Nightmares, which he had experienced in Canada, alternated with periods of insomnia. His headaches and sight problems continued. There were frequent further problems with memory and periods of what he called 'stupidity' or 'brain tiredness'. On one occasion JCC Davidson, Baldwin's confidant, currently Chancellor of the Duchy of Lancaster, found him lying on a sofa in Baldwin's room in a state of collapse. Baldwin, always amazingly tolerant of MacDonald's failings—perhaps because he had no burning desire to assume the burdens of office—said how useful it was that he still was in cabinet.

Collusive kindliness or not, the spectacle of MacDonald's declining health became an increasingly public one and a demeaning one—though it isn't clear whether he was entirely conscious of how serious it was. He was being referred to as 'Ramshackle Mac'. His physical decline was at least matched by his mental decline. He lost the thread of what he was saying. On one occasion he appeared indeed to have lost the power of speech altogether. In parliament this sad spectacle increasingly provoked not sympathy but derision. When he did speak, it was difficult to follow his line of thought, which had never been the most obvious quality of his oratory. His meaningless ramblings were openly mocked.

Baldwin was kind and supportive and often stood in for MacDonald, but he was well aware of what was happening: 'Poor old Ramsay was a doughty fighter in his early days; it was tragic to see him in his closing days as PM losing the thread of his speech and turning to ask why people were laughing.'[4] It was good of Baldwin to sustain MacDonald and not seek to propel him from the stage. He was the obvious successor, but he too was getting older: indeed, MacDonald thought he and Baldwin might retire together and that it would be Neville Chamberlain who would succeed him. But Baldwin was not totally bereft of an appetite for power. He was to have two years in Number Ten between MacDonald and Chamberlain.

*

Christmas at Lossiemouth as always revived him, but by the beginning of 1935 his doctor, Horder, was warning him that he could not go on forever. Maurice Hankey, the Cabinet Secretary, thought that he was too tired to continue. In his diary for 23 February 1935 MacDonald allowed himself to hope that 'freedom' was not far ahead. 'The allurements of the end become more enticing: Upper Frognal Lodge, the Hillocks, Spynie' where Margaret's ashes were buried.

*

The next great conference was of a different kind. An imperial economic conference opened at Ottawa on 21 July 1932. MacDonald wasn't present. The British delegation was headed by Baldwin but truly dominated by Chamberlain. This conference was to decide whether free trade was to be replaced by imperial preference. Such a development would fracture a government in which the free trade

HEALTH AND DIPLOMACY

Liberals would not remain. This worried MacDonald greatly. His position was invidious enough as it was. If the Liberals left and he was surrounded by nothing but Conservatives, any pretence of being a 'national' government would have gone. He was also concerned about his personal position. He knew he was already regarded as hanging on to office for its own sake, and he had no wish to appear even more limpet-like than he was already.

The conference did much less than was hoped. 'Enough discrimination was achieved', says Roy Jenkins, 'to give the Americans a running grievance, but not enough to produce any great stimulation of Empire trade.'[5] A scheme was devised which would involve higher tariffs on trade between the British Empire and the rest of the world. It wasn't the most dramatic of outcomes, but it was enough to shake out one component of the National Government. The official Liberals under Herbert Samuel, the purest supporters of free trade, left the government. The National Liberals, under Sir John Simon, felt able to remain.

Samuel had made it very clear what would happen, and MacDonald was desperate to avoid the secession and contain the unity of the government. He felt that its whole authority rested on the fact that it was a national coalition. Snowden thought that the Tories, now the anti-free trade party, were abusing their strength, and MacDonald was inclined to agree. He urged Samuel not to go. At the final cabinet meeting before the Samuelites departed, Baldwin with his fondness for nautical metaphors told them that they had 'signed on for the voyage'. Samuel replied by pointing out that it was the Conservatives who had refused to adhere to a common policy: 'All the sacrifices had come from the free traders.' The Samuelites left and the cabinet resumed after lunch without them. MacDonald said that he had thought of resigning but felt it was his duty to stay. Baldwin at his side on the bridge said that the Prime Minister 'had taken command of the ship for a definite purpose and must see it through'.* In his diary that night MacDonald was appropriately gloomy. He said he had never doubted his duty, but 'this [is] nae my ain hoose'.

---

* His final nautical metaphor was when he resigned as Prime Minister. He said that he would not spit on the deck or talk to the man at the wheel.

32

NATIONAL GOVERNMENT WITHOUT SAMUEL

After the withdrawal of the Samuelite Liberals, the National Government was not quite the same—just as MacDonald had feared. It was less national. MacDonald's dependence on the Conservatives was greater and more evident, and he didn't like that. He spoke about how he and Jimmy Thomas were 'two of us in the very curious position of being amongst the leaders of a party to which we do not belong and made responsible for a policy which we cannot control'.[1] MacDonald had the right, as Prime Minister, to demand a dissolution, and on one or two occasions he warned Baldwin that he would use that right.

Philip Snowden had stood down from the Commons at the November 1931 general election, but went to the Lords where he was Lord Privy Seal until he too resigned over the Ottawa Agreement. Churchill neatly but unkindly said that when Snowden took his seat in the Lords, he had 'marketed what might be called the surrender value of his life policy in socialism, on terms happily advantageous both to himself and to his country'.[2] MacDonald and Snowden had never been all that close, but they had been together for a long time and they shared a belief in balanced, Gladstonian finance.

So MacDonald was increasingly alone. He was also increasingly frail. His health troubled him in many ways. He was physically and spiritually exhausted and sometimes required medical stimulants; he frequently found himself despairing and depressed. In the revealing glare of modern politics he would not have remained in office.

*

He was, however, energised by travels abroad. Franklin D Roosevelt's inauguration as US President took place in March 1933. MacDonald was impressed by Roosevelt's tone but concerned by his lack of experience. He felt strong enough to visit Roosevelt in Washington just a few weeks after the inauguration. While he was there, the President's German Shepherd dog, 'Major', attacked him and ripped the seat out of his trousers. He was supplied with a replacement pair of trousers, and Major was exiled to Roosevelt's country home, Hyde Park, New York State. While he was impressed by the President's energy, he thought that the New Deal programme of government works was extravagant and over-ambitious, far from Gladstonian. The New Deal might perhaps have offered some lessons to Britain, but MacDonald learned nothing from it.

*

MacDonald's final appearance on the diplomatic stage was at Stresa, on Lake Maggiore, in April 1935, at a conference called to take stock of the implications of Germany's decision to rearm, introduce conscription and very evidently prepare for war. The conference was called by Mussolini, not yet happy with what he saw developing to his north. The outcome was the formation of an anti-German Front consisting of Italy, France and Great Britain. There was great promise here: had the Front held, Hitler would have been checked. But the Front didn't hold, not even for six months. It fell apart because Mussolini doubted Britain's commitment, and he was reinforced in his views when Sir John Simon went to Berlin for talks just before the conference and Britain signed a naval agreement with Germany just after it. Thus Mussolini found it convenient that Hitler would allow him to invade Abyssinia and that in return he would allow Hitler to annex Austria.

There is a tragic irony in the fact that MacDonald's long efforts on the international scene, starting with a desire to redress the foolish treatment of Germany in 1919 and ending now with a realistic attempt to thwart her renewed ambitions, were destroyed in just a few weeks and so unnecessarily. Because at Stresa, MacDonald had been very clear-sighted about the dangers posed by the rise of Nazism in Germany. He had appreciated what was happening from

NATIONAL GOVERNMENT WITHOUT SAMUEL

an early point. In 1933 he had referred to 'the flabby piety of pacifism'. He apprehended the novelty and nature of fascism as his appeaser colleagues in the National Government did not. Although he had consistently criticised the Versailles Treaty, he did not think that Hitlerism was a phenomenon which could be contained by redressing a few grievances. He was much more realistic than Chamberlain, and he did not view a German war as unnecessary and avoidable in the 1930s, as he had in the years before 1914.

It is important not to see his role in foreign affairs too much through the prism of his deteriorating health and vitality. While his personal authority had undoubtedly diminished at home, he was still known and admired on the foreign stage as no other member of a distinctly shabby cabinet was. It was regrettable that his Foreign Secretary was the National Liberal, Sir John Simon. As the historian Kevin Morgan said, 'Simon must have been suited for something, but not this.'[3] So MacDonald continued to cut a significant figure on the international scene. He still had sparkle. Clynes described the Prime Minister as 'the echo that was MacDonald', but that was truer of his performance in the Commons than abroad.

Indeed there had been no doubt that MacDonald would lead the delegation to Stresa. Anthony Eden, the Under-Secretary at the Foreign Office, recognised MacDonald's mastery in foreign affairs.[4] Baldwin was perfectly happy to be subordinate to MacDonald in general, and in foreign affairs he had no interest whatsoever. He could find his way around the continental spas and watering places, but otherwise Worcestershire was his world.

MacDonald had gone to the four-day conference at Stresa reluctantly. He came back, predictably, the worse of the trip. Ill and exhausted, he was still able to compose a useful memorandum for Baldwin's benefit as Prime Minister and to participate in the events in May that marked George V's Silver Jubilee. He wrote of a reception for the diplomatic corps on 8 May that 'the King's reply was a perfect expression of sovereign affection & solicitude. When he came to references & reminiscences personal to himself & the Queen his voice broke & tears stood in her eyes. Everyone deeply moved. Here the Empire was a great family, the gathering a family reunion, the King a paternal head.' Not the reactions of a revolutionary but of one simple and sincere man appreciating the same qualities in another.

*

Domestic politics in this period were less than heroic. Cooperative societies had hitherto been exempt from tax on their trading profits and investment income. It was suggested that the exemption was artificial and should be ended. MacDonald had enjoyed some support from the cooperative movement when he formed the National Government, and he had said there would be no tax on cooperative societies as long as he was a member of the government. Though he maintained that he had only been talking about the dividend paid to members, his pledge was an embarrassment. His fight was with the new Chancellor, the uncompromising Neville Chamberlain. Chamberlain refused to compromise and indeed threatened to resign. MacDonald gave way, but unhappily and blaming Chamberlain for intransigence.

Within a matter of weeks he received a further challenge on a financial matter. A large number of backbenchers demanded a free vote on an amendment to the Finance Bill which would repeal the land tax clauses of Snowden's budget of 1931.[*] MacDonald was not prepared to accept this, particularly so soon after his defeat on the cooperative taxes. Baldwin met the unhappy MPs and persuaded them to withdraw their amendment. This they did, but a year later the land tax clauses came up again. This time MacDonald was persuaded by Thomas to accept defeat.

*

The economy was beginning to recover. The recovery was hesitant: unemployment, though reducing after 1932, was still very high in certain areas, and it would be another year or two before the fall was evident; but the tide was turning. All the same, there were other

---

[*] Land values had soared while the rest of the economy stagnated in the early 1930s as a result of the building boom and the creation of new housing areas. Snowden had sought to tax resulting profits in line with the policy that had found favour with Labour and, indeed, Liberal governments from 1906 onwards.

reverses and embarrassments. MacDonald's general state of mind is reflected in a lengthy memorandum,[5] complaining about lack of discipline among the Conservative element in the House and about the fact that Conservative members saw themselves as Conservatives first and National representatives second. He argued that there was a lack of enthusiasm for the character that the government was tending to acquire, and there might even be room for a new party. His own future he thought, or threatened, would be to give up the premiership but remain in the government in a subsidiary position and, after that, to withdraw from political life altogether.

By the end of 1934 there was a question of Lloyd George's coming back into the government, largely as a result of the success of his campaign for a national development plan. Lloyd George could never be regarded as a spent political force. Even after 1940 Churchill regarded him as a potential threat. MacDonald had formerly been very hostile to Lloyd George, but on this occasion he contemplated the possibility of a rapprochement. It was Neville Chamberlain who killed the idea.

*

In the course of 1934 MacDonald saw that defence spending needed to be increased in the face of developments in Germany. His thoughts were in line with those of the Defence Requirements Committee (DRC), which was pressing for an increase. While he had been in Canada the negotiations with the DRC continued, and the cabinet took fright and cut back the scale of rearmament recommended by the committee. Soon after his return the cabinet was obliged to conclude that Germany would shortly have an army of 300,000 men as opposed to the 100,000 allowed by Versailles and that within a year Germany's air force would be as large as Britain's. MacDonald chaired a new cabinet committee, and despite opposition from Chamberlain, he succeeded in accelerating the expansion of the Royal Air Force. He took no pleasure in the need for spending on defence, but he could see that after a period of neglect action was needed.

And as 1935 began and Hitler became increasingly threatening, the need to focus on defence spending became more urgent. At the

THE CANCELLED PRIME MINISTER

East Fulham by-election in October 1933 a Conservative arguing for armaments had been defeated by a Labour candidate who secured a majority of 4,840 in what had been a safe Tory seat. In May 1935 the 'Peace Ballot' showed strong support for disarmament. Just before MacDonald retired as Prime Minister, the government published a White Paper, *Statement Relating to Defence*, one of the last documents he initialled as Prime Minister, which said that the government could 'no longer close its eyes to the fact that adequate defences are still required'. The difference between 1935 and 1914 was that MacDonald believed that Britain was now directly threatened as she had not been by the Kaiser.

MacDonald's initials were on the document, and it was on him that Labour and the Liberals turned their anger. He didn't like what he called 'the militarists', but he could see that much rearmament leeway had to be made good. He had none of Chamberlain's wilful optimism. When a plebiscite in the Saar* resulted in a huge majority in favour of return to Germany, he saw that war was not far away. The Defence White Paper, published on 4 March 1935, contained an unequivocal argument for serious preparation for war.

By now the date of Baldwin's succession had been pretty well agreed. On 28 May, MacDonald recorded a

> Committee of six leaders to discuss my resignation. Little ungracious. Agreed Baldwin sd. succeed I remaining in government provided it was to remain really National, test being distribution of offices & common policy for an election. This scene in my room of this gathering of the elders was queer. Baldwin sat as one troubled in spirit but almost dumb of tongue; ... Neville with an eye on Baldwin as though ready to pounce on him, like a man who sees things coming and knows that he need do nothing to help or hasten them.

*

MacDonald procrastinated over the timing, but he recognised that he had to go. He had a personal meeting with the King on 16 May.

---

* The Versailles Treaty provided that the area around the Saar, mineral-rich and ethnically German, together with bits of Bavaria, was mandated for fifteen years to a theoretically independent government and was occupied by League troops.

NATIONAL GOVERNMENT WITHOUT SAMUEL

The King accepted that MacDonald would resign but made it a condition, as he put it, that he should remain in the cabinet as Lord President so that he might often see him. The King knew that MacDonald would not take a peerage, but he pressed him to accept the Order of the Thistle. MacDonald replied he could not accept that his name should be prefixed by 'Sir' and said that he would value the offer as much as the ribbon itself. 'The King's words were those of a close personal friend.' The King told MacDonald that he understood perfectly well that he wouldn't want a title and said that if he were a self-made man the last thing he would want was a peerage. He couldn't understand why John Buchan wanted one on becoming Governor General of Canada.

The audience lasted for fifty minutes so that the King was quarter of an hour late for his next audience. He said he hoped that MacDonald might have

> seen me through, but I now know it is impossible. But I do not think it will be very long. I wonder how you have stood it—especially the loss of your friends & their beastly behaviour .... You have been the Prime Minister I have liked best; you have so many qualities, you have kept up the dignity of the office without using it to give you dignity.

MacDonald left for Lossiemouth on the night train.

There was a little pressure to stay on from some National Labour MPs, but there was no serious question of any change of plan. He agreed with Baldwin, who was 'troubled in spirit but almost dumb of tongue', that they would exchange places and that MacDonald would indeed become the Lord President of the Council, as the King had proposed. MacDonald thought this kept the national character of the government. But in truth he was in no hurry to disappear into a heathery gloom. At the final cabinet meeting on 5 June, Baldwin paid a routine tribute. There were a couple of dinners.

On 7 June 1934 he surrendered the seals of office, and Baldwin kissed hands and received them. Ramsay MacDonald's departure had been pretty downbeat.

33

DECLINE

The decline continued. MacDonald's golf was affected. 'My head & eyes refuse to concentrate. They refuse to think.' He was told that he was suffering from an overtired brain and was told to take six months' rest. He began an autobiography.

The remainder of MacDonald's political life was pretty grim. His health didn't revive when he surrendered the seals of office. What frustrated him most was that he wanted to continue to be influential in foreign policy, but he found that he just could not express himself comprehensibly. The Italian invasion of Abyssinia worried him. He felt that Britain was alienating Mussolini by her attitude. To his humiliation, Eden and Hoare said they were too busy to speak to him.

MacDonald always worried about the diminishing 'national' characteristic of the government. A year later, preparing to leave the cabinet entirely, he reflected that it was difficult for him to give 'a backing to the National combination as it had evolved under Mr B'.[1] The Conservatives wanted to consolidate their position now that they had their own man in Number Ten; and MacDonald's distaste for an early election was ignored. A general election was called in October 1935. MacDonald, now Lord President of the Council and still in the government, advised Baldwin to make rearmament the key point of the National Government manifesto. Baldwin chose not to. Indeed he told the public, 'I give you my word that there will be no great armaments.' He had observed the East Fulham by-election and the Peace Ballot. Later, in his 'appalling frankness' statement to the Commons, he said, 'Supposing I had gone to the country and said that Germany was rearming and that we must rearm, does anybody think that this pacific democracy would have rallied to that cry at that moment? I cannot think of anything that would have made the loss of the election from my point of view more certain.'* The outcome of the 1935 general election was satisfactory for the Conservatives. They still had a huge vote, although down 86 since 1931. The Simonite National Liberals were down two seats to 33. MacDonald's National Labour representation went down five to just 8. Labour itself, now led by Clement Attlee, had a very creditable increase in 102 seats, making a total of 154.

At a personal level the election was a disaster for MacDonald. It had been clear throughout the campaign that he was going to lose his seat. There was heckling and barracking and angry crowds. At least one meeting had to be abandoned. Hatred was untinged by sympathy for the old and broken man who had been idolised in his prime. MacDonald was shocked by the way he was seen by the electors. 'Some of the displays were absolutely bestial. Many of the faces of the women were lined with destitution; their eyes flamed & gleamed with hate & passion; their hair was dishevelled; their language filthy with oaths & some obscenity; they filled one with loathing & fear just like French Revolution studies.'[2]

He was warned that he should be prepared for defeat by at least 15,000. Malcolm MacDonald was also heading for defeat: 'Luck has been hard, and I cannot put my crushed feelings into thought. For myself I care nothing. I was prepared for myself, but not for him.' To make matters worse, his own opponent was his old protégé, Manny Shinwell. Shinwell received 38,380 votes; MacDonald less than half of that, 17,882.

He had been offered an alternative safe seat by a National Liberal MP but declined it, fearing that it would affect the outcome in other

---

* Thus the index entry in the first volume of his war memoirs: 'Baldwin, Stanley, confesses putting party before country'. The tone isn't characteristic: Churchill didn't nurse his wrath, and he didn't compile or sanction the index (see Williamson, 'Baldwin's Reputation', pp. 127–68). But he didn't repudiate it. What Baldwin said was not as disgraceful as it has seemed to be in popular memory; there was more nuance than history has chosen to record. Baldwin was partly to blame when he chose the words 'appalling frankness' to describe his admission to the House.

seats if he were seen to withdraw from Seaham. Before the election MacDonald's last duty as Lord President had been to attend at the swearing-in of Malcolm as a privy counsellor. Malcolm had just been appointed Secretary of State for the Colonies, the youngest member of the cabinet. It had been a proud occasion, although his father noted in his diary that Malcolm's coat fitted badly. Now Malcolm, like his father, lost his seat. But still MacDonald clung on. The King told him that he should remain in government and that he would be grieved and unhappy if he did not. The King said he did not expect to live for more than five years and that MacDonald could go after that. Baldwin asked him to come back via a by-election and MacDonald agreed, providing a seat could also be found for Malcolm. Malcolm was in due course found an alternative seat. Even more speedily, MacDonald himself came back to parliament with a Scottish Universities seat. The Combined Scottish Universities seat existed from 1918 to 1945. It was a three-member constituency, made up of former one-member constituencies for graduates of the four older Scottish universities. At general elections a single transferable vote was used; at by-elections the crude first-past-the-post method. The political flavour of the seat is reflected by the fact that MacDonald's three predecessors were Coalition Conservatives or Unionists, his successor a National Conservative; and that his fellow members were National Liberals and Unionists.

*

The King didn't last his five years: he died in January 1936. Just a few hours before he died, a Privy Council meeting was held at Sandringham so that the royal consent could be given to the proclamation setting up the Council of State which appeared to be necessary. MacDonald was present and was much moved by the King's incapacities. This final farewell has already been mentioned, but it's worth repeating MacDonald's words. They go to the essence of his relationship with the King, whose wishes had so significantly dictated MacDonald's conduct. Watching the King struggle to write moved him to tears.

> Then we began to walk out of the bedroom. At first the King took no notice but was told that we were going. He looked at us &

smiled. I was the last out & I shall never forget the look illuminated by affection (his eyes looked rather large) which he gave me & continued it as I went out & bowed a second time—my final farewell to a gracious & Kingly friend & a master whom I have served with all my heart.

But MacDonald's own situation was pitiable. He was pleased that Malcolm had received a ministry, and there were those old friends who continued to keep in touch with him. Otherwise he was pretty well ignored. He attended the Committee of Imperial Affairs and the Defence Requirements Committee and the cabinet itself. But in general he wandered through the Palace of Westminster, sometimes snubbed and otherwise ignored, hampered by failing eyesight and failing memory, sometimes with distressing and embarrassing results.

He was affected by the plight of his very old colleague Jimmy Thomas, who was found to have leaked budget secrets and to have accepted improper payments. Thomas had to resign from the cabinet and from the House. MacDonald entered very much into the family grief.

Just as he felt that Thomas had somehow been shabbily treated, he thought that he too was being slighted—even by Baldwin, who had been such a loyal subordinate for so long. His new distaste for Baldwin was partly based on the Prime Minister's weakness, as MacDonald saw it, in allowing himself to be pushed around by his party, notably Chamberlain, whom he saw as aggressively ambitious.

He found it difficult to dispatch business. He had problems with writing and even talking. But his perceptive insight in foreign affairs meant that he could see, as the Conservatives generally did not, the significance of the Spanish Civil War. He could see that the British policy of non-intervention assisted the dictators, and he complained that the cabinet could not see the drift to Nazism and the breakdown of democracy. In this he was ahead of most of his colleagues.

George VI was to be crowned in May 1937. Baldwin decided he would go after the coronation, and MacDonald came to the same conclusion. He attended his last cabinet on 12 May 1937. It was a particularly humiliating exit. Before it had finished, he asked Baldwin, still Prime Minister, if he could go early as the agenda was finishing. Baldwin told him he could. He sat on for a moment or two

DECLINE

and then left. That was that. On the following day he had an audience of the King. George VI offered him a peerage, as George V, Baldwin and Chamberlain had done. He declined again. On 28 May Baldwin tendered his own resignation and that of the government. That was the end of MacDonald's career as a minister, although he remained an MP for the rest of his life.

That was a very short period. He gave a farewell party at Frognal Lodge, where Sir Walter Citrine was the only other representative of the labour movement. When Citrine was leaving, he found MacDonald 'sitting at the top of the staircase, bending forward with his head between his hands'. 'O, I am tired,' he said.[3]

On 5 November, MacDonald and Sheila set off for South America in search of rest. It went badly from the start. When the ship called in at La Rochelle MacDonald was knocked down by a bicycle. On the following day he played deck quoits but felt seasick afterwards. On 9 November he had another game of quoits, and again felt the worse of it. At a quarter to eight that evening he died of heart failure.

A service took place in Hamilton, Bermuda, followed by a lying-in-state attended by thousands. His body was brought back to England on the Royal Navy cruiser *Apollo*.

MacDonald had been conceived in a farm bothy in Moray, but his funeral took place in Westminster Abbey on 26 November. The pallbearers included the Prime Minister, Neville Chamberlain, the Speaker, Sir John Simon, Lord De La Warr, Baldwin and Clement Attlee. The Archbishop of Canterbury gave the blessing and the names of those attending filled more than three columns in *The Times*, ranging from the Duke of Gloucester, representing the King, to members of Hampstead Rotary Club. Among old cabinet colleagues were Clynes, Mr and Mrs JH Thomas, Sankey, Greenwood, and Lord and Lady Londonderry. The *Civil and Military Gazette*, Lahore, reported that the proceedings concluded with 'a Scottish Dirge'. Almost certainly they were referring to the haunting lament 'The Flowers of the Forest', composed to mark the deaths of James IV and his followers, the flower of Scottish manhood, at the Battle of Flodden, a refrain so special that few pipers will play it except as a solemn act of remembrance.

After a private cremation service MacDonald's ashes were taken to Lossiemouth. There was a service in the Hillocks and then a procession moved to Spynie churchyard, where MacDonald was interred beside Margaret and David. His public persona had already been all but obliterated. Now the private man, too, disappeared into the mist.

34

JUDGEMENT

Ramsay MacDonald was one of Britain's longest-serving Prime Ministers. What were his achievements? He left his mark on foreign affairs. He was Britain's most effective Foreign Secretary of the inter-war years.

We have seen his astuteness in dealing with the actors on the European stage—his sensitive approach to French concerns and reducing tensions between France and Germany. His approach was personal and direct. His chemical connection with his interlocutors made things happen. His awareness of internal concerns in the United States was also unusual. He won the confidence of the US Secretary of State Henry Stimson and established a warm personal relationship with Roosevelt. It is notable that the United States was more suspicious of Britain *after* MacDonald's retirement. He understood and adjusted to American concerns about the League of Nations and the effect of sanctions. He was able to fight for Britain's naval interests without forfeiting American goodwill. DC Watt, reviewing the American archives, acknowledges that MacDonald never had to face the trials of the late 1930s. 'But, for all that, he emerges as a much more considerable figure in the field of foreign affairs than Simon, Hoare, or the young Eden ...; a worthy equal to Grey, Austen Chamberlain, or Curzon at their best.'[1] Looking at MacDonald's medical history against those of Ernest Bevin and Sir Stafford Cripps and of Sir Anthony Eden, Watt concludes that MacDonald's ill health may have been the result of the burden of foreign affairs.

If Hitler had not risen to power and resumed the interrupted war, MacDonald would have been seen as a hard-working and humane statesman who did much to make the unworkable settlement of Versailles work.

His domestic achievements, in terms of statute and structure, are pretty well non-existent. He gave a favouring wind to legislation for a federal India in the 1935 Government of India Act, but Churchill's obstructiveness and the outbreak of the Second World War stymied that.

In both Labour administrations a minority position obviously limited his capacity to pass grandiose legislation, and the nature of his position in the National Government was even more inhibiting. In any event he was not a radical or, at any rate by the 1920s, a socialist in any sense other than that he believed in progressive politics. He was not out to erect landmarks. David Marquand described him as 'an evolutionary utopian', and even that may be going too far. If he was a utopian, his idea of utopia was an existence not devised by Marx or any other theorists, not much more than a fair society. The route to it was a succession of little steps. 'One step! One step enough for me! Ah yes, my friend, as long as it leads to the next step.' He would quote from the hymn 'Lead, Kindly Light':

> Keep Thou my feet; I do not ask to see
> The distant scene; one step enough for me.

His great achievement was that Labour displaced the Liberal Party as the progressive alternative to the capitalist Conservative Party. That need not have happened. Labour could well have been subsumed into the Liberal Party. Many thought that would happen. Equally possibly, Labour could have withered away as irrelevant. The Liberal Party could have adapted, as many Continental parties did, to absorb the workers' vote. MacDonald's achievement, in his long years of work in the different strands of the Labour Party before he entered parliament and in the discipline which he imposed on the wilder elements of the parliamentary party thereafter, was to create a party that could last. He sought to demonstrate that Labour was ready for government and responsibility.

This book is an attempt to evaluate MacDonald's character and his actions. The most difficult part is exploring his reasons for

JUDGEMENT

assuming leadership of the National Government. He certainly thought that if he had not done what he did—accept personal and not party responsibility for the measures of 1931—the Labour Party's emergence as the second party of government would have been checked, perhaps forever. It was not, and that is because he had so established the Labour Party that it could survive the National Government years to form the victorious administration of 1945. On one occasion he described his role as that of a craftsman-creator, and if the durability of the Labour Party, despite 1931 and subsequent schisms and splits, continues to exist because of his craftsmanship, he would no doubt be pleased with what he had done.[2]

The opacity of his speaking style mirrored an intellectual vagueness. When the Labour Party drew up its programme in 1928, *Labour and the Nation*, the widespread reaction was that no one was much the wiser for reading it. Despite the fact that he had drafted it, RH Tawney pleaded with MacDonald to flesh it out with 'something concrete and definite about unemployment' in the subsequent election manifesto.[3] That wasn't MacDonald's way. He even told the Commons that he was 'one of those curious specimens of a Conservative who sits with the Labour Party. I am Conservative because I have a profound respect for historical institutions.'[4] He was saying that he was a pragmatist. He was pragmatic from the start. It didn't upset him that he should dress up to keep the King happy: the cavils of self-righteous colleagues seemed self-indulgent and unnecessary to him.

MacDonald had a high opinion of his own abilities. He was deprecating about the abilities of his colleagues both before and after the formation of the National Government. He criticised Labour politicians not because they were Labour, but because he didn't think much of most of them: in its early days, a new party will have people of pretty mixed abilities. But he was jealous of rivals, not just critical of unimpressive brains, and may have held back some people of real ability. Some have blamed MacDonald not so much for 1931 as for the two years before then, when, they have argued, the government was weak, unadventurous and timid.[5] But that scarcely does justice to the political situation, either in terms of Labour Party strength or of the forces that buffeted the institutions, politics and finance. Lord Skidelsky says that 'a Ministry of Economic Affairs plus an expansionist chancellor were indispensable: Bevin or Mosley in harness with Lloyd George at the Exchequer would have been the best combination',[6] but such a scenario was never possible. It is true that MacDonald's style of leadership, aloof and slightly contemptuous, did not make for dramatic or dynamic leadership, but it would have taken more than bravura to have reassured markets. The Labour leadership generally did give an appearance of senility, and many of its personalities were party veterans whose experience encouraged conservatism, but the primary purpose of Labour had to be to reassure; and MacDonald's success was to preside over a realignment in British politics which took place without the shocks and extremism that accompanied realignments in mainland Europe.

Was it a mistake for MacDonald to go into the National Government without his party? At a personal level it certainly was; his personal standing has never recovered. At a political level he sacrificed himself not only for the sake of his country, but also for the sake of saving his party from the contamination of cohabitation. His party was still there in 1940 and 1945, even if he has been cancelled, his image cut out of the Politburo Labour photograph. His misfortune in 1931 was to be at the fulcrum of the tension between theory and practicality, a tension that persists to the present day.

*

That misfortune was not of his making. There was no conspiracy or treachery. He made mistakes in his political career, as all politicians do. He was a poor delegator and didn't inspire personal loyalty among his colleagues. He had, however, a clear sense of what he wanted. His achievement was, more than that of anyone else, to make Labour the single progressive political party in Britain, disciplined, businesslike and practical. Most European countries at the beginning of the twentieth century had a multiplicity of groupings on the left, as did Britain. They still have them, ranging from the mildly liberal to quasi-communist, splitting the opposition to parties of the right.

What Britain has instead is best seen in its finest manifestations. The first is in the Labour element of the great war-time coalition,

JUDGEMENT

when arguably Churchill's most effective ministers, like Attlee, Bevin and Morrison, came from the ranks of a united and disciplined party which resisted internal dissension to prosecute the war. The second is the great administration under Attlee from 1945 to 1950, which radically reshaped Britain while unflinchingly opposing Communist Russia.

We have read that Keir Hardie at an early stage in MacDonald's career spoke of him in terms of Wren's gravestone: 'If you seek his monument, look around you.' When we think of Ramsay MacDonald and wonder what he should be remembered for, we should look at the great achievements of his party between 1940 and 1950. They would not have happened but for him.

NOTES

The James Ramsay MacDonald Papers are held in the Public Records Office, John Rylands Research Institute and Library at the University of Manchester. I have consulted extensively in MacDonald's diaries. To avoid unnecessary clutter I have not provided citations or dates in instances which are uncontentious. I repeat here the caution attached to the diaries which I quote in the text. 'These notes must not be presented as they stand. They are jottings to present for any future use feelings put down as I felt them at the moment and not final or considered conclusions.'

PROLOGUE

1. Note in pencil describing Curzon's interview with Lord Stamfordham, quoted in Dundas, *The Life of Lord Curzon*, vol. 3, p. 352.
2. Nicolson, *Curzon*, p. 355.

1. BACKGROUND AND BEGINNINGS

1. Elton, *The Life of James Ramsay MacDonald*, pp. 15–16.
2. *Sunday Express*, 9 June 1929.
3. Elton, *The Life of James Ramsay MacDonald*, p. 18.
4. Extract from Minute book of Alves Free Kirk Session, quoted in Marquand, *Ramsay MacDonald*, p. 5
5. Elton, *The Life of James Ramsay MacDonald*, p. 18.
6. Marquand, *Ramsay MacDonald*, p. 8.
7. The Royal Commission on the Employment of Children, Young Persons and Women in Agriculture, *Fourth Report* (HMSO, 1869), p. 35.
8. Royal Commission, *Fourth Report*, Appendix, Part II, pp. 27–8.
9. Skidelsky, *Politicians and the Slump*, p. 82.
10. Quoted in Watts, *Ramsay MacDonald*, pp. 12–13.
11. A Morgan, *J Ramsay MacDonald*, p. 13.
12. Cited in Cox, *A Singular Marriage*, p. 50.

13. K Morgan, *Ramsay MacDonald*, p. 89.
14. Jones and Middlemas, *Whitehall Diary*, vol. 2, p. 56.
15. Cole, *Beatrice Webb's Diaries*, pp. 121–2.
16. Ibid., p. 18.
17. MacDonald Papers, 3/49.
18. Macmillan, *The Past Masters*, p. 14.
19. Ibid., p. 89.
20. Ibid., p. 84.

2. A STEP TO THE SIDE

1. Quoted in Watts, *Ramsay MacDonald*, p. 9.
2. Watts, *Ramsay MacDonald*, p. 1.
3. Laski, *The Crisis and the Constitution*.

3. BRISTOL

1. Elton, *The Life of James Ramsay MacDonald*, p. 40.
2. Quoted in Davies, *To Build a New Jerusalem*, p. 56.
3. Shinwell, *The Labour Story*, p. 36.
4. Ibid., p. 36.
5. Marquand, *Ramsay MacDonald*, p. 18.

4. BEEFSTEAK PUDDINGS AND HOT WATER

1. K Morgan, *Ramsay MacDonald*, p. 15.
2. Marquand, *Ramsay MacDonald*, p. 20.
3. Elton, *The Life of James Ramsay MacDonald*, p. 58.
4. Ibid., pp. 58–9.
5. Letter to Mr Stewart, 18 September 1887, quoted in Marquand, *Ramsay MacDonald*, p. 21.
6. Marquand, *Ramsay MacDonald*, p. 23.
7. Hynes, *The Edwardian Turn of Mind*, p. 90.
8. Shinwell, *The Labour Story*, p. 35.

5. THE TESSELLATED PAVEMENT OF RADICAL POLITICS

1. Marquand, *Ramsay MacDonald*, p. 31.
2. *Clarion*, 7 February 1908.
3. *Oxford English Dictionary*.

NOTES pp. [45–72]

4. Elton, *The Life of James Ramsay MacDonald*, pp. 68–9.
5. Beatrice Webb, Diary, 18 October 1895, Passfield Papers, London School of Economics Library, Archives and Special Collections.
6. Beatrice Webb, Diary, 18 October 1896, Passfield Papers.
7. MacKenzie and MacKenzie, *The Diary of Beatrice Webb*, vol. 2, pp. 65–6.

6. THE STEPS OF THE BRITISH MUSEUM

1. Letters to MacDonald, June–July 1896, MacDonald Papers.
2. Cox, *A Singular Marriage*, pp. 60–5.
3. MacDonald Papers, 9 July 1896 and 15 July 1896.
4. Macmillan, *The Past Masters*, p. 86.

7. REFINING HIS PHILOSOPHY

1. Cole, *Beatrice Webb's Diaries*, pp. 117–18.
2. Williams, *A Pattern of Rulers*, p. 97.
3. Mackintosh, *Echoes of Big Ben*, p. 98.
4. A Morgan, *J Ramsay MacDonald*, p. 22.
5. KO Morgan, *Keir Hardie*, p. 142.
6. MacDonald to Herbert Samuel, 16 August 1895, quoted in Pelling, *The Origins of the Labour Party*, p. 167.
7. Quoted in *Labour Leader*, 13 March 1897.

8. SOUTH AFRICA AND BEYOND

1. Shaw to MacDonald, 20 November 1899, MacDonald Papers.
2. Marquand, *Ramsay MacDonald*, p. 67.
3. Quoted in Elton, *The Life of James Ramsay MacDonald*, p. 104.
4. *Labour Leader*, 21 April 1900.
5. Quoted in *ILP News*, April 1902.
6. Poirier, *The Advent of the Labour Party*, pp. 118–19.
7. MacDonald, *Socialism and Society*, p. 31.

9. WESTMINSTER

1. Jenkins, *Mr Balfour's Poodle*, pp. 10ff.
2. Elton, *The Life of James Ramsay MacDonald*, p. 133.
3. Cited in Bealey and Pelling, *Labour and Politics*, p. 155.

4. Shinwell, *The Labour Story*, p. 59.
5. Elton, *The Life of James Ramsay MacDonald*, p. 132.
6. Kirkwood, *My Life of Revolt*, p. 222.
7. *Socialist Review*, June 1911.
8. Hansard, 1911, vol. 27, cols. 114–19.
9. *Labour Leader*, 14 July 1911.
10. Nicolson, *King George V*, pp. 392–3.
11. Quoted in Snowden, *An Autobiography*.

10. FAMILY LIFE IN LOSSIEMOUTH

1. Private communication.

11. TRAGEDY

1. Quoted in Elton, *The Life of James Ramsay MacDonald*, p. 192.
2. Elton, *The Life of James Ramsay MacDonald*, p. 178.
3. Ibid., p. 194.
4. Katharine Bruce Glasier to MacDonald, 4 October 1911, MacDonald Papers.
5. MacDonald, *Margaret Ethel MacDonald*, pp. 54–5.
6. Elton, *The Life of James Ramsay MacDonald*, p. 199.
7. Diary, 26 September 1928 and 30 January 1929, MacDonald Papers.
8. Mrs Mary Agnes Hamilton became a Labour member of parliament. She differed with MacDonald over the events of 1931 and she described herself, even before then, as a 'loyal but critical follower'.

12. LEADER OF THE LABOUR PARTY

1. K Morgan, *Ramsay MacDonald*, p. 21.
2. Elton, *The Life of James Ramsay MacDonald*, p. 183.
3. Ibid., p. 186.
4. June 1910 (day of the month illegible).
5. Snowden, *An Autobiography*, vol. 1, p. 220.
6. Elton, *The Life of James Ramsay MacDonald*, p. 186.
7. Ibid., pp. 191–2.
8. Pelling, *The Origins of the Labour Party*, p. 226.
9. See Watts, *Ramsay MacDonald*, p. 27.
10. MacDonald, *The Socialist Movement*, pp. 148–9.

11. Quoted in Watts, *Ramsay MacDonald*, p. 31.
12. *Socialist Review*, October 1911.
13. Hansard, 1911, vol. 29, col. 1951.
14. MacDonald Papers, 30 July 1912.
15. Marquand, *Ramsay MacDonald*, p. 143.

13. MACDONALD'S LADIES

1. Marquand, *Ramsay MacDonald*, p. 148.
2. Pugh, *Speak for Britain!*, p. 205.
3. Marquand, *Ramsay MacDonald*, p. 406.
4. Interview with Iona Kielhorn.
5. Quoted from interview in Marquand, *Ramsay MacDonald*, p. 497.
6. 17 June 1935, Bibesco Papers, quoted in Marquand, *Ramsay MacDonald*, p. 687.
7. Sidney Webb, 'What Happened in 1931'.
8. Harold Laski in *Political Quarterly*, September 1932.
9. MacDonald to Londonderry, 16 February 1926, MacDonald Papers.

14. 1914: CRISIS

1. Elton, *The Life of James Ramsay MacDonald*, p. 226.
2. Quoted in Elton, *The Life of James Ramsay MacDonald*, p. 229.
3. Weir, *The Tragedy of Ramsay MacDonald*, p. 43.
4. Quoted in Weir, *The Tragedy of Ramsay MacDonald*, p. 48.
5. Snowden, *An Autobiography*.
6. Quoted in K Morgan, *Ramsay MacDonald*, p. 34.
7. Quoted in Elton, *The Life of James Ramsay MacDonald*, p. 266.
8. Elton, *The Life of James Ramsay MacDonald*, p. 259.
9. Diary, 25 October 1914, MacDonald papers.
10. Seely, *Adventure*, pp. 202ff.
11. MacDonald to Trevelyan, 5 August 1914, quoted in K Morgan, *Ramsay MacDonald*, p. 34.
12. Marquand, *Ramsay MacDonald*, p. 189.
13. *John Bull*, 20 and 22 February 1915.

15. HUMILIATIONS

1. Diary, 12 September 1914, MacDonald Papers.
2. Shinwell, *The Labour Story*, p. 49.

3. Ibid., pp. 49–50.
4. Cox, *A Singular Marriage*, pp. 686–9.
5. *The Press and Journal*, 19 December 1888; see McConnachie, *The Moray Golf Club at Lossiemouth*.
6. Beatrice Webb to Betty Balfour, 22 August 1913, Passfield Papers.

16. POLITICAL CHANGE

1. A Morgan, *J. Ramsay MacDonald*, p. 65.
2. Diary, 28 September 1915, MacDonald Papers.
3. Quoted in Watts, *Ramsay MacDonald*, p. 43.
4. See Taylor, *The Troublemakers*, p. 143.
5. *Forward*, 24 May 1919.
6. Diary, 9 October 1917, MacDonald Papers.
7. MacDonald, *Socialism after the War*, p. 41.

17. ABROAD AND IN THE WILDERNESS

1. *Leicester Daily Mercury*, 12 December 1918.
2. Letter to a friend, 18 August 1920, quoted in Marquand, *Ramsay MacDonald*, p. 241.
3. MacDonald, *Wanderings and Excursions*, pp. 57–61.
4. Marquand, *Ramsay MacDonald*, p. 270.

18. THE APPROACH TO POWER

1. Nevinson, *More Changes, More Chances*, pp. 315–16.
2. K Morgan, *Ramsay MacDonald*, p. 101.
3. Weir, *The Tragedy of Ramsay MacDonald*, p. 83.
4. *John Bull*, 16 June 1906.
5. Pugh, *Speak for Britain*, p. 165.
6. Quoted in Pugh, *Speak for Britain*, pp. 165–6.
7. Pugh, *Speak for Britain*, p. 164.
8. Quoted in Watts, *Ramsay MacDonald*, p. 55.
9. See Marquand, *Ramsay MacDonald*, p. 283.
10. Lyman, *The First Labour Government*, p. 8.
11. *The Labour Party's Aim*, pp. 13–14.
12. Diary, 1 January 1917, MacDonald Papers.
13. See Watts, *Ramsay MacDonald*, pp. 49–51.
14. Weir, *The Tragedy of Ramsay MacDonald*, p. 103.

NOTES   pp. [152–180]

15. Amery, *My Political Life*, vol. 2, p. 279; Nicolson, *King George V*, p. 404.
16. *The Times*, 17 November 1923.
17. *New Leader*, 23 November 1923.
18. *The Times*, 9 January 1924.
19. Butler, *The Electoral System in Britain*, p. 177.
20. Quoted in Lyman, *The First Labour Government*, p. 81.

19. GEORGE V

1. Nicolson, *King George V*, p. 383.
2. Ibid., p. 383.
3. A Morgan, *J. Ramsay MacDonald*, pp. 149–50.
4. Nicolson, *King George V*, p. 388n.
5. Clynes, Memoirs, pp. 343–4.
6. As has been noted, the protocol for his court forbade the presence of a party to a divorce, even the innocent party.
7. Nicolson, *King George V*, p. 388.
8. Quoted in Nicolson, *King George V*, p. 386.
9. Rose, *King George V*, p. 331.
10. Quoted in Watts, *Ramsay MacDonald*, p. 63.
11. Weir, *The Tragedy of Ramsay MacDonald*, p. 141.
12. Lyman, *The First Labour Government*, pp. 100–1.

20. REFLECTIONS FROM THE PINNACLE

1. Diary, 10 January 1924, MacDonald Papers.
2. Marquand, *Ramsay MacDonald*, p. 398.
3. MacDonald to Miss IM Drummond, 16 December 1925, MacDonald Papers.
4. Diary, 6 June 1926, MacDonald Papers.
5. Diary, 4 July 1926, MacDonald Papers.
6. Diary, 3 April 1927, MacDonald Papers.
7. Hamilton, *The Man of Tomorrow*, p. 174.

21. LABOUR IN POWER

1. Quoted in Watts, *Ramsay MacDonald*, p. 56.
2. Nicolson, *King George V*, p. 396.
3. Diary, 6 October 1930, MacDonald Papers.

4. Lyman, *The First Labour Government*, p. 100.
5. Marquand, *Ramsay MacDonald*, p. 299.
6. Churchill, *Great Contemporaries*, p. 223.
7. Lyman, *The First Labour Government*, p. 144n.
8. See Muggeridge, *The Thirties*, for a comparison of the two men.
9. Shinwell, *The Labour Story*, p. 123.
10. A Morgan, *J. Ramsay MacDonald*, p. 96.
11. *The Nation*, 2 February 1924, p. 627.
12. Marquand, *Ramsay MacDonald*, p. 307.
13. Interview with Iona Kielhorn.
14. Quoted in Marquand, *Ramsay MacDonald*, p. 357.
15. *The Times*, 18 January 1924.
16. Nicolson, *King George V*, p. 496.
17. Snowden, *Autobiography*, vol. 2, p. 631.
18. Hansard, 25 July 1924.
19. Torrance, *The Wild Men*, p. 94.

22. A MATINÉE IDOL ON THE WORLD STAGE

1. *The Times*, 23 July 1924.
2. Marquand, *Ramsay MacDonald*, p. 351.
3. Glasgow, *MacDonald as Diplomatist*, p. 230.
4. Nevinson, *Last Changes, Last Chances*, p. 309.
5. Shinwell, *Conflict without Malice*, p. 113.
6. Zimmern, 'The Prime Minister at Geneva', pp. 249–51.
7. Glasgow, *MacDonald as Diplomatist*, p. 41.
8. Diary, 27 September 1924, MacDonald Papers.

23. PROBLEMS CROWD IN

1. Weir, *The Tragedy of Ramsay MacDonald*, p. 160.
2. Grant to MacDonald, 5 and 8 February 1924, MacDonald Papers.
3. Torrance, *The Wild Men*, p. 39.
4. MacDonald to Grant, 27 April 1924, quoted in Torrance, *The Wild Men*, p. 65.
5. Marquand, *Ramsay MacDonald*, p. 366.
6. Jones and Middlemas, *Whitehall Diary*, vol. 1, p. 296.
7. Hansard, 1924, vol. 177, cols. 512–13.
8. Snowden, *An Autobiography*, vol. 2, p. 697.

9. A Morgan, *J. Ramsay MacDonald*, p. 103.
10. Quoted in Taylor, *The Troublemakers*, p. 97.
11. Ibid., p. 168.
12. Butler, *Electoral System in Britain*, p. 178.
13. Diary, 4 July 1926, MacDonald Papers.
14. Kirkwood, *My Life of Revolt*, p. 220.

24. OUT OF OFFICE

1. Quoted in Watts, *Ramsay MacDonald*, p. 81.
2. Diary, 3 December 1924, MacDonald Papers.
3. Marquand, *Ramsay MacDonald*, p. 419.
4. See Howell, *MacDonald's Party*, pp. 38–9.
5. Quoted in Cole, *Beatrice Webb's Diaries*, p. 63.
6. Bassett, *Nineteen Thirty-One*, p. 29.
7. Shinwell, *Conflict without Malice*, pp. 112–13.
8. Wertheimer, *Portrait of the Labour Party*, pp. 174–6.
9. David Marquand, '(James) Ramsay MacDonald', *Oxford Dictionary of National Biography* (online).
10. Middlemas, *The Clydesiders*, p. 79.
11. Shinwell, *Conflict without Malice*, p. 113.
12. Diary, 2 May 1926, MacDonald Papers.
13. Quoted in Watts, *Ramsay MacDonald*, p. 85.
14. Ibid., p. 88.

25. STOCKTAKE

1. Diary, May 1918, MacDonald Papers.
2. Morgan Phillips at International Socialist Conference in Copenhagen, June 1950, quoted in Phillips, *Morgan Phillips*, p. 162.
3. Donoughue, 'Harold Wilson'.

26. THE SECOND GOVERNMENT

1. Skidelsky, *Politicians and the Slump*, p. xii.
2. Diary, 5 June 1929, MacDonald Papers.
3. K Morgan, *Ramsay MacDonald*, p. 63.
4. Nicolson, *King George V*, p. 436.
5. Ibid., p. 435.

6. Quote from 'The Man Who Talks for Britain', *New York Times*, 29 September 1929.
7. Weir, *The Tragedy of Ramsay MacDonald*, p. 270.
8. Quoted in Marquand, *Ramsay MacDonald*, p. 572.
9. K Morgan, *Ramsay MacDonald*, p. 69.
10. Diary, 5 June 1930, MacDonald Papers.
11. K Morgan, *Ramsay MacDonald*, p. 66.
12. A Morgan, *J. Ramsay MacDonald*, p. 157.

27. CRASH

1. Marquand, *Ramsay MacDonald*, p. 518.
2. For a general discussion see King, *We Need to Talk about Inflation*.
3. PREM 11/2973, National Archives, Kew.
4. Quoted in Thorpe, *Supermac*.
5. Skidelsky, *John Maynard Keynes: Fighting for Britain*, p. 499.
6. Skidelsky, *Politicians and the Slump*, Appendix IV: Mosley Memorandum Material, pp. 407–8.
7. Macmillan, *The Past Masters*, p. 104.
8. K Morgan, *Ramsay MacDonald*, p. 68.
9. Easily confused with Lord Parmoor, mentioned above, who had also been put in the Lords by a grateful party—in his case, the Liberals in 1914.
10. MacKenzie and MacKenzie, *The Diary of Beatrice Webb*, p. 276.
11. Owen, *Tempestuous Journey*, p. 717.
12. See Williamson, *National Crisis*, pp. 229–52.

28. ECONOMIC CRISIS

1. Mowat, *Britain between the Wars*, p. 51.
2. MacDonald Papers, 1/260.
3. Marquand, *Ramsay MacDonald*, p. 611.
4. Snowden to MacDonald, 7 August 1931, MacDonald Papers, 1/260.
5. Nicolson, *King George V*, p. 458.
6. Diary, 20 August 1931, MacDonald Papers.
7. Diary, 22 August 1931, MacDonald Papers.
8. Cited in Marquand, *Ramsay MacDonald*, pp. 630–1.
9. Thorpe, *The British General Election of 1931*, p. 89.
10. See Skidelsky, *Politicians and the Slump*, p. 270 n. 2.

11. Sir Clive Wigram quoted in Nicolson, *King George V*, p. 464.
12. Quoted in Skidelsky, *Politicians and the Slump*, p. 279.
13. Weir, *The Tragedy of Ramsay MacDonald*, p. 369.
14. Quoted in Watts, *Ramsay MacDonald*, p. 111.
15. Malcolm MacDonald diary, quoted in Marquand, *Ramsay MacDonald*, p. 636.
16. Snowden, *An Autobiography*.
17. Weir, *The Tragedy of Ramsay MacDonald*, p. 383.
18. See Bassett, *Nineteen Thirty-One*, p. 141.
19. Weir, *The Tragedy of Ramsay MacDonald*, p. 386.
20. Ibid., p. 388.
21. Ibid., pp. 386–90.
22. Nicolson, *King George V*, p. 468.
23. Shinwell, *Conflict without Malice*, pp. 110–11.

29. REACTION

1. RM to Molly Hamilton, MacDonald Papers.
2. PRO 30/69/753, National Archives, Kew.
3. MacDonald Papers, 5/180.
4. Quoted in Watts, *Ramsay MacDonald*, p. 9.
5. Diary, 20 May 1934, 23 October 1933, 15 July 1934, MacDonald Papers.
6. Sidney Webb, 'What Happened in 1931'.
7. Nicolson, *King George V*, p. 465.
8. Ibid., p. 458.
9. Sidney Campion, quoted in Marquand, *Ramsay MacDonald*, p. 680.
10. Quoted in Watts, *Ramsay MacDonald*, p. 109.
11. Watts, *Ramsay MacDonald*, p. 110.
12. See generally on this issue Bassett, *Nineteen Thirty-One*.
13. Watts, *Ramsay MacDonald*, p. 115.

30. THE NATIONAL GOVERNMENT

1. A Morgan, *J. Ramsay MacDonald*, p. 207.
2. Quoted in Taylor, *English History*, p. 373.
3. Skidelsky, *Politicians and the Slump*, p. 393.
4. Marquand, *Ramsay MacDonald*, p. 662.
5. Diary, 29 October 1931, MacDonald Papers.
6. Cited in Marquand, *Ramsay MacDonald*, p. 708.

31. HEALTH AND DIPLOMACY

1. Diary, 20 January 1928, MacDonald Papers.
2. Diary, 30 November 1933, MacDonald Papers.
3. Diary, 22 and 23 March 1933, MacDonald Papers.
4. Quoted in Watts, *Ramsay MacDonald*, p. 134.
5. Jenkins, *The Chancellors*, p. 348.

32. NATIONAL GOVERNMENT WITHOUT SAMUEL

1. Quoted in Watts, *Ramsay MacDonald*, p. 129.
2. Quoted in Weir, *The Tragedy of Ramsay MacDonald*, p. 459.
3. K Morgan, *Ramsay MacDonald*, p. 79.
4. Eden, *The Eden Memoirs: Facing the Dictators*, p. 23.
5. MacDonald Papers, 5/196.

33. DECLINE

1. Diary, 18 May 1936, MacDonald Papers.
2. Diary, 15 November 1935, MacDonald Papers.
3. Citrine, *Men and Work*, p. 291.

34. JUDGEMENT

1. Watt, 'United States Resources', p. 70.
2. MacDonald, *At Home and Abroad*, p. 11.
3. Marquand, *Ramsay MacDonald*, p. 484.
4. Hansard, 22 February 1909.
5. See Skidelsky, *Politicians and the Slump*, pp. 389ff.
6. Skidelsky, *Politicians and the Slump*, p. 390.

BIBLIOGRAPHY

Amery, LS, *My Political Life*, vol. 2 (London, Hutchinson, 1953).
Bassett, R, *Nineteen Thirty-One: Political Crisis* (London, Macmillan, 1958).
Bealey, F and H Pelling, *Labour and Politics 1900–1906: A History of the Labour Representation Committee* (London, Macmillan, 1958).
Butler, D, *The Electoral System in Britain, 1918–51* (Oxford, Oxford University Press, 1953).
Campbell, J and R McLauchlan, *Haldane: The Forgotten Statesman Who Shaped Modern Britain* (London, Hurst and Co., 2020).
Churchill, WS, *Great Contemporaries* (London, Thornton Butterworth, 1937).
Citrine, WM, *Men and Work: An Autobiography* (London, Hutchinson, 1964).
Clynes, JR, *Memoirs, 1869–1937* (London, Hutchinson, 1937).
Cole, M (ed.), *Beatrice Webb's Diaries, 1924–1932* (London, Longman Green & Co., 1956).
Cox, J (ed.), *A Singular Marriage: A Labour Love Story in Letters and Diaries; Ramsay and Margaret MacDonald* (London, Harrap, 1988).
Dalton, H, *Call Back Yesterday: Memoirs, 1887–1931* (London, Frederick Muller, 1953).
Davies, AJ, *To Build a New Jerusalem: The British Labour Movement from the 1880s to the 1990s* (London, Michael Joseph, 1992).
Donoughue, B, 'Harold Wilson: A Flawed Political Genius?', Lord Speaker's Lecture, 2018, www.parliament.uk.
Dundas, JLD, *The Life of Lord Curzon*, vol. 3 (London, Benn, 1928).
Eden, A, *The Eden Memoirs*, vol. 1: Facing the Dictators (London, Cassell, 1962).
Elton, GE, *The Life of James Ramsay MacDonald (1866–1919)* (London, Collins, 1939).
Glasgow, G, *MacDonald as Diplomatist: The Foreign Policy of the First Labour Government in Great Britain* (London, Jonathan Cape, 1924).
Gwynne, SC, *Her Majesty's Airship: The Life and Tragic Death of the World's Largest Flying Machine* (London, Oneworld Publications, 2024).

BIBLIOGRAPHY

Hamilton, M, *Arthur Henderson: A Biography* (London, W Heinemann, 1938).

Hamilton, M, *The Man of Tomorrow: J Ramsay MacDonald* (London, Independent Labour Party Publication Department, 1924).

Howell, D, *MacDonald's Party: Labour Identities and Crisis, 1922–1931* (Oxford, Oxford University Press, 2002).

Hynes, S, *The Edwardian Turn of Mind* (London, Pimlico, 1991).

Jenkins, R, *The Chancellors* (London, Macmillan, 1998).

Jenkins, R, *Mr Balfour's Poodle*, 2nd edn (London, Bloomsbury Reader, [1968]).

Jones, T and K Middlemas, *Whitehall Diary*, vols. 1 and 2 (Oxford, Oxford University Press, 1969).

King, SD, *We Need to Talk about Inflation: Fourteen Urgent Lessons from the Last 2,000 Years* (New York, Yale University Press, 2023).

Kirkwood, D, *My Life of Revolt* (London, George G Harrap, 1935).

The Labour Party's Aim: A Criticism and a Restatement (London, George Allen and Unwin, 1923).

Laski, H, *The Crisis and the Constitution: 1931 and After* (London, Hogarth Press and Fabian Society, 1932).

Lloyd, T, 'J Ramsay MacDonald', in John P Mackintosh (ed.), *British Prime Ministers in the Twentieth Century* (London, Palgrave Macmillan, 1978).

Lyman, RW, *The First Labour Government, 1924* (London, Chapman and Hall, 1957).

McConnachie, J, *The Moray Golf Club at Lossiemouth, 1889–1989* (Moray, Moravian Press, 1988).

MacDonald, JR, *At Home and Abroad* (London, Cape, 1926).

MacDonald, JR, *Margaret Ethel MacDonald* (London, Hodder and Stoughton, 1912).

MacDonald, JR, *Socialism after the War* (Manchester, National Labour Press, 1918).

MacDonald, JR, *Socialism and Society* (London, ILP, 1905).

MacDonald, JR, *The Socialist Movement* (London, Williams and Norgate, 1911).

MacDonald, JR, *Wanderings and Excursions* (London, Jonathan Cape, 1925).

MacKenzie, J and N MacKenzie (eds.), *The Diary of Beatrice Webb, 1873–1892* (Cambridge, MA, Belknap Press of Harvard University Press, 1981).

BIBLIOGRAPHY

McKenzie, RT, *British Political Parties: The Distribution of Power within the Conservative and Labour Parties* (New York, St Martin's Press, 1955).

Mackintosh, A, *Echoes of Big Ben: A Journalist's Parliamentary Diary (1881–1940)* (London, Jarrolds, 1945).

Macmillan, H, *The Past Masters* (London, Macmillan, 1975).

Marquand, D, *Ramsay MacDonald* (London, Jonathan Cape, 1977).

Middlemas, RK, *The Clydesiders: A Left Wing Struggle for Parliamentary Power* (London, Hutchinson, 1965).

Morgan, A, *J Ramsay MacDonald* (Manchester, Manchester University Press, 1987).

Morgan, KO, *Keir Hardie: Radical and Socialist* (London, Weidenfeld and Nicolson, 1975).

Morgan, K, *Ramsay MacDonald* (London, Haus Publishing, 2006).

Mowat, CL, *Britain between the Wars, 1918–1940* (London, Methuen and Co., 1955).

Muggeridge, M, *The Thirties: 1930–1940 in Great Britain* (London, Hamish Hamilton, 1940).

Nevinson, HW, *Last Changes, Last Chances* (London, Nisbet and Co., 1928).

Nevinson, HW, *More Changes, More Chances* (London, Nisbet and Co., 1925).

Nicolson, H, *Curzon: The Last Phase, 1919–1925* (London, Constable, 1934).

Nicolson, H, *King George V: His Life and Reign* (London, Constable, 1952).

Norwich, JJ (ed.), *The Duff Cooper Diaries* (London, Weidenfeld and Nicolson, 2005).

Owen, F, *Tempestuous Journey: Lloyd George; His Life and Times* (London, Hutchinson, 1954).

Pelling, H, *The Origins of the Labour Party, 1880–1900* (London, Macmillan and Co., 1954).

Phillips, M, *Morgan Phillips: Labour Party Secretary, Socialist International Chairman* (Nottingham, Spokesman Books, 2017).

Poirier, PP, *The Advent of the Labour Party* (London, Allen and Unwin, 1958).

Pugh, M, *Speak for Britain! A New History of the Labour Party* (London, Bodley Head, 2010).

Rose, K, *King George V* (London, Weidenfeld and Nicolson, 1983).

Sacks, B, *J Ramsay MacDonald in Thought and Action: An Architect for a Better World* (Albuquerque, University of New Mexico Press, 1952).

BIBLIOGRAPHY

Seely, JEB, *Adventure* (London, William Heinemann, 1930).

Shinwell, E, *Conflict without Malice* (London, Odhams Press, 1955).

Shinwell, E, *The Labour Story* (London, MacDonald and Co., 1963).

Skidelsky, R, *John Maynard Keynes: Fighting for Britain, 1937–1946* (London, Macmillan, 2000).

Skidelsky, R, *Politicians and the Slump: The Labour Government of 1929–31* (Harmondsworth, Penguin, 1970 [1967]).

Snowden, PS, *An Autobiography*, 2 vols. (London, Ivor Nicholson and Watson, 1934).

Taylor, AJP, *English History, 1914–1945* (Oxford, Clarendon Press, 1965).

Taylor, AJP, *The Troublemakers: Dissent over Foreign Policy, 1792–1939*, The Ford Lectures delivered in the University of Oxford in Hilary Term 1956 (London, Hamish Hamilton, 1957).

Templewood, SJGH, *Nine Troubled Years* (London, Collins, 1954).

Thomas, JH, *My Story* (London, Hutchinson and Co., 1937).

Thorpe, CA, *The British General Election of 1931* (Oxford, Oxford University Press, 1991).

Thorpe, DR, *Supermac: A Life of Harold Macmillan* (London, Chatto and Windus, 2010).

Torrance, D, *The Wild Men: The Remarkable Story of Britain's First Labour Government* (London, Bloomsbury Continuum, 2024).

Watt, DC, 'United States Resources for the Study of British Foreign Policy, 1919–1939', *International Affairs*, vol. 38 (1), January 1962.

Watts, D, *Ramsay MacDonald: A Labour Tragedy?* (London, Hodder and Stoughton, 1998).

Webb, S, 'What Happened in 1931: A Record', *Political Quarterly*, January–March 1932 (also published as Fabian Tract no. 237).

Weir, L MacNeill, *The Tragedy of Ramsay MacDonald: A Political Biography* (London, Secker and Warburg, 1938).

Wertheimer, E, *Portrait of the Labour Party* (London, Putnams, 1929).

Williams, F, *A Pattern of Rulers* (London, Longmans, 1965).

Williamson, P, 'Baldwin's Reputation: Politics and History, 1937–1967', *Historical Journal*, vol. 47 (1), March 2004.

Williamson, P, *National Crisis and National Government: British Politics, the Economy and Empire, 1926–1932* (Cambridge, Cambridge University Press, 1992).

Zimmern, A., 'The Prime Minister at Geneva', in *Labour Magazine*, October 1924.

INDEX

Aberavon, Glamorgan, 140, 143–5, 231
Aberdeen, Scotland, 36, 131–2
Abnormal Importations Act (1931), 281
Abyssinia, 294, 301
Admiralty, 185, 188, 233, 241
Afan Sentinel, 145
Agadir crisis (1911), 111–12
agriculture, 6, 7–8
Aix-les-Bains, France, 152, 261
Albert Hall, London, 57, 154
Albert Victor, Duke of Clarence, 161
alcohol, 148, 187
Alexander, Albert Victor, 233, 243
All Souls College, Oxford, 11
Allen, Clifford, 120, 146, 215, 221
Allen, Lily, 82
Alves Free Kirk, Moray, 3
American Dollar Securities Committee, 257
Amery, Leo, 152, 213
anarchism, 60
Anderson, John, 251
Angell, Norman, 270
antiquarianism, 174

aristocracy, xiv, 10, 19, 32, 91–2, 101–10
Ark, 104
armed forces, 184, 187–9
Arnold, Matthew, 15
Asquith, Herbert, 78, 99, 105, 187, 190, 212
   general election (1910), 93
   general election (1918), 134, 135
   general election (1924), 156–7
   Labour electoral deal (1914), 100
   MacDonald Ministry, first (1924), 177, 184, 189, 192
   Prime Minister (1908–16), 93, 100, 101, 127–30, 184
   resignation (1926), 222
   Soviet negotiations (1924), 201, 208
   women's suffrage and, 138
Asquith, Violet, 78
Attlee, Clement, xiii, 16, 110, 178–9, 230, 251, 275, 302, 305, 309, 311
Auden, Wystan Hugh, 275
austerity, 21, 24, 247
Australia, 60, 79
Austria, 199, 255–6, 294

INDEX

Austria-Hungary (1867–1918), 163
Awakening of India, The (MacDonald), 79, 85

Bakunin, Mikhail, 137n
Baldwin, Stanley, xi, xii, 103–4, 144, 151–7, 221
   general election (1929), 232
   general election (1935), 301–2
   MacDonald ministry, first (1924), 169, 177, 209
   MacDonald Ministry, second (1929–31), 237, 239, 261, 263
   MacDonald's death (1937), 305
   National Government, first (1931), 152, 261, 263, 265, 266, 269, 271, 175
   National Government, second (1931–5), 282, 289–90, 295
   Prime Minister, first term (1923–4), xii, 151–7, 160, 196
   Prime Minister, third term (1935–7), 21, 185n, 298, 304–5
Balfour, Arthur, 19, 69, 74, 99, 104, 144, 196
Balliol College, Oxford, xii, 10, 74
Balmoral, Aberdeenshire, 159, 261
Bank of England, 24, 181, 248, 256, 258, 261, 263, 277
Bank of Scotland, 246

Barnard Castle by-election (1903), 68
Barnes, George, 94, 130, 132
Barrie, James, 10
bastardy, *see* illegitimacy
Battle of Cambrai (1917), 140, 188
Battle of Culloden (1746), 6
Battle of Flodden (1513), 305
Battle of Jutland (1916), 187
Battle of the Somme (1916), 206
Battle of Ypres First (1914), 119
Battle of Ypres Third (1917), 130
Bayswater, London, 51
Beatty, David, 1st Earl, 187, 189
Bedales School, Hampshire, 82
Belgium, 113–14, 117, 118–19, 121, 150, 197
Benn, Tony, 21
Benn, William Wedgwood, 243
Berengaria, 241
Berlin, Germany, 139
Bermuda, 305
von Bethmann Hollweg, Theobald, 79, 111
Betjeman, John, 168
Bevan, Aneurin, 76, 228
Bevin, Ernest, 138, 183–4, 216, 218, 219, 307, 310, 311
Bibesco, Marthe, 106, 179
Birkbeck Institute, 33
Birkenhead, Frederick Edwin Smith, 1st Earl, 104, 147n, 217
Blair, Tony, 217n
Blatchford, Robert, 42
Blenheim Palace, Oxfordshire, 10
Bloody Sunday (1887), 35

INDEX

Bloomsbury Group, 121
Board of Education, 182, 185
Board of Trade, 269
Bodkin, Archibald, 205
Boer War (1899–1902), 5, 63–7, 179
Bolsheviks, 130–31, 132, 133, 139, 141, 160
Bonar Law, Andrew, 128, 144–5, 150, 153
Bondfield, Margaret, 234, 248, 249, 260
Boswell, James, 136
bothies, xiii, 7–8, 12, 305
Bottomley, Horatio, 9, 121, 140
Bowes-Lyon, Elizabeth, 121
Bradford Observer, 61
Brancker, Sefton, 180
Bretton Woods system, 246
Brexit (2016–20), 282
Briand, Aristide, 243
Bristol, England, 25–9, 219
British Broadcasting Corporation (BBC), 174
British Empire, 180, 236, 238
   Imperial Conferences, 180, 238
   India, 60, 79, 85, 86, 98–9, 237–9, 282
   Ottawa Agreement (1932), 290–91, 293
   Statute of Westminster (1931), 239
British Museum, London, 50
British Socialist Party, 26, 72, 96, 99
British Workman's coffee taverns, 27
Britten, Benjamin, 7
Brocklehurst, Frederick, 65
Brockway, Fenner, 116, 146
Browning, Robert, 225n
Brüning, Heinrich, 255
Bryan, William Jennings, 60
Buchan, John, 146n, 186n, 299
Buchanan, George, 215
Buckingham Palace, London, 102, 166, 209, 266
Budget (1909), 79, 91, 130, 164
Budget (1924), 181
Budget (1925), 277
Budget (1931), 277, 296
Burnley by-election (1924), 184
Burns, John, 29, 42
Burns, Robert, 12, 13

Cairngorms, 83, 137
Calvinism, 11, 14
Cambridge University, 3, 12, 50, 71, 225
Cameron, David, 83n
Cameron, Samantha, 226
Campbell, John, 205–9
Campbell-Bannerman, Henry, 184, 187
Canada, 60, 79, 242, 289, 290–91, 293, 299
Canterbury, Cosmo Lang, Archbishop, 305
capitalism, 63, 75, 96, 150
Carlton Club, London, 144, 151
Carlyle, Thomas, 12, 54
Carpenter, Edward, 28
Cecil, Hugh, 91
Cecil, Robert, 131–2

331

INDEX

Celtic culture, 6, 19, 145, 174, 218
Ceylon, 110
Chamberlain, Austen, 307
Chamberlain, Joseph, 37, 69, 153
Chamberlain, Neville, 193, 259–65, 297, 298, 304
  Chancellorship (1931–7), 290, 296
  general election (1931), 280, 281
  Lloyd George overtures (1934), 297
  MacDonald's death (1937), 305
  Minister of Health (1924–9), 193
  Minister of Health (1931), 269, 281
  Munich Agreement (1938), 269
  National Government formation (1931), 259–65
  Nazi Germany, views on, 295, 298
  Ottawa Agreement (1932), 290
  succession, 288, 290
Chanak crisis (1922), 144, 239
Channel tunnel, 187
Chartist movement (1838–57), 15
Chelmsford, Frederic Thesiger, 1st Viscount, 185, 188, 189
Cheltenham College, 179
Chequers, Buckinghamshire, 83, 103, 105, 106, 197, 255, 277
China, 282

Christian Socialism, 14–17, 25, 34–5
Christian Socialist, 14, 34–5
Christianity, 5, 14–17, 46, 54–5
Church of Scotland, 5
Churchill, Winston, 82, 146n, 217, 221, 227
  Ark membership, 104
  Budget (1925), 24, 277
  Colonial Secretary (1921–2), 191
  free trade, views on, 252
  freelance journalism, 172
  general election (1923), 156
  India, views on, 253, 282–3, 308
  MacDonald ministry, first (1924), 181, 190
  MacDonald ministry, second (1929–31), 249
  Snowden, views on, 293
  strikes (1911), 97
  wartime coalition (1940–45), 310–11
Citrine, Walter, 305
Clarke, William, 59
Clyde engineers' strike (1915), 129, 130
Clynes, John Robert, 147, 148–9, 160, 166, 182, 213, 233, 295, 305
Co-operative Society, 187
Cole, George Douglas Howard, 175, 248
Committee of Imperial Affairs, 304
Committee of Imperial Defence, 187, 189

INDEX

Committee on Finance and Industry, 257
Commonwealth, 82
communism, 137–41, 210–12
Communist Party of Great Britain, 72, 205–8
Conflicts between Capital and Labour (Howell), 33
Congregationalism, 50
conscription, 118, 120n, 127–9
Conservative Party, 88–9, 96, 103, 221, 273–4, 308
   Asquith coalition (1915–16), 127–9
   Baldwin government (1923–4), 151–7
   Baldwin government (1925–9), 277
   Bonar Law government (1922–3), 150–51, 153
   general election (1885), 29
   general election (1906), 69
   general election (Jan 1910), 92
   general election (Dec 1910), 93
   general election (1918), 134
   general election (1922), 144–5
   general election (1923), 153–7, 177
   general election (1924), 212
   general election (1929), 231–2
   general election (1931), 273, 278, 279
   general strike (1926), 218
   House of Lords and, 91
   Lloyd George coalition (1916–22), 130, 132, 134
   MacDonald Ministry, first (1924), 189, 190, 200, 207–8
   MacDonald Ministry, second (1929–31), 237, 239, 248, 251, 252, 259–68
   National Government (1931–5), *see* National Governments
   People's Budget (1909–10), 79, 91, 130, 164
   Wages for Government Employees Bill (1910), 92
Constitutional Women's Suffrage Movement, 51
Cook, Arthur, 218, 220, 233
Cooke, Grace, 89
Coolidge, Calvin, 196
Cooper, Box and Company, 32
cooperative societies, 65, 94, 296
Coulard Hill, Lossiemouth, 13
Court of Criminal Appeal, 188
Covent Garden, London, 187
Creditanstalt, 255–6
Crewe, Robert Crewe-Milnes, 1st Marquess, 182
cricket, 12, 29n
Crimean War (1853–6), 163
Cripps, Stafford, 185, 269, 307
Crofton, Mordaunt, 25
Cunard Line, 241
Cunliffe-Lister, Philip, 269
Curragh mutiny (1914), 100
Curtius, Julius, 255
Curzon, George, 1st Marquess, xi, xii, 10–11, 151, 196, 307

Daily Citizen, 96

INDEX

Daily Herald, 96, 138, 177–8, 275
Daily Mail, 204, 210
Daily Telegraph, 94, 97
Daimler, 204, 207
Dalton, Hugh, 233, 236
Danton, Georges, 235
Davidson, John Colin Campbell, 1st Viscount, 289
Davidson, Thomas, 38
Dawes, Charles, 195, 240
Dawes Plan (1924), 195–9
Dawson, Bertrand Edward, 1st Viscount, 168
Dawson, Geoffrey, 261
Day-Lewis, Daniel, 82
Day-Lewis, Tamasin, 82
De La Warr, Herbrand Sackville, 9th Earl, 10, 101, 271, 305
decolonisation, 82
Defence Requirements Committee (DRC), 297, 304
Defence White Paper (1935), 298
Democratic Federation, 26–7
Derby, Edward Stanley, 17th Earl, 129
Dickens, Charles, xiii, 13, 54
Dickinson, Willoughby, 1st Baron, 271
diphtheria, 49, 85
Disraeli, Benjamin, 19, 227
Dock, Wharf, Riverside and General Labourers' Union, 42
'doctor's mandate', 278–9
Dolan, P.D., 218
Dollfuss, Engelbert, 288
Donoughue, Bernard, 228
Dover, Kent, 43–4, 46
Drainie, Moray, 10–11, 17
Drummond, Eric, 132
duchesses, 20, 101–10
Duke-Elder, Stewart, 289
Duncan, Andrew, 248
Dylan, Bob, 240

East Fulham by-election (1933), 298, 301
East Woolwich by-election (1921), 140
Echo, The, 67
Economic Advisory Council, 248
economic crisis (1930–31), xiv, 20, 232, 236, 245–53, 255–68
Economy Committee, 258
Eden, Anthony, 288, 295, 301, 307
Edinburgh Review, 59
Edinburgh University, 83
Edward VII, King, 92, 161, 162, 164, 165
Edward VIII, King, 152, 169
Edwards, Jack, 144
Egoist, The (Meredith), 16
eight-hour day, 44
elections
  1885 general election, 28–9
  1886 general election, 34
  1889 Elginshire & Nairnshire by-election, 15, 36
  1892 general election, 43–4, 46
  1895 general election, 44, 45, 46, 49, 61
  1900 general election, 66

INDEX

1903 Barnard Castle by-election, 68
1906 general election, 69–70, 71, 93
1910 January general election, 79–80, 91, 92; December general election, 93, 138
1918 general election, 134
1921 East Woolwich by-election, 140
1922 general election, 143–5
1923 general election, 153–7
1924 Burnley by-election, 184; general election, 210–12
1929 general election, 217, 231–3, 285
1931 general election, 20, 272, 273, 274, 275, 278–81, 293
1933 East Fulham by-election, 298
1935 general election, 21, 298, 301
Elgin, Moray, 6, 9, 125
Elginshire & Nairnshire by-election (1889), 15, 36
Elibank, Master of, *see* Murray, Alexander
Elizabeth, Queen Mother, 121, 162
Ellis, Havelock, 38
Elton, Godfrey, 1st Baron, 3–4, 22, 32–3, 71, 86, 88–9, 93, 95, 117
Emergency Powers Act (1920), 183
Eminent Victorians (Strachey), 165

England For All (Hyndman), 26
English Review, 155
Esher, Reginald Brett, 2nd Viscount, 162
Ethiopia, 294, 301
Eton College, Berkshire, xii, 10, 71
Euclid, 12
European Central Bank, 246
European Union (EU), 282

Fabian Essays in Socialism, 59
Fabian Society, xiii, 15–16, 27, 36–8, 43, 46–7, 59, 63–4, 76, 147
fascism, 236, 295
Fawcett, Millicent, 51
Fellowship of the New Life, 37–9, 46, 59
Finance Act (1930), 252
Finance Act (1932), 296
financial crisis (1930–31), xiv, 20, 232, 236, 245–53, 255–68
Finland, 286
First International (1864–76), 137*n*
First World War (1914–18), xi, 78, 82, 100, 103, 104, 112–21, 123–34, 163, 235–6, 288
  Battle of Cambrai (1917), 140, 188
  Battle of Jutland (1916), 187
  Battle of Ypres, First (1914), 119
  Battle of Ypres, Third (1917), 130
  conscription, 118, 120*n*, 127–9

Gallipoli campaign (1915–16), 243n
outbreak (1914), 112–21, 185
pacifism, 103, 117, 119, 120, 288
Palestine campaign (1915–18), 179
Siege of Kut al-Amara (1915–16), 3n
trade union activity, 129–30, 131
Fitzgerald, Charles L., 35
Fletcher, Horace, 147
Foot, Michael, 228
Forres, Moray, 240
France, 240, 307
  Agadir crisis (1911), 111–12
  Creditanstalt crisis (1931), 255–6
  First World War (1914–18), 111–12, 118, 119, 120, 185
  loan requests (1931), 260, 261, 277
  London Naval Treaty (1930), 243
  Paris Peace Conference (1919), 150, 179, 190
  Ruhr occupation (1923–5), 150–51, 152, 154, 195–9
  social democracy in, 228–9
  Stresa Front (1935), 294
  Treaty of Versailles (1919), *see* Treaty of Versailles
Francis-Williams, Edward Francis Williams, Baron, 58
Free Church of Scotland, 5, 216n
Free Kirk, Lossiemouth, 10, 54

free trade, 59, 74, 152–3, 252, 280–82, 290–91
Friedman, Milton, 246
Friends' Medical Corps, 119
Fry, Elizabeth, 186n

Gallipoli campaign (1915–16), 243n
Gandhi, Mohandas, 102, 282–3
Garsington Manor, Oxfordshire, 120–21
Garvin, James Louis, 199, 264
Gee, Robert, 140
general elections, *see under* elections
general strike (1926), 97, 218–20, 233
Geneva Disarmament Conference (1932–4), 287
Geneva Protocol (1924), 198, 199
geology, 13, 28, 33
George V, King, 19, 159–69, 191
  death (1936), 303–4
  general election (1910), 93
  general election (1924), 209–10
  MacDonald ministry, first (1924), 1, 156–7, 159–61, 191
  MacDonald ministry, second (1929–31), 233–4
  MacDonald's resignation (1935), 298–9
  National Government (1931–5), 159–60, 164, 259, 261, 262, 266, 274, 275
  Silver Jubilee (1935), 165, 295

INDEX

George VI, King, 304–5
George, Henry, 14, 26, 44, 50
Georgia, 139
Germany
    German Empire (1871–1918), 69, 79, 111–12, 113, 131, 133, 163
    Nazi Germany (1933–45), 286, 287–8, 294, 297–8, 301, 307
    Weimar Republic (1918–33), see Weimar Germany
Gibbon, Edward, 136
Gibson, Hugh, 240
Gissing, George, xiii, 31, 32
Gladstone–MacDonald Pact (1903), 68, 80
Gladstone, Herbert, 68
Gladstone, Margaret, see MacDonald, Margaret
Gladstone, William, 5, 12, 113, 114, 117, 143, 172, 181, 217, 218, 256, 293
Glasgow, George, 200
Glasgow, Scotland, 151
Glasier, Bruce, 26n, 46, 49–50, 69, 77, 87, 94, 96, 98, 136
Glasier, Katharine, 50, 88, 102, 108, 123
gold standard, 20, 24, 236, 257–8, 277–8, 285
Golders Green, London, 87
golf, 7, 78, 115, 125–6
Good Food Guide, 138
'Good-Bye My Fancy!' (Whitman), 121
Goodhart, Charles, 246

Gordon-Cumming, Cecily, 105–6
Gorell, Ronald Barnes, 3rd Baron, 271
Gosling, Harry, 141
Government of India Act (1935), 239, 283, 308
Gower, Patrick, 190
Grant, Alexander, 136, 203–5, 207, 241, 257
Gray's Inn Road, London, 31
Great Depression (1929–39), xiv, 20, 232, 236, 245–53, 255–68
Great Reform Bill (1832), 164
Greenwood, Arthur, 249, 305
Gregory Place, Lossiemouth, 81
Grey, Edward, 112–16, 307
Guild Socialists, 148
Guildhall Library, London, 33

Haddow, Martin, 272
Hailsham, Douglas Hogg, 1st Viscount, 185n
Haldane, Richard, 1st Viscount, 111, 169, 181, 184, 185, 187–9, 212, 233
Hales, Alfred Arthur Greenwood, 121
Half-Circle Club, 168
Halifax, West Yorkshire, 61
Hamilton, Bermuda, 305
Hamilton, Molly, 58, 89, 102, 108, 175, 271
Hampstead, London, 109–10
Hampstead Rotary Club, 305
Hankey, Maurice, 207, 290
Hardie, Keir, 26, 41, 46, 71, 74, 75, 93–4, 143

INDEX

appendix operation (1903), 61
death (1915), 118
general election (1985), 46
Gladstone–MacDonald Pact (1903), 68
illegitimacy, 46
ILP chairman (1893–1900), 45, 49, 60
ILP council resignation (1909), 93, 96
ILP council resignation (1909), 96
Italy trip (1904), 61
Labour Party establishment (1906), 72, 73, 94
Liberal electoral deal (1914), 100
LRC establishment (1900), 64, 65, 66
National Insurance Act (1911), 77
Socialist International congress (1896), 60
Union of Democratic Control, 111
women's suffrage, views on, 101
Hardy, Thomas, 165
Hardyman, Maitland, 120
Harrod, Roy, 247
Harrow School, Middlesex, 182
Hartshorn, Vernon, 237, 251–2
Harvey, Ernest, 261
Hastings, Patrick, 205–7, 209, 213
Heath, Edward, 171, 248
heavy oil, 179–80

Hegel, Georg Wilhelm Friedrich, 72, 150
Heidelberg University, 185
Henderson, Arthur, 68, 71, 73, 94, 115, 144, 146–7, 217
  Asquith coalition (1915–16), 127, 128
  Barnard Castle by-election (1903), 68
  Board of Education presidency (1915–16), 127
  Burnley by-election (1924), 184
  conscription, views on, 128
  constitution (1918), 133, 134
  Creditanstalt crisis (1931), 255
  Foreign Secretary (1929–31), 233–5, 238, 243, 255, 259, 261, 263
  Home Secretary, first term (1924), 182–3, 184
  Home Secretary, second term (1931), 261, 263, 270
  Liberal electoral deal (1914), 100
  Lloyd George coalition (1916–18), 130, 131, 132
  London Naval Treaty (1930), 243
  Russian Revolution (1917), 131, 132
Herbert, Jesse, 67, 68
Hereford, John Percival, Bishop of, 115
Herriot, Édouard, 197
Hewart, Gordon, 135
Highland Line, 1–2

338

INDEX

Highlands, Scotland, 1–2, 5–6, 20
Hillocks, Lossiemouth, 81, 83, 290, 306
Hitler, Adolf, 287–8, 294, 297–8, 307
Hoare, Samuel, 188, 264, 269, 283, 301, 307
Hoare, Simon, 259, 261, 264
Hobson, John Atkinson, 221–2, 236, 248
Hodge, John, 130
Home Rule Union, 34
Hoover, Herbert, 241, 255, 286
Horder, Thomas, 289, 290
House of Commons, 71, 74
   Select Committee on Home Work, 56
   union representation in, 42
House of Lords, 3n, 22, 67, 78n, 79, 184, 185, 253
   Osborne case (1909), 79–80, 86
   People's Budget (1909–10), 79, 91, 130, 164
   Taff Vale case (1901), 67, 75
Housing Act (1924), 192–3
Housing Act (1929), 237
Housing Act (1930), 237
Howell, George, 33
Howitt Road, Hampstead, 109
Hoxton and Haggerston Nursing Association, 51
Hyndman, Henry Mayers, 26–7, 28, 29, 45, 64
hypochondria, 34

illegitimacy, 1, 8–9, 13, 46, 49–50, 123–4

Illingworth, Percy, 100
Imperator, 241
Imperial Conference (1926), 180
Imperial Conference (1930), 238
Imperial Economic Conference (1932), 290–91, 293
Incitement to Mutiny Act (1797), 205
Independent Labour Party (ILP), 26n, 45–7, 49, 60–62, 63, 64, 72, 77, 94–6, 137–8, 144, 145, 221
   administrative council election (1921), 140
   Allen's resignation (1925), 215
   Big Four resignations (1909), 93, 96
   Communist International, relations with, 137–9, 140–41
   constitution (1918), 133–4
   First World War outbreak (1914), 115, 116, 117, 118
   general election (1906), 72
   general election (Dec 1910), 93
   general election (1931), 279
   Gloucester conference (1925), 215–16
   Let Us Reform the Labour Party (1910), 96
   LRC formation (1900), 64–6
   MacDonald ministry, first (1924), 178, 184
   National Government, first (1931), 273
   National Insurance Act (1911), 75, 76

INDEX

Russian Revolution (1917), 131
Scottish divisional conference (1927), 219
Socialism in Our Time (1926), 222
Independent Socialist Party, 59
India, 60, 79, 85, 86, 98–9, 237, 238–9, 282
   Government of India Act (1935), 239, 283, 308
   Round Table conferences (1930–31), 238, 282
India Office, 185
infiltrationism, 43
inflation, 246, 247
intellectualism, 174
International
   First (1864–76), 137n
   Second (1889–1914), 47, 60, 69, 79, 137n, 140–41
   Third (1919–43), 137–9, 140–41, 210
internationalism, 60, 111, 112
Iraq, 191
Ireland
   Curragh mutiny (1914), 100
   Home Rule movement, 34, 75, 100
   Partition (1921), 163
Irish Nationalists, 92, 93
Irvine, Ayrshire, 50
Irwin, Edward Wood, 1st Baron, 243n, 282
Islington, London, 34, 36
'It's All in the Game', 240
Italy, 61, 240, 243, 294–5

Jacobitism, 6

James IV, King of Scotland, 305
Jamieson, Neil, 21n
Japan, 240, 241, 243, 282
Jaurès, Jean, 54
Jenkins, Roy, 71, 178, 181, 291
Jenkins, William, 145n
Johannesburg, South Africa, 74
John Bull, 9, 121, 123
Johnson, Harry, 247
Johnston, Tom, 191, 249, 250
Jones, Thomas, 10, 192, 207–8
Joynson-Hicks, William, 153
Junior Carlton Club, London, 74
Justice, 28

Kapital, Das (Marx), 26
Keay, Seymour, 36
Kelvin, William Thomson, 1st Baron, 51
Kenya, 82
Kerensky, Alexander, 131
Keynes, John Maynard, 24, 182, 232, 236, 245–8, 249, 257–8, 287
Kielhorn, Iona, 83
Kilburn Liberal Club, 35
King's College, London, 51
Kingdom of Christ, The (Maurice), 15
Kingsley, Charles, 15
Kinnock, Neil, 21
Kirkwood, Davie, 73, 144, 145, 146, 177, 193, 214, 215, 270
Kirriemuir, Angus, 10
Kitchener, Herbert, 1st Earl, 128
Knox, John, 136

La Rochelle, France, 305

INDEX

Labour and the Nation (1928), 222, 223, 309
Labour and the New Social Order (1918), 133–4
Labour Electoral Association, 42–5
Labour Electoral Committee, 42
Labour Leader, 50, 65, 76, 128, 217
Labour Party, ix–x, xii, xiii–xiv, 20, 23, 64, 83–4, 95, 145–50, 308–11
   Asquith coalition (1915–16), 127–9
   Attlee government (1945–51), 178, 229, 230, 309, 311
   conference (1918), 133–4
   conference (1925), 139
   conference (1926), 221
   conference (1927), 222
   constitution (1918), 133–4
   establishment (1906), 72
   First World War outbreak (1914), 112–21
   general election (1918), 134
   general election (1922), 143–5
   general election (1923), 153–7
   general election (1924), 210–12
   general election (1929), 217, 231–2
   general election (1931), 20, 272, 273, 274, 275
   general election (Dec 1910), 93
   general election (Jan 1910), 79–80, 92

Labour and the Nation (1928), 222, 223, 309
Labour Party's Aim, The (1923), 148
leadership election (1911), 94–5
leadership election (1922), 148–9
Leicester by-election (1913), 99
Liberal electoral deal (1914), 100
Lloyd George coalition (1916–18), 130, 132, 134
MacDonald ministry, first (1924), *see* MacDonald ministry, first
MacDonald ministry, second (1929–31), xiv, 138, 182, 225
MacDonald's expulsion (1931), 20
Memorandum on War Aims (1917), 132
National Government (1931–5), *see* National Government
National Insurance Act (1911), 75–7
Third International, relations with, 137–9, 140–41
Trade Union Act (1913), 80
women's suffrage and, 77, 101, 138
Labour Party's Aim, The (1923), 148
Labour Representation Committee (LRC), 41, 64–6, 67, 68–9, 72, 93

INDEX

Lairig Ghru, Cairngorms, 83
Lake Maggiore, Italy, 294
land laws, 14, 26
Lansbury, Dorothy, 188
Lansbury, George, 76, 77, 96, 101, 115, 138, 141, 188, 216, 236, 249, 250
Lansbury's Labour Weekly, 138
Laski, Harold, 22, 107, 175
Lauder, Harry, 174
Lausanne Conference (1932), 104, 286
'Lead, Kindly Light', 308
League of Nations, 132, 198, 228, 238, 240, 287, 307
Leeds, West Yorkshire, 83
Lees, Edith, 38–9
Leicester, Leicestershire, 66, 67, 135
   by-election (1913), 99
   Children's Hospital, 56
Leicester Mercury, 65
Lenin, Vladimir, 131, 138, 141
Lerner, Alan Jay, 82
Let Us Reform the Labour Party, 96
Liberal Party, 15, 34–6, 59, 64, 71, 72, 96, 99, 134, 144–5, 150, 222–3, 308
   Asquith government (1908–1916), 77–8, 91–3, 99–100, 127–9
   First World War outbreak (1914), 112–14
   general election (1885), 29
   general election (1900), 66
   general election (1906), 69, 71
   general election (1918), 134
   general election (1922), 144–5
   general election (1923), 154–7, 177
   general election (1924), 212
   general election (1929), 232
   general election (1931), 279
   general election (Dec 1910), 93
   general election (Jan 1910), 79, 92
   Gladstone–MacDonald Pact (1903), 68, 80
   ILP, relations with, 61–2
   Irish Home Rule and, 34, 75
   Labour Electoral Association and, 42–3
   Labour electoral deal (1914), 100
   Labour Representation Committee and, 68–9
   Labour wing, 42–5, 71, 95, 99
   Leicester by-election (1913), 99
   Lloyd George coalitions (1916–22), 130, 132, 134, 135, 144, 183, 204, 239
   MacDonald Ministry, first (1924), 189, 190, 200–201, 207–8
   MacDonald Ministry, second (1929–31), 237, 248, 252–3, 259–68
   National Government (1931–5), *see* National Government
   National Insurance Act (1911), 75–7

INDEX

People's Budget (1909–10), 79, 91, 130, 164
Trade Union Act (1913), 80
trade unions and, 41
Yellow Book (1928), 222
Liberal Unionist Party, 37, 71
Life of James Ramsay MacDonald, The (Elton), 3–4, 22, 32–3, 71, 86, 88–9, 93, 95, 117
Lincoln, Edward King, Bishop of, 115
Lincoln's Inn Fields, London, 54, 56, 109
Liverpool Post, 97
living wage, 222
Llandudno, Clwyd, 180
Lloyd George, David, xii, 19, 130, 134, 135, 144–5, 151, 190, 222–3, 286, 297, 310
   cash for honours scandal (1922), 204
   Chanak crisis (1922), 144, 239
   coalition government (1916–18), 130, 134
   coalition government (1918–22), 135, 144, 183, 204, 239
   Edward VII's death (1910), 92
   Emergency Powers Act (1920), 183
   First World War (1914–18), 114, 129
   free trade, views on, 153
   general election (1910), 92, 99
   general election (1918), 135
   general election (1929), 232
   general election (1931), 279
   gold standard, views on, 236
   MacDonald Ministry, second (1929–31), 237, 249, 252–3
   MacDonald, relationship with, 78
   national development plan (1934), 297
   National Insurance Act (1911), 56, 75
   oratory, 227
   Paris Peace Conference (1919), 190
   People's Budget (1909–10), 79, 91, 130, 164
   Soviet negotiations (1924), 200–201
   Yellow Book (1928), 222
Locarno Conference (1925), 238
London, England, 31–4
   Bloody Sunday (1887), 35
   dock strike (1889), 41–2, 96
   Imperial Conference (1926), 180
   Imperial Conference (1930), 238
   Indian Round Table conferences (1930–31), 238, 282
   Naval Conference (1930), 242–3
   Poplar Order (1921), 192
London County Council, 36, 82
London Naval Treaty (1930), 242–3
London School of Economics, 22, 37, 59
Londonderry, Charles Vane-

INDEX

Tempest-Stewart, 7th Marquess, 103, 109–10, 305
Londonderry, Edith Vane-Tempest-Stewart, Marchioness, 102–5, 109–10, 161, 305
Londonderry House, London, 10, 103
Lossiemouth, Moray, xiii, 1–9, 13, 15, 22, 31, 33, 50, 53, 54, 57, 81, 83
    Field Club, 13, 28
    Fisheries and Community Museum, 81
    Hillocks, The, 81, 83, 290, 306
    holidays to, 190, 237, 257, 270, 272, 289
    housekeepers from, 102
    MacDonald's funeral (1937), 305–6
    Moray Golf Club, 7, 115, 125
'Lost Leader, The' (Browning), 225n
Lough, Thomas, 34–6

MacDonald, Alister, 82, 109, 136
MacDonald, David, 49, 82, 84, 85–6, 87, 94, 108, 116, 306
MacDonald, Ishbel, 8–9, 82, 83, 136, 167–8, 241, 265
MacDonald, James, 11
MacDonald, Joan, 82
MacDonald, John, 3–4
MacDonald, Malcolm, 3, 22, 82–3, 265–6, 268, 303, 304
MacDonald, Margaret, 49–56, 60, 67, 81, 82, 85–9, 102, 108, 136, 172, 306

MacDonald, Ramsay
    accent, 27
    antiquarianism, 174
    appendix operation (1904), 61
    aristocracy and, xiv, 10, 19, 32, 91–2, 101–10
    Asquith government (1908–1916), 77–8, 91–3, 99–100, 127–9
    Awakening of India, The (1910), 79, 85
    Baldwin government (1923–4), 152, 156
    Bibesco, relationship with, 106, 179
    biographies, 22–4
    birth (1866), xiii, 1, 81
    birth certificate, 3, 9, 123
    Bonar Law government (1922–3), 150–51
    Bristol period (1885–6), 25–9
    bronchitis (1927), 285
    Campbell-Bannerman government (1905–8), 71–2
    childhood, xii, xiii, 1–12
    Christian Christianity, 14–17, 54–5
    Christian Socialism, 14–17, 25, 34–5
    communism, views on, 137–41
    constitution (1918), 133–4
    David's death (1910), 85–6, 94, 108
    death (1937), 305
    depression, 34, 286, 293
    diaries, 12, 13, 55, 226
    duchesses, 20, 101–10

INDEX

East Woolwich by-election (1921), 140
economics, views on, 14, 16–17, 23–4, 35, 59
education, xii, xiii, 10–12, 174
Elginshire & Nairnshire by-election (1889), 15, 36
expulsion from Labour (1931), 20
Fabian Society membership, 36–9, 46–7, 59, 63–4
First World War (1914–18), see First World War
Foreign Secretary (1924), xi–xii, 184, 187, 190, 195–201, 307
freelance journalism, 172
general election (1892), 43–4, 46
general election (1895), 44, 45, 46, 49, 61
general election (1906), 69–70
general election (1910), 79–80
general election (1922), 143–5
general election (1923), 153–7
general election (1924), 210–12
general election (1929), 217, 231–3, 285
general election (1931), 20, 272, 273, 274, 278–81
general election (1935), 21, 298, 301–3
geology, interest in, 13, 28, 33
Gladstone–MacDonald Pact (1903), 68, 80
glaucoma, 286, 287

golfing hobby, 7, 78, 115, 125–6
Gordon-Cumming, relationship with, 105–6
Hamilton, relationship with, 58, 89, 102, 108, 175
health problems, 173, 285–6, 287, 288–90, 293, 301
House of Lords, views on, 91–2
hypochondria, 34
illegitimacy, 1, 8–9, 123–4
ILP membership, 45–7, 60, 64, 93, 140, 144, 145–7, 219–20, 229
India and, 60, 79, 85, 86, 98–9, 237, 238–9, 282, 308
internationalism, 60, 111, 112
Irish Home Rule, views on, 75, 100
Italy trip (1904), 61
land nationalisation, views on, 14, 26
leadership election (1911), 94–5
leadership election (1922), 148–9
Leicester by-election (1913), 99
Liberal electoral deal (1914), 100
Liberalism, 15, 43–4, 45, 78, 134
Lloyd George coalition (1916–22), 130
London, move to (1886), 31–4, 41

345

INDEX

Londonderry, relationship with, 102–5
Lough, secretary to (1888–92), 34–6
LRC formation (1900), 64–6, 93
Margaret, relationship with, 49–56, 60, 86–9, 102, 108
Moray Golf Club expulsion (1915), 115, 125
mother's death (1910), 85–6
moustache, xi–xii
musical taste, 174
National Defence (1917), 132
National Government (1931–5), *see* National Government
National Government, First (1931), *see* MacDonald Ministry, Third
National Government, Second (1931–5), 24, 104
non-intellectualism, 174
oratory, 143–4, 227, 286
pacifism and, 103, 117, 119
physical appearance, xi–xii, 65, 217, 286
Prime Minister, first ministry (1924), *see* MacDonald ministry, first
Prime Minister, fourth ministry (1931–5), *see* National Government, Second
Prime Minister, second ministry (1929–31), *see* MacDonald ministry, second
Prime Minister, third ministry (1931), *see* National Government, First
Rainbow Circle membership, 59
resignation (1914), 115
resignation (1924), 168, 208–9
resignation (1935), 298–9
Scottish Home Rule campaigning, 36
shyness, 27, 174
Socialism after the War (1917), 134
Socialism and Society (1905), 69
socialism, 15–17, 25–9, 34–9, 178
Socialist Movement, The (1911), 96
South Africa visit (1901), 60, 67, 74
South African War (1899–1902), 5, 63–4
spiritualism, 89
teaching career, 13, 17
Thomson, relationship with, 179
trade unions, views on, 96–8, 134, 147, 218
travels, 60, 67, 74, 79, 136, 139, 174, 285, 294–5, 305
treachery, accusations of, xiii, xiv, 16, 22, 23, 107, 310
Union of Democratic Control, 111
walking hobby, 13, 28, 125, 137, 174
Wanderings and Excursions (1925), 137

INDEX

wedding (1896), 54
women's suffrage, views on, 51, 67, 77, 101
MacDonald Ministry, First (1924), xiii, 102, 157, 159–60, 166–9, 171, 177–93, 195–201, 203–13
  armed forces and, 184, 187
  Campbell case, 205–9
  Grant baronetcy scandal, 203–5, 207, 211
  Housing Act, 192–3
  Iraq conflict, 191
  national dock strike, 183–4
  Ruhr negotiations, 195–9
  Soviet negotiations, 200–201, 208, 209
  Trade Facilities Act, 189
  trade unions and, 186
MacDonald Ministry, Second (1929–31), xiv, 138, 182, 225, 232–53, 255–68
  Creditanstalt crisis (1931), 255–6
  economic crisis, xiv, 20, 232, 236, 245–53, 255–68
  Finance Act (1930), 252
  India policy, 237–9
  Macmillan Report (1931), 257
  May Report crisis (1931), 257–68
  Mosley memorandum (1930), 249–51
  Trade Disputes Bill (1930), 253
  Unemployment Insurance Act (1929), 248–9
  unemployment policy, 232, 234, 235, 236, 237, 245–6

  US Navy negotiations, 239–32
MacDonald Ministry, Third (1931), *see* National Government, First
MacDonald Ministry, Fourth (1931–5), *see* National Government, Second
MacDonald, Sheila, 82, 262, 305
Mackintosh, Alexander, 58
Maclean, Donald, 260
Macmillan Report (1931), 257
Macmillan, Harold, 15–17, 55, 73, 171–2, 227, 247, 251
Macmillan, Hugh Pattison, 204, 257
Macmillan, Maurice, 15
Manchester Guardian, 249
Manchuria, 282, 287
Mann, Tom, 42, 46, 60, 96
Manning, Henry, 43
Markham, Frank, 271
Marks, George, 1st Baron, 271
Marquand, David, 4, 23–4, 50, 64, 146, 198, 245, 247, 258, 308
marriage, 1, 8
'Marseillaise', 57, 160, 210
Martin, Alec, 136
Marx, Karl, 26–7, 29, 72, 137*n*, 138, 308
Marxism, 14, 15, 16, 17, 26–7, 29, 42, 45, 46, 64, 72–3, 228, 308
Mary of Teck, Queen consort, 161
Masterman, Charles, 186
Matthew, Henry Colin Gray, 267

INDEX

Maurice, Frederick Denison, 15
Maxton, James, 146, 155, 180, 188, 191, 206, 209, 215, 216, 220–22, 233
May Report (1931), 257–68
May, George, 257
McVitie & Price, 203–5, 209, 211
McVitie, Robert, 203
'Melody in A Major' (Dawes), 240
Memorandum on War Aims (1917), 132
Memorial Hall, London, 65
Mensheviks, 139
Meredith, George, 16
Merrie England (Blatchford), 42
Merthyr Tydfil, Wales, 66, 143
Methodism, 46
middle classes, 1, 43
Middleton, James Smith, 109, 182
Middleton, Mary, 86, 87, 109
Military Service Act (1916), 128
miners, 41
Miners' Federation of Great Britain, 219
miners' strike (1984–5), 21
minimum wage, 221
Mitchell, Rosslyn, 125
Mitford, Nancy, 161–2
modernism, 162
monetarism, 246
Moray Golf Club, Lossiemouth, 7, 115, 125
Morel, Edmund Dene, 115
Morgan, Kevin, 9–10, 295
Morley, John, 1st Viscount, 112, 114

Morocco, 111–12
Morrell, Ottoline, 121
Morris, Tom, 7
Morris, William, 174
Morrison, Herbert, 233, 269, 276, 311
Mosley, Oswald, 59, 235–6, 249–51, 263, 310
Moss Bros, 169
moustaches, xi–xii
Munich Agreement (1938), 269
munitions workers' strike (1917), 129–30
Murray, Alexander, 1st Baron, 77, 78, 99
music, 174
Mussolini, Benito, 294
Mutual Improvement Society, 13

Namier, Lewis Bernstein, 3*n*
Nassau Senior Training Home, London, 51
National Administrative Council (NAC), 46, 60, 93, 219
National Cyclists' Union, 32
National Defence (MacDonald), 132
National Economy Act (1931), 277
National Executive Committee (NEC), 127, 128, 129, 156, 219, 236
National Government, First (1931), xiv, 20, 35, 110, 152, 225, 229, 259–68, 269–76, 308–10
 aristocracy and, 103, 107

INDEX

austerity, 24, 247
economic crisis, xiv, 20, 232
emergency budget, 277, 296
formation, 259–68
general election, 20, 272, 273, 274, 275, 278–81
George V and, 159–60, 159–60, 259, 261, 262, 274, 275
gold standard abandonment, 277–8, 285
Labour reaction to, 20, 35, 107, 138, 164, 269–76
National Economy Act, 277
National Government, Second (1931–5), 24, 104, 225, 279–99, 301, 308–10
   Abnormal Importations Act (1931), 281
   aristocracy and, 103, 107
   austerity, 24, 247
   defence spending increase (1934), 297
   East Fulham by-election (1933), 298, 301
   economic crisis, 232
   foreign policy, 282, 286–7
   'freedom to differ' (1932), 282
   general election (1935), 301–3
   Geneva Disarmament Conference (1932–4), 287
   Lausanne Conference (1932), 104, 286–7
   Manchuria crisis (1931–2), 282, 287
   Ottawa Agreement (1932), 290–91, 293
   Samuelite withdrawal (1932–3), 291, 293
   Statement Relating to Defence (1935), 298
   Stresa Front (1935), 294–5
   tariff reform, 281–2
National Health Service (NHS), 76
National Insurance Act (1911), 56, 75–7
National Labour, 270–71, 280, 299, 302
National Liberal Club, 36
National Library of Scotland, 203, 257
national minimum wage, 221
national railway strike (1911), 97
National Union of Women Workers, 56
nationalisation, 14, 26, 133–4
Naval Conference (1930), 242–3
Nazi Germany (1933–45), 286, 287–8, 294, 297–8, 301, 307
Nepal, 162
Netherlands, 131
Nevinson, Henry, 143
New Charter, The (MacDonald), 44
New Leader, 178
New Party, 251
New Statesman, 37
New York, United States, 60, 242
   Federal Reserve Bank, 260, 261, 263, 277
New York Times, 235, 242
Newnham College, Cambridge, 89
Newquay, Cornwall, 287

349

INDEX

Nicolson, Harold, 76, 162, 259, 268, 274
Nixon, Richard, 246n
Nobel Peace Prize, 240
nonconformism, 148
Nordic culture, 6, 218
Norman, Montagu, 181, 248, 261
North Sea, 5, 6
Northcliffe Alfred Harmsworth, 1st Viscount, 185, 210

Observer, 199, 264
Old Radicals, 44
Olivier, Sydney, 37
On England (Baldwin), 152
Order of the Thistle, 299
Orpheus Choir, 174
Osborne judgement (1909), 79–80, 86
Osmond, Donny, 240
Osmond, Marie, 240
Ossian, 5
Ottawa Agreement (1932), 290–91, 293
Oxford Dictionary of National Biography, 267
Oxford University, xii, 10, 11, 12, 71, 74, 82

pacifism, 103, 117, 119, 120, 148, 188
Paganism, 6
Palestine, 179
Palmerston, Henry John Temple, 3rd Viscount, 111, 235
Pankhurst, Emmeline, 101
Panther, 111

von Papen, Franz, 286
Paris Peace Conference (1919), 150, 179, 190
Parmoor, Charles Cripps, 1st Baron, 185, 256
Passfield, Sidney Webb, 1st Baron, *see* Webb, Sidney
Peace Ballot, 298, 301
Pensions Act (1929), 237
People's Budget (1909–10), 79, 91, 130, 164
Peterkin, James, 83
Pethick-Lawrence, Frederick, 67
Phillips, Morgan, 228
Picton-Turbervill, Edith, 101
Pigou, Arthur Cecil, 232
Plumstead Common, Woolwich, 120
Plutarch, 27–8
Poincaré, Raymond, xiin, 152, 196–7
Political Quarterly, 107
Politicians and the Slump (Skidelsky), 278
Pollitt, Harry, 205
Ponsonby, Arthur, 200, 201
Poor Law, 75, 272
Poplar Order (1921), 192
Portugal, 246
Postgate, Raymond, 138
poverty, 13, 20, 32–3, 44
Progress and Poverty (George), 14, 26, 44
Progressive Party, 36
Progressive Review, 47
prohibitionists, 148
Prudential Assurance Company, 257

INDEX

public schools, 82
pubs, 41

Queen's College, Oxford, 82

R101 airship, 179–80
radio, 144
Rainbow Circle, 59, 119n
Ramsay, Anne, 3, 4–5, 8, 33, 49, 52, 85–6, 116
Ramsay, Isabella, 4–5, 13, 33, 186
Ramsay, William, 4
rationalism, 15
Reading, Rufus Isaacs, 1st Marquess, 269
Red Clydesiders, 129, 130, 148, 150, 154, 177, 192, 193, 215
'Red Flag, The', 57, 128, 146, 160, 210
Reform Act (1884), 14
Reichstag Fire (1933), 288
Reith, John, 1st Baron, 174
Representation of the People Act (1918), 133
Richard, Cliff, 240
Rochester, Ernest Lamb, 1st Baron, 271
Rogart, Sutherland, 258
Roosevelt, Franklin, 144, 294
Royal Air Force (RAF), 179, 188, 191, 297
Royal Commission on Employment (1867), 7
Royal Corps of Commissionaires, 163
Royal Engineers, 179
Royal Institution, 51

Royal Military Academy, Woolwich, 179
Royal Navy, 185, 188, 233, 239–43
Royal Society, 51
Ruhr occupation (1923–5), 150–51, 152, 154, 195–9
Ruskin, John, 12, 15, 27, 54
Russell, Bertrand, 121
Russian Civil War (1917–23), 138
Russian Empire, 26, 113, 130, 163
Russian Revolution (1917), 130–32, 133, 160

Saar plebiscite (1935), 298
Sackville, Margaret, 101, 124
Sadler, Michael, 82
Sahara Desert, 174
Samuel, Herbert, 59, 61, 260, 262–5, 279, 281, 282, 291, 293
Sandringham, Norfolk, 161, 303
Sankey, John, 185, 233, 267, 269, 282, 305
Sassoon, Siegfried, 120
Saturday Review, 177
Scott, Walter, 5, 54, 136
Scottish Home Rule Association, 36
Scottish Land Restoration League, 50
Scottish Universities seat, 303
Seaham, County Durham, 231, 270, 280, 281, 303
Seamen's and Firemen's Union, 131

351

INDEX

Second International (1889–1914), 47, 60, 69, 79, 137n, 140–41
Second World War (1939–45), 236, 310–11
Seely, Jack, 78, 119
Sexton, James, 270
Sforza, Carlo, xiin
Shackleton, David, 73, 77, 94
Shakespeare, William, 13
Shaw, George Bernard, xii, xiii, 36, 39, 45, 47, 63, 147
Shinwell, Emanuel, 21, 26, 72, 103n, 124, 148, 266, 268, 269, 276, 302
Siege of Kut al-Amara (1915–16), 3n
Siege of Ladysmith (1899–1900), 5
Simon, John, 1st Viscount, 21, 273, 279, 282, 288, 291, 294, 295, 302, 305, 307
Singapore, 189
Sinking Fund, 182
Skidelsky, Robert, Baron, 232, 247, 278, 310
skilled workers, 41
Smillie, Robert, 186
Smith, Frederick Edwin, 104, 147n, 217
Smuts, Jan, 67
Smythson, 226
Snowden, Ethel, 147
Snowden, Philip, 22, 46, 71, 73–4, 96, 146, 147, 181–2, 215, 216, 217
  Budget (1924), 181–2
  Budget (1931), 277, 296
  Chancellorship (1924), 181–2
  Chancellorship (1929–31), 233, 237, 249, 256–7, 259, 296
  First World War outbreak (1914), 115, 116
  free trade, views on, 59, 281, 282
  general election (1924), 215
  general election (1931), 293
  illegitimacy, 46
  ILP chair (1903–6), 73
  ILP council resignation (1909), 93, 96
  ILP withdrawal (1927), 220
  leadership election (1922), 148
  Liberal electoral deal (1914), 100
  National Government, first (1931), 264, 266, 267, 269, 273, 274
  National Government, second (1931–5), 281, 282
National Insurance Act (1911), 76
Ottawa Agreement (1932), 293
Soviet negotiations (1924), 200
social democracy, 19, 24, 27, 34–5, 131, 228–9
Social Democratic Federation (SDF), 26–9, 45, 64–5, 72
Social Democratic Party of Germany, 69, 79, 112, 113, 126, 131, 139, 141

INDEX

socialism, 14, 15–17, 25–9, 34–9, 41–7, 51, 60, 64–6, 93, 156, 178, 221
  Christian Socialism, 14–17, 25, 34–5, 228
  Marxism, 14, 15, 16, 17, 26–7, 29, 42, 45, 64–5, 72–3, 228, 308
  social democracy, 19, 24, 27, 34–5, 131, 228–9
  trade unionism, *see* trade unions
Socialism after the War (MacDonald), 134
Socialism and Society (MacDonald), 69
Socialism in Our Time (1926), 222
Socialist Club, London, 50
Socialist International (1889–1914), 47, 60, 69, 79, 137*n*
Socialist Labour Party, 72
Socialist Movement, The (MacDonald), 96
Socialist Party of Great Britain, 72
Socialist Review, 97, 219, 220
Socialist Union, 35
Socialist Union of Young Men, 34–5
Society of Friends, 82
Sorel, Georges, 96
South Africa, 60, 67–8, 74
  Anglo-Boer War (1899–1902), 5, 63–7, 179
South Kensington Museum, London, 33
Southampton, Hampshire, 44, 46, 49, 61

Soviet Union, 160, 198, 199, 200–201, 208, 209, 210–12, 287, 311
Spanish Civil War (1936–9), 304
Spectator, The, 118, 177
Spey Bay, Moray, 126
spiritualism, 89
Spynie, Moray, 4, 6, 87, 88, 116, 290
Sri Lanka, 110
St Pancras Parliament, 36
St Paul's Cathedral, London, 95, 165
St Thomas's Hospital, London, 49
Stamfordham, Arthur Bigge, 1st Baron, 166, 191, 234, 262
Stanley, Venetia, 105
Starmer, Keir, 178
'Starving Poor of Old England, The', 45
State Socialists, 148
Statement Relating to Defence (1935), 298
Statute of Westminster (1931), 239
Stephen, Campbell, 215–16
Stevenson, Frances, 253
Stimson, Harry, 241, 243, 255, 258, 307
Stockholm, Sweden, 131, 132
Strachey, John, 59, 175, 236
Strachey, Lytton, 165
Stresa Front (1935), 294–5
strikes, 96–8
  Clyde engineers' strike (1915), 129, 130

353

INDEX

general strike (1926), 97, 218–20, 233
London dock strike (1889), 41–2, 96
munitions workers' strike (1917), 129–30
national dock strike (1924), 183
national railway strike (1911), 97
Taff Vale case (1901), 67, 75
suffragism, 51, 67, 77, 101, 138
Sunday Pictorial, 177
Sutherland, Millicent Sutherland-Leveson-Gower, Duchess, 10
Sweden, 97, 131, 132
Sweethillock Farm, Moray, 3
syndicalism, 96–8

'Ta-ra-ra-boom-de-ay', 43
Taff Vale case (1901), 67, 75
Tardieu, André, 243
tariffs, 69, 153, 182, 237, 248, 252, 280–82
Tawney, Richard Henry, 175, 309
taxation, 14, 181, 248, 257, 258, 259, 260, 296
Taylor, Alan John Percivale, 116, 138
Thackeray, William Makepeace, 54
Thatcher, Margaret, 174
Third International (1919–43), 137–9, 140–41, 210
Thomas, Ivor, 145
Thomas, James Henry, 107, 147, 167, 217, 232, 233, 234–5

leaks scandal (1936), 304
MacDonald ministry, first (1924), 184, 217, 233
MacDonald ministry, second (1929–31), 233, 234–5, 249, 251
MacDonald's death (1937), 305
National Government, first (1931), 264, 267, 269
National Government, second (1931–5), 282, 293
Thomson, Christopher Birdwood, 1st Baron, 106, 108, 179, 188, 191
Thoreau, Henry David, 12
Thorneycroft, Peter, 247
Thurtle, Ernest, 188
Tillett, Ben, 42, 45
Times, The, 97, 118, 146, 177, 261, 305
Town and Country Planning Act (1929), 237
Trade Disputes Act (1906), 75, 220
Trade Disputes Act (1927), 220
Trade Disputes Bill (1930), 253
Trade Facilities Act (1924), 189
Trade Union Act (1913), 80
trade unions, 10, 37, 41–2, 46, 71, 72, 93, 145–6, 218–20
  Clyde engineers' strike (1915), 129, 130
  First World War (1914–18), 129–30
  general election (1929), 217
  general strike (1926), 97, 218–20, 233

354

INDEX

London dock strike (1889), 41–2, 96
MacDonald Ministry, first (1924), 186
MacDonald Ministry, second (1929–31), 259–60
munitions workers' strike (1917), 129–30
national dock strike (1924), 183
national railway strike (1911), 97
Osborne case (1909), 79–80, 86
syndicalism, 96–8
Taff Vale case (1901), 67, 75
Trades Union Congress (TUC), 41, 57, 58, 64–5, 129, 156, 216, 219, 220, 259–60
Tragedy of Ramsay MacDonald, The (Weir), 22, 113, 143
Transport and General Workers' Union, 183, 219
Travellers Club, London, 261
Treaty of Brest-Litovsk (1918), 132
Treaty of Lausanne (1923), xi, xii
Treaty of Versailles (1919), 150, 179, 184, 190, 195–9, 294–5, 297, 308
  Dawes Plan and, 195–9
  Lausanne Agreement and, 104, 286–7
  reparations system, xi, 150, 195, 255, 286–7
  Saarland and, 298n
Trenchard, Hugh, 172
Trevelyan, Charles, 119, 182

Trevelyan, George Otto, 182
Trinity College, Cambridge, 182
Turkey, xi, 144, 239
two-power standard, 239–32
Tyrwhitt, Reginald, 189

Unemployed Workmen Bill (1906), 74
unemployment, 31, 75, 153, 181, 188, 193, 220, 223, 232, 234, 235, 236
  Great Depression (1929–39), 236, 245–6, 248–9, 257, 259, 260, 296
Union of Democratic Control (UDC), 111, 119n, 120, 123, 182
United States, 60, 114, 285, 294, 307
  Creditanstalt collapse (1931), 255
  Dawes Plan (1924), 195–9
  Geneva Disarmament Conference (1932–4), 287
  Lausanne Conference (1932), 286–7
  loan requests (1931), 260, 261, 263, 277
  Navy, 239–43
  New Deal (1933–8), 294
  Roosevelt's inauguration (1933), 294
unskilled workers, 41
Upper Frognal Lodge, Hampstead, 109–10, 290

Vickers, 179

355

INDEX

Victoria, Queen, 165
Vietnam War (1955–75), 245, 246n

Wages for Government Employees Bill (1910), 92
walking, 13, 28, 125, 137, 174
Wall Street Crash (1929), xiv, 236, 245
Wallace, Graham, 59
Wallas, Graham, 37
Wanderings and Excursions (MacDonald), 137
Washington Treaty (1922), 240, 241
Watkins, Alan, 230
Watt, Donald Cameron, 307
Watts, J Hunter, 28
Waugh, Evelyn, 227
Ways and Means Committee, 183
We Can Conquer Unemployment (1929), 223
Webb, Beatrice, 27, 36–7, 47, 160, 167, 222
  aristocratic circles, views on, 57–8
  Fletcherizing, 147
  general election (1923), 154
  golf, views on, 126
  Labour constitution (1918), 133–4
  MacDonald ministry, first (1924), 181, 213, 215
  National Insurance Act (1911), 75–6
Webb, Sidney, 27, 36–7, 47, 107, 146, 147, 167, 274
  Fletcherizing, 147
  general election (1929), 231
  Labour constitution (1918), 133–4
  MacDonald ministry, first (1924), 181, 183, 187
  MacDonald ministry, second (1929–31), 253, 256
  National Government formation (1931), 265
Wedgwood, Josiah, 148, 213
Weimar Germany (1918–33), 228–9, 307
  Creditanstalt crisis (1931), 255–6
  Lausanne Conference (1932), 104, 286–7
  reparations, xi, 150, 195, 255, 286–7
  Ruhr occupation (1923–5), 150–51, 152, 154, 195–9
  Treaty of Versailles (1919), *see* Treaty of Versailles
Weir, Lauchlan MacNeill, 22, 113, 143, 235, 248, 264–5, 267
Wells, Herbert George, xiii, 147, 162, 186n
Westminster Abbey, London, 305
Wheatley, John, 146, 148, 191–3, 213, 214, 215, 216, 220, 233
Whigs, 59, 72
Whitman, Walt, 121
Wigram, Clive, 262, 264
William IV, King, 164
Wilson, Harold, xiii, 228, 248, 273

INDEX

Wilson, Joseph Havelock, 42
Wilson, Woodrow, 132, 196
witchcraft, 6
Women's Industrial Council, 55–6
women's suffrage movement, 51, 67, 77, 101, 138
Wood, Edward, 68, 69
Wood, Kingsley, 207
Woodcraft Folk movement, 147
Woolwich, London, 120, 140
Woolwich Labour League, 35
Workers in the Dawn (Gissing), 31
Workers' Weekly, 205–8

working classes, 9, 41, 45, 51, 58, 65, 71, 221
Wren, Christopher, 95

Xi Jinping, 83*n*

Ye Olde Plow Inn, Buckinghamshire, 83
YMCA, 51
York Cottage, Sandringham, 161
Ypres, Belgium, 119, 130

Zilliacus, Konni, 82
Zinoviev letter (1924), 210–12